PHILOSEMITISM

Also by William D. Rubinstein

A HISTORY OF THE JEWS IN THE ENGLISH-SPEAKING WORLD Great Britain

BRITAIN'S CENTURY: British Political and Social History, 1815–1905

CAPITALISM, CULTURE AND DECLINE IN BRITAIN, 1750–1990

MENDERS OF THE MIND: A History of the Royal Australian and New Zealand College of Psychiatrists 1946–1996 (*with Hilary L. Rubinstein*)

THE JEWS IN AUSTRALIA: A Thematic History, Volume 2 1945–the Present

THE MYTH OF RESCUE: Why the Democracies Could Not Have Saved More Jews from the Nazis

Also by Hilary L. Rubinstein

MENDERS OF THE MIND: A History of the Royal Australian and New Zealand College of Psychiatrists 1946–1996 (*with William D. Rubinstein*)

THE JEWS IN AUSTRALIA: A Thematic History, Volume 1 1788–1945

Philosemitism

Admiration and Support in the English-Speaking World for Jews, 1840–1939

William D. Rubinstein
Professor of History
University of Wales
Aberystwyth

and

Hilary L. Rubinstein
Part-time Lecturer
University of Wales
Lampeter

First published in Great Britain 1999 by
MACMILLAN PRESS LTD
Houndmills, Basingstoke, Hampshire RG21 6XS and London
Companies and representatives throughout the world

A catalogue record for this book is available from the British Library.

ISBN 0-333-69950-5

 First published in the United States of America 1999 by
ST. MARTIN'S PRESS, INC.,
Scholarly and Reference Division,
175 Fifth Avenue, New York, N.Y. 10010

ISBN 0-312-22205-X

Library of Congress Cataloging-in-Publication Data
Rubinstein, W. D.
Philosemitism : admiration and support in the English-speaking world for Jews, 1840–1939 / William D. Rubinstein and Hilary L. Rubinstein.
p. cm.
Includes bibliographical references and index.
ISBN 0-312-22205-X (cloth)
1. Philosemitism—English-speaking countries—History—19th century. 2. Philosemitism—English-speaking countries—
—History—20th century. 3. Jews—Persecutions—History—19th century. 4. Jews—Persecutions—History—20th century. 5. English-speaking countries—Ethnic relations. I. Rubinstein, Hilary L.
II. Title.
DS141.R83   1999
305.892'4—dc21   98-52706
                                                                         CIP

© William D. Rubinstein and Hilary L. Rubinstein 1999

All rights reserved. No reproduction, copy or transmission of this publication may be made without written permission.

No paragraph of this publication may be reproduced, copied or transmitted save with written permission or in accordance with the provisions of the Copyright, Designs and Patents Act 1988, or under the terms of any licence permitting limited copying issued by the Copyright Licensing Agency, 90 Tottenham Court Road, London W1P 9HE.

Any person who does any unauthorised act in relation to this publication may be liable to criminal prosecution and civil claims for damages.

The authors have asserted their rights to be identified as the authors of this work in accordance with the Copyright, Designs and Patents Act 1988.

This book is printed on paper suitable for recycling and made from fully managed and sustained forest sources.

10 9   8   7   6   5   4   3   2   1
08 07 06 05 04 03 02 01 00 99

Printed and bound in Great Britain by
Antony Rowe Ltd, Chippenham, Wiltshire

For
Dorothy and Evelyn Bresner
Raymond Charles Duplain

Contents

Preface ix

Part I: Philosemitic Reactions to Jewish Crises

1. 'Barbarism and Bigotry': Philosemitism from the Damascus Affair of 1840 to the Moroccan Crisis of 1859   3

2. 'The Sympathies of All Good Men': Philosemitism from the Mortara Affair of 1858–9 to Romanian Persecution in the 1870s   22

3. 'The Imperishable People': Protesting against Pogroms and Persecution in Russia, 1881–1906   39

4. 'An Unspeakable Injustice': Philosemitism during the Dreyfus, Beilis and Frank Affairs, 1894–1913   59

5. 'The Inmost Heart of Hell': Philosemitism from the First World War to the Holocaust, 1914–45   79

Part II: A Typology of Philosemitism

6. 'The Spirit of the Age': Liberal and Progressive Philosemitism   111

7. 'The Deepest Debt': Christian Philosemitism   126

8. 'The Age-Long Dream': Zionist Philosemitism   149

9. 'The Glorious Inheritance': Conservative and Elitist Philosemitism   171

Epilogue

10. 'The Jewish Emergence from Powerlessness': Philosemitism in the Contemporary World, 1945 to the Present   189

Notes 204

Index 254

Preface

This book has two aims. The first is to draw attention to the existence of a persisting and virtually unknown tradition of philosemitism which manifested itself in Britain and elsewhere in the English-speaking world during every significant international outbreak of antisemitism during the century after 1840. The second is to offer a typology of philosemitism, distinguishing between varieties of support for the Jewish people. Accordingly, the book is divided into two parts, along those lines.

The opposite of hate, Elie Wiesel has observed, is indifference, not love. Indifference, in the present context, presupposes tolerance, that hallmark of a free society, which since the seventeenth century has enabled Jews to live in English-speaking lands in peace and security. But there has also been in those lands a strong tradition of philosemitism, which we define as support or admiration for the Jewish people by non-Jews, and which can reasonably be regarded as the reverse of antisemitism, hostility to or dislike of Jews. It is our belief that, particularly in the English-speaking world and perhaps elsewhere, philosemitism has been a significant force, the importance of which has been neglected to an astonishing extent in historical accounts of modern Jewry.

Compared with the thousands upon thousands of books and articles which have appeared in recent times about antisemitism (including the many hundreds on the Holocaust), virtually nothing whatsoever has been written about philosemitism. So far as we are aware, only two books have appeared in English on this topic: Solomon Rappaport, *Jew and Gentile: the Philo-Semitic Aspect* (New York, 1980) and Alan Edelstein, *An Unacknowledged Harmony: Philo-Semitism and the Survival of European Jewry* (Westport, Conn., 1982). While both, especially Edelstein's, are wide-ranging and valuable, neither uses primary sources or analyses the modern period in detail. Perhaps predictably, given the tendency of historians to dwell upon antisemitism, neither book is well known and the authors' viewpoints remain largely outside the mainstream of modern Jewish historiography. Throughout the century after 1840 rallies and petitions were the most frequently encountered modes of philosemitic protest; they were augmented by philosemitic books and pamphlets and other means of demonstrating solidarity with oppressed Jews. Most readers will know little, or possibly nothing, of these philosemitic activities: they are seldom referred to in histories of the Jews in Britain or the United States and have never before been treated comprehensively and in detail. Mention must be made, however, of Albert S. Lindemann, *The Jew Accused. Three Anti-Semitic Affairs (Dreyfus, Beilis, Frank) 1894–1915* (Cambridge, 1991), an excellent, much-needed account which examines philosemitic responses during those celebrated episodes.

In our view, much more attention should be paid by scholars to philosemitism than has hitherto been the case. A thorough account of the history of the Jewish people in modern times which focuses on antisemitism but which, as is typical, ignores philosemitism is, we believe, as one-sided as a history of capitalism which chronicles depressions, exploitations and bankruptcies but overlooks the affluence and technological innovation created.

The topic of philosemitism can be approached in various ways: for instance, by discussing the careers of leading philosemites and their writings, as Norman Rose did in his *The Gentile Zionists: a Study in Anglo-Zionist Diplomacy 1929–1939* (London, 1973). The way we have chosen is to organize this work into two parts. The first deals with the rallies, petitions and other forms of overt support given by non-Jews to the Jewish people during well-known outbursts of antisemitism between the Damascus Affair of 1840 and the Holocaust. We have here tried to indicate something of the remarkable range and depth of this support, and the sincerity obviously felt by philosemitic gentiles involved in those events. To any reader used to conceptualizing modern Jewish history in terms of the persecution and oppression of the Jews, persecution enjoying wide support, we venture to claim that the extraordinary depth, during times of antisemitism, of philosemitic support for Jews by prominent and influential non-Jews will seem well-nigh unbelievable. Indeed, it may well seem too good to be true, and many will surely ask wherein lies the small print, the sting in the tail, of these rallies and demonstrations. In the latter part of this book we deal with such groups as Christian conversionists and rightwing supporters of the Jews about whom these questions might well be asked. Suffice it to say that, with the rarest of exceptions, there was no sting in the tail of gentile support for Jews, and this evidently sincere and deeply felt sympathy for the Jewish people has surely to be taken at face value. The main reason why the attitude of gentile philosemites may seem so odd is, instead and quite simply, because they have been written out of history, and form no part, or a most marginal one, of the mainstream presentation of modern Jewish history.

In the second part of this work we attempt to offer a typology of the main varieties of philosemitism in the English-speaking world since 1840. It is clear that vocal and notable philosemites emerged from several different ideologies and perspectives, from viewpoints which themselves had little in common. Significantly, too, these perspectives spanned the whole political and ideological spectrum, most definitely including persons who were adherents of doctrines such as those of the British Conservative Party's imperially-minded rightwing or of intellectual Catholicism, which are seldom obviously associated with outspoken support for the Jewish people. Philosemitism in the modern English-speaking world, in other words, can readily be found along the entire ideological and theological spectrum, not merely among left-liberals, and is quite consistent with virtually every significant viewpoint which has emerged in the English-speaking world over the past 150 years.

Much of the evidence on which this work is based concerns Britain, for which unusually rich and comprehensive sources exist, and whose Jewish leadership was closely involved in responding to most of the seminal events in modern Jewish history. For the bulk of the period covered in this work, too, Britain was one of the world's greatest powers, a role it lost only after the Second World War. We have also focused, wherever possible, on American philosemitism, and have, as well, included a good deal of evidence from the Commonwealth, especially Australia, whose remoteness in fact enhances the value of the surprising range of philosemitism instanced there. We have not, however, examined philosemitism outside the English-speaking world, except in rare instances. In countries where the local tradition of antisemitism was so much more virulent than in the English-speaking world, local philosemitism raises a host of separate questions beyond the scope of this book, and also requires access to rare sources, in many languages. In all likelihood, however, the researcher will find an important tradition of philosemitism in virtually every country; the difference between this tradition in the English-speaking world and in countries such as Poland, Russia and Germany is that in the latter it was almost always weaker than were the forces of antisemitism.

We are also well aware that philosemitism and antisemitism existed side by side (together with considerable indifference to Jews) and that a comprehensive picture requires that both be considered. This book, however, discusses only philosemitism because virtually nothing has ever been written on the subject, and it is vital to place on record the strength of philosemitism, so often ignored. The present work should also be seen as forming part of a sequence of five books (the others authored by William D. Rubinstein alone), which comprise *A History of the Jews in the English-Speaking World: Great Britain* (London: Macmillan, 1996), *The Myth of Rescue: Why the Democracies Could Not Have Saved More Jews from the Nazis* (London: Routledge, 1997) and two forthcoming works, on antisemitism and on the history of the Jews in other English-speaking countries, especially the United States.

Over 100 years ago, the London *Jewish Chronicle* (13 November 1896) observed: 'an interesting paper might be written on the forgotten friends of Jewish progress in this country.' More often than not these people, who supported the cause of civil equality at home, championed the cause of persecuted Jews overseas; as well, many of them were regular donors to domestic Jewish institutions and charities. We are glad to have rescued a portion of them from what the *Jewish Chronicle* called 'the lumber room of our history'. Owing both to constraints of space and to the fact that the topic has been fairly well worked, we do not discuss non-Jewish support for Jewish political emancipation in Britain, except for the very occasional cursory and fragmentary reference. Such support was frequently manifested in civic rallies and in petitions to Parliament by town councils on behalf of an object finally achieved in 1858 when Baron Lionel de Rothschild was at last permitted to take his seat in the House of Commons as Britain's first Jewish MP.

We began to research this book in Australia, where we lived for many years and published widely on Australian Jewish history and affairs. We owe thanks to several persons and institutions in that country for encouragement, advice, or information: to Beverley Davis OAM, Honorary Archivist of the Australian Jewish Historical Society Victoria Inc., Dr Ray Duplain, Dr Philip Mendes, Colin Thornton-Smith, Dr Malcolm J. Turnbull, the State Library of Victoria, the Mitchell Library in Sydney, the J.S. Battye Library of Australian History, Perth, and the interlibrary loan service of Deakin University, Geelong. We are grateful, also, to the American Jewish Historical Society, to the Legislative Reference Library, Texas, Professor Mark Krupnick of the University of Chicago, Professor Frederick M. Schweitzer of Manhattan College, and to the following persons and institutions in Great Britain: C.M. Drukker, Honorary Secretary,

Preface

Jewish Historical Society of England, Dr Anthony Joseph, Miriam Rodrigues-Pereira, the staff of the National Library of Wales, especially Dr Lionel Madden, and the interlibrary loan service at the University of Wales, Aberystwyth. Our study has also benefited from material at the London Library, the Jewish Studies Library, University College, London, and the Parkes Library, University of Southampton. Special thanks are due to Gill Parry, who expertly wordprocessed the manuscript.

William D. Rubinstein
Hilary L. Rubinstein
Aberystwyth, Wales, 1999

Part I
Philosemitic Reactions to Jewish Crises

1 'Barbarism and Bigotry': Philosemitism from the Damascus Affair of 1840 to the Moroccan Crisis of 1859

In 1840 there were probably about 4,250,000 Jews in the world. About 80 per cent – roughly 2,975,000 – lived in Eastern Europe, where nearly all spoke Yiddish, the vernacular language of the Ashkenazi Jews of the Russian Pale of Settlement, Austria-Hungary and elsewhere. Probably around 5 per cent – roughly 700,000 – lived in the Afro-Asian world, chiefly Arabic and Ladino-speaking Sephardi Jews, while the remaining 15 per cent lived in Western Europe, the Americas and Oceania.[1] During the nineteenth century there was a remarkable population explosion among Europe's Jews. The world's Jewish population increased from 2,500,000 in 1800 to 7,750,000 in 1880, and to 10.5 million in 1900.[2] Nearly all of this expansion occurred among the Ashkenazi Jews of Eastern Europe. Sephardi Jewry in the Afro-Asian world hardly increased at all. As a result, Jews resident in the Near East and North Africa declined from 40 per cent of the world's Jewish population in 1800 to only 8 per cent in 1880, with Jews resident in Europe increasing from 59 per cent to 89 per cent in the same period.[3]

The disabilities suffered by Jews also differed from place to place. As a general rule, the further east one went, the greater the legal disabilities of Jews, and the further west one went, the fewer. By 1840, a greater or lesser degree of political equality had come to Jews in most European countries with the exception of Russia. Full civil rights had been granted to Jews in France in 1791. In Russia, the Jews had been granted a measure of civil rights, but full emancipation would not come until 1871 and the establishment of the German Empire. In Czarist Russia, the 'prison of nations', Jews (with a handful of exceptions) were compelled to live in the provinces of Russian Poland, Lithuania, Byelorussia, the Ukraine, Bessarabia and the Black Sea region, known collectively as the 'Pale of Settlement'. They also suffered from other forms of discrimination and oppression, including the liability of Jewish boys to be kidnapped and conscripted into the Czarist army for the extraordinary period of 25 years. (On the other hand, Czarist Russia did not interfere with the practice of the Jewish religion or unduly with Jewish education.) In the Ottoman Empire and elsewhere in the Moslem world, Jews (and Christians) were considered to be 'protected subjects' (*dhimmis*) provided they paid a special tax, the *jizya*. Jews were, however, discriminated against in a number of other ways, and remained outside the Islamic power structure. In practice, the treatment of Jews varied greatly with local traditions and the attitudes of local rulers. The middle and later nineteenth century saw a gradual easing of overt discrimination against Jews (the *jizya* was abolished in the Ottoman Empire in 1855, for instance) until the rise of modern Arab nationalism and hostility to Zionism at the end of the century.[4]

The English-speaking world was different. No overt laws of any kind against Jews existed in Britain after their readmission by Cromwell in 1656. In the 1660s Parliament debated, and rejected, a proposal to enact a special tax on Jews, similar to that which existed elsewhere in Europe. No attempts to enact specifically antisemitic legislation were ever again made in Britain. What discrimination existed in Britain was of a different kind, the inability of practising Jews to take the Anglican (or, after 1828, Christian) oaths necessary to hold some positions. The most famous such oath was that required to be taken by all newly elected members of Parliament. Until 1828, MPs were to testify their allegiance to the Anglican creed and, between 1828 and 1858, were required to swear an oath 'on the true faith of a Christian'. The efforts to change this oath (to 'so help me God') constituted the 'struggle for political emancipation' in Britain, finally won by practising Jews in 1858. Ironically, in 1858 Britain's Chancellor of the Exchequer was a converted Jew, Benjamin Disraeli.[5]

In the United States (and other 'pioneer' societies such as the Australian colonies) discrimination based on religion was forbidden by law. The American Bill of Rights, enacted in 1790, specifically forbade 'the establishment of a religion'. While some states established Protestantism as their official religion into the early nineteenth century, in practice there was no legal discrimination against Jews on religious grounds in the United States. There was, however, a measure of social and economic discrimination, much discussed by recent historians – although, as this work will show, there was also a considerable measure of philosemitism.[6] In Britain, there was little or no social discrimination of any kind against Jews. The English-speaking world almost entirely lacked the tradition of venomous popular antisemitism found in Central and Eastern Europe. Roman Catholics were the chief objects of religious hostility in both Britain and America, while, obviously, America's central racial problem had nothing to do with Jews.[7] In general, throughout the English-speaking world Jews were regarded as a small, low-profile minority who were seldom viewed by the Protestant majority in a dark light.

While enlightened opinion in the West looked ever more sympathetically at the question of full Jewish civil and political emancipation, a drama unfolded in the East which underlined assumptions of the benightedness of the region, galvanized western Jewish leaders into unprecedented political action, lobbying governments and forging alliances, and mobilized gentiles in Britain and the United States into mass displays of solidarity with Jewry. The Damascus Affair of 1840 marked a watershed in Jewish–gentile relations on both sides of the Atlantic: for apparently the first time in history, British and American gentiles held public rallies to press the cause of persecuted Jews overseas. It is thus appropriate to begin this history of philosemitism with that episode.

The affair in what was the administrative heart of Ottoman territory seized during the 1830s from the Porte's direct control by Turkey's viceroy in Egypt, Mehemet Ali, received much publicity in the West during the spring and summer of 1840. This followed the disappearance in February of a Sardinian Capuchin monk, Father Thomas, and his Arab servant. Both were allegedly last seen in or near the city's Jewish quarter. When they failed to return home a rumour flared, instigated by Greek Christians: the missing men had been murdered by Jews who drained their blood for use in the unleavened bread (*matzot*) eaten on the Passover festival. Suspicion fell on a Jewish barber; under torture, he implicated seven leaders of his community. Subjected to the most gruesome cruelties, all but two made false confessions. Three died from the sufferings inflicted; so did a young Jewish vendor who was called a liar and severely lashed for testifying that he had seen the missing men leaving town in a different direction. Anti-Jewish rioting broke out in Damascus and surrounding districts.[8] At almost the same time, though coincidentally, a similar (and more quickly resolved) case occurred on the island of Rhodes, a Turkish possession administered from Constantinople. This involved the disappearance of a boy from the majority Greek Orthodox population, the cry of ritual murder, the interrogation of Jewish communal leaders, the use of torture against the principal suspect and the sealing off of the island's Jewish quarter causing considerable hardship for its inhabitants.[9]

Among the first accounts of the Damascus Affair to reach the West were the despatches of the French Consul, Count de Ratti-Menton, who by an old Franco-Turkish treaty was entitled to protect Roman Catholic clerics in the Ottoman empire. He believed the ritual murder charge, and cooperated with the accused men's brutal native interrogators.[10] Before long, the occurrences in Damascus and on Rhodes found their way into western newspapers, and Jews and their religion came under close scrutiny. Extensive reportage of the incidents, particularly the long-running affair in Damascus, appeared in *The Times*. Although, in the pursuit of a thorough ventilation of the issue, it and some other British newspapers printed claims and counter-claims that Judaism entailed human sacrifice, almost all, regardless of political complexion or religious leaning, held the allegation to be preposterous, an echo of medieval calumnies against the Jews. The Tory *Morning Post*, soon to embark on its long reputation for anti-semitism (which in 1843 it protested, claiming 'perfect indifference' towards Jews) typified press comment when on 11 April 1840 it ascribed the accused men's confessions to 'atrocious cruelties' and stated that Christians, especially English ones, could not help but discount a story 'all the characteristics of which bear such evident ... exaggeration and inconsistency. It is a lamentable thing that the old story so often repeated during the Middle Ages should have been revived to satisfy the rapacity of barbarous authorities.'[11]

It says much for the rationality and enlightenment of British society that this attitude proved the predominant one, crossing political boundaries and withstanding published slurs on Judaism, although a tendency to treat the issue as an open question became discernible in *The Times*, which on 17 August conceded that irrespective of whether the Damascus prisoners had been 'justly or unjustly accused' they 'are entitled to a fair trial'.[12] In general, religious non-Jewish opinion in Britain took the ritual murder allegation for the myth it was – 'a mendacious calumny', to quote the Anglican *Christian Observer*. The *Protestant Magazine*, organ of the Protestant Association (an Evangelical body established in 1836 to press for legislation based on God's word) saw the Damascus Affair as indicative of 'unchanged Popery' and railed against Ratti-Menton. The Roman Catholic *Tablet* empathized with the accused, recalling that not so long ago 'in the cities of this very empire' some Protestants were prepared to believe that on Good Friday Catholics murdered children for ritual purposes: 'We too know what it is to be a minority ... Is it for us to be the ready receivers, on no evidence at all, of wholesale calumnies against others?'[13]

No one dismissed the allegation more devastatingly or effectively than the Reverend Dr Alexander McCaul, a graduate of Trinity College, Dublin, who from 1823 to 1830 had been stationed in Warsaw as representative of the London Society for Promoting Christianity Amongst the Jews. That organization, inaptly dubbed 'The London Jews' Society', had been founded in 1809 with support from both Anglicans and Nonconformists, but was an exclusively Anglican initiative from 1815. McCaul by 1840 was principal of the college for converted Jews run by the Society at its complex in 'Palestine Place', Bethnal Green, which comprised the Episcopal Jews' Chapel, schools and workshops.[14] Steeped in Jewish law and lore, as revealed in *Old Paths*, a weekly exposition of Judaism which he produced in the late 1830s, McCaul now swiftly issued a cogent and persuasive refutation of the ritual murder allegation in a booklet dedicated, with permission, to Queen Victoria. 'Time was', he declared,

> when to persecute and to oppress the Jewish people was regarded as one of the most effectual modes of defending the faith. Your Majesty has taught the nations a lesson of charity, as well as faith, by taking God's ancient people under your Majesty's special protection. [This was apparently a reference to Palmerston's instruction in January 1839 to Britain's foundation vice-consul in Palestine 'to afford protection ... generally' to the Jews of Palestine.] Whilst some of the powers of the earth have wavered, and continued to do homage to the spirit of unjust prejudice and the practice of persecution, to your Majesty's Government belongs the just praise of asserting the claims of justice and mercy, by interposing on behalf of the unhappy victims of religious hatred. All who are interested in the cause of suffering humanity, and anxious for the honour of Christianity, rejoice ... none ever conferred benefits upon Israel without a return of blessing from Him who hath said, 'I will bless them that bless thee.' (Gen. xii, 3)[15]

The booklet's authority is attested to, and its impact implied, in a contemporary review: 'It is strange that such a work should be called for in the present day; but the charge that has lately been made against the Jews, and the atrocious cruelties grounded upon it, are but too notorious, and it is well that its groundless and absurd nature should be exposed by the person of all others most capable of doing it. It would be a strange thing for the Jews to hold these doctrines and practice these rites, but stranger still that they should do it without his knowledge.'[16] It is notable that while McCaul was professionally engaged in converting Jews to Christianity, he was, however, a vigorous defender of Jews against antisemitism. This is perhaps paradoxical, but is nonetheless part of a common pattern which will be discussed more fully in chapter 7, dealing with Christian philosemitism.

Irrespective of party, politicians were generally dismissive of the allegations in Damascus and on Rhodes, and much concern was expressed for the Jewish communities involved. The Foreign Secretary, Lord Palmerston, a Whig, vowed his sympathy to a deputation from the Board of Deputies of British Jews who met him on 30 April, and, true to his word, he instructed Britain's envoys in Alexandria and Constantinople to register their country's strong feelings. The British consul-general in Alexandria was told to impress upon Mehemet Ali the 'extreme disgrace' into which his regime had plunged as a result of 'the barbarous enormities' at Damascus, which had been perpetrated not by 'an ignorant rabble' but by his officials – servants of a ruler 'who has prided himself upon promoting civilization'. The British government expected that those officials would be immediately dismissed and punished, and that 'the most ample reparation in his power' would be made 'to the unfortunate Jews'.[17] The Conservative leader of the Opposition, Sir Robert Peel, made his abhorrence of events known in two powerful parliamentary speeches.[18]

Ultimately, the renowned Anglo-Jewish philanthropist Sir Moses Montefiore undertook, with Adolphe Crémieux of France, a spectacular mission to the East which resulted in the release of the surviving accused and in the Sultan's issuance of a firman disavowing the ritual murder charge as a 'calumny'. (It was specifically for these efforts on behalf of persecuted Jewry that Queen Victoria, in 1841, granted Montefiore 'an especial mark of our Royal favour' concerning his coat of arms.)[19] Among those accompanying Montefiore was a future Lord Mayor of London, Alderman David Wire, known as 'a zealous friend to Judaism', who symbolized the change in attitude that had taken place within the City of London, illiberal towards Jews until the 1830s.[20]

Public meetings in which gentiles advocated Jewish emancipation were sometimes encountered in British towns and cities during the lengthy agitation which finally culminated in the right of Jews to sit in Parliament in 1858.[21] But the great meeting that took place at the Mansion House, headquarters of the Lord Mayor and Corporation of the City of London, on the afternoon of 3 July 1840 was, it seems certain, the first time a body of British gentiles assembled together on behalf of a persecuted foreign Jewry, and thus perhaps marks a turning-point in the history of philosemitism. That meeting reflected the City's new-found liberalism towards Jews and its esteem for Jewish merchants and brokers, like Montefiore, due to depart for the East; many of these were in the audience. It probably reflected, too, the popularity of the former Sheriff (Sir) David Salomons, destined to be London's first Jewish Lord Mayor, whose campaign in the 1830s and 1840s to be permitted to take the seat on the Corporation to which voters elected him was greeted with wild jubilation by gentile wellwishers when at last through Act of Parliament it succeeded.[22] (Salomons wrote a pamphlet describing events at Damascus which included a harrowing account by George Pieritz, a Jew-turned-Anglican missionary, of the tortures imposed; Pieritz's account also appeared in *The Times* of 4 July, helping to stir British opinion.[23])

The Mansion House meeting brought together London's mercantile and banking elite, and although a secular gathering, it was – whether by design or accident – ecumenical in nature, Anglicanism, Nonconformism and Catholicism being represented by the speakers.[24] These, similarly, reflected the entire spectrum of political opinion. The meeting demonstrated the City's solidarity with British Jews seeking justice for their co-religionists overseas and its rejection of an outmoded slur upon Judaism; it showed that Montefiore travelled not only with the blessing of British Jews. Although 'a considerable number' of leading Jewish merchants were present with their wives, it is probable that the bulk of those who ensured that the hall 'was crowded to excess' were gentiles. Certainly, gentiles dominated proceedings; they alone made speeches, and moved and seconded resolutions. While most of those present, including Members of Parliament, had direct connections with the City, in a foreshadowing of the broad base of representation seen at rallies of well-known people on behalf of Jews in future decades, it seems that prominent men from other fields, such as Thomas Campbell, a poet well known in his day who had helped to found the University of London, attended.[25]

Moving the resolutions were John Abel Smith, a banker and Liberal MP; Sir Charles Forbes, physician to the army; Samuel

Gurney, a Quaker banker and future Liberal MP; George Gerard de Hochepied Larpent, an East India merchant who would serve briefly as a Liberal MP; and Lord Howden, a distinguished diplomat. Seconding were future Conservative MP John Masterman, a banker and East India Company director; Dr (later Sir) John Bowring, the Benthamite economist, linguist and traveller with recent first-hand knowledge of Damascus who for many years edited the *Westminster Review* and was twice elected to Parliament as a radical Reformer; the Hon. and Rev. Baptist Noel, an Evangelical clergyman evidently related to Lord Byron; and Matthias Wolverley Attwood, a banker and Conservative MP. Other speakers included Alderman William Thompson, a wealthy ironmaster and shipowner who was also a Conservative MP (he opened the meeting in the temporary absence of its convenor, Lord Mayor Sir Chapman Marshall, who subsequently arrived together with other aldermen who had been detained on official business and took the chair); Alderman Wire; and the famous Irish 'Liberator', barrister and Reformer MP Daniel O'Connell, who had already spoken forcibly on the issue in the Commons.[26]

The five resolutions were carried unanimously. The main one recorded that the gathering

> has heard with the deepest emotion and with the greatest horror, the recital of the cruelties inflicted upon the Jews in the east, and hereby expresses its sympathy for the sufferers and its earnest hope that an immediate and impartial public investigation will take place so as to disprove in the face of the whole world the atrocious calumnies invented and propagated by their persecutors as a pretext for the infliction of cruelties almost unknown to the previous history of mankind.

The subsidiary resolutions condemned the use of torture to extract confessions as 'a relic of a barbarous age' and hoped that the entire world would soon enjoy the European system of 'a fair and impartial trial'; expressed 'deep regret that in this enlightened age a persecution should have arisen against our Jewish brethren, originating in ignorance and inflamed by bigotry' and anxiously prayed that 'through the diffusion of sound principles of religion in every country, all men may be considered as alike entitled to protection and to the benefit of just laws, impartially administered'; and praised the Foreign Secretary Lord Palmerston's 'prompt interference' in the situation and the concern expressed in Parliament by Peel and others.

It was also resolved that copies of the resolutions would be sent to British government ministers as well as to resident foreign envoys.[27]

A comparable public meeting was held in Manchester at the end of July, convened by the borough reeve, Sir Thomas Potter, in response to a requisition by citizens. Anglican, Nonconformist and Roman Catholic clergymen were among the speakers.[28]

Perhaps the most telling comments about these meetings were provided by German Jews. The Mansion House meeting, wrote one, showed that 'all the noblest men of England in all the religious confessions' upheld the Jewish cause. Another saw in the supportive stance of Peel and the British press proof that 'among the peoples of Europe it is only among the English that the pure love of humanity is firmly and organically rooted'. It was claimed that 'nowhere have so many laudatory judgments about the Jews been openly pronounced as at the great meetings in London and Manchester.'[29]

Similar protests took place in the United States. A meeting on 27 August 1840 at the Mikveh Israel Synagogue, Philadelphia, had been intended as an entirely Jewish affair until a local Episcopalian clergyman, the Reverend Dr Henry W. Ducachet, learned that it was to be held. He told its organizers of his 'sincere interest in the case of the afflicted descendants of Abraham, Isaac and Jacob (a noble ancestry)' and his conviction 'that the Christian community generally, and the Christian clergy especially, will gladly and generously cooperate with you in any plan you may adopt for their relief.' This did not convince the organizers to open the meeting to the general public, but Ducachet and two other clergymen were called upon to speak, Ducachet observing that 'for the first time in centuries, was a Christian minister addressing a religious assemblage in a Jewish Synagogue, a spectacle at once sublime and pleasing to humanity.'[30] In Charleston, South Carolina, a public meeting took place on 28 August under the aegis of Mayor Henry L. Pinckney, a member of the well-known Southern patrician family. Speakers included the Roman Catholic Bishop of Charleston, other Christian clergymen, and public figures. Appropriate resolutions were passed. A similar meeting occurred in Savannah, Georgia, on 3 September.[31]

American newspapers were almost invariably sympathetic and the government was supportive. 'In common with all civilized nations, the people of the United States have learned with horror the atrocious crimes imputed to the Jews of Damascus, and the cruelties of which they have been victims,' wrote Secretary of State John Forsyth. President Martin Van Buren 'fully participates in the public feeling' and 'has witnessed, with the most lively satisfaction, the efforts of several of the Christian Governments of Europe, to suppress or mitigate these horrors.' Through its Ambassador in Constantinople the country protested the use of torture; its Consul at Alexandria was instructed to do all he could to ensure 'that justice and humanity may be extended to these persecuted people, whose cry of distress has reached our shores.'[32]

The Damascus Affair occurred at a time of growing interest among gentiles for the idea of Jewish restoration. The phenomenon of 'gentile Zionism' has received much attention from historians.[33] Its various strands are discussed later in this volume. The Damascus Affair, played out as it was amid international tensions regarding the future of the Ottoman Empire, was widely interpreted as a major sign pointing the way to a Palestine repeopled with Jews. The Evangelical Lord Ashley (the courtesy title by which the great Tory social reformer the seventh Earl of Shaftesbury was then known) believed that 'The very insults, misrepresentations and persecutions of the Jews at Damascus bring forward the main question.'[34] Another leading Evangelical, the Reverend Edward Bickersteth, produced a treatise on Jewish restoration. He stated:

> The distressing tortures and persecutions of the Jews at Damascus and at Rhodes, have wonderfully spread and increased an interest in their behalf, and real sympathy for their sufferings. It has not only called forth the love of Christians, but also the benevolent interference of Christian governments in their behalf. And this has been so decided as may in all human probability help to prepare the way for their quiet, gradual, and safe return to their own country, and their protracted residence there.[35]

Yet another, the Reverend T.S. Grimshawe, told a receptive audience of Anglican clerics that 'the persecution of Rhodes and Damascus will probably be the last remnant of barbarous oppression prior to the restoration of the Jews.'[36] Once more, the ambiguity of the position of Evangelical philosemites seems apparent. While, certainly, their ultimate aim was the voluntary conversion of the Jews, their short-term goal was an amelioration of Jewish suffering, brought about if necessary by the active interference of the liberal Western powers, and, just as surprisingly, the restoration of Jews as Jews to Palestine.

The Times took note of this trend, by pointing out that Jews were, while not the sole, typically the first victims of the 'harsh and grinding system of misgovernment ... in Mahometan countries', and recalled that 'a community of English gentlemen have lately memorialized all the Protestant monarchs of Europe' regarding the restoration of the Jews. The paper could offer no comment on the scriptural interpretation which prompted that memorial – to which it had drawn attention on 9 March – and it regarded the issue as premature. But it did concede that 'a new element' had thereby been introduced into 'the Eastern question'.[37]

In 1843, three years after the Damascus Affair, two oppressive edicts regarding Jews, issued overseas, were reported in the British press and outraged non-Jewish opinion. The decree pronounced on 24 June 1843 at Ancona in the Papal States gave two months' notice of draconian restrictions to be imposed on Jews in that and eight other papal cities. Jews would be compelled to dismiss virtually all their Christian employees and would be unable to engage others. They would not be permitted to eat with Christians at public establishments outside the ghetto, to invite Christians to stay overnight inside the ghetto, nor to accept hospitality in Christian homes. Jews would not normally be allowed to spend the night away from the ghetto; those wishing to travel outside it required a licence. Jews would not be able to reside or trade in places possessing no ghetto. On pain of a hefty fine or seven years' imprisonment, Jewish dealers would have to surrender to the papal authorities their entire stock of Jewish ritual garments and all books irrespective of content. Next of kin arranging Jewish funerals would risk corporal punishment, and participants at such ceremonies would be heavily fined. Jews would also have to dispose of property yielding rents or interest. If this was not done within three months the papal representative would put such property to public auction.[38]

This decree, with its effective abolition of social contact between Jews and Christians and its assaults on the practice of Judaism, met such a storm of outrage from enlightened circles in Europe that it was suspended. Jacob Franklin, editor of the *Voice of Jacob*, one of two Anglo-Jewish newspapers established in the wake of the Damascus Affair – the other was a short-lived initial series of the *Jewish Chronicle* – was 'literally overwhelmed' with letters from gentile readers: 'One tone of plain spoken indignation pervades all.' An anonymous Anglo-Jewish commentator rejoiced that 'the whole press of England re-echoed with denunciations of the cruel policy.'[39]

Overwhelmingly, the British press deplored the fact that such unabashed persecution was still possible. The mood in both national and provincial newspapers was captured in a long editorial in the

Ipswich Express, which observed that the decree 'is calculated to force upon us the painful conviction that however we may flatter ourselves as to the light and civilization of the nineteenth century, the spirit of barbarism and of brutal and atrocious bigotry is not extinct in Europe'. It believed that if Roman Catholics in England were not imbued with such 'tyrannical hatred' towards others, this was 'much less to be ascribed to the liberality, Christian benevolence, and discretion of the ... Vatican, than to the innate love of liberty, to the generous and manly character which belong to all classes of Englishmen, without distinction, as well as to the beneficial influence of Protestant opinions and free institutions'. It was confident that if Britain had an ambassador at the Court of Rome, he 'would have been as successful in protecting the Israelites of Italy from oppression, as ... in the case of the persecuted Jews of Damascus, and other parts of the Turkish dominions' by injecting 'into the Papal councils, some small sense of political justice and religious liberty'. And it was sure that 'not a man in the United Kingdom' would fail to abhor the decree.[40]

Charlotte Elizabeth Tonna, the remarkable and influential Evangelical writer who edited the widely circulating *Christian Lady's Magazine* as well as (anonymously) the *Protestant Magazine*, called upon 'the Christians of England to make common cause with these persecuted "children of the covenant"' and devise some means of protecting them.[41] While Protestants recalled the Spanish Inquisition and the treatment of Jews in pre-Reformation England, Daniel O'Connell announced that, once satisfied that reports of the decree were true, he would, as a prominent Roman Catholic layman, remonstrate with the Vatican.[42]

On 2 May 1843, a Russian *ukase* ordered the 500,000 Jews living on the Pale of Settlement's borders with Austria and Prussia back into the heartland. Although issued earlier than the Ancona decree it failed immediately to arouse British gentile opinion, undoubtedly because it lacked the obvious atavistic quality of the decree and was at first accepted for what the Czarist authorities claimed it was: a necessary precaution against smuggling. But with subsequent reports that those affected faced probable destitution, being permitted to enter only a prescribed list of localities in the Pale where poverty and overcrowding were rife, that deportations were proceeding, and that a minimal number of Jews had been engaged in contraband, a great surge of pro-Jewish feeling became apparent.[43] The *Morning Herald* expected such a response from its countrymen, and endeavoured to lay the true picture of Jewish distress in Russia before them. *The*

Times pointed to the 'dreary future' awaiting those expelled from the borders, who 'have been plunged into such nameless desolation that the language of the tenderest compassion can find no words for it.'[44] Declaring that 'evil to the Jewish people' would rebound upon the perpetrators, the *Britannia* hoped God would 'raise up aid to the oppressed in their hour of need ...'[45] The *Christian Lady's Magazine*, denouncing 'one of the most barbarous acts ever perpetrated even by a northern Czar', characteristically reproduced from the *Voice of Jacob* commentary and foreign press reports on the measure.[46]

Much thought was given to the best means for securing revocation of the *ukase*. 'Amicus Judaeorum', writing in the *Guernsey Star*, advocated public meetings and the preparation, 'by men high in rank and station', of 'a strong but respectful memorial' to be presented to the Czar 'through some powerful and influential channel, as might yet arrest this evil, and prevent the infliction of this great injustice upon an unoffending people'. That paper's editor trusted in the efficacy of 'promptly expressed' public opinion and the power of the press, and believed that 'the Jews throughout Europe ought to bestir themselves with all their power', enlisting the aid of well-disposed legislators, so that pressure might be brought to bear upon Russia.[47] The *Morning Herald* considered that journalistic persuasion, rather than a direct approach from 'private individuals, however numerous or important', would weigh with the Czar and prove less counterproductive. A direct approach might prompt intransigence, but press commentary travelled far, and would 'provoke an echo even in the bosom of the haughtiest autocrat'.[48]

'Did not public opinion save the Jews of Damascus?' mused Jacob Franklin. 'Has not public indignation been instrumental in at least suspending the [Ancona] decree?' Hearing that the *ukase* had been suspended, he praised 'the warm and ready sympathy which this impending calamity has evoked on all sides' and acknowledged 'an eminent debt of gratitude' to the press. He was relieved that public meetings, with 'the risk of irritating language by unguarded orators', had been avoided.[49] Events had convinced the hitherto sceptical and suspicious editor that in Britain 'true' friends to Jewry were 'numerous,' that

> It is no longer to be doubted that the desire to aid the Jews prevails extensively ... there are powerful Gentiles whose impulses have always been to operate concerning Israel ... the friends of Israel can meet to proffer sympathy and aid, on principle, and with a

general reference to the oppressions under which our people, as Jews, labour in various parts of the world ... Let us then, like wise men, recognize that there is a common ground for the Jew and the Christian ... it is only the neglect of our own people to step forth boldly and say how and where their national interests may be served and defended.[50]

He hoped all professed friends of Jewry would 'not hang back from giving practical evidence of their sincerity – as auxiliaries, not as unlicensed intermeddlers or apostatizers'.[51]

For Franklin, Charlotte Elizabeth Tonna 'stands forth pre-eminently' among Jewry's friends.[52] She now responded eagerly to his challenge to 'the philanthropist, whose heart yearns to the sufferer' and 'the Christian, who owes to the Jews ... the hope that is within him ... to memorialize the powers or the people which oppress that ancient race',[53] heartily commending to her readers 'this good work, of which the object is to influence foreign states by a strong public expression of the feeling which Englishmen cannot but entertain'.[54]

Mindful that the *ukase* was only temporarily stayed, Mrs Tonna, during the Czar's private visit to Queen Victoria in July 1844, composed a petition to him on behalf of his 'oppressed and burdened Jewish subjects' and zealously obtained signatures from influential practising Christians: peers, prelates, Members of Parliament, privy councillors and others. Czar Nicholas received this petition from Lord Ashley.[55] Mrs Tonna also strived for an 'auxiliary' on the lines suggested by Franklin, which to quote Ashley – with whom she raised the matter in May 1843 – would join Jews in determining 'the best mode of ameliorating the civil condition' of oppressed Jewries.[56] A year after that discussion she reported that 'a very decided step has been taken by a party of independent gentlemen in London ... preparations are being made to follow it up in other parts of the country.'[57] It is likely that those involved included many if not all the petitioners, and were largely members or supporters of the Protestant Association. Mrs Tonna felt that in view of the persecution in Russia and the Papal States, 'ought we not to be more than passively watchful of what befalls our brethren? Ought we not to be prepared to act, as far as circumstances may enable us, in their defence and in their behalf?'[58] But for reasons which remain unclear, the Board of Deputies rebuffed this initiative. It might have suspected ulterior conversionist motives despite the fact that these were painstakingly disavowed; or perhaps it felt that since the offending edicts were suspended, there was sufficient time to secure their removal through diplomatic and lobbying efforts conducted by the likes of Montefiore.[59]

Meanwhile, disaster had again struck the Jewish world. In August 1844 a French fleet bombarded the Moroccan seaport of Mogador. The panic-stricken Moors fled, leaving the Jews, locked inside their quarter, to the mercy of Berber hill tribes who overran the undefended town. For several days the tribesmen plundered the quarter, attacking and robbing its inhabitants indiscriminately. Many women and girls were carried off to be raped. A number of Jews were slaughtered. Refugees, huddled in the countryside, faced starvation; all, regardless of former income, were destitute.[60]

William Willshire, a local businessman who acted as British Vice-Consul, wrote to a prominent London Jew of the 'horrible treatment' endured by the Mogador Jews and of their 'strong demands upon the sympathies and charity of an enlightened and religious public ... your co-religionists and the public in general.'[61] He was not disappointed, for when details of the outrages reached the press, British gentiles were among the contributors to a fund for the Jews of Mogador set up by an Anglo-Jewish committee chaired by Montefiore.

Mrs Tonna put herself in the forefront of fundraising efforts:

> We hope there is not a family in which some responsive voice will not be heard, some mite, however trifling, contributed to alleviate the heart-rending misery ... We hope [reports from Mogador] will be read ... with much intercessionary prayer, and alms such as each can afford ... Let us swell, as we can, the portion sent to them ... for they are 'the children of the prophets, and of the covenant which God made with their fathers ...'[62]

The donations poured in: £1 from Mrs Tonna herself, ten shillings from Captain Henry Downes RN, £1 from a John Beecher of Coniston, Lancashire; £2 from Captain Groves FRS; £4 collected by a Mrs Stapleton at Dartmouth; £5 from a Mrs Roberts of Bath, and so on. Many gentiles contributed anonymously: 'A Christian Lady at Plymouth ... M.A.B. "in acknowledgement of her debt to Israel" ... A Clergyman's Widow ... Lover of Israel, Huddersfield ... A friend to Israel ... A few friends from Boston upon Humber.' The donations cited were passed to the fund by Mrs Tonna, who collected a total amount unsurpassed by any Jew.[63] For several decades gentiles had been (and would continue to be) among the donors to Anglo-Jewish communal causes – schools, hospitals, specialized charities, philanthropic institutions, even synagogue building funds – in many cases on a regular basis.[64] But the Mogador fund is, if not the earliest, then certainly among the earliest occasions on which British gentiles subscribed money for distressed Jews overseas.

That example would be repeated during the following decade. In 1854 Chief Rabbi Nathan Adler and Sir Moses Montefiore launched an appeal on behalf of 'famishing' Palestinian Jewry, whose usual aid from their Russian co-religionists had been cut off by the Crimean War. The *Jewish Chronicle* expressed 'delight' at the huge number of gentile respondents: 'Our Christian brethren contributed largely' to the final amount.[65] Donations came from all components of the United Kingdom, including obscure rural areas, and from people in all walks of life, clerical and lay, military and civilian, titled and downright humble. Amounts ranged from £52 and 10 shillings given by the Merchant Taylors' Company to 'A Christian's Mite' of one shilling.[66] Donors included people well known to the Jewish community as allies, such as that tireless advocate of Jewish settlement in Palestine, former Governor of South Australia Colonel George Gawler, who gave ten guineas; the City of London's official solicitor, Charles Pearson, a veteran contributor to Jewish domestic appeals and a familiar face at Jewish charitable functions who gave five guineas; and at least three of the speakers at the Damascus rally (Abel Smith, who gave £25, and Attwood and Wire, who each gave £5). The Dowager Countess of Ashburnham sent five guineas; her servants managed a total of £1 14 shillings. 'The Railway Servant, Tring Station' (serving Lord Rothschild's country seat) sent £1. The Royal Sussex Lodge of Freemasons, Jersey, named in memory of a philosemitic son of King George III, donated £2. The Bishop of Bangor gave £5, as did the Mayor of Sheffield. There was the usual crop of anonymous donors: 'A Protestant ... A Poor Man of the Christian Community ... Christian Friends, near Portsea ... A Christian Widow and Her Son ... A Lover of Jews (Dumfries).'[67]

A group of London Welshmen collected £30 for the fund at a special meeting organized by the Reverend John Mills, a Welsh Calvinistic Methodist minister. He had been one of the seven-man executive (comprising, it must be noted, both Christians and Jews) of the Association for Promoting Jewish Settlement in Palestine,[68] which furnished two other speakers at the meeting: *Jewish Chronicle* editor Dr Abraham Benisch and (Sir) Hugh Owen of the Poor Law Board, future founder of the University of Wales. Mills was also the author of two recently published books about Anglo-Jewry's history, customs and institutions. He 'felt a more than ordinary interest in Jewish affairs; and has had greater intercourse with British Jews than, probably, any other minister in the United Kingdom.'[69] He would shortly tour Palestine, eagerly recording his impressions.[70] At this meeting, he and Benisch were, respectively, mover and seconder of a resolution sympathizing with 'the poor and oppressed condition of the Jews in the East, but especially in Jerusalem'. A further resolution, declaring 'That the present distressed and lamentable condition of the Jews in Jerusalem has peculiar claims on our sympathy, not only on the score of common humanity, but also on the benevolence of Christianity, which ... inculcates kindness to every human being, independent of creed or colour', was moved by a black Canadian, the Reverend S.A. Ward, seconded by the Reverend Thomas Phillips of the British and Foreign Bible Society.[71]

Non-Jews in the colonies also gave generously to the appeal. For example, in remote Hobart, Tasmania, where a total just exceeding £727 was raised towards the Australian total of £8,000, at least 165 gentiles donated amounts of £1 or more, while subscriptions of less than that sum totalled just over £53. The town's mayor gave £10. The donors' list was headed by Lieutenant-Governor Sir William Denison, the Anglican Bishop of Tasmania, and other prominent people. A public meeting in Sydney soliciting donations was chaired by Sir Charles Nicholson, Speaker of the New South Wales Legislative Assembly. It was addressed by fiery Presbyterian cleric and radical politician Dr John Dunmore Lang, who moved the resolution, considering it the 'duty' of Sydneysiders to 'cordially and liberally' join their Jewish fellow-citizens in the appeal, by the Roman Catholic Archdeacon of Sydney, and another parliamentarian. Gentiles donated in Melbourne; a local Jew wrote that 'Many kindhearted Christians in this city had frequently requested to be allowed to assist the Jews in various undertakings'. The Adelaide appeal was supported by South Australia's Governor, Sir Henry Edward Fox, and by leading citizens including clergymen of various denominations.[72] (This generous response from Australians, involving the convening of public meetings addressed by prominent non-Jews, was repeated in 1861–3 when a long-staying rabbinical emissary from Palestine sought funds for a charitable project, and again during the Relief Fund for Palestinian Jewry in 1865–6, which was also liberally subscribed by gentiles in Britain and other parts of the Empire.[73])

In October 1859, amid fears of a war between Spain and Morocco, several hundred Jews from Tangier, afraid that they would be attacked by Berber hill tribesman as the Jews of Mogador had been in 1844, sought British protection. A Royal Navy steamer took them to Gibraltar, whose Governor, Sir William Codrington, welcomed them 'in a manner which makes us feel the blessings of true charity and English rule', to quote a Gibraltar Jew. British officials and senior naval personnel involved in the rescue operation proved invariably kind; some were singled out for special praise. Codrington ordered tents and blankets, while a relief committee of British 'gentlemen imbued with noble feelings of charity,' including Catholic and Protestant clerics and headed by a naval captain and a colonel in the artillery, swung into action.[74]

In November the British Board of Deputies appointed a relief committee of its own, and appealed for donations to Jews everywhere, and to 'benevolent communities and persons, without distinction of creed, whose philanthropy may induce them to proffer assistance'.[75] Hundreds of British gentiles high and lowly, urban and rural, answered the call. Again, donations poured in from all parts of the United Kingdom, from non-Jewish individuals and firms, in sums large and small. There was a sprinkling of Members of Parliament, both Liberal and Conservative; several peers; clerics including at least one bishop; army and navy officers; doctors, lawyers and other professionals; civic dignitaries including several mayors, deputy mayors and sheriffs; the Canterbury Lodge of Freemasons and the Lodge of Benevolent Goodfellows; private companies and banking establishments in both London and the provinces. Among the latter, large donations of £20, £10, or ten guineas were not uncommon. There were the anonymous whose aliases left no doubt as to their non-Jewish identity. And as well as men and women of rank, means and influence, there were many of modest income who gave what they could, including parishioners answering pleas from their clergymen, and even groups of schoolchildren. Some local newspapers encouraged fund-raising efforts.[76]

The *Jewish Chronicle* took heart from the very large number of non-Jews who responded. It drew attention to those in Lancaster, where only a solitary Jew resided: 'Honour to [him] for having so nobly represented the cause of his distressed co-religionists, and still more honour to his Christian fellow-townsmen for having so humanely responded to his call.'[77] As in previous appeals gentile donors came forward from surprising places, such as Carnarvon and small towns in North Wales, the Isle of Man, Dumfries and rural Scotland as well as Ireland, and one may only speculate as to how they learned of the appeal; perhaps they were among the *Jewish Chronicle*'s Christian subscribers. That newspaper, at any rate, was delighted:

> Rich and poor, Jew and Gentile, are equally ready to participate in this work of charity. The cry of distress resounding from Gibraltar has called forth an outburst of sympathy, the depth and universality of which refreshes and enlarges the heart, showing as it does that in the cause of humanity we all know how to sink all sectarian differences, and only to feel as brethren, as children of the God of mercy.[78]

2 'The Sympathies of All Good Men': Philosemitism from the Mortara Affair of 1858–9 to Romanian Persecution in the 1870s

As an infant Edgardo Mortara (born 1851), son of a Jewish lace merchant at Bologna in the Papal States, fell ill. His family's teenaged Catholic servant girl, fearing that he would die and his soul be damned, secretly baptized him. Although she was a lay person her action was valid in canon law, but since the boy recovered she kept her deed to herself. However, in 1858 one of Edgardo's young brothers died before the girl had a chance to repeat her action. Upset, she confided everything to a neighbour, who informed a priest. He, in turn, notified the Archbishop of Bologna who, without attempting to ascertain the veracity of the girl's claim, had Edgardo removed from home by gendarmes on the evening of 24 June and taken to a hostel for converts in Rome.[1]

Vainly did his parents and their allies plead for Edgardo's return. In April 1859, Sir Moses Montefiore arrived in Rome with the intention of interceding with the Vatican, but neither Pope Pius IX nor Cardinal Antonelli, the papal Secretary of State, would grant him an audience. Their position was fixed: the Catholic Church could not return a child brought within its saving fold to parents who remained outside it. To do so would be a betrayal of the Church's responsibility to one of its own and a transgression of canon law. Edgardo Mortara remained a Catholic and never returned to his family. He grew so attached to the new faith in which he was carefully nurtured that he took holy orders, dying in Belgium only in 1940 after a long clerical career.

The Archbishop's highhandedness was consistent with a principle laid down by an eighteenth-century pope, that 'in cases where baptism has been validly, but perhaps illicitly, administered to Hebrew infants ... all such are to be separated from their relations and educated in the Christian faith.' Similar instances had, within fairly recent memory, occurred at Ancona, Ferrara and Modena. But they apparently attracted little publicity.[2] Edgardo's abduction, however, followed as it was by his anguished father's spirited attempt to get him back and the alerting of Jewish communities outside Italy, received considerable attention in the press. As always, manifestations of philosemitism at times of crisis in the Jewish world depended upon such crises being brought to public notice, which in practice meant the notice of the literate. The fate of Edgar, as the boy became known in English-speaking lands, became a *cause célèbre*, and in many countries gentiles, predominantly liberals and non-Catholics, were engaged in the crusade to have him restored to his family.

During the struggle to have him returned, central to what unfolded as the Mortara Affair of 1858–9, the Anglo-Jewish community organized no public protest. Its hopes were pinned on the efficacy of a face-to-face meeting between Sir Moses Montefiore and the Pope, and in December 1858 the Board of Deputies authorized its chairman's journey. Since the Affair occurred at a period when the influence of missionary Evangelicalism within the Church of England was at its peak, Jews certainly feared the influence of conversionists in any organized inter-faith activity on Edgar's behalf. The *Jewish Chronicle* carried several features and editorials urging caution regarding communal cooperation with Christians in the Affair, which might be used by conversionists to further their aims.[3] Perhaps Anglo-Jewry also felt that to seek more help from British liberals, who had already performed yeoman service in the fight for Jewish parliamentary emancipation (achieved the year the Affair broke), would be excessive. However, the Affair coincided also with the zenith of both an aroused Protestant anti-Catholicism in Britain and of mid-Victorian liberalism. Consequently, there was unprecedented activity by influential British Protestants and also by liberals on Edgar's behalf. As one British gentile observed: 'The sympathies of all good men are with [the Jews] in this case, and no right-minded Christian will refuse his aid.'[4] The strength of Protestant feeling on the subject could go was captured by the London *Daily Telegraph*:

> The Papal government seems determined to refuse all concession in the case of the young Mortara. Threats, entreaties, prayers, all are alike thrown away ... Its only answer to outraged Europe is, that

Roman Catholicism is above all natural right, and that 'parental affection is a Pagan prejudice.' France is the only European power in a position to bring the Papal government to its senses, and unless she vigorously sets about the task we may assume that this language will be kept up to the end. So much the better, perhaps, for the world at large and civilisation. Rome will only the more speedily hasten to her fall ... May we live to see the day!⁵

The *Jewish Chronicle* implored the Archbishop of Westminster, Cardinal Wiseman, and his Catholic clergy in Britain to 'break an ominous silence which may be construed into approbation'. It urged them, with their continental counterparts, to issue a joint appeal to the Pope asking not only for Edgar's return to his parents but also for renunciation of the papal principle which led to his abduction. Montefiore's Board of Deputies, too, tried to stir the conscience of Catholics, sending an account of the kidnapping which appeared in *The Times* on 9 September 1858 to some 1,800 priests throughout the United Kingdom.⁶ But the only priest prepared to break ranks was Dr George Oliver of Exeter, who described the abduction as 'an abominable act ... a nefarious transaction' since 'A father has a natural right over his children, and without his free consent, it is unjustifiable in a Christian to attempt to baptise them.'⁷

On 29 October 1858 the Evangelical Alliance, meeting in Liverpool under the chairmanship of the Earl of Roden, passed a resolution 'unsolicited by the British Jews, and instigated only by their own feelings of jealousy for the honour of the Christian name, indignant at the prostitution of that name to the purposes of oppression, and especially grieved that it should be rendered odious to the ancient people of God, before whom they desire that the Christian faith should never appear but in its own characteristics of love, generosity and freedom'. Moved by the Alliance's President, Sir Culling Eardley (himself of part-Jewish extraction through his maternal descent from the eighteenth-century financier Sir Sampson Gideon) and seconded by the Reverend Dr Pomroy, Secretary to the American Board of Commissioners for Foreign Missions, the resolution recorded 'sympathy' with Edgar Mortara's family, 'so cruelly treated', its hopes for his restoration to them, and its disavowal of the 'shameless' action which recalled 'the ecclesiastical tyranny of former ages'. This resolution was sent to Montefiore, and Eardley arranged for 50 newspapers containing reports of the meeting to be delivered to the Board of Deputies in case they proved useful in its campaign to have

Edgar returned home.[8] He wished a grateful Montefiore 'speedy and entire success' in the matter. 'I have reason to believe that among Christians of every shade there is a widespread feeling of indignation at the conduct of the Court of Rome,' he assured him.

> Generous Roman Catholics in France especially join with us in disavowing and condemning it.
>
> We shall be glad to be informed whenever it is decided what further steps shall be taken by the Jews of Europe. We shall, as soon as we know our intentions, inform our friends in various countries concerning them, and request their sympathy.[9]

Anticipating that Montefiore would visit the Emperor of France, Napoleon III, to plead with him to exert pressure on his papal ally, Eardley swung the Evangelical Alliance, dedicated to the cause of religious liberty, into a well-coordinated back-up campaign. The Alliance arranged to send a deputation to Paris in support of Montefiore. The Lord Mayor of London, David Wire, who had travelled with Montefiore to the East in 1840, undertook to accompany the deputation along with the Provost of Edinburgh. It was expected that the Lord Mayor Elect of Dublin would do so too. The Alliance hoped that its overseas subsidiaries – in the United States, France, Germany and elsewhere – would also send spokesmen to Paris.[10]

Meanwhile, in the winter of 1858, a committee chaired by Wire with Eardley as his deputy organized a petition 'signed by Protestant archbishops, bishops, former lord chancellors, eminent statesmen, and numerous personages public and private' for presentation to the Emperor. (Similar addresses in support of religious liberty were prepared by Protestant organizations in the United States, France, Holland, Switzerland, Piedmont, Hungary and Turkey.) 'It was felt,' explained Eardley,

> that such an appeal to the Emperor in support of a similar one from the Jews of Europe, would be gratifying to the French nation. We were also assured that the Emperor would appreciate it. He has more than once declared that the French flag should not float over ecclesiastical despotism at Rome.

News that Montefiore intended to visit not Paris but the Vatican scuttled the plan. Eardley was philosophical: 'If you fail at Rome, your case will be all the stronger for your going, after all, to the Emperor. Real Christians will not be the less ready to support you then than now; and, in the meantime, it may not be useless for it to be known that the Protestants are resolved to sustain the Jews in their just claim.'[11]

On 3 November 1858 the Committee of the Protestant Association, which had concerned itself with the plight of overseas Jewry during the 1840s, sent a memorial to the Foreign Secretary, the Earl of Malmesbury, urging the British government to consider how its influence 'exercised so often with success in defence of civil and religious liberty and the rights of the oppressed, may be now exerted for the restoration of the child ... to his parents at Bologna, and that steps may be taken accordingly.' The signatories 'strongly object to the principle that the mere fact of a Jewish child having been baptised with or without its own consent, or the consent of its parents, should entitle the clergy, ministers, inquisitors, or other agents, or officers of the papacy to take such child away from parental control, believing ... that such a course is in direct violation no less of natural rights than of the principles of civil and religious liberty.' The memorial was forwarded to Malmesbury by the Association's Chairman, James Lord.[12]

A similar document was sent on 19 November to Lord Malmesbury by the Edinburgh-based Scottish Reformation Society under the chairmanship of J.H. Balfour. The latter noted in a separate letter that the signatories regarded the treatment of Edgar as 'a breach of all human right, a startling exhibition of assumption and intolerance, which, unless checked, may expose every British subject or others beyond the pale of the Church of Rome to be treated in the same manner.'[13]

On 2 December a comparable memorial was sent to Malmesbury by the Committee of the Protestant Alliance. A letter written a few days later by that body's President, the Earl of Shaftesbury (formerly Lord Ashley) explained:

> Your memorialists participate in the general feeling of indignation which has been expressed, both in this country and abroad, in reference to the case of Edgar Mortara, who has been forcibly removed by the authorities at Rome, and placed in a Romish seminary for education; notwithstanding the earnest protest of his parents. The fact that the child has, through the instrumentality of a Roman Catholic nurse, been secretly baptised, even if it can be proved, your memorialists cannot regard as a justification of this flagrant invasion of parental rights and religious freedom.
>
> Your memorialists venture to hope that it may not be deemed inconsistent with the position which her Majesty's government

maintain in relation to the Papal government to express their distinct disapproval of this act of cruelty, and use what influence may be practicable in restoring the child to his parents.[14]

Meanwhile, early in December 1858, a public meeting to protest Mortara's abduction was held at Chelsea under the auspices of the South-west London Protestant Institute. The principal speaker was a clergyman, and a resolution was passed condemning the action of the papal authorities. Colonel C.S. Vereker, in the chair, declared that across Europe the Mortara family's plight was 'arousing the indignation and exciting the heartfelt sympathy of all independent men, be they Protestant or Catholic'. Britons had an obligation to speak out.

> It would surely be a deep and indelible disgrace to us in this Protestant land if we did not raise our voice in the cause of civil and religious liberty ... The whole world looks to the course taken by England in such matters as this. It therefore behoves Englishmen and Englishwomen to exert themselves on behalf of the afflicted and oppressed, of whatever creed or persuasion they may be. It behoves them ... to stand forward in defence of the rights of man. Would I could say that the government of this country had taken a manly course by remonstrating against the cruelty perpetrated, and by endeavouring to procure the restoration of the little Jewish child to its afflicted parents, not of course, by direct means – for that would be impossible, owing to this country not holding diplomatic relations with the court of Rome – but indirectly through some Roman Catholic governments with which we are on terms of amity.

In his replies to the organizations which had contacted him on the subject, Lord Malmesbury had observed that since France and other Catholic states had failed to influence the Vatican, an approach from the British government was unlikely to be effective. Vereker took the point, but believed that for honour's sake if nothing else, Malmesbury should have registered Britain's protest as soon as the abduction became known, instead of sitting on the sidelines awaiting events.[15]

Early in February 1859 'a large and influential meeting' of Marylebone residents was held under the auspices of the National Protestant Society to hear Dr Charles Lemprière, Fellow of St John's College, Oxford, deliver an address 'enthusiastically cheered throughout' in which he stressed 'the duty of crying aloud against the monstrous outrage of the Mortara tragedy'. He declared that 'it was to England the eyes of the world were turned whenever a question of thraldom and oppression was mooted ... It was our mission to proclaim the rights of man to the civilised world.' He was supported by three laymen.[16] The main vehicle for non-Jewish protest in Britain was the petition mentioned by Eardley in his letter to Montefiore in December 1858, which was held in abeyance once the latter's intention of journeying to Rome was revealed. With the failure of Montefiore and the Board of Deputies to procure Edgar's release, the petition, evidently more numerously signed in the meantime, was presented in October 1859 to the French Ambassador in London, representative of the country ostensibly best placed to make the Pope see reason. Noting that Montefiore's visit to Rome was ineffectual, the petition stated:

> Whereas it is a dishonour to Christianity in the eyes of Jews among all nations that the seizure and detention of Edgar Mortara should be supposed to be consistent with the principles of the Christian religion.
>
> Now we, the undersigned British Christians, do hereby protest and declare that the proceedings of the Pope of Rome in taking away the Jewish child ... from his parents, and educating him in the Roman Catholic faith, are repulsive to the instincts of humanity, and in violation of parental rights and authority, as recognised in the laws and usages of all civilized nations, and, above all, in direct opposition to the spirit and precepts of the Christian religion.[17]

This document attracted hundreds of influential signatories: the list of 459 in *The Times* occupied almost one and a half columns of tiny print (it ended '&c.,' implying more names). It is thus historically significant in being perhaps the first mass petition signed by numerous important and well-placed gentiles to protest against wrong being done to a Jew. Its signatories included the Archbishops of Canterbury, York and Dublin, with 19 bishops. (Conspicuously absent was the Bishop of London, Dr Archibald Campbell Tait, who explained that the abduction 'was but part and parcel of the system of Rome, and that were he to protest against every unjustifiable act of the Papacy he should have nothing else to do but continuously to protest.'[18]) Many other very senior Anglican clergymen signed, along with a number of nonconformist ministers. The Dukes of Beaufort, Cleveland, Leeds and Wellington signed, as did the Marquis of Cholmondeley, ten earls including Shaftesbury, as well as Lord Brougham and other peers. The final count was said to include 36 Members of Parliament: the printed list contained two short of that figure, drawn from all parties. There were 11 Conservatives including Sir Brook Bridges, Lord Ernest Bruce, Sir Charles Burrell, J.S. Erle-Drax and T.B. Horsfall; 20 Liberals including Lord Ashley (the Tory Shaftesbury's heir), the Hon. F.W.F. Berkeley, Adam Black (the well-known publisher), Lieutenant-General E.P. Buckley, the Hon. Frederick Calthorpe, J. Henry Gurney, Samuel Gurney, (Sir) William Hutt, the Hon. Arthur Kinnaird, Admiral Sir Charles Napier, Lord Alfred Paget, and (Sir) Titus Salt (the famous manufacturer); two Reformers and one old-fashioned Whig.[19].

David Wire, Lord Mayor of London, headed the list of English civic dignitaries who signed. These included Benjamin Scott, Chamberlain of the City of London, several provincial alderman and municipal officeholders, and the mayors of 55 English towns large and small, crisscrossing the map from Bodmin to Berwick-on-Tweed, from Carlisle to Dover. There were, from Scotland, the Lord Provosts of Edinburgh and Perth, and the Provosts of nine towns, from Annan just inside the Border to Tain in the far north-west, even Kirkwall in the Orkneys; the Lord Mayor of Dublin, the Mayor of Derry and an alderman of Cork; and, from Wales, the Mayors of Brecon, Cardigan, Haverfordwest, Pembroke, Pwllheli and Tenby, as well as an alderman of Llanidloes.

An equally impressive number of signatories were drawn from 'all professions and the higher classes of the realm'.[20] These included doctors, lawyers, bankers, military and naval officers, and people evidently of private means. A wide range of localities was represented, including remote Stromness, also in the Orkneys. Officials of many religious and ecclesiastical bodies signed: predictably, the Evangelical Alliance, its offshoot the Working Men's Education Society, the Protestant Alliance, the Protestant Association, the Reformation Society – and many more, such as the Congregational Union of England and Wales, the Lord's Day Observance Society and the British and Foreign Bible Society.[21]

'The Christian protest bears the property and intelligence of Protestant England,' enthused a non-Jewish regular reader of the *Jewish Chronicle*, Samuel Smith of Sedgley, near Wolverhampton, who that same year collected small sums from townspeople for the Jews of Morocco Relief Fund. 'I am thankful to Almighty God that I am spared in my old age to see such a manifestation of England's Christian love in behalf of the plundered parents and the helpless child.' He intended to distribute 1,000 copies of the printed petition among his parish's 40,000 residents. 'May the blessing of Him who appeared to Moses in the bush ... ever rest on his ancient people.' He wrote to the Bishop of London registering his disapproval of that prelate's refusal to sign the petition and begging him to reconsider: 'It is, my lord, an act of Christian unity which will be enrolled in the archives of heaven ... The names of Abraham, Isaac, and Jacob are engraved on my heart.'[22] Like many gentiles, Smith was an avowed admirer of Montefiore's exertions on behalf of the Jewish people: 'The life and memory of Sir Moses Montefiore belongs to eternity ... Although of a different persuasion, my devotedness to [him] has been of long standing.'[23]

On 7 November this petition was presented to the Foreign Secretary, Lord John Russell, by 'a numerous and influential deputation' from Lord Mayor Wire's 'Mortara Committee'. Wire was indisposed, and another intending delegate, former Lord Mayor of London Sir James Duke, was also unable to be there. Duke's name did not appear in the list of petitioners printed in *The Times*, nor did those of certain other delegation members such as James Lord, Chairman of the Protestant Association, the Mayor of Rochester and several clergymen. Presumably, these people had signed the petition after it went to press, or as signatories on behalf of religious and ecclesiastical bodies whose involvement had been noted in the newspaper. The delegation, led by the committee's Vice-Chairman, Sir Culling Eardley, included a Major-General Alexander, ex-Quaker City businessman and future Conservative parliamentarian R.N. Fowler, Samuel Gurney MP and Benjamin Scott. A strong letter of support had been received from Lord Stratford de Redcliffe, until 1858 Britain's Ambassador in Turkey; 'many noblemen and gentlemen had sent in letters or cards ... showing the interest taken in the subject in the provinces.'[24]

Noting that 'all Europe rang' with the 'infamy' of Edgar Mortara's abduction, the delegation urged the British government to 'bring the subject of the Papal treatment of the Jews' before any nations which might be involved in the future of the Italian states, so that 'the long-oppressed and down-trodden race of Israel might be released from that religious oppression.' Russell, known as a good friend to Anglo-Jewry and to all liberal causes, readily agreed that 'the real justice of the case ... needs no argument'. But he pointed out that not all European nations took as liberal a view of human and Jewish rights as Britain and France, making concerted action difficult, and Britain had no real hope of influencing a foreign power with such an intransigent view of the righteousness of its own cause as the Vatican.[25]

Towards the start of the Affair, when plans were being made by Jews to approach the Vatican, the *Jewish Chronicle* had remarked that 'it will become the Christians of England to render them moral support', quickly adding that 'Christians will require, and have required, no request from Jews to induce them to move in the matter'.[26] Its confidence had been amply realized. While appreciating that the obstacles outlined by Russell would probably prove insuperable, it had the satisfaction of knowing that 'the sea of public opinion' surrounding the case 'rolls on majestically'. It regarded Wire and his committee warmly, and felt sure 'That there are high-standing influential men of acknowledged liberalism who stood aloof from the protest, merely because they did not deem it comprehensive enough …' The only effective means of obtaining justice for the Mortara family rested with the forthcoming Congress of European powers, called to settle the future of Italy, which should establish 'liberty of conscience, in the full sense of the word, as an international law of the civilised world'.[27] Many aspects of the efforts by British gentiles on behalf of Mortara are extraordinary and should be highlighted. While Jews such as Montefiore of course attempted to identify sympathetic British Christians and use their efforts in Mortara's cause, the agitation in support of the boy cannot simply be described as an agitation masterminded by the Jewish community. Many – perhaps most – of the sympathetic Christians involved came forward voluntarily and often spontaneously. Secondly, the efforts on Mortara's behalf contained an important anti-Catholic component, in which the Catholic Church's attitude was seen as a relic of medieval barbarism, with both antisemitism and the backward features of Catholicism viewed as utterly contrary to the progressive spirit of the age, in contrast to Protestantism, which was sympathetic to Jews, and which, precisely owing to its progressive, enlightened nature, certainly eschewed antisemitism. Thirdly, on the scale of calamities which have befallen the Jewish people down the ages, the Mortara Affair was surely a trivial one, yet by the late 1850s, in Britain at any rate, it became virtually a national *cause célèbre* and evoked an unprecedented effort by sympathetic Christians. By this time, for a sector of Britain's Protestant Establishment, support for Jews and opposition to antisemitism had become almost a test of enlightenment.

The next few decades saw further crises in the Jewish world. There was the plague and famine in the Holy Land leading to the successful appeal of 1865; a serious pogrom at Odessa in 1871, concerning which the Evangelical Alliance cooperated with the AJA; and anti-Jewish riots involving blood libels at Marmara and Smyrna, which were promptly suppressed by Turkish troops. Aside from these, the next big crisis to receive publicity in Britain occurred in Romania. For most of the nineteenth century the Jews of that country faced antisemitism as pernicious as it was tenacious. Discriminatory legislation began in 1804. Although the Romanian provinces formed part of the Turkish Empire, Russia, whose troops occupied them for several decades prior to the Congress of Paris (1856), wielded considerable influence. In order to check this influence, Britain and the other powers at the Congress, which followed the Crimean War, placed the Danubian provinces of Moldavia and Wallachia comprising Romania under their guarantee and restored Bessarabia to Moldavia; the Sultan, to whom Romania paid an annual tribute, reserved the right of controlling the country's foreign policy but granted it autonomy in internal affairs.[28]

Restrictive ordinances against Romanian Jewry were based on Russian models. Violence and arbitrary expulsions occurred. Romanian Jewry, numbering perhaps 200,000 by the 1870s as a result of a substantial immigration into Moldavia which had occurred over the past century, was split into the foreign-born under the protection of foreign consuls and the native-born. But the law denied citizenship to both communities. Their situation improved somewhat between 1859 and 1866 under the liberal Prince Alexander, but when (following his deposition) reports of its deterioration reached the West, Sir Moses Montefiore visited Bucharest in 1867 for personal talks with Alexander's successor, Prince Charles, who assured him that there was no cause for anxiety.[29]

In February 1872 at the Romanian town of Ismail just inside Bessarabia, a Lithuanian-born Jewish convert to Christianity, in conspiracy with Romanian or Russian antisemites, stole sacred items from the local cathedral and blamed Jews. First, he implicated his employer, a Jewish tailor, and then the rabbi and warden of the Ismail synagogue. Their presumed guilt led to riotous attacks on Jews, which quickly spread from Ismail to neighbouring settlements resulting in deaths and injuries. A total of five Jews were accused; all entirely innocent, they were convicted by a Romanian court and sentenced to three years' imprisonment, while arrested rioters went free. By the time the apostate confessed his crime and the attacks were quelled, considerable damage had been done to Jewish communities in Romania and to that country's image in the Western world.[30]

The London-based Anglo-Jewish Association (AJA), one of the two principal Jewish humanitarian aid agencies to whom the Jews of Ismail appealed for relief, publicized an eyewitness account of the riots:

> The mob, fanaticised by the priests and instigated by villainous intriguers ... hastened from house to house and pitilessly assaulted frail old age and defenceless women; they spared not even the babe at the breast ...
>
> Our helpless brethren were brutally ill-treated, wives and daughters were outraged ... houses were pillaged, our sanctuaries desecrated, and Scrolls of the Law carried off. Even the dead were disturbed in their resting-places ... Many succumbed under their wounds ... the sick are huddled together on straw mats ... Hundreds of ill-used creatures, stripped almost naked, wander about the streets, homeless and starving ...[31]

The Romanian disturbances, which coincided with a worsening of the Jewish condition in neighbouring Serbia, also in defiance of the Congress of Paris, were widely condemned in Britain by Jew and gentile alike. The hand of Russia was believed to be at work behind the scenes, and it was rumoured that Russian officials signalled the mobs to attack. There was resentment that the Romanian regime, upheld by courtesy of the European powers, permitted such savagery to occur. And the violence brought Romania's antisemitic legislation under scrutiny. The London *Daily Telegraph*, for example, with a sympathy characteristic of the British press, deplored the status of Romanian Jewry:

> As aliens they can hold no landed property, not even on lease; they cannot fill the humblest civil office; they are shut out from every profession down to that of apothecaries and teachers. While bound to serve in the army, no price, no degree of bravery or merit, would procure them a commission in it. Their conduct in Roumania, at the present day resembles that of the Jews during the middle ages. In default of a Ghetto, they are liable to be thrown into prison and maltreated, with the view of extorting false evidence of conspiracies hatched by the police themselves. Such is Roumania today, and she calls herself Christian, and exists by the patience of Europe.[32]

When in April 1872 Sir Francis Goldsmid MP, President of the Romanian Committee of the AJA, raised the treatment of Romanian and Serbian Jewry in the Commons, several non-Jewish members made speeches condemning the persecution and calling for action. The Welsh Liberal Henry Richard led them in declaring their abhorrence and detestation of the atrocities ... which were a stigma and a disgrace to the century in which we lived. The records of every age and country showed that no more loyal, industrious and useful members of the community could be desired than were the Jews whenever a fair opportunity was allowed them, and that they were capable of winning the highest distinctions in philosophy, literature, art, and politics ... An appeal to the whole civilised world was the best course to be adopted.

Lord Enfield, the Liberal Under-Secretary of State for Foreign Affairs, maintained that Britain 'had a right to demand ... perfect political liberty' for the Jews of the affected Balkan States. William Wheelhouse (Conservative) observed that if Romania and Serbia continued to flout their treaty obligations, tough measures by Britain would be required. Philip Muntz (Radical), George Dixon and John Whitwell (both Liberal) also championed the Jews.[33]

Some Jewish leaders insisted that Montefiore had made headway during his visit to Bucharest in 1867 and that what was needed now was not a public meeting on the lines of the one held in 1840, which might alienate the Romanian regime and prove counterproductive, but another personal approach.[34] The *Jewish Chronicle* saw things differently: a public meeting would bring together Britons 'regardless of distinction of creed, community, personal or party feeling or political views [to] publicly ratify the expression of English opinion distinctly uttered by the press' and would thereby 'convince the Roumanian government that the people of England are in earnest in their outcry against acts of oppression'.[35] This was the view taken by the AJA after powerful persuasion by one of its brightest luminaries, (Sir) John Simon MP, and accordingly a meeting was convened by Lord Mayor of London (Sir) Sills Gibbons.[36]

The meeting took place in the Mansion House on 30 May, and like the relief fund for Romanian Jewry set up by the AJA it received generous support from non-Jews. So many distinguished gentiles attended that reporters did not list them all. They included 34 Members of Parliament (of all affiliations, Liberals with City interests predominating), peers and other titled persons, representatives of City firms, bankers including the Governor and other officials of the Bank of England, alderman and other City office-holders. Many letters apologizing for absence and upholding the aims of the meeting were received: for example, from the Bishops of Exeter and Peterborough, Liberal MP Jacob Bright and Lord Houghton, a liberal-minded former Conservative MP. The latter repeated the words of Hastings Russell, the new Duke of Bedford: 'I take great interest in the old race and old religion, and the most painful interest in the fact that my Christian brethren have ever made persecution and tyranny part of their religious practice.'[37]

Opening the meeting, Alderman (Sir) William Lawrence MP (Conservative) observed:

> In this country and in this city pre-eminently, the Jews had been placed on an equal footing ... and in protesting in this country and in this city ... we wished to show to the Roumanians and to all the world that if any insult was offered to the Jews in Roumania or elsewhere, we felt it was an insult offered to ourselves. Those [attending] were present, not merely as a number of individuals, but as representing the City of London, and indeed the whole people of this country ...[38]

A clear indication of the climate of British opinion had to be sent to Whitehall, to Romania (where three of the five accused remained in jail), to Russia with its suspected involvement in the disturbances, and to Turkey, the power with ultimate control over Romania. Therefore, influential non-Jews of all parties took centre stage, the only Jewish speakers being Sir Francis Goldsmid and Alfred de Rothschild, who, respectively, moved and seconded the fourth and final resolution, expressing thanks to all those who made the meeting a success.

In centre stage Shaftesbury moved the first resolution, which like them all was carried unanimously: 'That this meeting protests against the outrages committed on the Jews in Roumania, as a disgrace to modern civilization, and deeply sympathizes with the unhappy sufferers.' In his speech he observed that the occurrences were a disgrace,

> not only to modern civilization, but to Christianity, and to everything that would exalt and dignify man (loud cheers.) We should be distressed to hear of outrages perpetrated on any class of people in any country whatsoever; but much more were we called upon to express our sympathies in the present instance; for here the sufferers were an ancient nation of great note and fame, who occupied a most distinguished position in the pages of the world's history, and who stood on the civil rights that were accorded to them by the Powers of Europe (cheers) ... They had done nothing whatever to promote those terrible outrages, which could only be traced to the jealousy which the Roumanians entertained for a

people remarkable for their industry, their truth, and their submission to all the principles of just government in whatever country they might be placed in (cheers) The only remedy ... was for this country and all civilized nations to raise their voice against such proceedings ... Although it was but a small section of the Hebrew people for whom the meeting was now pleading, yet ... they were the descendants of an ancient and famous race, whose glories were not surpassed in all the world's history. They were not behind in any quality that dignified and adorned men and women in any walk of life; and were these people to be put down and treated with scorn and cruelty by a handful of the most contemptible creatures on the face of the earth? (cheers). We had all a deep interest in the millions ... of Jewish people who were making their way in every part of the world. The time might yet come when they would resume their former position among the nations of the earth, and it was to be hoped that the time was not far distant when they would resume ... the position of a distinct people and nation – with its proper government, and would vie with all the other peoples and nations of the world in every glory and grandeur which could dignify the human race.

The resolution was seconded by Liberal MP Robert Wigram Crawford, who said that while he generally opposed interference in the affairs of other countries, in view of the Treaty of Paris this was 'an exceptional case' and Turkey should be asked to exercise its suzerainty over Romania. The Bishop of Gloucester and Bristol, Dr C.J. Ellicott, moved the second resolution: 'That justice demands the relief and indemnity of those who have suffered, or are suffering, in person or property, and the effectual protection of the Roumanian Jews against future outrage, by securing to them, in accordance with existing Treaties, equality of rights with their fellow citizens.' Seconding was R.N. (later Sir Robert) Fowler MP (Conservative), who had signed the Mortara petition.

Liberal MPs Kirkman Hodgson and Edward Baines, supported by Sir Thomas Fowell Buxton, a former parliamentarian of their own party, respectively moved and seconded the third resolution. This thanked the British government for already giving 'timely aid' to the victims of the disturbances through its Consul in Bucharest, and urged it to demand that in order to safeguard the rights of Romanian Jewry, the Congress of Paris 'unite in a joint representation to the Roumanian Government' and take 'such other means as may be deemed available.' It also nominated a 32 man delegation to convey the meeting's feelings to the Foreign Secretary, Earl Granville. The non-Jews nominated included landowner Sir Charles Trevelyan, whose son, a Liberal MP, was also at the meeting, and W.H. Smith, founder of the famous bookselling and stationery chain, who was a Conservative MP. The others were parliamentarians: those already mentioned as having spoken at the meeting, plus Sir Thomas Bazley, Humphrey Crum-Ewing, Lord Henley, Arthur Kinnaird, Sir John Lubbock, Anthony Mundella, Henry Richard, Peter Rylands and James White (all Liberals).[39] 'What was needed was an expression of sympathy on the part of our Christian fellow countrymen; and this was given with generous energy and unmistakable force,' enthused the *Jewish Chronicle*.

The great meeting at the Mansion House has an importance which can scarcely be over-estimated. In the greatest city of the greatest empire in the world, an expression of opinion has gone forth, which reflects the views of this powerful and good English nation, and which cannot – which dare not be – lightly regarded. A prelate of the National Church, a peer of the realm, the Lord Mayor of the great commercial metropolis, and a nobleman of great literary reputation [Lord Houghton], are representative exponents of English society, and they speak its voice ...

It was, indeed, a gratifying spectacle to see our Christian brethren united with us in this cause ... Humanity is a doctrine and practice of Christian Englishmen: and to them the voice of oppression serves as a call for redress ...[40]

Amelioration of the lot of Romanian and Serbian Jewry was accomplished in 1878 with the clause regarding the rights of minorities insisted upon at the Congress of Berlin. The role of the United States, whose House of Representatives had in May 1872 passed a resolution directing President Ulysses S. Grant to protest at the outrages perpetrated on the Jews of Romania, must not be overlooked. Many Jews had never forgiven Grant for his order, during the Civil War, expelling Jews from the military district under his command for allegedly flouting Treasury Department trade regulations, an order swiftly rescinded by President Abraham Lincoln. Since then, Grant appeared anxious to make amends. He was close to the prominent Jewish lay leader Simon Wolf, and in 1870 appointed as American Consul in Bucharest a Jew, Benjamin Peixotto, who served with great effect until 1876. Grant's Secretary of State, Hamilton

Fish, made clear the administration's support for the Jews in several pronouncements which have been noted by historians.[41]

In Britain, as part of a campaign to put the issue of Balkan Jewry squarely on the agenda of the Congress of Berlin, a public meeting addressed by John Simon was held on 16 January 1877 at Bedford, chaired by the Mayor and attended by prominent townspeople. Suitable resolutions were proposed by Bedford's Conservative MP, Captain F.C. Polhill-Turner, by an alderman and a Christian clergyman. They were seconded by a senior army officer and two clergymen, one of whom proudly announced that he had trudged miles to be there.[42]

The public meeting as a weapon in the fight for Jewish rights abroad had been pioneered by the City of London. Intended not as an empty gesture, but as a potent way of demonstrating the extent of pro-Jewish feeling among the British commercial and political elite, both to the government at home and persecutory regimes abroad, it aimed to exert genuine pressure, and for that reason brought together speakers of prestige and influence and packed the platforms with public figures. No longer confined to the City of London nor indeed to the metropolis, but meaning still to showcase prominent gentile supporters of Jews – drawn now from a variety of fields of endeavour including the arts and academia – and act as an important lobbying agent, it would feature largely in efforts by gentiles in Britain and other English-speaking countries on behalf of oppressed Jewries overseas in the years ahead.

3 'The Imperishable People': Protesting against Pogroms and Persecution in Russia, 1881–1906

On 1 March 1881 the relatively liberal Czar, Alexander II, was assassinated by terrorist revolutionaries. In the ensuing climate of bewilderment and anxiety, a wave of pogroms swept across southern Russia. Commencing in comparatively mild form at Elizavetgrad on 15 April, they assumed more serious character at Smela ten days later, at Kiev on 26 April and at Odessa on 3 May, causing considerable destruction, outrage, injury and loss of life. What began in the urban centres spread to the countryside, so that during the spring and summer of 1881 southern Russia was in the grip of anti-Jewish violence, known to us as pogroms, unprecedented in the Czarist Empire.

Economic resentment on the part of peasants, itinerant workers and migratory unemployed (in many cases often the worse for alcohol) towards Jewish merchants and shopkeepers in what was an area of high population density and competition for employment, seems to have been the root cause of the pogroms. Although the pogroms began during Easter Week, religious antisemitism appears to have been of peripheral significance. Direct evidence that the Czarist authorities orchestrated the anti-Jewish rioting is lacking. Indeed, the pogroms seem to have taken the government by surprise, and made it fear a general attack on order and property. It was in the government's interest to quell the riots as swiftly as possible, and this, apparently, was done.[1]

The assassinated Czar had yielded some benefits to certain sections of Russian Jewry. He had abolished the odious cantonist system, whereby young Jewish boys had been conscripted for a minimum of 25 years of military service. He had eased the entry of Jews into institutions of higher learning. He had permitted selected categories of Jews – university graduates, wholesale merchants, manufacturers and guild-artisans – to reside outside the 15 provinces constituting the

Pale, in whatever part of the Russian Empire they chose (which for most inclined to relocate meant Moscow, St Petersburg and Kharkov).[2] Following the pogroms of 1881, the government of his successor, Alexander III, accepted recommendations that the causes of tension between Jews and non-Jews should be removed. Hence the 'May Laws' of 1882, which forbad any further shift of Jews from the cities and *shtetlakh* of the Pale into the countryside, prohibited Jews from purchasing or renting property in rural localities, and prevented Jews from trading on Sundays or Christian holidays. Police and other local officials were effectively empowered to interpret these regulations as they thought fit, which led to arbitrariness in their enforcement and consequent uncertainty. Pogroms were not halted by these laws: there were further outbreaks in March 1882 and July 1883, and, far east of the Pale, an isolated incident in July 1884.[3]

In Britain there was considerable outrage among gentiles at the pogroms of 1881 and their successors, and the reports from Russia attempting to justify the violence were deeply deplored. It was widely feared in Britain that the revocation by the new Czar, Alexander III, of previous reforms would cause further misery for Russia's oppressed Jews and a sympathetic response by British philosemites was not slow in coming. Spearheading the British campaign on behalf of Russian Jewry and bringing the issue before influential public opinion was *The Times*, the *Jewish Chronicle* later recalled, which

> became the mouthpiece for voicing British indignation against the treatment of the Jews abroad. Between 1880 and 1883, at least thirteen leading articles were devoted to the subject, besides innumerable reports and notes. Its protests against the pogroms in Russia could not easily have been more outspoken.

The Times published an account of the wrongs endured by the Jews of Russia, written at its request by the well-known Jewish historian and commentator Joseph Jacobs: 'This timely publicity was largely responsible for the importance which the question immediately attained in the eyes of the world.'[4]

As a result of such items, in January 1882 a great meeting to protest at the sufferings of Russian Jewry took place at the Mansion House under the chairmanship of London's Lord Mayor, future Conservative MP (Sir) John Whittaker Ellis. It had been requisitioned by 38 prominent gentiles, including five who had played active parts in the 1872 protest regarding Romanian Jewry: Shaftesbury, the Bishop of Gloucester and William Lawrence MP, all of whom had spoken at the meeting held that year, and MPs Sir John Lubbock and Henry Richard, who had been delegation members. Other requisitioners were 15 further MPs from across the political spectrum; the Archbishop of Canterbury, Dr Tait; the Bishops of London, Oxford and Manchester; the Roman Catholic Archbishop of Westminster, Cardinal Manning; five further high-ranking Anglican clergymen; leading Unitarian divine Dr James Martineau; Lords Mount-Temple and Scarsdale; and four distinguished intellectuals, Matthew Arnold, Charles Darwin, Master of Balliol Dr Benjamin Jowett, and the scientist Professor John Tyndall.[5]

True to the nature of such meetings, Jewish notables attended, but gentile public figures dominated proceedings. The crowded hall held non-Jewish peers and peeresses, MPs of all parties, and clergymen of various denominations, as well as the Governor of the Australian colony of Victoria and the Canadian High Commissioner. Indeed, the roll-call bid fair to resemble a 'Who's Who' of British Society, a characteristic repeated on comparable occasions in subsequent decades.[6] Many of those present, such as Baroness Burdett-Coutts and (Sir) William Soulsby, were familiar to the Jewish community as its champions. The immensely wealthy and legendarily philanthropic Baroness, 'a lifelong friend of the Jewish cause', was on intimate terms with several Anglo-Jewish leaders. In 1859 her £50 had been an outstandingly generous donation to the Jews of Morocco Relief Fund. In 1877 she sent £200 worth of warm fabric for the exclusive use of Jewish victims of the Russo-Turkish War. Her proposal that ancient aqueducts at Jerusalem be restored at her expense, so that the Jews of that city would be ensured water, was rebuffed by the Ottoman authorities.[7] Soulsby, a long-serving London alderman, was one of the Jews' tried and tested allies in the City, and was knowledgeable in the history of Jewish emancipation.[8] Yet Robert Browning, well-remembered for several poems sympathetic to Jews and widely, though erroneously, believed to have been of Jewish extraction, was the only celebrity present whose demonstrative philosemitism is generally known. Browning's fellow poet, Algernon Swinburne, had that same month penned a sonnet entitled 'On the Russian Persecution of the Jews', and the well-known novelist Charles Reade, contemptuously dismissing the Russian peasantry, 'lawfully outwitted' by the Jews, announced:

> If by any chance this recent outrage should decide the Jewish leaders to colonise Palestine ... let us freely offer ships, seamen,

money – whatever we are asked for. It will be a better national investment than Egyptian, Brazilian, or Peruvian bonds.[9]

Among those unable to attend who sent messages of solidarity were Britain's richest landed proprietor, the Duke of Westminster, Lord Kinnaird, Poet Laureate Alfred (Lord) Tennyson, the Bishop of Exeter, the noted Baptist preacher the Reverend C.H. Spurgeon and several MPs. One of the latter, the Liberal (Sir) Henry Fowler (later a senior Cabinet minister), expressed a widespread sentiment: 'It is the duty of Englishmen, irrespective of creed or party, to utter their strongest protests against this brutal and barbarous persecution. If the Russian government have sanctioned, connived at, or condoned these fiendish cruelties, no considerations of a political or dynastic character should be allowed to stifle the voice of England.'[10] The rationale behind the public meeting was articulated by one of the principal speakers, Lord Shaftesbury. He described it as a great 'moral weapon' whose wielders might justly anticipate ultimate victory, for although its deliberations might be treated with contempt by those it sought to influence, 'the power of any constantly repeated affirmation of a great principle founded upon justice and humanity' could not be perpetually disregarded, even by absolute rulers.[11]

The five resolutions were carried unanimously. Non-Jews introduced the first four. Shaftesbury, seconded by the Bishop of London, Dr John Jackson, moved the main one, which declared that 'the persecution and outrages which the Jews in many parts of the Russian dominion have for several months suffered are an offence to civilization to be deeply deplored.' Moved by Cardinal Manning, seconded by Canon F.W. Farrar, the second resolution disavowed any claim to interfere in the domestic affairs of foreign nations and recorded its desire for the continuation of cordial Anglo-Russian relations, observed 'that the laws of Russia relating to Jews tend to degrade them in the eyes of the Christian population, and to expose [them] to the outbreaks of fanatical ignorance.' Manning's stirring denunciation of Russian persecution and tribute to Jewish public achievements included lines recalled for decades to come:

> There is a Book ... which is common to the race of Israel and to us Christians. That Book is a bond between us, and in that Book I read that the people of Israel are the oldest people upon the earth. Russias and Austrias and Englands are but of yesterday compared with the imperishable people which – with inextinguishable life and immutable traditions, and faith in God and in the laws of God,

scattered as it is all over the world, passing through the fires unscathed, trampled into the dust and yet never combining with the dust ... lives on still a witness to us, a witness and a warning. We are in the bonds of brotherhood with it.[12]

The third resolution requested the Lord Mayor to transmit the resolutions to Prime Minister Gladstone and Foreign Secretary Earl Granville 'in the hope that her Majesty's Government may be able, when opportunity arises, to exercise a friendly influence with the Russian Government' on behalf of Jews. It was moved by Liberal MP and author James (later Lord) Bryce, seconded by the aristocratic Liberal MP Edward Lyulph Stanley. The fourth resolution established a fund for the relief of Russian Jews, including refugees, and aimed at effecting long-term amelioration of their situation. It was moved by J.G. Hubbard, a Conservative MP, seconded by Liberal MP William Fowler. Moved and seconded by prominent Jews, the fifth resolution acknowledged the sympathy towards Russian Jewry 'shown by all classes in this country'.[13]

The ensuing 'Mansion House Fund' on behalf of Russian Jewry was chaired by Lord Mayor Whittaker Ellis with Soulsby as Honorary Secretary. Its non-Jewish members were Cardinal Manning, the Bishop of London, the Roman Catholic Bishop of Salford (later Cardinal Vaughan), Canon Farrar, Canadian High Commissioner Sir Alexander Galt, Liberal MP Samuel Morley, Conservative MPs Sir Robert Carden, William Cotton, R.N. Fowler and J.G. Hubbard, future Conservative MPs Henry Hucks Gibbs (later Lord Aldenham) and (Sir) Reginald Hanson, future Lord Mayor Alderman (Sir) John Staples, a sheriff and a colonel. (The preponderance of Tories reflected the political changeover that had occurred during the previous decade in the City of London, with which they were connected, many as aldermen. It is important to note that the City's change of allegiance from Liberal to Conservative certainly did not result in any diminution in its support for oppressed Jewry.) Within a few weeks the Fund committee had appointed a sub-committee 'to deal with the Jewish refugees [from Russia] now in Galicia, by selecting the place or places in which agricultural settlements might be formed' and appointed writer, traveller and Zionist Laurence Oliphant as its commissioner in Brody and Lvov. His task was to divide the refugees into occupational categories and select those suitable for agricultural work in the New World from those better suited to traditional employment in Europe and the British colonies.[14]

Altogether, the Mansion House Fund received over £100,000, mainly, it seems, from gentiles, enabling it to send several thousand refugees to the United States and Canada and aid many more. Some gentiles had not waited for the Fund; a collection of nearly £35 made at St Jude's Anglican Church, Southsea, for example, had been handed to officials at the Mansion House meeting.[15] Much of the total subscribed was raised through public meetings under civic auspices featuring gentile speakers held at over 40 locations throughout Britain. These ranged from major towns and cities such as Birmingham, Leeds, Liverpool, Manchester, Cardiff, Swansea, Edinburgh, Glasgow and Dublin, to smaller places such as Ashton-under-Lyne, Brighton, Dover, Falmouth, Stroud and Merthyr Tydfil; three separate meetings were held in the Potteries alone.[16] Resolutions at these meetings were often modelled on those at the Mansion House. Typically, the Mayor or Lord Provost presided, and speakers were local notables and clergymen, including parliamentarians and bishops. Messages of support were received from MPs and other influential wellwishers unable to attend.[17]

A number of prominent Oxford graduates meanwhile called for a public protest meeting under university auspices. They included Matthew Arnold, Robert Browning, former Liberal MP Sir George Bowyer and sitting Liberal MP Sir Horace Davey QC, the Archbishop of Canterbury and the Lord Chief Justice (Lord Coleridge). But resident members of the university, who sent over £200 to the Mansion House Fund, determined instead upon a memorial of solidarity to Chief Rabbi Dr Nathan Adler. The initiators of this document were Dr Edwin Palmer, Archdeacon of Oxford, Canon of Christ Church and ex-Professor of Latin (who framed it) and President of Trinity College Dr John Percival, a future Bishop of Hereford. It expressed sorrow and amazement at events in Russia and the earnest hope that equality before the law would soon be the lot of every citizen of every land, regardless of 'race or creed'.[18] This document was signed by 245 resident members of the university, including the Vice-Chancellor, no fewer than 18 heads of colleges, 25 professors and numerous fellows and tutors. Among its famous signatories were C.L. Dodgson (Lewis Carroll), Benjamin Jowett, T.H. Green and Max Müller. Rather than entrust it to the post, Palmer insisted on carrying it to London himself. A separate protest against the pogroms, signed by 1,589 Oxford undergraduates, was sent to Whittaker Ellis and his committee.[19]

Canon Farrar, who addressed the Mansion House meeting, contributed a very long and extraordinarily philosemitic article to the press, drawing attention to the oppression of Jews not only in Russia but in other parts of Europe. Appearing in diverse newspapers, it undoubtedly helped to raise public awareness of the issue, which many clergymen made the subject of sermons. Articles detailing the Jews' plight appeared in serious political and literary journals.[20] A Scottish gentleman, Robert Macfie, was so moved by the plight of Jews abroad that he added a codicil to his will:

> Whereas I have great sympathy with those poor Jews who are being persecuted by mushroom autocrats in Europe ... I instruct my trustees to keep an eye upon such cases, and I empower them ... to expend out of the trust funds under their charge such sum or sums not exceeding in all £5000, besides any interest, for ... granting to or expending as they shall deem best for behoof of any Jew or Jews who shall be at the time in circumstances similar to those hereinbefore indicated by me, and shall be ... deserving of assistance, such sum or sums as to my trustees shall seem suitable.

In 1899 following Macfie's death the money was distributed among the London Jewish Board of Guardians, the Russo-Jewish Committee and several subsidiary claimants. 'Mr Macfie's legacy serves as a pleasant indication of the broadness of mind and toleration prevalent in this country.'[21]

Protests by gentiles at the pogroms extended throughout the English-speaking world, even in the unlikeliest places. A striking example of the ubiquity of public speech and action on behalf of persecuted Russian Jewry may be found in remote Australia, whose six colonies comprised a total population of two million, of whom only about 9,100 were Jews. Outrage regarding the pogroms was quick to manifest itself, and public meetings were held in Melbourne, Adelaide and Sydney in August 1881 – that is, before their British counterparts. At each meeting motions were passed deploring events in Russia, establishing a relief fund, and appointing a committee to administer it.[22] Resolutions at the Melbourne meeting were moved almost exclusively by well-known non-Jews: distinguished barrister and politician Sir George Verdon, a parliamentarian, a history professor, two physicians and the Mayor. The latter had convened the meeting and presided. He was also appointed co-Treasurer of the relief fund committee, whose other members included Verdon and two further parliamentarians, one of them a future premier of the colony of Victoria.

The pattern of mainly non-Jewish sponsorship of resolutions was repeated in Adelaide and Sydney. In Adelaide the four non-Jews concerned were the South Australian Minister for Education, a Presbyterian Hebraist and Biblical scholar, a prominent physician who was also a leading Catholic layman, and the politically rather conservative Attorney-General (Sir) John Downer, who would later serve as premier of the colony. Chairing the meeting as well as the relief fund committee was the Mayor. Other non-Jewish committee members were Downer, renowned Chief Justice Sir Samuel Way and two parliamentarians.[23] Liberal statesman Sir John Robertson, who delivered an emotional speech and was already known for his support of Jewish causes, chaired the Sydney meeting. The platform was packed with prominent parliamentarians including the conservative-leaning Sir George Reid, a future prime minister of Australia. Non-Jewish sponsors of resolutions were the eminent Catholic liberal barrister and politician William Bede Dalley, whose zealous eloquence was the highlight of the gathering, (Sir) Thomas Buckland, a prominent Anglican businessman and pastoralist, a senior Anglican clergyman and a leading Presbyterian minister. Included on the relief committee were Robertson, Dalley, Buckland and six senior parliamentarians.[24] All three relief funds were generously subscribed, from rural as well as urban areas. And with the opening of Britain's Mansion House Fund in January 1882 Australian fundraising recommenced. A number of public meetings, addressed by parliamentarians, clergymen, and other non-Jewish local notables, took place in country towns such as Bendigo and Ballarat. Donations were liberally forthcoming.[25]

Public protest meetings and fundraising also occurred in the United States. On 1 February 1882 a huge non-Jewish demonstration of sympathy took place in New York, with the Mayor presiding. Among the capacity crowd were numerous men of note, both Democrat and Republican: public figures such as former Secretary of State Hamilton Fish, lawyer and diplomat Joseph H. Choate, former Attorney-General Edwards Pierrepont, and bankers and industrialists, many of them household names. (A rumour that former president Ulysses S. Grant was present proved false, but he evidently supported the cause.) Over 30 distinguished figures headed by Fish were named vice-presidents of the meeting. Speakers were famed lawyer William M. Evarts, who was a former Attorney-General, Judge Noah Davis, and three prominent clergymen: two Presbyterians and one Methodist Episcopal. Ex-Minister to Russia John W. Foster had intended to address the meeting, but urgent business kept him in Washington. A letter from him, robustly denouncing Russia's treatment of Jews, was read out to 'frequent and hearty applause'. Resolutions were enthusiastically adopted. They registered 'sadness and indignation' at the pogroms, called for 'just and impartial treatment' for Russian Jewry, deplored Russia's reversion to 'medieval persecution', sympathized with American Jews 'in their sorrow for their afflicted brethren in Russia', and appealed to the United States government to prevail upon Russia to cease oppressing its Jewish subjects.[26] Several months later a three-day festival in aid of Russian Jewish refugees arriving in the United States was held in New York, with leading gentiles playing highly visible roles.[27]

At Philadelphia on 15 February 1882 a meeting chaired by the Mayor made provision for Russian Jewish refugees due to disembark there. All speakers except one were non-Jews. Resolutions were passed sympathizing with Russian Jewry, requesting Pennsylvania's state legislature to protest Russian persecution, and appealing to benevolent Philadelphians for aid in receiving the refugees.[28] A mass rally to protest at the oppression of Russian Jewry and provide for their relief was held on 4 March in Philadelphia with philanthropist John Welsh presiding in the presence of Pennsylvania's Governor. Chief Justice George Sharswood and many other distinguished non-Jewish attendees played official roles. All but one of the speakers were gentiles: a general, the Protestant Episcopal Bishop, the Methodist Episcopal Bishop, a Baptist clergyman, a Roman Catholic priest (whose Bishop sent a message of support) and a former mayor.[29]

These meetings were replicated elsewhere in America, whose 'people ... have heard with great regret the stories of the sufferings of the Jews in Russia,' as Secretary of State Frederick T. Frelinghuysen observed (following a pro-Jewish joint resolution of Congress) when instructing the American envoy in St Petersburg to decide how effective it would be to lay his country's expectations that the persecution should cease before the Czarist authorities.[30] The Russian Refugee and Colonization Fund, headquartered in New York, was generously subscribed by non-Jews, with individual donations from wealthy men sometimes reaching four figures.[31]

Meanwhile, the curtailment of Jewish residency rights enshrined in the May Laws of 1882 had caused considerable hardship for tens of thousands. In 1887 Jews already living in the countryside were prohibited from migrating from one village to another. The policy of forcing the great majority of Jews into the already overcrowded towns caused widespread pauperization, and economic ruin faced people summarily expelled from centres outside the Pale, and thus deprived of their livelihood, as occurred, notably, to the Jews of Moscow and St Petersburg in 1891. At the beginning of the 1890s numerous localities, one after another, were classified as villages, and closed to fresh Jewish settlement.

The deteriorating condition of Russian Jewry led to a great protest meeting on 10 December 1890 at London's Guildhall under the presidency of Lord Mayor Sir Joseph Savory 'to express public opinion upon the renewed persecution to which millions of the Jewish race are subjected in Russia under the yoke of severe and exceptional edicts and disabilities'. This extraordinary meeting was probably attended or explicitly supported by more eminent and influential British persons than any held previously to protest at the oppression of Jews. Indeed, it is difficult to find a British meeting on a controversial foreign subject during the entire nineteenth century which enjoyed the support of so many distinguished men and important opinion-leaders. It was requisitioned by 85 distinguished non-Jews: peers, senior clergymen, naval and military figures and 24 parliamentarians of various political allegiances. Several, such as Sir John Lubbock MP, James Martineau, Benjamin Jowett, Cardinal Manning, Archdeacon (formerly Canon) Farrar and Lord Addington (formerly J.G. Hubbard MP) had been among the requisitioners of the 1882 meeting. Some of the others, such as Matthew Arnold and Baroness Burdett-Coutts, had attended that meeting or, like the Duke of Westminster and the Reverend C.H. Spurgeon, would have done so if not prevented by other matters. Among the requisitioners was Conservative MP Whittaker Ellis, who as Lord Mayor had presided over the 1882 meeting. The Archbishop of Canterbury (Dr Edward White Benson), headed the list of Anglican clergymen, including several bishops. The Dukes of Abercorn, Argyll and Newcastle, the Marquises of Abergavenny and Ripon, Earl Spencer and the Earl of Meath, inaugurator in 1892 of the Empire Day movement, were among the nobles on the list. It also included such household names as Lord Tennyson, the celebrated Poet Laureate, artist Sir Frederic (later Lord) Leighton, novelist (Sir) Walter Besant, Professor Thomas Huxley (Darwin's famous defender), Liberal MP John Bright and future Viceroy of India Lord Curzon, at that time a Conservative MP. As one signatory, leading Welsh nonconformist the Reverend Hugh Price Hughes, remarked at the meeting, no Lord Mayor had received a requisition 'more influentially signed'.[32] 'The monster meeting ... was a success in every sense of the term,' reported an eyewitness.

The historic hall was crowded from end to end ... The aristocracy of talent, as well as of birth, were there, and the oratory reached a scale of merit which has rarely been equalled even in the House of Commons ... It is, of course, impossible, without sinking to the level of a catalogue, to give any idea of the numbers of representative men and women present. Three, however, will suffice as a sample of the gathering – Lady Burdett Coutts, Professor Huxley and 'General' Booth.[33]

The Duke of Somerset, the Earls of Aberdeen, Dartmouth and Portsmouth, Earl Waldegrave, suffragist (Dame) Millicent Fawcett and novelist George Meredith were among the many sending messages of support.[34]

The first resolution adopted by the 1890 protest meeting deplored the harsh disabling legislation specifically aimed at Russian Jewry, since 'liberty is a principle which should be recognized by every Christian community as among the natural human rights'. It was moved by the Duke of Westminster 'in a long, and weighty, and diplomatic speech' ('diplomatic' because organizers were keen to avoid antagonizing the Czar). The Duke was seconded by 'England's greatest orator', Dr William Boyd Carpenter, the Bishop of Ripon, who 'delivered himself of an outburst of eloquence, in which probably even he surpassed himself'. The second resolution proposed that a respectful memorial should be addressed to the Czar, signed by the Lord Mayor on behalf of the citizens of London, requesting the repeal of all legislation discriminating against Jews. It was moved by the Earl of Meath, seconded by Conservative MP Sir Robert Fowler (who since the 1872 meeting had received a baronetcy). Following custom, the third resolution thanked the Lord Mayor for convening the meeting; its proposer was Liberal MP Sir Joseph Pease, seconded by that tireless advocate of Imperial Federation, Conservative MP Sir John Colomb. All resolutions passed unanimously.[35]

Cardinal Manning, who was too ill to participate, wrote in his customary stirring fashion that intervention in the domestic affairs of Russia was warranted by the penal laws which 'justify the words that "no Jew can earn a livelihood," and that "they are watched as criminals"'. The 'great and primary laws of human society', the 'broad and solid base of natural law' upon which 'the jurisprudence of European civilization rests', had been violated. Thus 'it is not only sympathy but civilization that has the privilege of respectful remonstrance.'[36] This reasoning, and a protest against antisemitism signed by scores of

Russian literary figures led by Count Leo Tolstoi, encouraged the meeting to proceed with its own petition to be conveyed by deputation to the Russian sovereign:

> Five million of your Majesty's subjects groan beneath the yoke of exceptional and restrictive laws. Remnants of a race whence all religion sprang – ours and yours, and every creed on earth that owns one God – men who cling with all devotion to their ancient faith and forms of worship, these Hebrews are in your Empire subject to such laws that under them they cannot live and thrive.
> ...
> Sire! ... we beseech your Majesty to repeal those laws that affect these Israelites. Give them the blessing of equality! In every land where Jews have equal rights the nation prospers ...[37]

It was signed 'on behalf of the Citizens of London' by Sir Joseph Savory. The Duke of Westminster would have gladly accepted the 'privilege' of taking it to St Petersburg but for his ill-health and advanced age. The men intended for the task were the Earl of Meath and Sir Joseph Pease, who had proposed and seconded the relevant motion. When Pease had to defer owing to business pressures, his place was taken by solicitor and shipowner Sir Albert Rollit, a future Mayor of Hull and Conservative MP.[38]

The plan of handing the petition to the Czar, however, was aborted following advice from the British Ambassador in St Petersburg, who wrote on 21 January 1891 that Alexander regarded the deputation 'as an outrageous piece of interference'.[39] Meath and Rollit needed much persuading by a regretful Savory and the Russo-Jewish Committee of the AJA not to travel as planned. Had they gained access to the Czar, the petition 'from the citizens of the greatest city in the world ... would ... have been a weapon of such moral force as to be well-nigh irresistible,' reflected the *Jewish Chronicle*, 'but it is a subject for both pride and gratitude that such distinguished Englishmen should have been found not merely willing, but anxious, to approach the Emperor of Russia as bearers of the British message of mercy on behalf of the persecuted Jews.'[40]

The Archbishop of Canterbury had written privately to the Czar's chaplain and confessor urging the cause of Jewry; he was rebuffed. Queen Victoria took a sympathetic interest in Russian Jewry. One might speculate as to the reason: possibly it was because of her close relationship with her former Prime Minister, Benjamin Disraeli; possibly because of the long-standing anti-Russian stance of much of the Court and the 'Establishment', owing to rivalry over the future of Turkey; possibly as a result of her earlier exposure to the views of Charlotte Elizabeth Tonna, whose *Christian Lady's Magazine* she received. She wrote to the Czar pleading with him 'in the name of humanity to put a stop to the barbarous legislation which disgraces his Empire', and it was perhaps with tempered optimism that Savory despatched the petition to St Petersburg. 'I need hardly assure your Majesty that the Memorial is not addressed from any political or religious considerations, but solely in the feeling that an expression of friendly interest in the welfare of the Jews in Russia by the City of London will have ... gracious and generous reception,' he explained to the Czar in a tactful covering letter.[41]

It was to no avail: letter and petition were peremptorily returned, apparently unread, via the Russian Ambassador in London. This contemptuous reception had perhaps been foreshadowed by the 'bitter and spiteful' reaction in the Russian press regarding the Guildhall meeting: 'Russia is not a British colony ... If the whole of Europe were turned into a pro-Jewish meeting, Russia would still remain self-contained and independent,' and the warning by a British consul in Russia that the criticism voiced at the Guildhall had provoked considerable acrimony in the country and 'nothing but harm could rise from such a meeting'.[42] But annoying the Russians could also be interpreted as a vindication: 'Nothing can better prove the wisdom of those public meetings in England than ... the fact that Russian nobles kept the Press cuttings [describing them] in their drawers for years, and brought them out [in indignation] whenever they saw an Englishman.'[43]

The Guildhall rally was followed by public meetings at Manchester, Birmingham and Bristol, requisitioned by influential citizens. These meetings featured prominent non-Jewish speakers and passed appropriate resolutions. The meeting at Bristol, for example, was initiated by about 100 well-known non-Jews with local connections, including the city's two MPs, a judge, civic officeholders, bankers, merchants and clergymen. Held on 30 January 1891, the meeting, chaired by the Mayor, was addressed by the High Sheriff, by Liberal Unionist MP Lewis Fry, wealthy businessman J. Storrs Fry, the High Sheriff, Anglican Bishop Ellicott, the Roman Catholic Bishop of Clifton, and four others, including two clergymen.[44]

Earlier, 1,200 people had attended an open air demonstration in the East End organized by the Working Men's International Club. Owing to its flirtation with Nihilists, this rally was disdained by established Anglo-Jewry. Chaired by an official of the London County Council, it was addressed by free-thinker Dr Edward Aveling, Eleanor Aveling (Edward Aveling's wife and Karl Marx's daughter) representing female trade unionists, and William Morris, Oxford-educated poet, interior designer and socialist, in addition to three Russian dissidents.[45]

Awareness of the plight of Russian Jewry, and appreciation of the positive qualities of Jews, was also undoubtedly stimulated by articles in leading periodicals. At the request of the Russo-Jewish Committee, novelist (Sir) Hall Caine, who wrote *The Scapegoat*, a novel with a Jewish theme, undertook in 1892–3 a fact-finding mission to Russia.[46]

In the United States numerous influential non-Jews were among over 400 signatories to a petition addressed to President Benjamin Harrison and Secretary of State James G. Blaine to win over Czar Alexander III, Queen Victoria, the Czar, the Sultan, the Austro-Hungarian Emperor, the King of Italy and the Queen Regent of Spain to the idea of imminently holding a conference on the condition of 'the Israelites, and their claims to Palestine as their ancient home; and to promote in all other just and proper ways the alleviation of their suffering condition.' Drawn up on the initiative of Chicagoan W.E. Blackstone, a devout lay Methodist who had recently returned from the Holy Land, the petition was circulated in Chicago, New York, Boston, Philadelphia, Baltimore and Washington. It was signed by congressmen, governors, mayors, judges, publishers, industrialists, financiers, philanthropists and clergymen. The 413 eminent signatories included future president William McKinley, leading businessmen J. Pierpont Morgan, John D. Rockefeller and Cyrus McCormick, Supreme Court Justice Melville W. Fuller, celebrated evangelist Dwight L. Moody and Cardinal Gibbons of Baltimore.[47] Gibbons, 'the most popular Catholic prelate in the States', matched his British equivalent, Cardinal Manning, in vigorously decrying antisemitism.[48] Harold Frederic, American-born London correspondent of the *New York Times*, contributed to that paper a series of articles sympathetic to Russian Jewry, which later appeared in book form and made a great impact. Other articles supporting Jews appeared in various journals.[49]

Over a decade later, from 19–21 April 1903 during the reign of Czar Nicholas II, a terrible pogrom, infamous even today, raged at Kishinev, capital of the Russian province of Bessarabia, in the wake of a ritual murder allegation following the killing of a Christian boy. The carnage, torture, mutilation and rape left 47 Jews dead, 424 injured, hundreds of homes destroyed and shops looted. There were fears that it presaged a repetition of the violence of 1881, and when the outside world learned of the pogrom it typically reacted with the same horror and condemnation as before: Russia, observed a British newspaper aptly, was 'standing at the bar of public opinion in Europe and America charged with conduct unworthy of a Christian and civilised Government of modern times'.[50] 'Can nothing be done to stop the printing and circulation of these horrible fabrications [the blood libel]?' asked the Irish nationalist politician and journalist Michael Davitt in a letter to *The Times*. He had been sent to investigate anti-semitism in the Kishinev region by two New York newspapers owned by William Randolph Hearst, and would immediately publish a book bringing the pogrom in its harrowing detail before a wide readership.[51] Sir Horace Rumbold, British Ambassador to Vienna, had at the time of a blood accusation in Bohemia in 1899 joined forces with Lord Rothschild and two prominent Roman Catholic laymen, the Duke of Norfolk and Lord Russell of Killowen, in attempting to destroy the ritual murder myth, and to that end he had talks with the papal nuncio in Vienna. Rumbold now proposed that the Pope and the Czar should combine in a public disavowal of the myth, to discredit it once and for all.[52] *The Times* led the rest of the British press in condemning the outrages, and many sympathetic letters from gentiles appeared. Non-Jewish names occurred in the lists of subscribers to a relief fund aimed primarily at Jews.[53] A mass demonstration in the East End held by Jewish Bundists and Russian dissident groups, chaired by J.F. Green, Secretary of the International Peace and Arbitration Association, received support from Labour MP Keir Hardie and socialist activist H.M. Hyndman.[54] But to widespread dismay, London's Jewish Lord Mayor, Sir Marcus Samuel, with the blessing of Anglo-Jewry's principal bodies and the *Jewish Chronicle*, declined to call a great public meeting in the City on the grounds that it would be inappropriate and ineffective.[55]

Evidently, Australians did not take their cue in such matters from the Motherland: to the envy of many Britons, Jew and non-Jew alike, there were public meetings in Melbourne, Sydney, Adelaide and Ballarat, featuring noted non-Jewish speakers, clerical and lay. 'Public opinion is a force that runs far, touches strange chords of influence, and makes itself felt in strange quarters,' wrote the well-known Methodist educator and writer on imperialist themes who urged Melbourne's rally. 'It would be something to show that such acts of monstrous cruelty, even on the other side of the world, awaken echoes of indignant abhorrence here.' An appeal in Melbourne 'to all friends of humanity' for donations to a relief fund made by the city's Jewish ministers was generously answered by gentiles throughout Victoria.[56]

American non-Jewish revulsion at the Kishinev pogrom has been extensively documented: throughout the United States countless editorials, sermons and appropriate resolutions adopted by diverse organizations denounced the violence and demanded justice for Russian Jewry. Relief committees were set up. Numerous public meetings took place across the country, featuring prominent gentile speakers such as mayors, legislators, judges, bankers, businessmen, clergymen and others well-known and well-respected in public or professional life. Such meetings occurred not only in cities with substantial Jewish populations, such as New York, Chicago, Philadelphia and San Francisco, but at places like Fort Smith in Arkansas, Sioux City in Iowa and Tecoma in Washington.[57] New York's was a typical, if spectacular, example. It was convened by 48 prominent citizens (all but two of them gentiles) headed by distinguished non-Jewish lawyer Paul D. Cravath, and including such familiar names as philanthropist George Foster Peabody, politician and writer Carl Schurz and publisher Charles Scribner. Some had participated in the 1882 protest; others were to be in the forefront of future initiatives on behalf of Jews. Chaired by Mayor Seth Low, this meeting at Carnegie Hall on 27 May 1903 attracted 3,500 people, and was addressed by four noted gentiles led by ex-President Grover Cleveland.[58] At these meetings, resolutions typically condemned the horrors, expressed sympathy for the victims, and demanded that the government remonstrate with its Czarist counterpart in the cause of Russian Jewry. Sometimes they went further, as at the meeting at Des Moines, Iowa, chaired by the State Governor and featuring the Chief Justice, another judge and two clergymen on its non-Jewish panel of speakers. Among its resolutions was one specifically assuring the persecuted Jews of Russia 'that America offers them a home'.[59]

A mammoth petition condemning Kishinev prepared by the Independent Order of B'nai B'rith for presentation to the Czar was circulated during July in 36 states and territories and obtained 12,544 signatures, the majority of them non-Jewish. Signatories included 37 congressmen, 22 state governors, 11 state chief justices, 150 mayors, 514 clergymen including 10 prelates and numerous representatives of other walks of life, including the public service, the military, banking, business, education, journalism, farming and the higher professions.

The Russian government refused to receive it, but President Theodore Roosevelt, who declared that no recent event had affected him more than the Kishinev horror, ensured that the petition was preserved in the State Department archives.[60]

Between 1903 and 1906 pogroms in Russia varied in frequency and ferocity, but there were certainly hundreds of them, and the death toll in 1905 was particularly high.[61] Yet again, gentiles in English-speaking countries protested anti-Jewish atrocities. The timing of these protests in the case of Britain is especially noteworthy because 1905 also witnessed the enactment of the Aliens Act which limited Russian Jewish migration (and other forms of European migration) to a perceptible extent.[62] The central form of agitation in Britain on behalf of persecuted Russian Jewry was a large protest meeting which deliberately included many influential gentiles from the 'Establishment' as well as notable British Jews. Held at the Queen's Hall, Langham Place, London, on 8 January 1906, it was presided over by Lord Rothschild and comprised a galaxy of prominent gentiles including senior clergymen, numerous peers, MPs and leaders of the Bar and business life as well as most Anglo-Jewish leaders. A letter was read out from the Archbishop of Canterbury, Dr Randall Davidson, unable to be present, who asserted that 'the sympathy which England feels for the members of the Jewish race who have recently suffered so terribly is wide and deep, and it is of the very essence of our Christianity to express it by word and act.' He had written to the Metropolitan of St Petersburg urging in the name of Christianity that no further 'tragedies and misdeeds' reoccur. Telegrams of support were also read out from the Prime Minister, Sir Henry Campbell-Bannerman, Conservative opposition leader Arthur Balfour, Joseph Chamberlain and the Duke of Devonshire. Balfour stated that 'the treatment of their Jewish citizens by European nations, from medieval times onwards, is certainly the darkest blot on the history of Christendom', while Chamberlain termed the pogroms 'an indelible disgrace upon our Christian civilisation'. Letters were also read out from numerous other distinguished supporters of the rally unable to attend, including the Lord Chief Justice, the Bishop of London, the Headmaster of Eton, the Vice-Chancellor of Cambridge University, George Bernard Shaw and Sir Edward Poynter, President of the Royal Academy.[63]

As before, the January 1906 rally passed a series of resolutions supporting the oppressed Jews of Russia. The first resolution proclaimed on behalf of 'all Englishmen, without distinction of creed or party,' its 'deep indignation and horror at the organized massacres and outrages' which 'are an offence to civilization and a disgrace to humanity, and ... its keen sympathy with the survivors' and with the victims' families. It was moved by the Bishop of Ripon, who reprised the dynamic performance he had given at the 1890 rally; seconding him was Conservative MP and sometime Solicitor-General Sir Edward Clarke KC. The second hoped that Russia would soon be free of internal strife and would then grant equal rights to Jews as the sole remedy against further outbreaks of antisemitic violence. It was moved by the Roman Catholic Archbishop of Westminster, Cardinal Bourne, seconded by famous colonial administrator Lord Milner. The third requested the chairman to forward the resolutions to the Prime Minister and Foreign Secretary in anticipation of an opportunity for the British government 'to exercise a friendly influence' upon the Czarist regime. It was moved by the Reverend Dr R.F. Horton, President of the Free Church Council, seconded by Lord Kinnaird. The fourth, giving the usual vote of thanks to the chair, was moved by Conservative MP Sir Joseph Dinsdale and seconded by former Conservative MP Lord Glenesk, proprietor of the *Morning Post*.[64]

In Australia, a wide range of individuals and organizations denounced Czarist persecution. New South Wales state parliamentarian Dr Richard Arthur, head of the newly formed Immigration League of Australia, advocated Jewish refugee settlement. Following overtures from several sources, Prime Minister Alfred Deakin cabled Downing Street advising that Australian public condemnation of the pogroms was unanimous, and that all state premiers were united on the issue.[65] Deakin's actions allayed plans for public protest meetings in Melbourne and Sydney convened by the respective lord mayors. However, the relief funds for survivors of the pogroms opened in both cities attested to the strength of gentile sympathy, and many distinguished names were among the donors. A meeting in Sydney organized by the Jewish community received expressions of solidarity from non-Jews. The City's Anglican Archbishop convened and chaired a protest meeting addressed by senior clergymen of various denominations.[66]

Perth and Adelaide had already held public protest meetings under mayoral auspices. At Perth the many non-Jewish dignitaries who packed the platform heard the grand old man of Western Australian Jewry laud the support of non-Jews throughout the English-speaking world, and they heard strong speeches from local non-Jewish notables representing all major denominations: the city's Anglican

Archbishop, two other clergymen, four parliamentarians, one ex-parliamentarian, and the Mayor-elect. A particularly stellar cast followed Adelaide's Mayor in condemning the outrages: South Australia's socialist Premier, Thomas Price, Liberal opposition leader Richard Butler, the Roman Catholic Archbishop (Dr John O'Reily), the Anglican Honorary Canon, the President of the South Australian Council of Churches, and a prominent merchant, philanthropist and Congregational lay leader. Price was instrumental in convincing Deakin to contact Downing Street. As in 1881, these public meetings predated the London one. The philosophy behind them was eloquently put by veteran philosemite O'Reily:

> Our voice may count but for little. The chorus made up of many voices may count for much. In every quarter of the civilised world Russian wrongs to the Jews excite indignation and regret. From every quarter comes Christian expostulation – a plea for justice for a much injured race ... our words will endure; and moving in union with other words spoken in a thousand places will not be void of their effect.[67]

A public meeting in Ottawa to protest the pogroms was addressed by Canadian Prime Minister Sir Wilfrid Laurier. He stated that Jews who chose Canada as a refuge would find a 'hearty welcome' and he was 'proud to assert the brotherhood of man and the fatherhood of God'.[68] Considerable sympathy for Russian Jewry manifested itself in the United States, through newspaper editorials and other means. As in Great Britain, a relief fund was generously subscribed. The philanthropic industrialist Andrew Carnegie donated $10,000:

> The terrible crimes being committed ... might lead one to lose faith in humanity ... Do not be discouraged ... we must ... finally reach the true conception of the brotherhood of man.[69]

Mark Twain, giving a special recitation, joined a number of non-Jewish performers who volunteered their services at a special benefit matinée before an upper-middle class audience in New York: it raised $3,000. America's Vice-President, Charles Warren Fairbanks, sent $100 to the fund in his home town, Indianapolis.[70]

Prominent non-Jews addressed a huge protest demonstration in New York organized by the Jewish Defence Association. They included two Baptist ministers, Madison C. Peters, author of *Justice to the Jew* (1899) and other philosemitic books, and Robert S. MacArthur. Both had been busy in the protest over Kishinev, and both proved tireless in the present campaign, MacArthur declaring: 'if I had a thousand voices I would lift them all up in behalf of this ancient, this noble, this marvellous people.'[71] The titular head of the American Episcopal House of Bishops, Archbishop Tuttle of Missouri, based in St Louis, where several non-Jews addressed a big protest meeting, sent a cable message to the Metropolitan of St Petersburg similar to that despatched by the Archbishop of Canterbury. It expressed his Church's horror at the atrocities and its wish to do everything possible to assist the survivors.[72] Representative Allan L. McDermott of New Jersey, who was terminally ill and unable to attend to Congressional business, made a surprise appearance on the floor of the House to make a long, impassioned speech on behalf of Jews. He ascribed their persecution in Russia and elsewhere to the stereotype that Jews, rather than Romans, killed Jesus, and pleaded for a change in Christian attitudes.[73] A joint resolution of Congress proclaimed that 'The people of the United States are horrified by the reports of the massacre of Hebrews in Russia on account of their race and religion, and that those bereaved thereby have the hearty sympathy of the people of this country.' Introduced on 22 June 1906 into the Senate by Anselm J. McLauren of Mississippi and into the House by Robert G. Cousins of Iowa, it passed without debate. (This was not a foregone conclusion; a resolution introduced the previous year, condemning the shooting of demonstrators outside the Czar's palace in St Petersburg, failed to pass.) The resolution was signed by President Theodore Roosevelt, who regretted that in practical terms there was little the United States could do to influence Russia.[74] Despite the realities constraining him, American Jews presented Roosevelt with a specially commissioned gold medal 'in recognition of his humane endeavours on behalf of the Jews oppressed in other lands'; a similar medal was presented to ex-President Cleveland.[75] Nowhere in the English-speaking world is it in fact possible to find anything generally except deep and certainly sincere sympathy for the plight of Russia's Jews persecuted by the Czarist regime.

4 'An Unspeakable Injustice': Philosemitism during the Dreyfus, Beilis and Frank Affairs, 1894–1913

During the two decades preceding the First World War three Jews, Alfred Dreyfus in France, Mendel Beilis in Russia, and Leo Frank in the United States, were tried for heinous crimes which they did not commit amid circumstances so sensational that they have passed into history as 'Affairs'. While, in the cases of Dreyfus and Frank, the precise role and nature of antisemitism is arguable,[1] all three wrongfully accused men were met by a torrent of sympathy and demands for justice from non-Jews.

As recounted many times, Captain Dreyfus was an Alsatian-born Jewish officer on the French General Staff, personally unpopular, who in 1894 was accused of selling military secrets to Germany. A list of secrets offered for sale, discovered by intelligence officers and known as the *bordereau*, appeared to be in his handwriting. and he was arrested. In December he was unanimously convicted by a military tribunal on a charge of treason, publicly stripped of his military insignia and imprisoned for life on Devil's Island off the coast of French Guiana. Dreyfus's conviction hinged essentially upon the handwriting on the *bordereau*. This meagre evidence was reinforced by dramatic testimony given at the trial by Commandant Henry, an intelligence officer who claimed that a secret agent of proven reliability had named Dreyfus as the traitor, and by the contents of a dossier compiled by intelligence officers and passed to the judges by the Minister of War. This dossier contained a document identifying the traitor as an officer with the initial D. In the interests of national security, Henry was not pressed to provide the informant's name, and, extraordinarily, the defence was not permitted to examine the dossier.

Early in 1896, a new head of military intelligence, Colonel Picquart, concerned that military secrets continued to be leaked to Germany, re-examined the *bordereau*. He was struck by the similarity of the handwriting to that of Commandant Esterhazy, a high-living intelligence officer whose mounting debts might indeed make paid espionage a tempting proposition. Although he disliked Dreyfus, Picquart made known his suspicions. They were not welcomed by the Army, jealous of its honour and apprehensive regarding the political implications that a wrongful conviction of Dreyfus might possess. But eventually, in January 1898, Esterhazy was tried. Almost immediately after that officer's prompt acquittal, the novelist Emile Zola, acting on little more tangible than a hunch, issued the famous treatise entitled *J'Accuse*, in which he alleged a conspiracy by the Minister of War and the top echelons of the Army to convict an innocent Dreyfus.

Later in the year, it was discovered that Henry had forged evidence against Dreyfus; having confessed, he killed himself. Esterhazy fled to Britain, where he confessed to writing the *bordereau*. Dreyfus, whose family and friends had from the beginning campaigned to prove his innocence, was brought back from Devil's Island and retried, again by military tribunal, at Rennes in the late summer of 1899. By a majority of three, his five judges, unwilling to jeopardize the honour of the Army, especially given the German military threat, pronounced him guilty, adding the curious rider 'with extenuating circumstances', and sentenced him to ten years in prison. Faced with a phenomenal outburst of incredulity and anger from the captain's now numerous French supporters, known as Dreyfusards, and outraged opinion around the world, the French President granted him a pardon and he was released. Total exoneration waited until 1906.[2]

Since its heyday in the late 1880s and early 1890s the antisemitic movement in France, symbolized most notoriously by Edouard Drumont and his book *La France Juive*, had remained relatively dormant. Modern scholarship has considerably modified and perhaps discredited an earlier assumption, fed by some of Dreyfus's earliest supporters like Joseph Reinach, that antisemitism lay at the root of the Affair.[3] Dreyfus himself and his defence lawyer resolutely rejected attempts to portray him as a Jewish martyr, framed by antisemites, and in the early stages many Jews accepted his guilt. It was later that the country became polarized into pro- and anti-Dreyfus camps, and the intervention of Zola, as detested by the right as he was admired by the left, accelerated that process. By and large, those believing in Dreyfus's innocence derived from the liberal, anti-clericalist left, and those holding him guilty from the Ultramontane right. Developments in the affair – Picquart's intervention, then Zola's, even Esterhazy's confession – persuaded many people that a Jewish plot was afoot to entice recruits into the crusade to prove Dreyfus innocent, and that those who aided that cause had been duped or bought. Accordingly, assaults on Jews and attacks on Jewish property broke out in over 70 locations in France, and anti-Jewish riots on a far worse scale erupted in Algeria, where antisemitism ran deep.[4]

The Dreyfus Affair is commonly considered to have been among the most significant progenitors of rightwing nationalist antisemitism in modern European history and is, of course, often credited with converting Theodor Herzl (who witnessed Dreyfus's trial and degradation) to political Zionism, with momentous long-term results. Yet the Affair can be viewed not only as evidence of the growth of antisemitism in its modern racial-nationalist form even in Western Europe, but as a demonstration of the strength of philosemitism and of the forces opposed to Dreyfus's arrest and conviction. It should not be forgotten that in France itself the Affair led to a major electoral victory for the left and the Dreyfusards, resulting, among other things, in the disestablishment of the Catholic Church in 1904.

It is no exaggeration to say that throughout the English-speaking world public opinion was overwhelmingly, indeed almost unanimously, in favour of Dreyfus once it became clear that he was almost certainly the victim of a terrible injustice based to a significant degree on the perceived antisemitism of the French military officer class, backed by much of the Catholic Church and the extreme right. This pro-Dreyfusard sentiment appeared strongly from the beginning of 1898 and gathered momentum with the Rennes verdict in September 1899. Declaring that Dreyfus's fate had become 'a concern for humanity at large', novelist David Christie Murray, who had turned his amateur graphologist's eye to reproductions of the *bordereau*, became one of the first well-known Britons to crusade for justice. In January 1898 he gave a public lecture in London before a 'large and keenly attentive audience' including judges and other members of the legal profession who cheered his arguments in support of Dreyfus. Christie Murray also proposed a declaration of solidarity with Zola, charged with libel as a result of *J'Accuse*, to be signed by British writers. But while 'innumerable' people supported the project in principle, and many were willing to sign, it was reluctantly abandoned for fear that foreign intervention might antagonize the French and do more harm than good.[5] Also in 1898 the poet George Barlow brought out a book on the Affair. He deeply deplored the role of antisemitism, on which he placed central emphasis.[6] Several detailed articles championing Dreyfus appeared during 1898 and the following year in Leopold Maxse's *National Review*, which is generally viewed as one of the main sources of right-wing British nationalism with an anti-'alien', antisemitic edge. Notable articles in the periodical came from Maxse himself, the scholar F.C. Conybeare, and top civil servant Sir Godfrey Lushington. The latter also appealed to public opinion on behalf of Dreyfus in an extensive review of the Affair published in *The Times*.[7] A Jewish commentator traced the sympathetic attitude of the British press to well before the Rennes verdict, and praised especially Emily Crawford, Paris correspondent of the London *Daily News*:

> No one can estimate the great debt we owe to Mrs. Crawford, for the remarkable articles that have day in, day out, appeared from her pen. And these articles have not been designed merely to instruct and enlighten public opinion here, they have been reproduced in the French papers ... Any Jew reading the almost violent leaders in the *Daily News* on this case must have felt how safe were the causes of truth and justice in the hands of the British people.[8]

With the Rennes verdict rage erupted 'not only in the press, which had fought such a ... valiant battle on behalf of Dreyfus, but wherever Englishmen congregate; in the churches, in the theatres, in private gatherings and in public.'[9] Editorials, special features and letters to the press throughout Britain denounced the verdict; a Cardiff newspaper, for instance, declared that 'As part of the campaign against Jews the persecution of Dreyfus ... has only served to unite them for a purpose the nobility of which must command the sympathy of people of all creeds'; while the *Spectator* warned Britons to ensure that antisemitism did not spread to their shores.[10] Pro-Dreyfus sermons flowed from numerous Christian pulpits, while resolutions condemning the French court were passed by institutions ranging from the Cambridge University Union to the Amalgamated Society of Railway Servants.[11] A Newcastle shipowner captured the popular mood when he predicted that 'hundreds of thousands of Englishmen would refuse to tread the soil of France' and that he would advise others to do as he intended, and boycott the Paris Exhibition of 1900 unless 'Dreyfus was acquitted, and acquitted with honour'.[12] Booked excursions to France were indeed cancelled; 90 British manufacturers withdrew from the Exhibition and others threatened like action. The first firm to register for the Exhibition, a South Wales building goods company, which had been allotted prime space, had won a gold medal previously in Paris and had expectations of doing so again, unhesitatingly withdrew, explaining: 'At present ... we do not attach any value to any French judicial award, nor will we even appear to court one.' For emphasis it added: 'no member of this firm is a Jew.'[13] At concerts, French performers were booed off the stage, and pro-Dreyfus tableaux were enacted at several theatres. At one London music hall a verse sympathetic to Dreyfus was incorporated into an existing popular song; following the final line, 'Be he Jew, be he Gentile, let the man have fair play', the 'vast audience' spontaneously rose, cheering tumultuously.[14]

The London *Daily Chronicle* found that the 'profound emotion' to which the verdict gave rise had 'no parallel in our experience of modern political affairs' and 'animates the entire country without distinction of class or party'.[15] Well-known champions of Dreyfus included the Duke of Westminster, the Marquis of Londonderry, Holman Hunt, Mrs Patrick Campbell, the novelists Marie Corelli and Edna Lyall, the crusading journalist W.T. Stead and the expatriate Australian diva (Dame) Nellie Melba. Most of these, and others of eminence, had spoken out well before the verdict.[16] Earl Beauchamp complained that the 'Fraternity' in France's trio of ideals 'excluded the Jew', while the Earl of Crewe supported continuing attempts by French Dreyfusards to clear Dreyfus's name completely.[17] Virtually the entire British 'Establishment' was pro-Dreyfus. The author and poet Hilaire Belloc, certainly a lurid and pronounced antisemite, attributed his failure to secure election as a Fellow of All Souls in the late 1890s to the fact that he was a vocal anti-Dreyfusard, perhaps the only one prominent at Oxford at the time.[18]

Yet, paradoxically, there was resistance in influential quarters – noticeably *The Times*, which had itself condemned the Rennes verdict as 'the grossest ... the most appalling prostitution of justice which the world has witnessed in modern times' – to holding a great protest meeting in the City of London on the grounds that it would be improper to question the legal system of a friendly foreign power. This attitude, which held sway owing to anxiety that offending the French government would drive it to intransigence and disadvantage Dreyfus, also prevented protest meetings under mayoral auspices at provincial centres: the Mayor of Portsmouth, for example, though personally sympathetic, refused to comply with a numerously signed request for a civic protest. However, there are signs that such meetings would have proceeded had Dreyfus not been swiftly pardoned and released.[19]

Mass outrage found outlets. An address of sympathy to Dreyfus's much admired and long-suffering wife, organized by the *Daily Chronicle* in lieu of an earlier proposal to petition the French government for Dreyfus's release, obtained 112,130 signatures, including those of peers and senior military and naval officers.[20] A meeting in London held by two rather obscure Christian organizations to affirm 'belief in the innocence of the military martyr' and extend 'warmest sympathies with him and his family in their suffering', attracted 4,000 people.[21] A 'splendid demonstration of national conscience' in Hyde Park on Sunday, 17 September, drew a total crowd of 80,000 in which 'All types of Jew ... stood side by side with all types of non-Jew – Church of England clergymen, Nonconformist pastors, Catholic priests, soldiers and sailors, professionals and workmen, Tories and Radicals, religionist and infidel'.[22] Consisting of parallel sessions, this 'mass meeting of the citizens of London' was addressed by innumerable speakers, virtually all non-Jews. This motley collection included the Liberal (later Labour) W.G. Steadman MP, who laid considerable emphasis on antisemitism as a culprit in Dreyfus's plight, an alderman, clergymen, retired military officers, trades unionists and feminists. Messages of support were received from various people, ranging from the actress Ellen Terry to the future Labour MP Keir Hardie. The Liberal Party leader and future prime minister (Sir) Henry Campbell-Bannerman joined the official procession on its way to the park and listened intently to the speeches.[23]

Two resolutions were passed. The first recorded 'deepest sympathy' to Dreyfus and his wife, assuring them 'that wherever the English tongue is spoken there is admiration and gratitude for the splendid courage and noble example they have shown amidst unparalleled persecution.' The second expressed 'abhorrence' of French officers who had 'sullied the uniform they wear in the long and desperate fight with truth and innocence', congratulated Zola and other prominent Dreyfusards 'for the splendid resistance they have made to military and sectarian fanaticism', and appealed to the French government 'to act according to the best traditions of free and generous France by releasing and rehabilitating Captain Dreyfus before it is too late'.[24] All this occurred amid wild enthusiasm. An elated participant reported:

> Almost every speaker gave expression to the opinion that Dreyfus would not have been persecuted as he had been, were he not a Jew. Never have I heard the name 'Jew' so loudly and enthusiastically

cheered ... not a single voice in all that vast multitude was raised in opposition or derision ... Cheer after cheer went up as the Resolution of sympathy with Captain and Madame Dreyfus was put to the meeting ... In no other country in the world not even perhaps in democratic America would it have been possible for such a demonstration to have been held, without inciting some counter demonstration against the race to which the hero and heroine of the day belonged.[25]

In the United States, before the Rennes verdict Democratic presidential candidate William Jennings Bryan was among those who publicly championed Dreyfus. Sympathetic pieces appeared in newspaper columns.[26] Upon receipt of the verdict mass anger reigned. Public protest meetings featuring non-Jewish speakers were held in many locations. There were calls for the American government to intervene. Episcopalian clergymen in San Francisco, for instance, urged President McKinley 'to take such action toward a reversal of the sentence as is possible and compatible with the diplomatic relations existing between the two nations'; while similar resolutions were passed by the congregation of Plymouth Church, Brooklyn, following speeches by Dwight L. Moody and others.[27] Among the many messages of sympathy to Dreyfus and his wife was one from the Bishop of Albany (William C. Doane) and other vacationers at a resort in Maine. They assured Madame Dreyfus: 'The heart of the whole world is toward you. The trial has made evident the innocence and the noble character of your husband, and the great public, which has followed this struggle with anguish, now renders to him and to his children the honor for which he has struggled till now, for which he is still struggling in France.'[28] The *New York Times* denounced the 'narrow and detestable race prejudice' and the 'cowardice and cruelty' which had arisen among the 'naturally gallant' French.[29]

Numerous Americans resolved to boycott the Paris Exhibition; there were many tearings of the French flag. In Chicago, a non-Jewish manufacturer sacked every Frenchman in his workforce, and vowed never to employ any again.[30] A crack swordsman of Kansas City, Captain Thomas Phelan, challenged the villain Esterhazy to a duel. Residents of the small, remote rural Kansas town of Belleville announced that they would subscribe towards Phelan's travel costs; if he killed Esterhazy they would double the amount.[31] Citizens of Wichita deliberately demonstrated their solidarity with Dreyfus by electing a Jewish girl as their carnival queen; non-Jewish aspirants were eclipsed as 'enthusiasm for her ran over the city like wildfire'.[32] In a cable, the townsfolk of Oswego, Wisconsin, told Dreyfus that they hoped he would be pardoned, adding a 'cordial invitation' for him thereafter to make his home among them.[33] Everywhere, the 'unanimity and intensity' of public sympathy for him was remarkable: 'From the newspapers, from public men, from church congregations, from theatre audiences, and from all places where people assemble, as well as from every individual who has favoured the rehearing of the trial, arises an unbroken chorus of amazement and disgust [at] what is universally regarded here as an unspeakable injustice.'[34]

Enormous support for Dreyfus was evident throughout the rest of the English-speaking world, particularly following the Rennes verdict. Extraordinarily, in Australia townspeople in two very small country settlements in separate colonies were the first to denounce that verdict, in cables to *Le Figaro*.[35] Protest meetings under civic auspices were held in country towns as well as cities such as Melbourne, Sydney and Perth. Many messages of sympathy were cabled to Madame Dreyfus, notably from both houses of the Victorian legislature. Some Australians went further. Residents of the country town of Bendigo, for instance, cabled the French Prime Minister expressing their 'hope that France will do justice'.[36] As well as sending a cable to Madame Dreyfus, the people of Geelong contacted the French President; when they heard of Dreyfus's pardon and release they enabled the Mayor, through public subscription, to advise *Le Figaro* that this turn of events was unsatisfactory: 'The citizens of Geelong, Australia, ask, in the name of God and humanity, that the innocent be exonerated and the guilty punished.'[37] Across the Tasman, almost every member of the New Zealand Parliament signed a cable of sympathy to Madame Dreyfus.[38] From South Africa 'universal indignation' was reported; the Canadian press was 'practically unanimous' in condemning the verdict.[39]

As in the case of Dreyfus, the Beilis Affair of 1911–13 is almost as notable for the philosemitism it kindled as for the antisemitism that prompted it. Mendel Beilis, a Jewish clerk in a Kiev brickworks, was charged in August 1911 with the ritual murder of a twelve-year-old Christian boy whose badly stabbed body had been discovered in March. Police were initially satisfied that the killers belonged to an underworld gang known to the boy and upset with his threat to reveal their loot to the authorities. But at the funeral leaflets blaming the Jews were distributed, and the ensuing agitation by organized antisemites led to the trumped up charge against Beilis. His trial was postponed until September 1913 while the prosecution constructed its flimsy indictment. During a trial lasting 34 days the case against him unravelled, and on 28 October he was acquitted.[40]

Beilis's arrest and trial led to an international outcry. In Russia itself, liberals – and occasionally reactionaries – criticized the obviously fabricated indictment, engineered for political ends and with the potential to unleash further pogroms. The centrepiece of the Russian protest movement was a denunciation of the blood libel signed by 159 eminent non-Jews: members of the Council of State and of the Duma, academicians, intellectuals, lawyers, scientists, writers and artists. Signatories included names internationally renowned, such as the novelists Maxim Gorki, Counts Aleksei and Lev Tolstoi and the poet Alexander Blok.[41] Similar documents were issued in Germany, bearing additional signatures from Denmark, and in France. Again, those signing were non-Jews eminent in public and intellectual life, the professions, science and the arts. There were also senior Christian clergymen.[42]

In Britain, a parallel statement of outrage was issued in May 1912, to coincide with the date originally scheduled for the trial. Public support for Beilis by influential Englishmen probably eclipsed anything ever seen before, even the philosemitic response to the Russian May Laws. Denouncing the charge as a 'relic of the days of Witchcraft and Black Magic, a cruel and utterly baseless libel on Judaism, an insult to Western culture, and a dishonour to the Churches', the protest noted that 'among the ignorant and inflammable populace of Eastern Europe, the "Blood Accusation" has often given rise to terrible outbreaks of mob violence against the Jews.' It was signed by 240 influential persons. This extraordinary list included the Archbishops of Canterbury (Davidson) and York (Lang), the Roman Catholic Archbishop of Westminster (Cardinal Bourne), numerous Anglican bishops and other senior clergymen and representatives of nonconformist bodies; politicians including former prime ministers Lord Rosebery and Arthur Balfour, Sir Edward Carson, Austen Chamberlain, Ramsay MacDonald and James Lowther, Speaker of the House of Commons; other public figures such as Lord Mayor of London Sir Thomas Crosby, the Duke of Norfolk and the Earls of Cromer and Selborne; legal luminaries including members of the High Court of Justice and the Court of Appeal; Field Marshal Earl Roberts and other senior officers from the armed services; academics, principally professors from the universities of Oxford, Cambridge and London, including such renowned scholars as A.V. Dicey, Sir Charles Harding Firth, Sir James Frazer, Sir James Murray and two members of the Darwin family; the presidents of the Royal Colleges of Medicine, Physicians and Surgeons; the presidents of cultural organizations such as the British Association, the Royal Society, the Royal Academy, and bodies representing sculptors, architects and specialist painters; the Master of the King's Music and representatives of the Royal College of Music, the Poet Laureate and such household names from art and literature as Lawrence Alma-Tadema, Arthur Conan Doyle, John Galsworthy, H. Rider Haggard, Thomas Hardy, Frederic Harrison, Anthony Hope, Montague Rhodes James, Jerome K. Jerome, John Masefield, Sir Arthur Quiller-Couch, George Bernard Shaw and H.G. Wells; the President of the Institute of Journalists and the editors or other representatives of leading journals including the *Quarterly Review*, the *Edinburgh Review*, the *Fortnightly Review*, the *Spectator*, the *Nation* and ten London daily newspapers; and official representatives of Australia, New Zealand and South Africa. A number of the signatories, including Lord Milner and painter (Sir) Ernest Waterlow, had been active in the Jewish cause on past occasions. Yet several others, such as eugenicist Karl Pearson, are sometimes seen as flirting with antisemitism.[43]

A contemporary commented incisively on these petitions:

> It is in the signatures ... that their chief importance lies. Not only is every name that of a non-Jew, but the long lists read like a roster for each country of its men of eminence in the professions, arts, sciences, and industries ... All of the worthier walks in life are represented by its notabilities, and if any are missing they could only be discovered by a laborious search through the biographical dictionaries.[44]

Also in 1912, a protest rally was held in the East End of London, comprising many of the people who had staged protests there in 1906 against the pogroms, such as the union organizer Herbert Burrows and feminist Charlotte Despard. Presiding was J.F. Green of the Society of Friends of Russian Freedom. The renowned socialist H.M. Hyndman was among the speakers, and supportive messages were received from many leaders of the Labour movement.[45]

When the Beilis trial opened in 1913 protests intensified. Condemnatory resolutions were passed by diverse organizations, ecclesiastical and lay. Countless editorials and articles deploring the charge appeared in the press, both in Britain and the Dominions. The consensus was manifest in the *Sydney Morning Herald*: 'In the name of Christianity and every faith which numbers among its tenets justice and truth, liberty and toleration, protest is due against a condition of affairs in which these infamous things are possible.'[46] Outrage was expressed from numerous Christian pulpits, and the headquarters of the Salvation Army in South Africa, reflecting a widespread fear that pogroms would ensue, urged its London counterpart to 'exercise your influence to avert such a calamity and protest at action so totally opposed to the teachings of Christ'.[47] A Jesuit priest, Father Herbert Thurston, renewed his longstanding publicity crusade against the myth of ritual murder. He was echoed by the Roman Catholic press. Numerous newspapers and periodicals, religious and secular, national and provincial, went out of their way to stress Judaism's aversion to shedding blood.[48]

The petition aside, the main British vehicle for condemning the Beilis trial was a mammoth interdenominational rally in London on 28 October 1913 arranged by the English Zionist Organization and featuring, apart from Sir Francis Montefiore, presiding, exclusively non-Jewish speakers. Hours before the meeting Farringdon Street was thronged with eager participants; the main venue became so packed that a simultaneous overflow meeting became necessary. Even so, 'there was a crowd unable to obtain admission which would have been sufficient to fill both halls twice over.'[49] Many prominent non-Jews attended, and letters of encouragement were tabled from numerous signatories to the petition who could not be there as well as from other wellwishers such as Joseph Chamberlain and Andrew Bonar Law. The latter wrote: 'From the time of Constantine until the present day the unfair treatment to which Jews have been subjected in many European countries has been a blot on our civilization and a discredit to our religion.'[50] This collection of letters was described as 'the most remarkable in its catholicity of any that we have recorded on the occasion of a public demonstration'.[51] Later, non-Jews including Conservative MPs Leslie Scott and Richard Chaloner expressed disappointment that they had not known that the rally was to be held: 'it is important that every public man and lawyer should make known his abhorrence of such slanders on a great and noble race,' maintained Scott, a leading barrister.

The main speaker was the eminent jurist Professor A.V. Dicey, who had written the introduction to a recent book detailing the severe legal disabilities facing Russian Jewry.[52] He moved the unanimously carried sole resolution of 'this meeting in the City of London of persons of all denominations' which condemned the 'revival of the calumny' of ritual murder as likely to 'foster outrage and violence' against the Jewish race, 'a sentiment diametrically opposed to the best teachings of every religious faith.' The resolution invited 'the moral support of the civilized world' for any measures the Russian government might take to shield the Jews 'from further obloquy, insult and hurt'. It was seconded by Conservative MP (Sir, later Viscount) George Cave, a future Home Secretary and Lord Chancellor who became Chancellor of the University of Oxford. Other speakers were two Liberal MPs, (Sir) G.H. Radford and W.S. Glynn-Jones, a Jesuit priest and a Salvation Army colonel representing General Booth, who was overseas. A Christian clergyman was the impromptu main speaker at the overflow meeting. Accounts of proceedings were telegraphed to Russia.[53]

Many non-Jewish sympathizers joined a mass demonstration intended for Jews in Trafalgar Square on 2 November, and there were also protest meetings in the provinces. A civic meeting of 2,000 including many non-Jews at Leeds, chaired by a non-Jewish magistrate in the absence of the Lord Mayor, and attended by an MP and prominent citizens, was addressed by Christian clergymen and other gentiles. At a meeting of 3,000 Glaswegians chaired by Sir John Ure Primrose, a former Lord Provost, the main resolution was moved and seconded by the Roman Catholic Archbishop of Glasgow and a senior Church of Scotland minister; other speakers were Christian clergymen and two non-Jewish professors. Over 1,000 citizens of Sheffield, including many noted figures, attended a demonstration addressed by senior clergymen. A great rally at Manchester, chaired by the Lord Mayor and addressed by two prelates, other clerics and the Mayor of neighbouring Salford, went ahead despite Beilis's acquittal, in protest at the notion of ritual murder, which had not been repudiated by the Russian authorities. Impromptu protests were made at Nottingham and elsewhere.[54]

As with previous instances of antisemitism overseas, comparable protests occurred throughout the English-speaking world. In the United States, an open letter to Czar Nicholas II, dated 31 October 1913, was signed by 74 leading clergymen of various denominations and localities. Foreseeing an outbreak of anti-Jewish violence triggered by the impending verdict, they implored the Czar to halt proceedings against Beilis and endorse the *ukase* issued by Alexander I in 1817 against the blood libel. They assured the Czar that the libel was 'unfounded'; it had been declared 'a baseless and wicked invention' in four papal bulls and had been condemned by several former Central and Eastern European rulers. Thorough investigations by theologians and other scholars had entirely discredited it.[55] Signatories to this letter included Catholic and Episcopal prelates such as Cardinal Farley and Dr David Greer, both of New York, *Catholic Encyclopedia* Editor-in-Chief Charles G. Herbermann, leaders of the Presbyterian and Methodist Churches including Syracuse University's Chancellor James R. Day, spokesmen for the Congregational Churches and of the Churches of Christ, and the Georgia-based Bishop J.S. Flipper of the African Methodist Church. The State Department declined to transmit their protest on the grounds that the Russian government had refused to accept such documents, so it was left at the Russian embassy in Washington with a request that it be conveyed to the Czar.[56]

American outrage at the Beilis Affair was displayed in other ways. 'It is not the obscure prisoner at Kieff alone who is sure to be the victim of persecution,' averred the *New York Times* in a typical press reaction,

> it is all the members of the Jewish race. And in every land where that race is an integral part of the body politic, among the people who live with them the sense of systematic resentment is strongly felt. It has found expression from all classes, all sects, all nationalities.[57]

The country's ethnic press was also sympathetic. Its umbrella organization, representing 600 newspapers in 29 languages with a circulation of over 18 million, registered its concern: the Kiev charge 'may discredit a race which is of great service to the world, and, furthermore ... there is no foundation to it'.[58]

Organizations ecclesiastical and secular, including stage legislatures, issued expressions of solidarity with the accused and anger at the ritual murder allegation. For example, relevant resolutions were passed by the Episcopal Convention in New York, the New York State House of Assembly, the Albemarle Association and the Liberal Ministers' Club, Philadelphia, while Esperantists in New York concurred with a protest by their movement worldwide originating in Bohemia.[59] The United States Senate adopted a strongly worded resolution introduced on 22 October 1913 by Senator J. Hamilton Lewis of Illinois. Champ Clark, Speaker of the House of Representatives, characterized the Kiev trial as 'the most preposterous and monstrous performance of this age', having 'no parallel since the days of witchcraft'.[60]

Public protest meetings featuring non-Jewish speakers were held in many cities. For instance, an overflowing meeting in Chicago was addressed by the celebrated social worker Jane Addams and Christian clergymen. Over 2,000 citizens of Cleveland representing virtually every denomination attended a meeting chaired by ex-Judge F.A. Henry, featuring several gentile speakers. The students and faculty of the College of the City of New York held a mass rally addressed by four non-Jewish senior academics.[61]

In Canada, too, there was widespread indignation. Mass protests were staged in several places. 'As usual, in most liberal actions, the West leads the way,' was one comment when Winnipeg pioneered the trend. Over 6,000 people, including parliamentarians and civic officials, attended a rally there which passed a resolution declaring the blood accusation baseless. Similar resolutions were passed by Toronto civic officials on the motion of a non-Jewish alderman and at a public meeting in Montreal.[62]

The last in this trilogy of trials occurred in Atlanta, Georgia, where on 26 April 1913 a fourteen-year-old white girl was strangled in the basement of the pencil factory where she worked. There had been many recent unsolved attacks on women in Atlanta, including 18 murders, and police came under intense pressure to make an early arrest. Immediate suspicion fell on the black nightwatchman who discovered the body, but police attention quickly shifted to Leo Frank, the superintendent of the factory, which was owned by his uncle. Born in Texas of German Jewish parents, Frank was brought up in Brooklyn and graduated from Cornell University. A Georgia resident since 1908, he was married to a girl from a prominent Atlanta Jewish family, and was President of the local B'nai Brith organization. He was tense and nervous in manner, and his behaviour under questioning gave the impression of guilt. He had been one of the few people in the factory on that fatal Saturday when the girl had come to his office to collect her wages, and was unable to provide a satisfactory account of his whereabouts during the vital hour which medical expertise indicated as the probable time of her death.

Tried amid a climate of mob hostility, Frank was found guilty in August 1913 on the specious, well-rehearsed evidence of a black sweeper at the factory (a convicted thief who was almost certainly the real murderer) and sentenced to hang. He then embarked upon a lengthy appeals procedure. A request for a new trial was rejected by the original judge, but Georgia's governor, John M. Slaton, who detected in the prosecution testimony major discrepancies which had been overlooked, signed a commutation order. For this he was widely reviled, and state troopers had to disperse an angry crowd which attacked his residence. Not long afterwards, on 17 August 1915, Frank was abducted from prison by vigilantes and hanged from a tree near his alleged victim's home. Her true killer was never brought to justice.[63] This was probably the only occasion in American history when a Jew was lynched by a mob, and certainly the best-known such incident. Coming at a time of heightened social antisemitism in the United States, it aroused considerable fear among many American Jews.

Although it was extraordinary for a southern court to convict a white man, Jew or gentile, on the testimony of a black one, the role of antisemitism in the Frank Affair, especially in the early stages, should not be exaggerated: five Jews sat on the grand jury that indicted him. Jews were long established in Georgia, and had produced some of the state's most respected citizens. Governor Slaton noted this following Frank's conviction, and pointed to the fact that his own long-standing law partner was Jewish. 'I don't want the impression to go out that the State of Georgia and the Governor of Georgia could not give justice to a Jew ... Frank shall not be a victim of injustice simply because he is a Jew.'[64] Despite occasional incidents, the South was not pervasively antisemitic; indeed, it has been argued that a philosemitic tradition prevailed.[65] Southern Europeans were far more frequently the targets of southern prejudice than Jews, to say nothing of southern violence: a number of Italians had been killed by lynch mobs, often on trivial grounds.[66] Moreover, though there were in Atlanta many rumblings about Eastern European non-Jewish immigrants, who were resented by the city's newly industrialized poor as job competitors, little was said about Jews.[67]

Slaton offered an analysis of the Frank Affair which matched that of dispassionate observers: 'It is true that a certain kind of prejudice has risen in the South against Frank, but it is the prejudice of the employe[e] against the employer. The fact that the head of a large factory is accused of attacking a girl, one of his employees, has been sufficient to give rise to this kind of prejudice.'[68] Clearly, Frank's status as an industrialist and employer from the North was a greater factor in arousing prejudice towards him than was his Jewishness. Although the epithet 'damned Jew' was bandied about in Atlanta during the trial, it was pointed out by an objective analyst that had he been Italian, 'damned Guinney' would have been heard.[69] The impoverished tenant farmers who had become reluctant industrial workers and urban slum dwellers resented the economic necessity for their womenfolk to toil in factories. Frank was portrayed as an exploiter of cheap female labour. Moreover, factories were widely believed to be immoral places, unfit for respectable females. This belief was fuelled by (unsubstantiated) claims that Frank made improper advances towards the girls he was supervising. He was unjustifiably rumoured to have a history of perverted sexual behaviour, which poisoned the atmosphere in which he was tried. Also against him was an unappealing personality and an unattractive physical appearance.[70]

As early as September 1913 local Jews had requested the distinguished constitutional lawyer Louis Marshall, President of the American Jewish Committee, to intervene in the 'American "Dreyfus" case that has just developed in Atlanta.' Other Jewish leaders in the North were similarly approached. But all moved cautiously, loath 'to be considered as championing the cause of Jews who are convicted of crime'.[71] When, during the appeals procedure, they did get involved and a fund to meet Frank's legal costs was started, many Georgians angrily assumed that rich Jews from outside the state were using their wealth to purchase a guilty man's acquittal.[72]

At the same time, there was considerable non-Jewish support for Frank throughout the United States, including Georgia. In March 1914 the *Atlanta Journal* declared that he 'has not had a fair trial. He has not been fairly convicted, and his death ... will amount to judicial murder.' It demanded a fresh trial.[73] Others in the state echoed that call. French-born Professor Joseph Lustrat of the University of Georgia likened the prejudicial public feeling surrounding the case to that which doomed Dreyfus: 'I do not claim that Frank is innocent, but I claim that he ought to be given a fair chance to prove his innocence.'[74] E.H. McMichael, Acting Speaker of the Georgia House of Representatives, who had attended the trial, was ashamed that he had begun to assume Frank's guilt 'not from facts and testimony, but by popular belief and hostile feeling manifested by the crowd'. Frank deserved another hearing: 'The Constitution of our State guarantees to every man, white or black, high or low, Gentile or Jew, an absolutely fair trial.'[75]

Denying a fresh trial, Judge Leonard Roan admitted that he did not know whether Frank was 'innocent or guilty', which prompted one Atlanta newspaper to ask: 'is it not time to pause before legal murder is added to the long list of other crimes in our state?'[76] Many Georgians agreed, although an Atlanta woman, describing Jews as 'God's own chosen ones', was not alone in her claim (in a pro-Frank article in the *New York Times*) that 'no one has yet dared publicly to express his belief in Frank's innocence without being accused of having been bought with Jewish money.'[77] An apparently non-Jewish former state resident, appealing for clemency in an open letter to Governor Slaton, insisted that the fierce hostility to Frank which had gripped sections of Atlanta was not shared in other Georgian cities, where the 'sole evidence' of the principal prosecution witness would have failed to convict.[78] The *New York Times* believed that 'intelligent' Atlantans were unaffected by the prejudice of the 'raging mob' and coaxed them to speak out: 'It is difficult to imagine how a community can place a more indelible stain upon itself than by sending an innocent man to death through its own passion and clamour.'[79]

Speak out they did. By mid-May 1915, following Roan's decision,

> Thousands of Atlanta businessmen, including practically every banker in the city ... have signed their names to petitions pleading for a commutation of Leo M. Frank's death sentence ...
>
> There are said to be several hundred petitions in circulation in Atlanta alone, while there are hundreds of others in the State. Petitions and letters flood Governor Slaton's office with each incoming mail. It is predicted that there will be over a million names submitted ... in appeal for ... life imprisonment.[80]

Among the petitioners was a member of the prosecution team, and requests for commutation were received that spring and summer from distinguished legal authorities in Georgia, some bluntly stating their belief in Frank's innocence. They included ex-justices of the state Supreme Court.[81] 'We know that the rank and file of the Atlanta bar are convinced that Frank's trial was unfair, and we believe that the rank and file of the entire Georgia bar are of the same opinion,' declared the *Atlanta Journal*, itself demanding clemency. 'With the utmost conservatism we can go further and say that a great majority of the people of Georgia feel that Frank's guilt has not been proved beyond reasonable doubt, and that a great many of them consider him innocent.'[82]

Christian clergymen in Atlanta, feeling 'grave doubt as to his guilt', presented a petition of their own. Their representative, an Episcopalian who counted Governor Slaton among his congregants, informed the official commutation hearing: 'We appeal on moral grounds and for justice. We appeal ... against the prejudice of Gentiles against Jews.' In several Atlanta churches prayers for the

Governor's divine guidance were said, so that he would 'save the good name of the State'. The Georgia Society of the State of New York, consisting of native Georgians and others connected with the State, also approached Slaton.[83]

Across the United States a similar pattern emerged:

> What we now see is a simultaneous and spontaneous movement ... in which all sorts of people unite – to impress upon the [Governor of Georgia] the adverse view of the trial and conviction taken literally by hundreds of thousands. This they do in part by resolutions adopted at great public meetings, in part by petitions signed by long lists of names and still more by individual telegrams and letters ... declaring strong doubt of Frank's guilt or strong belief in his innocence, and asking, as an emergency measure, that his sentence be commuted to life imprisonment in order that opportunity may be provided for the future vindication so confidently expected.[84]

Spearheading demands for a new trial were Jane Addams, the noted naturalist John Burroughs, Thomas Edison and, perhaps surprisingly, Henry Ford, who would later propagate (and eventually, possibly owing to Edison's influence, repent of) antisemitism. All sorts of people proclaimed their belief in Frank's innocence, from the socialist leader Eugene V. Debs to the opera star Geraldine Farrar.[85] Investigative reports favourable to Frank carried by several newspapers boosted the cause.[86]

The fight for Frank's life was fought in editorials, correspondence columns, and Christian pulpits. 'The outcries of the mob ... were not against Frank – it was a cry against the Jew,' thundered that stalwart philosemitic crusader Madison Peters.[87] Public meetings calling for clemency, involving non-Jewish speakers who cited antisemitism as a factor in Frank's conviction, were held in several cities; that at Rochester, New York, for example, was convened by a citizen's committee headed by the Mayor and comprising educators, business and professional men. About 1,000 people attended the meeting in Minneapolis, necessitating an overflow function.[88] Two huge non-sectarian rallies were held in Chicago. The first, reputedly 200,000 strong, was addressed by judges, clergymen and other prominent non-Jewish Chicagoans. The second was held under the auspices of 50 Jewish and general women's organizations.[89] 'The appeals in behalf of Frank from outside the State are a remarkable feature of the case,' observed the entirely sympathetic *New York Times*. 'They have come from everywhere and from all sorts of conditions of men.'[90] In an unprecedented development, the Governors of Arizona, Louisiana, Maine, Michigan, Mississippi, North Dakota, Oregon, Pennsylvania, Texas, Virginia and West Virginia departed from convention and brought pressure to bear on their Georgian counterpart. Resolutions urging clemency were passed by the state legislatures of Louisiana, Michigan, Pennsylvania, Tennessee, Texas and West Virginia, as well as by many groups, some not readily associated with this activity, including the American Medical Association, the Columbus Chamber of Commerce, the Cincinnati Businessmen's Club, the Chicago Chapter of the Daughters of the Confederacy, the Illinois Bankers' Association and women's groups.[91]

Frank was inundated with correspondence from supportive strangers, and over 75,000 letters and telegrams had been received in the Governor's office by mid-May, fewer than 20 urging the death penalty. Altogether, over two million people pleaded for Frank, some on forms specially printed by newspapers in several cities.[92] Among the public figures who interceded with Slaton were the influential Senator W.E. Borah of Idaho – who was to emerge as a firm friend of Zionism – and scores of his congressional colleagues including senators from Colorado, Connecticut, Illinois, Indiana, Louisiana, Mississippi, Missouri, Nevada, Texas and Georgia itself; ex-Senator and former Secretary of State Philander C. Knox; ex-Governor of Ohio and former Ambassador to France Myron T. Herrick; Frank Walsh, Chairman of the United States Industrial Relations Commission; Frederick A. Delano of the Federal Reserve Board; mayors from coast to coast; and numerous judges and clergymen.[93]

Across the country hundreds of petitions were organized on Frank's behalf. They came from alumni of his alma mater, Cornell, from the San Diego Theosophical Society, 'the big towns of Illinois and Indiana and 100 places', and so on. The organizers of a petition in Waco, Texas, explained that they acted 'as Gentiles upon our own initiative in the interest of ... fairness in behalf of our fellow-man.'[94] In New York City a petition organized by the Women's Peace Society obtained 800,000 signatures. Over one million people signed petitions in Illinois. A monster petition organized in Chicago obtained 600,000 signatures. It was carried to Chicago by a hand-picked delegation consisting of Judge John N. O'Connor, Chief Justice of the Illinois Criminal Court, a Baptist pastor and the non-Jewish representative of women's organizations.[95] A petition organized in Boston, bearing 50,000 signatures, was taken to Atlanta by ex-Governor of Massachusetts Eugene N. Foss, two leading Boston journalists, and a prominent Rhode Islander.[96] 'Memory is searched in vain,' marvelled the *New York Times*, 'for a criminal case in which a verdict of conviction aroused anything even approaching ... the dissatisfaction which is felt'; the enormous support Frank received was unprecedented in American legal history.[97]

The philosemitic response to the Frank case, as with the Dreyfus and Beilis affairs, occurred at a time when most historians believe that antisemitism fanned by ubiquitous Social Darwinist assumptions about the inequality of races was stronger than at any time since the Enlightenment. The range and depth of philosemitism might, however, indicate that this familiar view needs to be considerably modified, and that the forces of friendship and admiration for Jews were also strong.

5 'The Inmost Heart of Hell': Philosemitism from the First World War to the Holocaust, 1914–45

Philosemitic activity not merely continued to exist but arguably intensified during the interwar and wartime period. At first, gentile supporters of Jews found themselves responding to physical Jew-hatred in what came to be known as the 'zone of antisemitism,' the newly independent Slavic nations of Eastern Europe. Later, of course, philosemites found themselves confronted with ideological and institutionalized prejudice of monstrous proportions in a nation hitherto regarded as perhaps the most cultured in Europe. Philosemites were also, during the 1920s, championing their Jewish fellow-citizens of English-speaking countries against widespread accusations flung from the extreme right that Jews were agents of Bolshevism, and, during the 1930s, against the tirades of antisemitic demagogues such as Sir Oswald Mosley in Great Britain and Father Charles E. Coughlin in the United States. They also defended Jewish refugees from Nazism against the aspersions of people opposed to offering haven. The record of philosemitism during this period must be set against the heightened antisemitism which manifested itself during the interwar years, culminating in the Holocaust. As always, this record is much less well known, and it is especially important that at least its main strands be set out since they occurred during this darkest of dark times.

Non-Jews in Britain, the United States and other western countries condemned the pogroms which erupted in Eastern Europe from 1919 to 1920, perpetrated by forces under the command of Ukrainian nationalist leader Simon Petlura, and demanded that the civil and political rights of Jews be guaranteed in the peace settlement. At Westminster, champions of the cause included MPs of all parties, including such long-standing philosemites as Conservatives Lord Henry Cavendish-Bentinck, Lord Robert Cecil and W.G.A. Ormsby-Gore, Liberals J.M. Kenworthy (Labour from 1926) and J.D. Kiley, and Liberal defector Josiah Wedgwood, who voted Labour from mid-1919 and became an Independent Labour member in 1931. Most of those named were keen Zionists, remaining loyal to the Zionist movement during the vicissitudes attending it between the Balfour Declaration of 1917 and the MacDonald White Paper of 1939. Strikingly, only Kiley, who represented Whitechapel, sat for a constituency with a significant Jewish population.[1]

Protest meetings featuring prominent gentile speakers were held in several major cities in mid-1919. The Lord Mayor of Cardiff, for example, chaired the meeting in his city. Local Liberal MP Sir William Seager and Baptist Theological College Principal William Edwards were the major speakers, echoed by other non-Jews. Messages of solidarity were received from the local Conservative MP, from three Welsh bishops and from the Principal of the University College of Wales at Cardiff.[2] At Glasgow's protest meeting, the speakers were former Lord Provost Sir Samuel Chisholm and an ex-baillie. Belfast's, chaired by Conservative MP Sir William Whitla, was addressed by Christian clergymen. In a message of support, T.H. Burn MP denounced 'the slaughter of an ancient race'. Professor Dicey, the Archbishop of York and several non-Jewish MPs of all parties sent similar messages to Manchester's protest meeting. Hull's, chaired by the Sheriff, was addressed by three Christian clergymen and a senior Salvation Army figure.[3] A large gathering at Leeds, where, earlier, veteran Labour organizer Tom Mann had spoken at a protest by trades unionists, was addressed by local Liberal MP Robert Armitage and other non-Jews. Presiding was Leeds University Vice-Chancellor Sir Michael Sadler, who several years later was among the 51 prominent people who signed a letter to *The Times* defending the work of sculptor Jacob Epstein against criticism redolent of anti-semitism.[4] Scores of non-Jews attended special services for victims of the pogroms, held on 26 June 1919 at synagogues across Britain.[5] Two huge protest demonstrations held that same day in London under Jewish auspices were addressed, respectively, by J.M. Kenworthy and by J.D. Kiley and H.N. Brailsford, a journalist and Labour MP who had visited Poland and been appalled by antisemitism there. Messages of sympathy were received at both rallies from Dicey, the Archbishop of York, several MPs of all political complexions, and a businessmen's organization. The Labour Party, in annual conference, transmitted its unanimously passed resolution condemning the atrocities.[6] In April Kiley, with lawyer, churchman and Conservative-turned-Labour politician Lord Parmoor, had addressed a protest in

London convened by the Zionist Organization. Gentile outrage was also expressed in other forums.[7] In the United States many prominent non-Jews denounced the pogroms. Distinguished jurist and recent presidential candidate Charles Evans Hughes, a future Republican Secretary of State and federal Chief Justice, was principal speaker at a protest demonstration in New York's Madison Square Garden, also addressed by the Mayor. State Governor Alfred E. Smith, Senator William M. Calder and ex-Secretary of the Treasury William G. McAdoo were among those who sent messages of sympathy.[8] A subsequent meeting held at Carnegie Hall to protest at atrocities in the Ukraine had Secretary of the Navy Josephus Daniels, a cardinal, the Mayor and the State's Lieutenant-Governor among the speakers. Similar meetings were held in other great American cities.[9] Also forcefully condemning the pogroms were ex-President William H. Taft, Champ Clark, former Speaker of the House of Representatives, congressmen of diverse political allegiances and church bodies.[10] Long known as a 'tried and proven friend of the Jewish people',[11] Taft in 1921 vigorously condemned the dissemination in Henry Ford's *Dearborn Independent* of the notorious Czarist forgery *The Protocols of the Elders of Zion*. Ridiculing the notion of 'a Jewish conspiracy to seize the world', Taft went on to ask how anyone could believe that 'Jewish bankers and businessmen' held national governments in thrall when half of world Jewry were 'suffering from pogroms and persecution [and] starvation'.[12] His speech prompted the formation of a Committee of Religious Minorities, which issued a manifesto against prejudice and discrimination based on race or creed. Taft was among its signatories, who included former Secretaries of State William Jennings Bryan and Robert Lansing. Another signatory was Charles W. Eliot, a former president of Harvard University, who thus signalled his disapproval of the quota system on Jewish admissions operated by Harvard and certain other universities at that time.[13] (In 1929 an abortive scheme was started by non-Jews mindful that the quota system was preventing numerous Jews from gaining a higher education for a Jewish University of New York, towards which an anonymous gentile pledged $200 000.[14])

Taft, Bryan and Lansing were among the 121 eminent Americans who signed a keynote petition (made public on 3 January 1921) decrying 'the appearance in this country of what is apparently an organised campaign of anti-Semitism, conducted in close conformity to and [in] cooperation with similar campaigns in Europe' – a reference to Ford and the *Protocols*. 'Anti-Semitism is almost invariably associated with lawlessness and with brutality and injustice,' it continued. 'We believe it should not be left to men and women of the Jewish faith to fight this evil, but that it is in a very special sense the duty of citizens who are not Jews by ancestry or faith.' It lauded the contribution of Jews to national life since the inception of the Republic, and called upon non-Jews, especially 'moulders of public opinion – the clergy and ministers of all Christian Churches, publicists, teachers, editors and statesmen – to strike at this un-American and un-Christian agitation.'[15] The petition was organized by the leftwing author John Spargo; 'no Jewish person or society had anything to do with its preparation or publication.'[16] President Woodrow Wilson insisted that his name be added to the list of signatories, who comprised Secretary of State Bainbridge Colby and serving or former Cabinet secretaries, as well as a distinguished array of American leaders and opinion-makers such as senior clergymen, educators, editors, lawyers and businessmen. They included Jane Addams, Ray Stannard Baker, Nicholas Murray Butler, Paul D. Cravath, Clarence Darrow, W.E.B. Dubois, Robert Frost, Charles Dana Gibson, John Haynes Holmes and Cardinal O'Connell. Many signatories were no strangers to the Jewish cause, having been in the forefront of protests over Russian persecution; many were to crusade prominently against Nazi antisemitism.[17]

During the Nazi era, when the eyes of the free world were focused on Germany, injustices against the Jews of Poland also attracted attention in the West. A meeting in June 1937, convened under Jewish auspices in London to condemn the pogrom in Brest-Litovsk, received messages of sympathy from leading politicians of all parties and from the Archbishop of Canterbury and other prelates.[18] The installation that year of the so-called 'ghetto benches' for Jewish students at Polish universities drew strong protests. The National Union of Students and student bodies at several British universities passed condemnatory resolutions, sent to the Polish Ambassador in London. The Students' Union Council of the University College of South Wales at Cardiff, for example, expressed 'horror and disgust' and called on the Polish government 'to take immediate steps to bring about the cancellation of this discriminatory and barbarous measure'.[19]

In the United States, protests against the ghetto benches came from such bodies as the American Federation of Teachers, the American Youth Congress, and the American section of the International League for Academic Freedom.[20] Perhaps the most striking American protest was that issued on 20 December 1937 by the Institute for International Education, 'intended as a tribute to Jewish teachers and students in this evil day when their place in the life of scholarship is threatened with extinction'. It was signed by 179 non-Jewish scholars including five Nobel Prize winners, 59 university and college presidents, and 107 deans and professors. Institute President Dr Stephen Duggan observed that 'if time was not an element, it is evident that the appeal would as readily have been published with a thousand ... signers.' A week later a statement by the American Writers Committee to Aid the Jews in Poland was issued. Its 33 signatories included such famous names as Van Wyck Brooks, Archibald MacLeish, Lewis Mumford, Clifford Odets, Genevieve Taggard and Thornton Wilder.[21]

The rise of Nazi Germany, with its brutal and extreme anti-semitism, produced in English-speaking countries countless examples of philosemitism, so that only the most significant can be noted here. Many readers, accustomed to perceiving the 1930s as leading to the 'abandonment of the Jews' by 'bystanders' in the democracies during the Holocaust, may be surprised to learn of the depth of empathy for persecuted German Jewry and the genuine detestation of Nazi anti-semitism displayed, not least by the British 'Establishment'.

A most striking early example of the British elite's abhorrence of Nazi antisemitism and sympathy with the victims occurred at the Queen's Hall, London, on 27 June 1933. An impressive array of prominent non-Jews attended, comprising

> Every section of British public life, lay and spiritual, distinguished representatives of all political parties, of all the professions, leaders of present-day British opinion and outstanding members of every section of the great British public ...
>
> Two hours before ... a number of people had formed a queue outside ... And as the hour drew near for the meeting to begin those on duty at the various entrances were almost overwhelmed and swept off their feet by the crowds clamouring to get in.[22]

The distinguished attendance included such household names as Margot Asquith, Sir Wyndham Deedes, royal physician Lord Dawson of Penn, Sir Ernest Benn, H.A.L. Fisher, G.P. Gooch, C.E.M. Joad, Hugh Seton Watson and Wickham Steed. Chaired by former Liberal MP and Solicitor-General Lord Buckmaster, the meeting unanimously endorsed the sole resolution, moved by the Archbishop of Canterbury (Dr Cosmo Gordon Lang), supported by a Beilis protest veteran, the Reverend Dr J. Scott Lidgett, representing the Free Churches, and the Earl of Iddesleigh, representing Britain's Roman Catholics. While disclaiming any intention to interfere in another nation's internal affairs, and stressing the desire to preserve cordial Anglo-German relations, the resolution proclaimed its 'duty' to observe that 'the discrimination now being exercised against the Jews in Germany is contrary to the basic principles of tolerance and equality which are accepted by the modern world in relation to the treatment of religious and racial minorities.' Its cautious wording, and the 'measured and moderate' tone of the addresses, failed to conceal the depth of indignation felt by all the speakers.[23]

Feelings on the issue ran high in other forums. A mass meeting at the same venue brought together representatives of major national youth organizations including the National Union of Students, the British Federation of University Women, the Students' Christian Movement, the YMCA and political affiliates. Chaired by Blanche Dugdale, niece of Earl Balfour and herself an ardent Zionist, it included speeches from a Labour MP and ex-minister Isaac Foot, the Past Principal of Somerville College, Oxford and a London University professor. It passed unanimously an appeal to German youth to try to stop their country's persecution of Jews.[24] Civic demonstrations of protest featuring prominent non-Jewish speakers, and uniting gentile public opinion across party and sectarian lines were held at numerous locations across Britain. A meeting at Portsmouth Guildhall, for example, chaired by the Lord Mayor, was addressed by a local Liberal MP, the Anglican Bishop and Provost, the President of the city's Free Church Council, the Principal of the Municipal College and the Headmaster of the Grammar School.[25] Another, at Nottingham, chaired by the Principal of the local University, was addressed by, among others, two local MPs, Holford Knight KC (Labour) and (Sir) T.J. O'Connor (Conservative) and two bishops. 'On the platform were representatives of the Anglican, Roman Catholic, and Free Church bodies, and of the three principal political parties, as well as of the professional, industrial, and commercial life of the city.'[26] A comparable meeting at Newcastle upon Tyne, with the Lord Mayor presiding and the Anglican Archdeacon of Northumberland moving the resolution condemning Nazi Germany, received messages of sympathy from 19 regional MPs as well as the Marquis of Londonderry, Lord Ravensworth and Lord Joicey (two local colliery owners), Sir Charles Trevelyan, the Bishop of Newcastle and the Roman Catholic Bishop of Hexham.[27]

Such meetings appear to have been supported as enthusiastically in locations where the Jewish population was sizeable as in those where it was negligible. For example, 3,500 people attended a meeting at Manchester Free Trade Hall, chaired by the Lord Mayor and featuring among the entirely non-Jewish panel of speakers the Bishop of Manchester, the Roman Catholic Bishop of Salford and the editor of the *Manchester Guardian*.[28] A meeting at Pontypridd, chaired by the President of the local League of Christian Churches and attended by MPs and public figures of all political complexions, saw 3,500 people fill the Town Hall to hear keynote speaker George Lansbury MP speak with feeling of his regard for Jews and denounce their persecution, while 'a still larger number' of people milled outside: 'Undoubtedly the whole of the Welsh valleys were aroused in sympathy with the German Jews.'[29]

Outrage in Parliament at Nazi antisemitism was near-universal. In April 1933 a House of Commons all-party committee, with Oliver Locker-Lampson as Secretary, was formed to monitor the treatment of Jews in Germany. Its members included the Duke of Devonshire's heir, Lord Hartington, Earl Beauchamp's heir, Lord Elmley, Rear-Admiral (Sir) Murray Sueter, J.W. Hills, the Hon. (Sir) Richard Denman, Dingle Foot and, perhaps surprisingly in view of the sometimes harsh treatment of Jews in his novels, John Buchan (later Lord Tweedsmuir), who had demonstrated his sympathy towards persecuted Jewry as far back as 1905.[30] Certain MPs, representing various political outlooks, are noteworthy for the passion and effort they devoted to the cause of persecuted Jewry and the plight of refugees. To the names of Locker-Lampson, Viscount (formerly Lord Robert) Cecil, Sir Austen Chamberlain, J.M. Kenworthy and W.G.A. Ormsby-Gore, all mentioned previously, may be added those of Vyvyan Adams, Robert (later Lord) Boothby, (Sir) Patrick Hannon, George Jones, Holford Knight, George Lansbury, Eleanor Rathbone and Josiah Wedgwood (a by no means exhaustive list). The concern of such people was certainly not confined to speeches: they also consistently attempted to find effective ways to mitigate Nazi antisemitism and to provide refugees with havens.

Early in 1933 Oliver Locker-Lampson wrote a remonstratory letter to Hitler; two other Conservative MPs, Sir Philip Dawson and Patrick Hannon, sent a comparable communication to President von Hindenberg pleading for German Jewry.[31] Around the same time, Locker-Lampson and Labour MP Herbert Morrison, along with the editors of the Anglican *Church Times*, the Roman Catholic *Tablet* and the *Methodist Times*, addressed a big Jewish protest meeting in the City of London.[32] Throughout the 1930s and 1940s Locker-Lampson was even busier on platforms in support of German Jewry than he had been on specifically pro-Zionist ones in the 1920s. He, Vyvyan Adams, and Kenworthy, were among the Conservative MPs most vocal in the call to fling the gates of Palestine wide open to refugee immigration.

There were condemnatory statements by churchmen of all denominations. Dr Hensley Henson, Bishop of Durham, was 'on the public platform and in the pulpit, in the Church Assembly and in the House of Lords',[33] a particularly doughty champion of Jewry. He wrote a memorable introduction to a book describing Nazi antisemitism published in 1936: 'We find ourselves looking on a woeful spectacle of oppression – cold, cunning, complete, covering every part of social life, closing every door or escape, pursuing the innocent, the helpless, the humble, the educated, even the illustrious members of the persecuted race with a merciless boycott from the cradle to the grave ...'[34] When a Jewish deputation called at his home in 1938 to honour him for his 'distinguished defence' of their people, he was embarrassed that the representatives 'of an ancient and famous race' should acknowledge his 'petty service'. But he was delighted to 'welcome a company of Israelites to his house' on terms of 'really deep and genuine' empathy with them. He advised them to 'take comfort in the thought that in your hour of extreme anguish and difficulty you are being borne by a great volume of sympathetic feeling which I suppose at no previous time in the history of mankind would have been possible.'[35]

In 1933 MPs Holford Knight and Sir George Jones (Conservative), along with the Earl of Listowel, a Jesuit priest and an army major, were appointed by the World Alliance for Combating Anti-Semitism to a new internal committee intent on marshalling anti-Nazi gentile opinion worldwide into a coordinated campaign of support for persecuted Jewry. The cause was, said Knight, the 'public duty' of 'all men and women of goodwill'.[36] He and Jones had been active in the cause for some time. Earlier in the year, for instance, they had been among the prominent non-Jewish speakers at a mass protest meeting in Whitechapel which was also addressed by an Anglican cleric, the Editor of the *Catholic Herald* and the local MP. In the chair was Lord Mount Temple, President of the Emergency Committee for German Jewry.[37] Later, in protest at escalating persecution, Mount Temple resigned his chairmanship of the Anglo-German Fellowship.[38] Early in 1933, in revulsion at German Jew-baiting, a group of non-Jewish

Fleet Street journalists formed an organization known as 'Friends of Jewry', pledged to counter prejudice. It obtained an immediate gentile enrolment of 400. Two founders, George Nicholson and John Murray, embarked on a sympathetic history of Diaspora Jewry. It took the form of a novel in order to influence as wide a readership as possible.[39]

The British press as a whole expressed 'a damning indictment'[40] of Nazi antisemitism. Soon after Hitler's assumption of power, the *Daily Mirror*, for example, observed:

> In spite of protests from men and women of every form of religious belief throughout the world ... Amidst the astonishment of the civilised world [Berlin] is placarded with denunciations of Jews; Jewish employees are being dismissed; Jewish shops are surrounded by gangs ... in the bully's uniform. The idiotic belief that all Jews are plotters or 'traitors' is thus to be instilled ... into the best-educated nation in Europe – as though the German people were back in the days of pre-war Russian pogroms, or further back in the night of the Middle Ages! It cannot be necessary to remind any but lunatics that the superstition that 'traitors' within a nation are often or invariably Jews is as false as to assert that witches or wizards are responsible for the influenza. Imagine ... our own Disraeli as the victim of a pogrom![41]

Primarily targeting Jews, the Central British Fund for the Relief of German Jewry, opened in 1933 for the maintenance of refugees, received 'support and encouragement from non-Jews of all classes'. Messages accompanied many donations, such as: 'I hope you believe that all Christians are not like the Germans'; 'I trust you will be able to collect enough money to settle the greater part of Palestine with your nation'; and 'always have we had a deep regard for your nation, and with the little we are able to give are extended our prayers and sympathy.'[42] In 1933 four organizations opened a joint appeal, the German Refugees Assistance Fund. They were the Academic Assistance Council, under the presidency of Lord Rutherford, the International Student Service under the presidency of Professor Ernest Barker, the International Committee for Securing Employment for Refugee Professional Workers, with which Lord Cecil and Liberal Party Vice-President Margery Corbett-Ashby were prominently connected, and the Germany Emergency Committee of the Society of Friends, chaired by Professor G.B. Jeffery. The Archbishops of Canterbury and York, Lord Buckmaster, Sir Austen

Chamberlain, Dame Sybil Thorndike, Edith Lyttleton, H.A.L. Fisher and the Reverend J. Scott Lidgett helped to launch it, and the long list of eminent people subsequently commending it to the general public included the Earl of Lytton, Lord Parmoor, Sir Wyndham Deedes, (Sir) Gilbert Murray, Eleanor Rathbone MP, Sir Michael Sadler, Sir Josiah (later Lord) Stamp, H.G. Wells and the Vice-Chancellors of Oxford, Cambridge and London universities.[43]

Incredulity that Nazi Germany had turned on one of the most talented and valuable sections of its population was commonplace. There was considerable sympathy for expatriate Jews associated with culture and learning who suddenly found themselves stateless; for many people they symbolized the refugees as a whole. When, in 1933, the conductor Bruno Walter, whose accomplishments were no longer wanted by his homeland, took to the platform at the Queen's Hall to conduct the London Symphony Orchestra, both audience and musicians 'sprang to their feet, and there was a mighty roar of cheering' which had as much to do with the persecution he endured as with his talents: 'rarely has a conductor had so enthusiastic a reception.'[44]

Einstein, already an icon, was taken as the embodiment of the refugees' plight although he was in fact a Swiss citizen. He was in the United States when the Nazis seized power and deprived him of his post at a German university. In New York he was given a tickertape parade, and when he visited Britain in 1933 under the auspices of various refugee-aid associations he was fêted. Prominent non-Jewish intellectuals and public figures joined the vast throng which honoured him at a meeting in London's Royal Albert Hall chaired by Nobel Prizewinning physicist Lord Rutherford. As Einstein stepped onto the platform, the hall 'resounded' to 'the cheers of 10,000 people ... the tornado of applause taking some moments to subside.' A collection was taken for the Refugee Assistance Fund, one of the largest opening donations coming from Locker-Lampson, whose advice to Jewish refugees was:

> Be not afraid! You have stood beside the grave of every one of your oppressors in turn ... I prophecy that you will rise to glory under the banner of the British Empire.

Other speakers included Sir William Beveridge, Sir Austen Chamberlain and Lord Buckmaster.[45] Einstein's case was frequently invoked, Locker-Lampson going so far as to describe him as 'the greatest saint' he had ever met.[46]

Concern for the best minds in Germany resulted in the foundation in 1933 of the Academic Assistance Council (renamed the Society for the Protection of Science and Learning) by Rutherford, Beveridge, G.M. Trevelyan, Lionel (later Lord) Robbins and others, specifically to assist refugee scholars. Those signing its initial statement to the press included such eminent names as the poets Lascelles Abercrombie and A.E. Housman, J.S. Haldane, the Biblical scholar Sir George Adam Smith, British Museum Director Sir Frederic Kenyon, Sir Michael Sadler, banker Sir Josiah (later Lord) Stamp, Lords Buckmaster and Cecil, and several Nobel Prizewinning scientists: Sir William Bragg, Sir Charles Sherrington, Sir Joseph Thompson and Lord Rayleigh. The Council found posts for a remarkable number of refugee scholars, at a time when there were fewer than 20 universities in the British Isles, all with rigid hierarchical structures, and managed placements overseas for many others.[47] The Archbishop of York (Dr. William Temple) and Sir Frederic Kenyon became, respectively, President and Chairman of the Society for the Protection of Science and Learning. In its endeavour to find new posts for displaced German Jewish scholars and scientists it too was extraordinarily successful: 'amongst those whom we have been privileged to help are men and women whose intellectual gifts and genius form part of the cultural wealth of the world.'[48] British intellectuals and people involved in the arts displayed much fellow-feeling for their persecuted German-Jewish counterparts. In 1933 an appeal on behalf of a distinguished physiologist, sacked from his research job in Berlin because of his Jewishness, was signed by 20 senior academic British scientists in related fields, mainly at Oxford and Cambridge. 'It seems to us that Britain would be well advised to make it clear that those whose intellects are to be accounted as among the finest in Germany today and who, simply because they happen to be Jews, are being dismissed from their posts, would find here safe refuge and opportunities for continued scientific activity.'[49] That same year at London University, where a students' meeting addressed by Professor J.B.S. Haldane had issued a resolution of protest against the persecution of German Jewish scholars, a number of professors agreed to a small voluntary tax on their incomes to help such scholars, deprived of their own livelihoods.[50] Similar manifestations of outrage and support were forthcoming from other British universities, continuing throughout the Nazi period.

A formal economic boycott of Nazi Germany was pressed by some sections of Anglo-Jewry from the beginning of Hitler's regime as a possible means of easing the persecution. There was, however, resistance to the idea, some Jewish leaders arguing that a boycott would be likely to exacerbate the difficulties facing German Jewry. Some believed that in any case it would not be effective. Not until late in 1934 did the Board of Deputies (half-heartedly) adopt the proposal. But a boycott was advocated from the first by many prominent non-Jews, including Attlee, Dingle Foot, Sir George Jones, Kenworthy, Locker-Lampson, Lord Ponsonby and Wedgwood. A big meeting in London in March 1933 chaired by the Haham (chief rabbi of the Sephardi community), Dr Moses Gaster, called unanimously for a boycott as well as a liberal asylum policy in Britain and Palestine. The main speakers were non-Jews: Lord Marley, Chairman of the Parliamentary Advisory Council of the ORT, the Society for Jewish Handicraft which provided vocational training in Central and Eastern Europe, and left-wing journalist Hannen Swaffer. Following the *Anschluss* in 1938, Wedgwood was in the vanguard of those loudly repeating demands for action.[51]

Outrage at the Nuremberg Laws, promulgated in 1935, was demonstrated at a huge rally in Hyde Park under the auspices of the British Non-Sectarian Anti-Nazi Council to Champion Human Rights. It featured numerous distinguished non-Jewish speakers including the Earl of Kinnoull, Lord Marley, Sir Walter Citrine, J.B.S. Haldane, Sylvia Pankhurst and, from the House of Commons, Attlee, Wedgwood, Eleanor Rathbone, W.J. O'Donovan and the newly elected Socialist D.N. Pritt KC. A veteran of the Dreyfus protest movement, the 91-year-old feminist leader Charlotte Despard, travelled from Belfast especially to deliver her forceful speech.[52]

Following the *Anschluss* (March 1938) a Sunday was set aside for intercession services at British synagogues to express solidarity with the Jews of the expanded *Reich*. Noted gentiles attended these services in their hundreds, and churches of all denominations held parallel intercession services of their own. At Birmingham, whose Lord Mayor in 1933 had emphasized his city's solidarity with Jewry by going to a synagogue service with his aldermen, Jews and Christians held a joint service at the Parish Church, attended by almost 2,000 people. The services at Leeds were followed by a huge protest rally at which the principal speakers were the Bishop of Durham and Sir James Baillie, Vice-Chancellor of Leeds University.[53]

In order to raise funds for Jewish child victims of Nazi persecution, a major exhibition of Jewish art was held in London in May 1938. The Duchess of Atholl and Margot Asquith, both outspoken foes of Nazi persecution, helped to organize it, with encouragement from prominent figures including Lady Diana Cooper, Dame Sybil Thorndike, Sir Arbuthnot Lane and Sir Ronald Storrs. It was the first in a series of exhibitions paying tribute to the attainments of the Jewish people in various fields of endeavour. 'In these days of Anti-Semitism,' explained a supporter, Arthur Henderson MP, 'it is only just that attention should be called to the remarkable contributions of this gifted race in the realms of religion, music, science, literature and the drama.'[54]

At a demonstration against Fascism by the Association of Writers for Religious Liberty in June 1938, addressed by established literary figures such as John Brophy, C. Day Lewis, Rose Macaulay and Sylvia Townsend Warner, (Sir) Compton Mackenzie, speaking as a Catholic, made the 'greatest impression' with his 'fiery impassioned protest against Fascist persecution, which was seen in its most bestial form in the persecution of the Jews'.[55] Other well-known authors, loudly championing the Jewish cause included E.M. Delafield, E.M. Forster, Desmond MacCarthy, J.B. Priestley and (Dame) Rebecca West.[56]

In the wake of *Kristallnacht* (9–10 November 1938) Harold Nicolson could observe: 'British opinion has revolted with force and unanimity against the persecution of the Jews in Germany.'[57] Politicians, including Cabinet ministers, spoke out. Bodies representing all shades of opinion, including town councils, passed protest resolutions. Some, like the Durham Miners' Association, called on the British government to suspend relations with Germany until the latter ceased to persecute Jews. Groups of private citizens made representations.[58]

Ecclesiastical bodies passed condemnatory resolutions. The Chief Rabbi was bombarded with appropriate messages from Christian individuals, churches and religious organizations. Clergymen forwarded donations from congregants (sometimes unsolicited) to the appeal funds. As before, special services of intercession for Jews under Nazism, held in synagogues throughout Britain, saw large attendances of non-Jews. At Cardiff the synagogue was so full of both Christians and Jews that many sympathizers could not gain admittance; leading medical practitioner G.N.W. Thomas, staunchly philosemitic, spoke from the pulpit at the minister's invitation. The service at Liverpool was attended by the Lord Mayor in official regalia, along with other members of the Corporation.[59]

In a letter to *The Times* the Archbishop of Canterbury denounced the 'deeds of cruelty and destruction' and expressed the expectation, handsomely fulfilled, that churches throughout the country would pray for German Jewry.[60] Opening the autumn session of the Church Assembly, he asked the gathering to stand in silent prayer for the victims of Nazism.[61] During the Abbey Armistice Day Service, the Dean of Westminster interpolated a special prayer for the Jews. Many parish churches did likewise.[62] Later, the General Assembly of the Church of Scotland, which heard Moderator Dr James Black deliver a moving eyewitness account of the plight of German Jewry, passed a resolution asking the British government 'by itself or in concert with other Powers, to come to the rescue of refugees in their imminent peril'.[63] The Reverend Rees Howell, Director of the Bible College of South Wales, Swansea, announced the College's readiness to house 100 Jewish refugees, and aid the settlement in Palestine of many more.[64]

Fifteen leading barristers of the Temple, including Stafford Cripps and Norman Birkett, signed an open letter of protest at the suffering of 'hundreds of thousands of persons merely because of their race'.[65] A letter recording 'our solemn protest, before the conscience of civilisation, against the persecution of the Jews in Germany' appeared in the same newspaper above well-known names in the worlds of politics, learning and the arts.[66] In apparent seriousness, George Bernard Shaw suggested that the League of Nations should immediately establish a committee, assisted by a team of international psychiatrists, to declare German and Italian antisemitic measures the result of 'pathological phobia'. Then, Hitler and Mussolini would 'either have to cancel the measures or stand before Europe as certified lunatics. That is a position which no Leader can afford.'[67]

Students at many universities passed protest resolutions. Those at Cambridge sent a letter to the German Ambassador signed by representatives of a broad cross-section of university clubs and societies registering 'horror and revulsion' at the 'terrible suffering', the 'barbarous violence and cruel legislation inflicted without mercy or justification on the Jews of Germany'.[68] Oxford undergraduates wrote to their university's Chancellor, Foreign Secretary Lord Halifax, stressing that everything that Britain could do to stop 'one of the most barbarous and cowardly persecutions' in history should be done.[69]

In December 1938 a mass assembly of 8,000 people under the presidency of former Labour Lord Chancellor Lord Sankey was held in London's Royal Albert Hall. It gave unanimous approval to the sole resolution: 'That this great meeting of British citizens, representative of all religious bodies and all schools of political thought, strongly protests against the religious and racial persecution which is taking place throughout Germany, and pledges itself to support every legitimate form of action likely to alleviate the suffering of all the victims of such persecution.' Speakers were senior representatives of the major parties and churches: former Colonial Secretary and lifelong philosemite Leopold Amery MP (Conservative), Herbert Morrison MP (Labour), Sir Archibald Sinclair (Liberal) – all three of whom called for relaxation of restrictions on Jewish immigration into Palestine – as well as the Archbishop of York, Cardinal Hinsley, the Moderator of the Free Church Council (Dr Robert Bond) and the Liberal intellectual Lady Violet Bonham Carter. Lloyd George and Attlee sent letters of support, while Lord Dunsany, an Anglo-Irish writer of conservative bent, contributed a philosemitic poem.[70]

Many similar functions were held elsewhere. For instance, Glasgow's Lord Provost convened a protest meeting 'representative of the town council, the University and the Churches'. At the request of representative citizens he sent a message to Prime Minister Neville Chamberlain denouncing Germany's treatment of Jews and requesting that the British government make official representations.[71] At Cardiff, Daniel Hopkins MP and city councillors addressed a protest organized by the local Jewish community, which called on Britain to stand by the spirit of the Balfour Declaration. Hull's 'mainly non-Jewish' meeting featured the Lord Mayor, Lord Strabolgi (J.M. Kenworthy), two MPs and Christian clergymen among the speakers. And at Leeds University the well-known literary scholar Professor Bonamy Dobree presided over a big demonstration.[72]

British newspapers stressed the need, now, for 'practical help'.[73] *The Times* observed:

> it is certain that foreign indignation counts for no more immediately ... The education of one people by the opinion of other peoples is a vain hope, and denunciation is an empty indulgence ...
>
> Sympathy with the Jews demands something more than that ... It is not to be believed that the nations which feel this sympathy cannot find the means of assisting unwanted citizens to leave Germany and of providing the territory in which these Jews can found a liberated community and recover the right to live and prosper.[74]

Numerous ordinary Britons, including the the father of future Prime Minister Margaret Thatcher, a grocer in Grantham, boarded refugees at their homes. A letter to the Evian Conference on Refugees in July

1938, urging a 'comprehensive and generous decision translated into immediate action', was signed by a number of well-known people including Lord Horder, Sir Norman Angell, Margot Asquith, Margery Corbett-Ashby, Lady Isobel Margesson, D.N. Pritt KC MP and Viscountess Rhondda.[75] The *Lancet* rejected notions that refugee doctors were taking jobs away from British medical practitioners, and advocated a generous intake in the name of traditional British tolerance.[76]

From 1933 onwards, Britain tacitly relaxed restrictions on alien immigration operating since 1919 in order to admit significant and growing numbers of German (and, later, Austrian and Czech) Jews, whose numbers are usually estimated at about 60,000. Another 25–30,000 or more emigrated to the Dominions, and over 100,000 to Palestine until the 1939 White Paper, issued in response to Arab pressure, limited overall Jewish immigration to 75,000 over the next five years, although contrary to popular belief it did not result in a decline in numbers coming from Germany until the outbreak of the war made it impossible for Jews to leave Germany. (About 240,000 emigrated to the United States, and 100,000 elsewhere.) Given the panic occasioned by *Kristallnacht* and its signals that all Jews had to leave Germany, the resettlement of German (and other Reich) Jews was being accomplished in a *relatively* generous and orderly manner. It is a fact that about 72 per cent of Germany's Jews managed to emigrate from that country until the Nazis forbade them to leave, as well as about 65 per cent of Austria's Jewish population in the short pre-war period following the *Anschluss* in March 1938. It seems clear that on a *per capita* basis Britain (with the Dominions) took more refugee Jews than any other country, including the United States: the British government always had wide discretionary powers to admit refugees (as it were) surreptitiously, powers which did not exist in the United States, where immigrant quotas, set by Congress, could not easily be varied by clandestine means. From 1933 the Board of Deputies of British Jews entered into a semi-secret agreement with Whitehall whereby Britain would admit significant numbers of German Jews so long as the Jewish community paid the entire cost of their resettlement, obviating the need for any explicit change in the country's refugee laws which would be openly debated, potentially giving rise to heightened antisemitism. In 1938–9, too, as the British government closed the gates of Palestine to significant Jewish migration, it opened the doors to Britain increasingly wider, as the floods of refugees unleashed by *Kristallnacht* became an overwhelming tide. By mid-1939

Jewish refugee migration to Britain was both generous and successful. At the back of this unique example of generosity towards refugees at this time was revulsion, especially by the 'Establishment', at Nazi antisemitism. Hostility to Nazi antisemitism might also have been one significant factor, of course among other significant factors, in Britain's decision to stand alone against Germany after the fall of France. No refugee who reached Britain without a visa was turned back.[77]

Liberal Party leader Sir Archibald Sinclair reflected the feelings of countless Britons irrespective of party when he declared that there was now an 'urgent need for tackling vigorously the problem of refugees and for the generous fulfilment of British obligations to World Jewry ... under the Palestine Mandate.'[78] A Commons non-party amendment tabled by Josiah Wedgwood, regretting 'that in view of what has happened in Germany during the last week, H.M. Government has not yet seen fit to allow the Jewish refugees from Germany increased facilities to go to Palestine during the next six months' was signed by 38 MPs, all but one non-Jewish (17 Labour, seven Conservative, seven Liberal, four Independent and three National Liberal, allied with the Conservatives).[79]

A resolution giving wholehearted support for the Fund for Refugees set up by former Prime Minister Lord Baldwin in a radio appeal in December 1938 was passed unanimously at a meeting of leading Jews and non-Jews convened at the Mansion House by London's Lord Mayor, Sir Frank Bowater. A comparable meeting, involving non-Jewish speakers, was held in Manchester.[80] In December 1938 a number of distinguished personalities in the art world, including Sir Muirhead Bone, Sir Kenneth (later Lord) Clark, Augustus John, Dame Laura Knight, Henry Moore and Paul Nash, issued an urgent appeal on behalf of German Jewish artists who had taken refuge in Czechoslovakia but now faced probable deportation to concentration camps in their homeland. The appeal aimed to settle these refugees in Britain or other countries, and asked for 'money, guarantors, and hospitality'.[81] Bone, John, Moore and five other prominent non-Jews constituted the Artists' Refugee Committee.[82]

Concerned that the refugee influx might lead to an upsurge in domestic antisemitism, a number of representative Anglican clergy and laity issued a repudiatory statement at the end of 1938. Although confident that the national 'sense of justice' and the 'abundant kindliness' of Britons would predominate, they felt compelled to express the feeling of the vast majority of Christian English people, that, in whatever form and however modified it may be, anti-Semitism remains wicked folly, utterly opposed to the spirit and letter of the teaching of our Lord.

... We would assure our Jewish fellow countrymen that we have the fullest appreciation of the contribution that they have made and are making, in various ways, to the national life.

Headed by the Archbishop of York and the Bishops of Chichester, Bradford and Bristol, the signatories included Dr W.R. Matthews, Dean of St Paul's, Dr H.L. Goudge, Regius Professor of Divinity at Oxford, Lord Wolmer, George Lansbury, Sir George Arthur, Lady Cynthia Colville, Dorothy Sayers, Sybil Thorndike and the editors of the *Record*, the *Church Times* and the *Church of England Newspaper*.[83]

British Foreign Secretary Anthony Eden's disclosure in the House of Commons on 17 December 1942 that the Allies had irrefutable confirmation of the wholesale extermination of Jews in Nazi-held Eastern Europe was met with a revulsion and sorrow that started in the chamber itself:

> The House had listened in an almost over-powered silence, broken at moments, with gasps, as the Secretary of State for Foreign Affairs, in measured phrase and thundering emphasis, recounted the diabolical crimes of rapine and mass murder wreaked upon millions of innocent Jewish men, women and children ... The torrent of questioning that followed Mr. Eden's declaration that the United Nations resolved to exact retribution on the satanic criminals of Nazi Germany, had reached its climax of indignation. Suddenly, from an obscure corner near the Speaker's Chair, the quivering voice of a small man [Labour member W.S. Cluse] was barely heard to ask that the House of Commons might rise in sympathy with the Jewish people and in protest against Nazi infamy. A murmur swept through the packed benches – a murmur of approval, as well of sheer surprise that so great a gesture should have come from a man – a working man – so unobtrusive.
>
> The House of Commons rose. The British Cabinet, complete save for the Prime Minister himself, rose. The Distinguished Strangers, conspicuous by the tall, gaunt figure of Lord Simon, the Lord Chancellor, rose. With bowed heads 300 men and women stood in silence.[84]

Across Britain, resolutions condemning Nazi barbarity were passed by numerous non-Jewish organizations. The Press bellowed its outrage. In verses entitled 'The Jews' Christmas 1942' describing with harrowing accuracy scenes which became generally familiar from newsreels after the war, the writer Sir John Squire penned a 'flaming denunciation':

> ....
> Did ever any man in any clime
> However animal or infidel
> Conceive such horrors as this monstrous time?
> We gaze into the inmost heart of Hell.[85]

Leaders of all the major Christian denominations expressed sorrow; many services of intercession were held. The Archbishop of Canterbury (Dr Temple) had recently presided at a meeting of the Royal Albert Hall calling attention, with the aid of continental speakers Jan Masaryk and Jacques Soustelle, to the Nazi atrocities against Jews. Congregationalist Dr J.S. Whale, Moderator of the Free Church Assembly, Roman Catholic Bishop Dr David Mathew and Lord Cecil also spoke.[86] The common reaction of both clerics and laymen alike to Eden's revelations was that of the Bishop of London (Dr Arthur Winnington-Ingram), who spoke of the 'horrible sense of impotence ... to bring help to those who suffer', yet trusted that Britain and the Allies would 'freely and gladly' offer refuge 'to all who can escape and remove themselves from the clutches of this Nazi terror'.[87] 'The greatest crime in history is now being perpetrated,' declared the Archbishop of York, 'the deliberate extermination of the Jews of Europe.' He felt that repeatedly broadcasting Allied warnings to those ordering the atrocities and those committing them that 'sure punishment' awaited them 'may possibly act as some deterrent'. He realized that 'it is only by victory that we shall be able to save the victims of this awful tyranny.'[88] Yet he maintained: 'We must do all we can in the name of Christianity and humanity to save at least a remnant from these foul murderers.'[89]

Although Jews under Nazi occupation were entrapped, prisoners of a psychopath intent on killing them all, many non-Jews viewed them as if they were refugees or potential escapees who could, and emphatically should, be rushed to safety – in Britain, in Allied and neutral countries, and in Palestine. Demands by non-Jews for action of this kind quickly followed Eden's announcement: from MPs, clerics and other public figures such as Sir Wyndham Deedes and Major-General Sir Neill Malcolm, from various organizations, from specially convened civic protest meetings including ones in provincial centres such as Derby, Grimsby and Huddersfield, and a huge rally at Manchester University chaired by the Vice-Chancellor and featuring prominent non-Jewish speakers.[90] Seventy-eight per cent of respondents to a Gallup Poll in 1943 answered affirmatively the question: 'Do you think that the British Government should or should not help any Jews who can get away?' This was the largest positive response ever recorded in a Gallup Poll in Britain.[91] A motion tabled in the House of Commons in February 1943 called 'for immediate measures on the largest and most generous scale compatible with the requirements of military operations and security, for providing help and temporary asylum to persons in danger of massacre who are able to leave enemy and enemy occupied countries.' The signatures of its sponsors – Professor A.V. Hill, Colonel Victor Cazalet, Sir Patrick Hannon, Robert Morrison, Eleanor Rathbone and Graham White – headed the list of 233 names from all parties.[92]

In 1943 such people, who felt the agony of the Holocaust to their souls, established the National Committee for Rescue from Nazi Terror under the presidency of the Marquis of Crewe. Its driving forces were the publisher Victor Gollancz, one of only six Jewish office-bearers, and Eleanor Rathbone, a Vice-President. Among those who held either the post of Vice-President (35 in all) or comprised its ten-person Executive Committee (chaired by Labour MP David Grenfell) were Archbishops Temple and Garbett, ex-Archbishop Lang, Cardinal Hinsley, the Moderator of the Church of Scotland, Lord Sankey, Sir William Beveridge, Quintin Hogg (later Lord Hailsham), Harold Nicolson, Frank Pakenham (later Earl of Longford), the Reverend James Parkes and Lady Violet Bonham Carter. A pamphlet outlining its 12-point proposals appeared in April 1943; a revised edition was published the following January. Slightly modified, these proposals were published in 1944 under the title *Continuing Terror*.[93]

A meeting chaired by Sir William Beveridge at Oxford in 1943 passed a resolution condemning the 'meagre action' taken by the government. It was subsequently signed by 'ninety of the best-known Oxford names' including many heads of colleges.[94] A letter to *The Times* in February that year called on Whitehall to urge the German government to permit Jews to leave Nazi-occupied lands, to offer joint Allied protection to Jews freed or escaping from such lands, to persuade neutral countries to receive 'as many Jewish refugees as possible', and similar measures. It was signed by numerous celebrities, including George Bernard Shaw, Beatrice Webb, Lord Sankey, Gilbert Murray and Harold Nicolson.[95] A dramatic demonstration of elite outrage was a cable sent to Anthony Eden, then in Washington, on 20 March 1943 assuring him 'of the fullest support of public opinion in this country for treating [the] problem as one of extreme urgency ... British conscience so deeply stirred that [the] country [is] prepared for any sacrifice consistent with not delaying the victory.' It was signed by 206 persons, including the leaders of virtually every Christian denomination, the Lord Mayors of nearly every large city, the heads of most Oxbridge colleges, the Chancellors and other officials of nearly every university, most trade union leaders, and luminaries of British science, literature, music and art.[96] These appeals demonstrated both the deep humanitarianism of the British intelligentsia – even rather unexpected figures – as well as, tragically, the futility of the concept of rescue.[97]

Parallel patterns of protest occurred in the United States throughout the Nazi era. A huge demonstration under Jewish auspices in New York's Madison Square Garden in March 1933 was addressed by Alfred E. Smith, Bishop William T. Manning and Mayor John P. O'Brien.[98] A little later, the Reverend John Haynes Holmes and a number of judges, lawyers and public officials were some of the recognizable non-Jews among a 100,000-strong Jewish-organized protest parade through New York led by Major-General John F. O'Ryan. Prominent non-Jewish speakers addressed the marchers at their destination.[99] Around that time, 1,200 American clergymen representing 26 denominations signed a petition to the leaders of various Protestant sects in Germany: 'We deplore the consequences that must fall upon the Jews, and upon Christendom, which permits this ruthless persecution ...'[100] A protest against the ousting of Jewish judges and lawyers in Germany was issued by 51 American legal luminaries. Among them were former Secretaries of State Elihu Root and Bainbridge Colby, former Attorney-General George W. Wickersham, former Secretary to the Treasury Ogden L. Mills, former Counsellor to the State Department Frank L. Polk, former Governor of New York Charles S. Whitman and ex-Ambassador to Germany James W. Gerard.[101]

From the beginning, Nazi treatment of Jews was vehemently denounced by the American press.[102] Journalist Dorothy Thompson, expelled from Germany owing to a series of condemnatory eyewitness reports she sent to a Jewish daily in New York, wrote a chapter in a book exposing Nazi excesses published in 1934. Other well-known non-Jewish contributors included Alfred E. Smith and John Haynes Holmes.[103] Following the *Anschluss* in 1938 Dorothy Thompson devised a plan to enable Jews desiring to emigrate from Germany to take capital with them.[104] Meanwhile Anne O'Hare McCormick, foreign affairs commentator on the *New York Times*, argued that if necessary the United States should make a 'spectacular gesture' and admit every refugee from the *Reich*.[105] Dorothy Thompson's husband, the novelist Sinclair Lewis, showed his contempt for Nazi race laws along with the equally non-Jewish dramatist Sidney Howard. When asked for confirmation of their 'Aryan' status by an impresario in Berlin, who wanted to produce Howard's stage adaptation of Lewis's novel *Dodsworth*, the two men replied:

> We fear that with deep regret we shall be unable to give you certificates guaranteeing that we are Aryans. Who knows what ancestors we may have had in the last few hundred years? We really are as ignorant of them as even Hitler of his. In answering please use our proper legal names – Sidney Horowitz and Sinclair Levy.[106]

The non-sectarian Anti-Nazi League was set up in 1933 to campaign for a boycott of German goods, and similarly constituted anti-Nazi bodies sprang up across the United States. In 1934 eight distinguished jurists, including Clarence Darrow and Senator Edward P. Costigan, established in New York an unofficial Commission of Inquiry into Nazi persecution.[107] American churches maintained their relentless denunciations, and many secular bodies, including the American Federation of Labor, opposed their country's participation in the Berlin Olympics.[108] In 1937 an enormous anti-Nazi rally held in New York under Jewish auspices was addressed by John W. Lewis, Chairman of the Committee of the Industrial Organization, and General Hugh Johnson, former administrator of the National Recovery Administration; supportive messages were received from seven state governors and 50 members of Congress.[109] With the *Anschluss* and the terrors of *Kristallnacht* outrage intensified. In November 1938 innumerable protest meetings uniting Jews and non-Jews were held throughout the country; one in New York, attended by 30,000 people, received messages of solidarity from the governors of 19 states.[110] American churches declared Sunday, 21 November a national day of prayer for the victims of Nazi persecution.[111] In response to the *Anschluss* President Roosevelt announced that from 1 July 1938 the annual immigration quotas for Germany and Austria would be combined, providing a total of 25,947, in order to maximize the chances of refugees from Austria wishing to enter the

United States.[112] Noting that American opinion had been 'deeply shocked' by *Kristallnacht*, Roosevelt declared: 'I myself could scarcely believe that such things could occur in a twentieth century civilization,' and he recalled his country's Ambassador and Trade Commissioner from Berlin.[113]

For decades the concept of a Jewish national home in Palestine had found favour with influential non-Jewish Americans.[114] A joint resolution of Congress approving the Balfour Declaration, moved by Senator Henry Cabot Lodge and Representative Hamilton Fish, had been signed by President Harding in 1922.[115] A Pro-Palestine Committee founded during Nahum Sokolow's visit to the United States in 1932 was headed by Vice-President Charles Curtis, with prominent senators W.E. Borah and William King among the influential members.[116] Reports in 1938 that Britain intended a drastic curtailment of Jewish immigration into Palestine caused an enormous outpouring of indignation in the United States from Jew and non-Jew alike. President Roosevelt received a joint petition signed by 51 senators, 194 members of the House of Representatives, and 30 state governors, supporting his administration's representations to Britain on the matter. 'The fate of great numbers of men, women, and children, who are being persecuted solely because of their faith and race, must arouse the deepest compassion in the hearts of all civilised men and women,' the petition said in part. 'If our Government can, in this critical hour in the history of the Jewish people, help keep the one door through which oppressed Jews have entered into freedom and hope, we shall have rendered an historic service to the cause of enlightened mankind.'[117] Roosevelt received over 100,000 messages to that effect, many from non-Jewish individuals and organizations. They included 'scores' of university presidents supported by numerous faculty members; religious bodies ranging from the National Council of Catholic Men to the Federal Council of Churches of Christ, the largest organization of Protestant Churches in the country; resolutions from public meetings, including a gathering of black New Yorkers, and from some state legislatures.[118] Thirty-six Christian spokesmen, Catholic and Protestant, mainly senior clergymen, but including several distinguished laymen, cabled British Prime Minister Neville Chamberlain appealing to him to hold fast to the Balfour Declaration:

> Hundreds of thousands of Jews now in Palestine have staked their lives and fortunes on their faith in Great Britain. In reliance on

British honour millions of Jews have entrusted the destiny of their people to the British Government. Into the foundations of the Jewish National Home they have poured blood and treasure, and their magnificent accomplishments, material and spiritual, have won the high regard of the Christian world. Not only have the Arab people in Palestine greatly benefited by the administration of the Mandate, their political, civil, and religious rights have been fully protected, but they have freely enjoyed all the fruits of Jewish achievement.

Today, in their hour of agony, the persecuted victims of blind hate look to Palestine as their chief and almost sole hope. The abandonment by Great Britain of her pledges to the Jewish world would reduce them to despair. In our solemn judgment, such a course would be regarded by the entire world as a surrender to the forces of violence and hatred now sweeping the world; it would be a blow to Christian honour, and a most damaging blow to the prestige of Great Britain, which holds this honour in her keeping.

Signatories included such stalwarts of the Jewish cause as John Haynes Holmes, who had written a pro-Zionist book, and Alfred E. Smith.[119]

The newspaper tycoon W.R. Hearst, meanwhile, urged that Germany's former African colonies, forfeited in the First World War, be mandated to Britain, France and the United States as a Jewish national home. Subsequently, the Portuguese and Belgian colonies could be purchased. 'Africa was rapidly becoming a second America. The Jews would create one of the great nations of the earth.'[120] The British White Paper of 1939 prompted outrage from 150 members of Congress including almost the entire Foreign Affairs Committee of the House of Representatives, headed by Hamilton Fish. He urged 'no retreat, no compromise, and no surrender to British betrayal of promises and pledges'; while Senator William King of Utah observed: 'As long as the Jews continue to answer White Papers with further colonisation and broader settlement activities, what they have so gloriously built in Palestine will endure long after the Hitlers and Mussolinis have passed from the earth.' Numerous editorials condemned the White Paper as 'a second Munich'.[121]

Following confirmation in December 1942 of the extermination of European Jewry, 62 senators and 182 members of the House of Representatives signed a statement of support for their country's 'declared and traditional policy' regarding Palestine.[122] The following

March, the New York State Legislature unanimously adopted a resolution of sympathy and called for the admittance to Palestine of 'as many as will be required by the urgent situation of the Jewish people'.[123] Congress, apparently more realistic regarding rescue – calls for which were numerous – unanimously passed a resolution introduced by Senator Alben W. Barkley which condemned the 'mass murder of Jewish men, women, and children', and asked that Palestine be opened to large-scale Jewish immigration after the war.[124] Following a proclamation by Governor Thomas E. Dewey, 9 March 1943 was observed throughout New York State as a day of mourning for slaughtered European Jewry. Hundreds of non-Jews participated in a packed memorial meeting in Madison Square Garden; comparable meetings were held in Chicago, Washington and elsewhere.[125] At the beginning of 1944 the National Committee against Nazi Persecution and Extermination of the Jews was founded in Washington under the presidency of Supreme Court Justice Frank Murphy. It aimed 'to rescue those who may yet be saved' and to fight domestic antisemitism. Its members included Roosevelt's Vice-President, Henry Wallace, Assistant Attorney-General Norman A. Littell, Eric A. Johnston, President of the United States Chamber of Commerce, former Republican presidential nominee Wendell Willkie, the governors of Massachusetts, Wisconsin and Utah, and senior clergymen. At about the same time, in January 1944, President Roosevelt created the War Refugee Board, a body specifically founded to save the lives of European Jews. Some historians have claimed that it rescued 200,000 Jews from death at the hands of the Nazis, although this claim appears greatly exaggerated. Since Europe's Jews were the prisoners of a psychopath who was going to kill all of them, there was, in fact, very little that the Allies could do apart from win the war.[126] There were also calls for stateless and Palestinian Jews to be permitted to form a Jewish Army fighting alongside the Allies. This scheme, which also had its British supporters, was championed by, among others, Senators Barkley and Edwin C. Johnson, Congressman Will Rogers, Governor Chase Clark of Idaho and Pierre van Paassen, who chaired the American Committee for a Jewish Army.[127]

In Canada there were similar developments, with Nazi persecution roundly denounced.[128] Immediately following *Kristallnacht* 35 protest meetings were held across the country: 'not for many years has Canadian sentiment been so deeply stirred.'[129] At Toronto, whose City Council unanimously passed a resolution urging the Canadian

Prime Minister to protest to the German government against racial and religious persecution, 17,000 people crowded into the Maple Leaf Gardens for a demonstration which saw thousands more turned away. There were speeches from the 94-year-old former Chief Justice of Ontario, Sir William Mullock, from Sir Robert Falconer, former President of the city's university, and from the painter Sir Wyly Grier. A similar meeting at Halifax, Nova Scotia, was addressed by the Chief Justice and the President of Dalhousie University. At Kingston the main speakers were a Roman Catholic titular archbishop and the Principal of Queen's University.[130] Considerable indignation was also voiced in French Canada, generally depicted as a particularly unpleasant hotbed of antisemitism.[131] Few of the speakers appear to have been of French extraction; the percentage of protestors of such extraction is unclear. A huge meeting took place in Montreal chaired by a Chief Justice of Quebec Superior Court. A meeting in Quebec was addressed by the Minister of Commerce, a judge and an Anglican archdeacon. Students at McGill University in Montreal raided the premises of a private German club, screaming abuse and wreaking havoc.[132]

Substantial support for persecuted Jewry circulated in Australia during these dark years. Former Acting Prime Minister W.A. Watt, a veteran of the Kishinev protest, moved the resolution of outrage at a rally in Melbourne in April 1933, convened by the Jewish community to raise funds for German Jewish relief. Other non-Jewish speakers included a state Cabinet minister, a leading barrister and the President of the State Council of Churches, while the platform was filled with dignitaries including politicians, businessmen and senior officers of the city's university. Messages of sympathy, which came from all the main Christian denominations, included a tribute to Jewish prominence 'in the political, social, artistic, and industrial activities' of Australia from future Prime Minister (Sir) Robert Menzies, who described himself as 'an admirer of Jews' keen intellect, marked industry, generosity, and domestic loyalty'.[133] A similar rally in Sydney, convened by the Lord Mayor, was addressed by non-Jewish public figures in the presence of many more. The main resolution was moved by State Premier (Sir) Bertram Stevens, seconded by the President of the New South Wales Legislative Council, Sir John Peden, who to frequent applause eloquently denounced the persecution of a people 'great in mind and national spirit and in the service they had rendered to the world'. Protest meetings were also held in Brisbane and elsewhere, and they reoccurred in reaction to

Kristallnacht.[134] At the start of the Nazi era former Australian Prime Minister S.M. (later Lord) Bruce demonstrated his goodwill towards Jewry while heading his country's delegation to the League of Nations in Geneva. He readily allowed a rabbi, a combative political Zionist, to act as the delegation's official spokesman on Palestine. In 1938, as High Commissioner in London, Bruce urged the Australian government to admit 30,000 refugees from Nazism over the next three years, a number subsequently fixed at 15,000.[135]

One of the strongest displays of philosemitism in Australia across the political divide involved the attempt between 1939 and 1944 by the Freeland League for Jewish Colonization to persuade the Federal Government to agree to a semi-autonomous Jewish refugee settlement of some 50,000 persons in the sparsely populated Kimberley region of the country's far north-west. The impetus had come from two Australian non-Jews, the ex-Chairman of the Australian Meat Board and the Editor of the *British Australian and New Zealander*, both of whom saw the plight of Jews under Nazism as an opportunity to populate Australia's vulnerable northern coast, but with whom the humanitarian factor also weighed heavily.[136] In 1944, after much stalling, the proposal was finally rejected by the Federal Government on the traditional grounds of Australia's opposition to group settlements of non-Britons, but not before it had received widespread public endorsement. Western Australia's Premier, whose state was responsible for the Kimberley region, was an early convert to the scheme, which was warmly advocated in a lengthy public statement issued by 14 prominent non-Jewish Western Australians headed by the Anglican Primate of Australia.[137] Subsequently manifestos of support for the scheme were issued in Melbourne and Sydney, signed by about 100 non-Jewish opinion leaders, their names a veritable 'Who's Who' of the nation's elite. There were luminaries of the Bar, politics, academia and the business community, as well as labour leaders and representatives of women's groups.[138] Some were seasoned campaigners in the Jewish cause. The scheme received considerable support from other prominent non-Jews, from the press and from many of the respondents to a Gallup Poll taken in 1944.[139] Much interest also attached to a possible subsidiary or alternative scheme for a Jewish refugee settlement in Tasmania. That proposal was lobbied for energetically by its initiator, the son of a noted non-Jewish mining industry figure; he lost his life in pursuit of it.[140]

News of mass killings of Jews in Europe was met with horror and demands for rescue. A public meeting was held in Sydney in

November 1942, for example, to condemn the atrocities. It was opened by the Lord Mayor. Other non-Jewish speakers included: a future leading minister in Menzies' Cabinet, (Sir) Eric Harrison, at that time a New South Wales Liberal politician; a state Labor colleague very active in support of Jews; the Anglican Archbishop of Sydney; and Josiah Wedgwood's daughter Camilla, a University of Sydney academic. Messages of solidarity were read from Prime Minister John Curtin and Minister for External Affairs Dr H.V. Evatt (who in 1947 would be President of the UN Ad Hoc Committee on Palestine which decided on the Partition of Palestine and thus the creation of the Jewish State), the Roman Catholic Archbishop of Sydney and the British High Commissioner.[141] Rescue was the purpose of the Australia-Palestine Committee formed in 1941 under the joint chairmanship of C.V. Pilcher, Anglican Bishop Coadjutor of Sydney, who was ubiquitous on pro-Jewish platforms, and of a distinguished non-Jewish research scientist, as well as of the Pro-Palestine Committee formed in Melbourne that same year under the chairmanship of a non-Jewish university professor. These committees were composed of several prominent non-Jews, including the respective state premiers on opposite sides of politics, (Sir) William McKell and (Sir) Albert Dunstan.[142] The Sydney-based Australian Council for Jewish Rights, founded in 1943 by a group of non-Jews including Pilcher and Camilla Wedgwood, had as central aims the combating of antisemitism, the postwar settlement of Jewish refugees in Australia, and 'to undertake all possible efforts in order to rescue as many as possible of the millions of Jews now doomed to certain extermination in Nazi-dominated Europe'.[143]

One positive response to Nazism was the consolidation in the English-speaking world of Jewish–Christian relations. The trend had been pioneered in the United States since the 1890s, especially during the 1920s. That country's chief organization promoting Jewish–Christian understanding, the National Conference of Jews and Christians, was founded in 1927. In 1937–8 its title was changed to reverse the order of the final nouns. It marked its first decade with a four-day conference at which speakers included powerful magazine publisher Henry Luce, James M. Gillis, Editor of the *Catholic World*, other prominent non-Jewish editors, and James L. McConaughy, President of the American Association of Colleges.[144] Church bodies and related organizations had issued denunciations of domestic antisemitism and resolutions of support for Jewish Americans in response to Henry Ford's Jew-baiting. At the beginning of 1921, for instance, a meeting in Chicago of 400 Protestant ministers adopted a resolution condemning antisemitism and calling on church members to repudiate it; Supreme Knight James A. Flaherty of the Knights of Columbus ordered 2,200 lecturers belonging to that leading Roman Catholic fraternal order actively to combat Jew-hatred.[145] In 1926 the American Christian Fund for Jewish Relief, aiming to raise $25 million for destitute Jews in Eastern Europe, was launched at New York's Cathedral of St John the Divine by the Wesleyan General John Pershing, the Roman Catholic Major-General John O'Ryan and the Congregationalist Dr Samuel Parkes Cadman, with Episcopalian Bishop Manning presiding. Launching the fund in Philadelphia, Cardinal Dougherty remarked that Christians owed a duty to Jews 'for unjust persecution and for the Jewish contribution to civilization'.[146] Cadman was one of the official Christian signatories to a denunciation by the Permanent Commission on Better Understanding between Christians and Jews in America (founded in 1927) of a blood libel raised by a foreign immigrant at Massena, New York, in 1928 when a small girl went temporarily missing.[147] One of the major pioneers of dialogue, the great Protestant theologian Reinhold Niebuhr of Detroit, was instrumental in founding the American Palestine Committee in 1932 and the Christian Palestine Committee in 1942.[148]

In February 1938 a manifesto disavowing antisemitism as a 'sin', 'unChristian', 'a denial of the fundamental principles on which this nation was founded', issued by the Greater New York Federation of Churches to 'their brethren and fellow citizens of Jewish race and blood', was signed by over 200 clergymen of 14 denominations. The following month a manifesto issued by the National Conference of Jews and Christians in response to the *Anschluss* was signed by 99 Protestant, Catholic and Jewish leaders. It asserted that the three faiths 'stand together on common ground in defending human rights and liberties'.[149] In 1939 a Committee of Catholics to Fight Anti-Semitism was formed in New York to counter the propaganda of Jew-baiting 'radio priest' Father Charles E. Coughlin. With Dr Emmanuel Chapman, Professor of Philosophy at Fordham University, as Executive Secretary, this large and enthusiastic committee of clergy and laity boasted among the latter New York State Assemblyman Robert F. Wagner, playwright Emmet Lavery, author Theodore Maynard and former heavyweight boxing champion Gene Tunney.[150] Initiatives against antisemitism were also made by the Sons of Italy Grand Lodge, with 200 branches, and by Protestant denominations.[151]

In Britain efforts by clergymen to educate Christians in the practices and beliefs of Jews and dissipate prejudice also accelerated during the interwar period, especially after the rise of Nazi Germany. Increasingly, rabbis and other Jewish spokesmen were invited to address church groups on issues of Jewish concern. Sidney Dark, editor of the influential Anglican *Church Times*, wrote for popular consumption two books highly sympathetic to Jews, one with *Sunday Times* columnist Herbert Sidebotham.[152] The Anglican Reverend James Parkes played a pivotal and illustrious role in promoting understanding. In lectures and publications he waged unremitting war on antisemitism, surviving an assassination attempt in Geneva by the Nazi Antisemitische Weltdienst in 1935. With the Methodist Reverend W.W. Simpson, he was a driving force in the foundation in 1942 of the Council of Christians and Jews in reaction to Nazi barbarism.[153] In Australia, the New South Wales Council of Christians and Jews was formed in 1943 under the presidency of Sydney's Anglican Archbishop. A Sydney clergyman, the Reverend Burgoyne Chapman, waged a tireless paper warfare against antisemitism.[154] Jewish–Christian dialogue was also actively fostered in Canada during the Nazi era, while in South Africa a Society of Jews and Christians, headquartered in Johannesburg, established branches in other centres during the late 1930s.[155]

Between 1933 and 1945 the democracies were faced with the coming to absolute power, first in Germany and, after 1939, in most of continental Europe, of the most fanatical antisemite in history. Contrary to the widespread depiction of the democracies' response to Hitler's antisemitism as weak and inadequate, most of Germany's Jews were rescued while there was still time and before anyone could have realized that Hitler was bent on continential genocide. After 1939 and the start of the war rescue became impossible, except by winning the war and ridding the world of the Nazi scourge. This the Allies did, thus saving the lives of the three million Jews of Europe who survived the war, and of the half million in Palestine, all of whom would surely have perished had not the democracies fought and destroyed Hitler's monstrous regime.

Part II
A Typology of Philosemitism

6 'The Spirit of the Age': Liberal and Progressive Philosemitism

It is fruitful to divide the notable philosemites of the English-speaking world into a number of types, and the next four chapters will examine the typology which, we believe, best explains and accommodates the most frequently encountered varieties of philosemitism: liberal and progressive, Christian, Zionist and conservative/elitist. Obviously, these are at best only rough guides. An individual philosemite might well be categorized under several of these headings, while another may well fit under none. Nevertheless, we believe that this is the most useful way to classify the leading philosemites of the century between 1840 and the Second World War, with many examples of all these types. The post-1945 period presents special problems of it own, and for that reason we have preferred to treat it separately as the final chapter of this book.

It is probably fair to say that the plurality of vocal and active philosemites can best be classified as liberals and progressives, committed to defending Jews against oppression because their human rights were violated. By and large (and with many exceptions) philosemitism was strongest in societies, like Britain and the United States, where liberalism was strongest. (Conversely, antisemitism was strongest, generally speaking, in societies where the Anglo-American tradition of liberalism was weakest.) The force and importance of liberal philosemitism was also strongest in Britain and the United States because the influential elites of those countries were often liberal and had certainly internalized the liberal values of tolerance and pluralism. Thus, the Whig aristocracy in Britain, dominant in politics during much of the nineteenth century, and the leadership of both the Democratic and Republican Parties in the United States, were firmly committed to tolerance for Jews. For many liberal philosemites, hostility to Jews was atavistic, a relic of the barbarism of carlier, benighted ages, now made happily uncommon by the steady march of civilization and its values. Often, philosemitism was seen as a component of the liberal Christian values of fairness and justice which many who were liberals in the English-speaking world espoused. For instance, Lady Violet Bonham Carter (daughter of H.H. Asquith, Britain's Liberal Prime Minister from 1908–15) denounced Nazi antisemitism in the following terms:

> We honour your race, whose genius has given so much to the world. We reverence your faith, from which our own was born. We share your suffering. We salute your courage. But there is one thing you cannot share with us – our shame. Shame that a nation which for centuries has at least called itself a Christian nation should outrage justice, gentleness and mercy, should violate every canon of our Christian faith.[1]

Those were the sorts of words spoken by countless philosemites irrespective of type. But what, in particular, drew liberals to the cause was an ideological world view which regarded all men as equal, religion as a purely private matter and ethnic distinctions (at least among persons of European descent) as irrelevant. This attitude underlay the campaign, during the 'age of reform' which witnessed the first of the great pro-Jewish rallies in Britain, to allow Jews elected to Parliament to take their seats by swearing an oath acceptable to and binding upon them. As Macaulay observed in 1831:

> The points of difference between Christianity and Judaism have very much to do with a man's fitness to be a bishop or a rabbi; but they have no more to do with his fitness to be a magistrate, a legislator, or a minister of finance, than with his fitness to be a cobbler. Nobody has ever thought of compelling cobblers to make any declaration on the true faith of a Christian …[2]

In British colonies such as Jamaica and Australia, where Jews took their place as legislators long before they were permitted to do so in the mother country, this liberal attitude was apparent essentially from the start, while the American Constitution, which provided a definition of citizenship that in no way excluded Jews, infused successive generations with the conviction that secular liberalism was the very touchstone of political morality.[3] This underlines the useful if perhaps exaggerated distinction by political scientist Hans Kohn between the type of nationalism found in continental Europe and that found in the modern English-speaking world plus post-revolutionary France. In the former, nationality was seen as essentially ethnic/religious in nature, with minority groups (especially Jews) treated as always suspect if not alien; in the latter, all residents of the country have been regarded as equal citizens.[4]

The Damascus rally of 1840, the forerunner of many held under the auspices of the Lord Mayor and Corporation of the City of London in support of persecuted Jews overseas, reflected the transition occurring within a powerful institution from what Jewish commentators described as 'the stronghold of obsolete laws and the hotbed of prejudices' to 'a stronghold of religious, no less than of civil, liberty'.[5] Within the recent memory of participants at the rally, the Corporation's illiberal laws had prevented Jews from opening retail premises within the boundaries of the square mile under its jurisdiction, while the restrictive practices of the City livery companies, from which Jews were effectively disbarred, impeded the spread of useful trades among the Jewish community. No Jew could hold municipal office.[6]

By the time of the rally most of the Jews' disabilities in the City had disappeared. In 1830 they obtained the right to establish retail outlets there with the passage of an Act giving them the freedom of the City. It was engineered by a future Chief Justice, Thomas (later Lord) Denman, who as Common Sergeant was the second most senior legal officer in the City, supported by the City Solicitor, Charles Pearson, who was instrumental in getting the City's schools opened to Jews. When, in 1835, David Salomons was elected Sheriff of London, an Act of Parliament was passed enabling Jews to assume that office without subscribing to the Christian form of the requisite oath. Owing to the opposition of the Court of Aldermen, to which Salomons was initially elected that same year, he could not take his place as an alderman until the passage of a parliamentary Act in 1845 similarly relieved persons elected to municipal office of the obligation to swear 'on the true faith of a Christian'.[7] By 1840 a discernibly liberal ethos prevailed in the City as a result of its transformation from a trading area dominated by closed, monopolistic livery companies and often narrow-minded small private firms into the great financial centre of the world, a cosmopolitan hub in which bigotry sat uneasily, and which archetypal liberal David Wire described as 'the emporium of commerce, the home [*sic*; hope?] of the slave, the teacher of nations, and the promoter of universal love, universal happiness, and universal peace.' The City's 'best sympathies' were accordingly inclined 'to support ... our elder brothers in the faith'.[8] By the time Wire and other City personalities took up the cause of Damascus Jewry the City had joined battle for Jewish parliamentary emancipation at home – a measure the *Stock Exchange Journal* described as 'some atonement to a cruelly persecuted race' – and it demonstrated its goodwill decisively in 1847 when it first elected Baron Lionel de Rothschild to represent it at Westminster.[9] Nor was the City's now pervasive liberalism undermined by the Conservatives who came to dominate it later in the century, for they too shared its essential ethos; there were, of course, City Conservatives at the 1840 rally.

As early as 1796 a pamphlet issued in London demanded the 'equal participation of our civil rights' for a people whose 'skill and ingenuity' had brought considerable commercial benefits to the country. Citing also their good conduct as citizens, the anonymous author – who was compared to C.W. von Dohm in Prussia and Abbé Grégoire in France as a major prophet of enlightenment regarding Jews – maintained that 'where the greatest toleration of religious principles exists, there can be as little danger to be apprehended from the Jews as from the Quakers, or any other sect.'[10] In 1801 an understanding Chairman of the Commission of Magistrates decreed that Jewish inmates of Bridewell prison within the City be excused from work on their Sabbaths and festivals.[11] And a few years later the Duke of Sussex and two other sons of King George III were taken to a Friday evening service at the Great Synagogue, Duke's Place, by the influential financier Abraham Goldsmid.[12]

For the Duke of Sussex that visit marked the beginning of a close association with Anglo-Jewry which ended only with his death in 1843. By 1817 he had become patron of the Jews' Hospital, Mile End, having apparently donated to its funds as early as 1807, the year following its establishment as an almshouse for the Ashkenazi aged poor and for boys and girls of similar background who were there taught handicrafts before apprenticeships or domestic positions were sought for them. He learned Hebrew from a Jewish tutor, acquired a library of Hebraica, and studied the Torah daily with an eminent Jewish instructor. A staunch ally of progressive causes, the Duke was always willing to listen to Jewish grievances, and said explicitly on several occasions that he opposed conversionism. He refused to meet any Jew who had accepted Christianity. On the day of his burial a special prayer for him was offered in London's synagogues, the interiors of which were draped in black. Four eminent Jews, including Montefiore and Salomons, attended the funeral by invitation, and in his memory Anglo-Jewry established Sussex Hall, the so-called Jews' and General Literary and Scientific Institution.[13]

As a Whig, the Duke enjoyed enormous popularity among the

middle classes. He was, moreover, England's premier Freemason. With its Judaic concepts and imagery, Freemasonry might have stimulated his philosemitism as well as that of others; certainly in English-speaking lands it welcomed Jews into its ranks, thereby aiding their integration into society.[14] His patronage of Jews' Hospital played a significant part in lowering barriers between Jew and gentile in the City, and created a climate of cordiality which enabled him successfully to persuade his contacts there to relax municipal restrictions disadvantaging Jews.[15] As the hospital's patron Sussex regularly inspected its facilities, conversed with its inmates – he told the children to cling through life to their Jewish heritage – attended its synagogue and presided over its annual dinners. On these occasions he brought 'many personal friends, whom he interested in his good work', and thus the annual dinners came to be attended by 'persons of rank and influence', who followed his example in making generous contributions to the hospital's coffers.[16] On his death, his equally well-disposed brother, the Duke of Cambridge, succeeded him as patron. Cambridge subsequently became patron also of the Western Jewish Girls' Free School and – like the Queen Dowager (Adelaide), the Duchess of Kent (Queen Victoria's mother) and the Duke of Buccleuch – a patron of the Jews' Orphan Asylum.[17]

The great pro-Jewish rallies in the City of London thus occurred against an ever-strengthening background of elite involvement in the Jewish cause: gentiles of means and influence supported the fund-raising appeals of Jewish schools and philanthropic institutions of all kinds, and attended their annual festivities. This went far beyond reciprocity for the evenhandedness displayed by wealthy Jews towards charitable endeavours, whereby people such as Montefiore donated to general causes as well as Jewish ones. From the 1840s onwards, donors' lists of Anglo-Jewish institutions, large and small, prominent and obscure, contained score upon score of gentile names. Among the City and Bank of England officials, bankers, stockbrokers and merchants who contributed to those institutions were many of the speakers and other participants at the rallies, as well as other philosemites such as Lord John Russell. He presided over the annual dinners of the Jews' Free School. Many were regular donors, in some cases to a range of institutions; amounts given were often astonishingly generous. Several donors had business connections with Jews. A few remembered Jews in their wills.[18]

The rationale for such interaction was voiced by the Duke of Sussex: the Jews were governed by 'the Old Covenant', he by 'the New', yet the tenet of both was 'Fear God, Honour the King, and Love thy Neighbour as thyself'.[19] Nor was such interaction confined to London. Some gentile donations to metropolitan Jewish charities came from the provinces, and from the early 1840s Jewish philanthropic societies in Liverpool, Birmingham and Portsmouth welcomed gentiles at their annual dinners. Those at Portsmouth appear to have been particularly convivial affairs, with speeches from local gentile civic leaders, clergymen, parliamentarians and officers in the armed services, many toasts, and the presence of captains and lieutenants from visiting foreign warships (Russians were pointedly banned).[20]

Since the eighteenth century a number of writers, of fiction and non-fiction, had been endeavouring to foster an improved climate for Jews by countering negative stereotypes of them. Maria Edgeworth noted that Jews were too frequently depicted as 'of a mean, avaricious, unprincipled, treacherous character', whose manner, appearance and speech 'were mimicked and caricatured, as if to render them subjects of perpetual derision and detestation'.[21] There is no doubt that the interaction with Jews experienced by gentiles at Jewish charitable functions – reinforced by the realization that Jews' philanthropy was not confined to their own community – helped to foster tolerance by dissolving stereotypes and frequently led to admiration of Jews: 'it is only on such occasions that the middle classes of the Gentiles, who generally come into contact only with the lower class of the Jews, become better educated of the nation, and learn to respect them.'[22]

A noted humanitarian, Lord Dudley Stuart, knew little of Anglo-Jewry until he was taken to the Jews' Hospital by the Duke of Sussex and began contributing to communal charities. Jews were, he found, 'a worthy set of people ... exceedingly tolerant, the essence of kindheartedness, liberality and generosity'.[23] A reporter who attended the annual dinner of the Jews' Free School in 1854, when Earl Granville stood in for Lord John Russell, wished that opponents of Jewish parliamentary emancipation were present:

> They would have seen a bearing in speech and act as distinctly English as in any British Christian assembly; every speaker instinctively claiming Britain as his country, and every listener being especially vociferous on the enunciation of any patriotic and particularly John Bull sentiment. They would have seen 600 boys and 300 girls – clean, neat and healthy – educated in honest handicrafts, plain useful knowledge, music, design, and Hebrew; not to become mere exchangers, but *producers*.[24]

The *Jewish Chronicle* praised the spectacle of Jew and gentile 'mingling together in social harmony ... for the noble purposes of charity' as 'a glorious mark of the triumph of civilisation'.[25] During the 1840s that newspaper stressed the existence of an 'Increased Liberality of Feeling' between the two communities.[26] The signs of gentile goodwill were becoming ever more apparent. More and more of them were – in a theme which developed into a philosemitic cliché – paying public tribute to the Jews as honest, peaceable, patriotic, outstandingly moral citizens, who did not mistreat their wives or neglect their children, seldom drank to excess or ran foul of the law or became a charge on the parochial authorities.[27] A conviction was abroad that, to quote a Mayor of Portsmouth, discrimination against Jews was 'not only unjust to the latter, but adverse to the spirit of the age'.[28] Liberalism was abundant. When, in 1843, Montefiore, accompanied by prominent gentiles including Wire and local dignitaries, made his way in procession from Birmingham's synagogue to the site of a Jewish school whose foundation stone he had come to lay, 'among all the crowd (consisting chiefly of the lower classes) which lined our way, there was not heard a single expression derogatory to Jews or Judaism; there was not a single countenance disgraced by a trait of derision.' At the banquet following the ceremony, presided over by the Mayor, 'all sects and callings, all parties and divisions, religious and political' were represented; there were heartfelt philosemitic speeches; during the toast to Montefiore and his wife 'every hand was waving, every glass ringing, every face flushed with joy [and] veneration'.[29]

Leading citizens of Birmingham hosted a dinner for their city's first Jewish councillor, an active charity worker. Repeated cries of 'Shame, shame' greeted his references to the persecution of Jews throughout history and in his native Russia: 'here I stand surrounded by an assembly principally composed of good and enlightened Christians – Englishmen, who have invited me here to ... do me honour.'[30] Birmingham, Portsmouth and Southampton had effectively waived the obligation for civic officials to swear the Christian oath, although until the Act of 1845 abolishing that requirement the presence of Jews on town councils was technically illegal. In 1843 Portsmouth's future first Jewish Mayor – 'whose fitness for the Council has been proved, and whose conduct as a tradesman and a townsman stands so high in the estimation of all'[31] – unexpectedly lost his seat on the council despite the uncanvassed votes of the Mayor, the Governor of the garrison, the town's commercial elite and numerous army and navy officers. Many supporters had been deterred by a sudden rumour that he faced a £50 fine for every council decision in which he participated (a penalty which few townspeople wished to see enforced). The following year he was decisively returned against a High Anglican churchworker in a campaign entirely free from antisemitism. To his amazement church bells pealed in triumph at the result. 'This is a conclusive proof, that all those religious prejudices are gone, and men are now judged by their conduct.'[32] When the funeral cortège of a member of the same civic-minded family passed through Southampton in 1846, non-Jewish shopkeepers closed their doors in a mark of respect 'seldom paid to one of their own creed'.[33] In 1851, when David Salomons contested the parliamentary seat of Greenwich against a non-Jew of the same party, a local gentile firm paid for three omnibuses to ferry his supporters to the poll; his victory was celebrated by one non-Jewish admirer with 121 (*sic*) rounds from a canon![34] By that time, Jewish parliamentary emancipation could count on the votes of one archbishop, several prelates and over 130 temporal members of the House of Lords.[35] And one of the Jews' most faithful champions in the Commons, the radical Thomas Duncombe, set to work on a sympathetic history of Anglo-Jewry.[36]

Liberal philosemitism was also consolidated elsewhere in the English-speaking world by the perception of Jews as worthy citizens. In frontier societies such as the American West, Canada, South Africa and Australia, their contributions to burgeoning economies and emerging towns were generally appreciated, and they were typically accepted as fellow pioneers of settlement and civilization. A newspaper in New South Wales, for example, averred:

> The Hebrews of this colony, as of every other locality in the British dominions, have established for themselves as a body, a reputation for general morality, integrity, and munificent generosity, which vies with, and in some instances, shames the best efforts of the communicants of other spiritual denominations ... They are the last against whom the intolerant advocates of invidious disqualifications, and obsolete arbitrary distinctions, should be permitted to prevail.[37]

Another, contrasting the licentiousness and brutality which, it claimed, too often characterized life in the outback, wished that Jews could administer the colony, and disseminate their moral code.[38]

When H.N. Brailsford wrote around the time of the Beilis Affair that 'The progress of any European society towards civilisation may be measured infallibly by its treatment of its Jews', he was voicing what had become a commonplace, an opinion that had impressed itself upon the liberal British mind during the emancipation struggle.[39] Those who flocked to the rallies fundamentally believed, in the words of Sir Archibald Sinclair, who led the Liberal Party during the Nazi era, that 'Governments will learn that there is no national defence against the moral indignation of the world, and in the long run the cause of tolerance will prevail.'[40] An important element – indeed, almost a defining characteristic – of liberal philosemitism was the conviction that antisemitism was atavistic, an unconscionable throwback to a benighted era. It was in particular strongly associated in the minds of many liberals with the horrors of the Inquisition, and the Roman Catholic Church was frequently seen as the chief culprit in keeping it alive. Many liberals saw it as a component of a much wider persecution by the Vatican of both Protestantism and free thought, and it was accordingly to be condemned as part of a general attack upon religious 'superstition', as during the Damascus, Mortara and Dreyfus Affairs.

That antisemitism was centrally atavistic was repeated from one philosemitic demonstration to the next. For instance, the Damascus rally expressed 'deep regret' that an anti-Jewish persecution had erupted 'in this enlightened age'.[41] Sir Fowell Buxton, at the 1872 rally, lamented that the 'revolting ... cruelties' of Ferdinand and Isabella had been 'paralleled in this century'.[42] Lord Bryce told its 1882 counterpart: 'It is, indeed, enough to make one blush for modern civilization to think that a people like the Jews ... should be subjected to such terrible persecutions'; while the parallel Oxford protest mentioned 'the unreasoning antipathies and savage cruelties of the Middle Ages'.[43] The 1890 rally resolved 'that in the last decade of the nineteenth century religious liberty is a principle which should be recognized by every Christian community as among the natural human rights'.[44] The Board of Aldermen of New York, in a motion condemning the Kishinev pogrom, declared: 'The forces of bigotry, prejudice and intolerance are repugnant to the emancipated intelligence of the modern world and antagonistic to the conscience of free institutions.'[45] Balfour told Parliament in 1905 that 'The medieval treatment of the Jews was a permanent stain on European annals' – a view widely echoed, not least by the novelist George Meredith, a persistent denouncer of Russian antisemitism, accounts of which 'disordered' his mind.[46] The Beilis protest of 1912 referred to 'the days of Witchcraft and Black magic'.[47] During the 1930s many felt, with American Secretary of the Interior Harold Ickes, that comparisons with the Middle Ages were inadequate, for Nazi persecution recalled rather the bestial days of barbarism.[48] In a representative comment, W.P. Crozier, Editor of the *Manchester Guardian*, declared it 'immeasurably shocking that Germany should be turning its back on the whole principle of equality between races and religions, and should apparently be marching back into the Dark Ages'.[49]

'It is a proud and honourable thing for a powerful government and a great people to interest themselves in the affairs of the suffering and feeble, wherever they are found, and by whomsoever they may be oppressed,' observed a liberal newspaper in 1862 during an anti-semitic episode in Tunis which had merited the attention of the British government.[50] This humanistic approach propelled liberal and progressive philosemites, many of whom were likely to support a range of enlightened causes, and were to be found on platforms and in movements championing, for example, the rights of slaves, Armenians and Bulgarians. Two days before they demonstrated on behalf of Damascus Jewry, O'Connell, Samuel Gurney, Bowring and Fowell Buxton had attended the first anniversary meeting of the Society for the Extinction of the Slave Trade.[51] The Duke of Westminster, who presided over the 1890 rally, had performed the same role at a great meeting in 1876 on behalf of the persecuted Christians in Bulgaria.[52] Shaftesbury told the 1882 rally: 'It is not simply because those who are persecuted are Jews that we are met here; Englishmen would feel the same sympathy for Buddhists, Mahomedans, or Pagans.'[53] Lord Parmoor, denouncing the pogroms of 1919, explained that 'injustices of this kind were not a question of special nationalities, but everyone who loved liberty in its true sense desired to protest against gross injustices of this character.'[54]

At the 1840 rally David Wire specified 'liberality' as a principle which brought the protesters together.[55] The same principle induced him to organize the 1859 Mortara protest, and liberals as well as Protestant activists were well represented among its signatories.[56] At the 1882 rally Shaftesbury, while acknowledging the 'deep special feeling towards the Hebrew race' felt by himself and many others, observed to loud cheers that the 'one grand universal principle' uniting the participants was 'deep regard for the rights of the human race ... it is the desire of every true Englishman that every one should be as free and happy as he is himself.'[57] At the comparable Sydney protest the liberal statesman Sir John Robertson remarked that 'It is difficult to believe that ... in great civilized countries, any section of the people should be so insulted, outraged, and persecuted, for their religious opinions' – a view widely echoed.[58]

The liberal outlook was clearly articulated in the opening resolution at the 1890 Guildhall rally, which declared that 'religious liberty is a principle which should be recognized by every Christian community as among the natural human rights.'[59] It was widely endorsed in other statements, for example in messages of support from the Duke of Argyll, a confirmed humanitarian ('There can be but one feeling among all parties and among all Churches in these islands against every form of persecution on account of religious belief') and Lord Tennyson ('I ... loath every kind of persecution').[60]

It was given broad expression in the Kishinev protests of 1903, for example, by New York's Mayor Seth Low at his city's rally: 'We are here to respect one another; whatever be the creed, whatever the race, whatever the belief, we are of one blood, one before God and humanity.'[61] And it was a cornerstone of the protests in 1905–6, as enunciated, for example, by Adelaide's Mayor Theo Bruce at his city's rally (they protested 'as members of the human family, and ... because they had the advantage of living under the British Crown and of enjoying ... religious freedom and tolerance'[62]) and by Canadian Prime Minister Sir Wilfrid Laurier at Ottawa's: Jewish immigrants to Canada would find 'a hearty welcome' in a land with institutions

> in which there are equal rights for all, and under which every man, no matter what his origin, his creed or his race may be, is sure to find an equal share of liberty, of justice, of equity, and of sunshine. I am here as a citizen of Canada because I believed it my duty to be here, when as a Canadian and a British subject one must be proud to assert the brotherhood of man and the fatherhood of God.[63]

Lord Buckmaster described the 1933 major rally as essentially one by 'independent and fair-minded' non-Jews 'against the cruelty and wrong of an injustice the burden and bitterness of which they will never be called upon to share' and declared that his feelings would be as strong if the world owed no debt to the 'genius of Jews'.[64] Professor Walter Murdoch, a tireless Australian champion of Jewish refugee settlement, felt 'a burning pity and a fierce rage' because the Nazis' victims were 'human beings like ourselves'.[65]

At the same time, Murdoch and many other philosemites of his ilk acknowledged the Jewish people as what Professor Gilbert Murray called 'the protomartyr' in the annals of human suffering.[66] Moreover, several philosemites of the liberal or progressive type had a close interest in Jews and Judaism. The affinity with Jews on the part of Robert Browning, who attended the 1882 rally, is well known. Less well known, perhaps, is the 'friendly interest in Jewish affairs' taken by Lord Leighton, a requisitioner of the 1890 rally, who was an honoured guest at communal functions,[67] and the fact that Lord Tennyson, who constantly expressed sympathy for persecuted Jews, derived inspiration for some of his poems by reading the Old Testament in Hebrew, and studied Spinoza.[68] Matthew Arnold, who protested against Russian persecution, had a long and cordial association with the Jewish community through his work as a Government Education Inspector, and he counted several Rothschilds and Montefiores among his personal friends. He, too, read the Bible in Hebrew, and the eagerly sought opinions of E.O. Deutsch, Talmudic scholar at the British Museum, made an impact on him.[69] Thomas Huxley was justly described as 'an agnostic with a strong leaning towards Judaism' and he attested to that – and his admiration for Jews – several times in his writings. In 1882 he demonstrated his solidarity with persecuted Jewry by attending the consecration of the St John's Wood Synagogue, an occasion which deeply impressed him, and he would have spoken at the 1890 rally, of which he was a requisitioner, but for the state of his health.[70] Other examples of this sort of philosemite could be given. Nor did a liberal outlook regarding Jews necessarily entail a liberal outlook regarding other peoples. Many of the speakers and other participants at the Australian pro-Jewish rallies, for example, were active campaigners for an immigration policy which excluded Asiatics in order to safeguard wages; few dissented from such a policy once it was in place.[71] In the United States, especially in the South, it was one thing to champion Jews, quite another to champion blacks.[72]

Among the supporters of Jews in their tribulations were members of other minority groups, whose philosemitism was presumably honed by their own experience of oppression or marginalization. They included such American blacks as the abolitionist Frederick B. Douglass, educator Edward Blyden, Bishop Flipper, and singer Paul Robeson, as well as groups of Chinese in the United States and Australia who protested at the Kishinev massacre. They also included Irish nationalists, such as the Australian Sir John O'Shanassy, who mentioned the Irish situation when he donated to Russian Jewish relief in 1881, and John Redmond, who in expressing 'deepest sympathy' over the pogroms of 1905–6, noted: 'Ireland has learned from persecution to sympathize with the persecuted.'[73]

Nevertheless, liberals and progressives were represented among those demonstrators on behalf of oppressed Jewry who had shown in the past that they were personally not immune from prejudice towards Jews to some degree. They included Michael Davitt, who frankly and shockingly justified antisemitism in some cases, for instance where Jews were 'foes of nationality' or agents of 'unscrupulous capitalism', Arnold White, who lent his written support to the 1906 rally, H.G. Wells, who signed the Beilis protest, and Wickham Steed and Beatrice Webb, who condemned Nazi persecution. During the 1930s many people of various political complexions, including G.K. Chesterton, Agatha Christie and Dorothy Sayers, thoroughly repented of their previous anti-Jewish prejudice, and actively endeavoured to make amends.[74] Socialists were especially likely to harbour ambivalent feelings towards Jews, championing the downtrodden 'Jewish masses' under Czarist rule, and *Reich* Jewry during the 1930s under Nazism, yet all too often exhibiting 'rich Jew anti-semitism' in their representation of Jews as plutocrats. In 1907, for instance, the annual conference of the British Social Democratic Federation denounced the recent pogroms in Russia while simultaneously describing the Jewish members of the Commons as agents of 'the capitalist classes', in politics 'for social advancement and personal profit'.[75] Defending Leo Frank, the socialist *New York Call* explained: 'It is not because this man is a Jew ... that we interest ourselves in his behalf, but because of the dubious character of the "justice" meted out to him.'[76] These sorts of people loved Jews when they were victims; their attitude is best described, in the phrase that Gladstone used about himself, as 'anti-anti-semitism'.[77] Such support was obviously less inclined to be steadfast than that based on a positive appreciation of Jews as citizens, colleagues and companions, on admiration for what they had achieved and what they had contributed to society, which, as shown, was the hallmark of a great deal of liberal philosemitism (as well as of other strands of philosemitism outlined in this work).

More widely and generally, the attitude of the extreme left, especially that of Marxist leaders, parties and movements, to Jewish persecution and indeed to Jewish identity, has attracted a good deal of attention from historians. Most agree that the extreme left's attitude was, at best, ambiguous, and at worst little different from the hostility of right-wing antisemites.[78] Certainly the history of the Jewish people in the Soviet Union and its satellites was catastrophic, with leaders of that country building on the legacy of Czarist antisemitism while introducing elements of their own. Similarly, extreme left-wing Trotskyite and other fringe Marxist parties became renowned for the ferocity of their anti-Zionism (especially after 1967, but stemming from an attitude adopted while Trotsky was still alive), which, in its centrality, and rhetorical extremism, seemed to many Jews to cross the border to the openly antisemitic.[79] The extreme left's traditional difficulties with Jewish identity has many facets. Judaism as a religion is – as are all religions – an 'opium of the people'; Zionism was long seen as a component of reactionary 'bourgeois nationalism'; the Jewish people were often seen as having survived into modern times largely because of their status as outcast financiers. Yet, because of the seeming force of Establishment antisemitism, strong sympathy and identification with the extreme left was a common and typical response of Jewish intellectuals and secularized youth throughout the world, especially during the interwar years and particularly in the 1930s, the 'devil's decade', when fascism and economic depression were ubiquitous.[80] The love affair between a major segment of Jewry and the extreme left is reminiscent of what is often said about the 'symbiosis', from the Enlightenment until Hitler, between German Jewry and Germany, that the Jews' affection for Germany was, unfortunately, almost wholly unreciprocated. The Communist Party and other Marxist groups were quite happy to welcome Jewish support, provided that Jews slavishly toed the party line. Nevertheless, and despite everything which might be said of Marxists' hostility to Jewish demands, in some times and places Marxists did act as important and visible champions of oppressed Jews when such championship appeared to be uncommon. Most strikingly, perhaps, this occurred during the 1930s in the East End of London, where the largely non-Jewish British Communist Party was extremely active in a range of activities on behalf of East End Jewry, forming tenants' organizations and rent strikes in protest against slum housing conditions and, in particular, helping to head the movements of protest against Sir Oswald Mosley and his British Union of Fascists.[81] Communists played an especially important role in organizing the celebrated 'Battle of Cable Street' in October 1936, when a large contingent of Mosley's Blackshirts were forcibly prevented from marching through a heavily Jewish area of Whitechapel, perhaps the only time that the extreme right and left came into physical conflict in modern British history and one of the few occasions during the decade of rampant fascist triumph that the forces of 'progressive' anti-fascism seemed to prevail.[82]

Much of the support given by secularized and intellectual Jews to the Soviet Union and to Western Communist parties vanished with the Nazi–Soviet Pact of 1939; it re-emerged during the Second World War after Germany launched its unprovoked attack on the Soviet Union in June 1941, and especially with knowledge of the genocide of Eastern European Jewry, but then declined with the Cold War and the fierce antisemitism of Stalin's postwar years and of the post-Stalinist Soviet Union until the rise of Gorbachev. Briefly, in 1947–8 the Soviet Union shifted its foreign policy so that it favoured the creation of the State of Israel, but for most of the next four decades, and especially after the 1967 Six Day War, the Soviet Union was among Israel's bitterest enemies. In general, the extreme left, especially its Communist and Marxist groupings, have been less sympathetic to ameliorating the oppression of Jews in the postwar world than any other component of the political spectrum except the antisemitic extreme right. It is notable for producing either seldom or never any significant examples of most of the other strands of philosemitism which are discussed in this work. On the other hand, as leftists and 'progressives', Marxists believe in human equality, however nominally and theoretically, and oppose ethnic oppression, and thus must always oppose overt antisemitism, at least on paper.

7 'The Deepest Debt': Christian Philosemitism

Throughout the period covered in this book, most philosemites in the English-speaking world were, nominally at least, Christian. This chapter is concerned with avowed practising Christians, those who were clearly animated in their activities on behalf of Jews by their Christian principles. Christianity was an important element in philosemitism for a number of reasons which are not difficult to understand. Judaism is the ancestral religion of Christianity, and Jews were the first people to be vouchsafed the Divine revelation which Christians believe culminated in the life and mission of Jesus. While most Christians had long believed that the 'New Covenant' of Jesus had superseded the 'Old Covenant' of Moses, increasingly many Christians concluded that, on the contrary, God's Covenant with the Jewish people had never been annulled. To them, in a sense, an attack upon Jews was also an attack upon Christianity, especially as modern ultra-nationalistic and racially motivated antisemites were often explicitly pagans who held all religions in contempt and despised the message of mercy and love in Christianity. Secondly, Christians were explicitly enjoined to assist the weak and downtrodden and thus were called upon to support Jews oppressed by their government or a foreign power. Thirdly, antisemitism, when it was enunciated and practised by men who claimed to be Christians, in fact was a severe embarrassment and reproach to the world's enlightened Christians, since it was so obviously inconsistent with the basic principles of the Christian religion. Fourthly, Protestants in the English-speaking world long associated antisemitism with the superstitious barbarisms of the Roman Catholic (or, occasionally, Eastern Orthodox) Church, and saw the apparent propensity of Roman Catholic (and Orthodox) societies to treat Jews as second-class citizens as further evidence of the inferiority of Catholic (and Orthodox) Christianity to Protestantism. In general, the more reformed and free from pre-Reformation belief and practice the Christian sect, the more philosemitic it was, although there were, of course, many exceptions. The Presbyterian Church in Scotland and overseas, and smaller and less dogmatic sects such as the Quakers and Unitarians were in general more philosemitic than other strands within Protestantism, although again this was often a matter of degree and of the propensity of individual activists to involve themselves in assisting persecuted Jews. While, prior to the 1960s, Protestants as a rule were more sympathetic to Jews than were Catholics, there were also a surprisingly large number of the latter who actively opposed antisemitism and supported oppressed Jewish communities. A fifth element in Christian philosemitism is to be found in the fact that some of the smaller Protestant sects saw themselves as literally the successors to the ancient Israelites, not in the sense of supplanting a now-displaced group formerly chosen by God, but as a kind of modern parallel to them; members of these sects were often deeply fascinated by the Jewish people and by contemporary Jews as the modern representatives of the ancient Israelites. A sense of affinity with Jews was enhanced, among the smaller Protestant sects, by a common history of persecution. Together, these factors which engendered Christian philosemitism were extremely powerful, and often more than balanced whatever religious antisemitism remained in the English-speaking world after the early nineteenth century.

It is frequently difficult to separate these factors in a clear-cut way. For instance, at the 1882 London rally the Bishop of London lamented that 'they who perpetrated these atrocities are men who bear the name of Christians'.[1] At its 1890 counterpart the Bishop of Ripon declared that 'It was to affirm the principles of Christianity and of humanity that the meeting had been called together'.[2] 'If putting on sackcloth and ashes, and walking ... with lighted candles, could express the feelings of shame felt by the Christian people, they should do it,' announced the Methodist minister who organized Melbourne's Kishinev protest meeting in 1903.[3] Deploring the pogroms of 1906 the Bishop of Oxford wrote: 'we Christians ... cannot deny or forget that those on whom this storm of cruelty has broken suffer thus because they are Jews, at the hands of men who bear our Master's name ... how ashamed we are and how we would retrieve ... the dishonour brought on our faith.'[4]

Russia's revival of the charge of ritual murder was 'deplorable from the standpoint of true religion, of humanity, and of civilization, and abhorrent to the spirit of Christianity,' wrote the 74 leading American ecclesiastics who protested at the Beilis prosecution to the Czar 1913.[5] A joint statement against antisemitism issued by the heads of the Anglican, Roman Catholic and Free Churches in Britain in 1938 affirmed that 'racial hatred and discrimination' were 'contrary to the spirit and teaching of our Lord Jesus Christ'.[6] 'It is inconceivable,' observed the Bishop of Johannesburg that same year, 'that anyone who prides himself on being a Christian can be an anti-Semite.'[7] And so on. Repeatedly, Christians proclaimed their sympathy because Jews were fellow human beings deserving of humane treatment, and who moreover were 'beloved for their Father's sake'.[8]

But, as noted, for numerous Christians, including many who spoke thus, solidarity with Jews ran far deeper. Judaism was the fount of Christianity; Jews could not be regarded merely as followers of one world faith among many. Between the expulsion of Jews from England in 1290 and their resettlement, the country had undergone a Protestant Reformation which was conducive to a climate of philosemitism. For with the Reformation the Bible had embarked upon its role as what T.H. Huxley called 'the national epic of Britain', so closely did Britons identify with the story of Israel in its pages.[9] The seed had been sown by Henry VIII when he ordered a vernacular translation to be placed inside every English church, and it flourished with the Jacobean version. The influence of the Bible – of the Hebrew scriptures – upon the British people, even those who were not particularly religious and read the sacred text primarily as literature, became almost symbiotic. As Josiah Wedgwood explained:

> The Anglo-Saxon, more than any other race, wants to sympathise with the Jews ... no doubt we understand the Jew better than can those to whom the Old Testament is not familiar from infancy. To the foreigner the word Jew is a hissing in the street; to us the word suggests Solomon and Moses, and a thousand cradle stories. So often have we used their names for our own children that they seem now to be our fathers, especially our Puritan forefathers ... Towards such a people one has a feeling almost of awe, they are so well known.[10]

Countless Britons must have identified with Israel against Pharoah and Haman, and, by extension, with the contemporary descendants of Israel against their latterday persecutors. The influence of the Bible upon Britons was frequently commented upon. Dr Abraham Benisch, newly arrived in Britain, marvelled shortly after the Damascus Affair at 'the generosity, liberality, and simple manners of a nation whose chief model is the Bible'.[11] This emphasis made philosemites of numerous individuals. As David Katz observes, 'devotion to Scripture often rubbed off on the descendants of the biblical heroes described therein, even to the extent of producing a certain esteem for the Jews and their culture, with or without the desire to see their ultimate conversion to Christianity.'[12]

The Bible made a powerful impact in this regard on innumerable people and the Biblical inheritance cast lustre on modern Jewry in the eyes of many Christians, fascinated that the descendants of the patriarchs and prophets walked among them. Whenever the Victorian writer Leigh Hunt, imbued with images of ancient Israelites, encountered 'a Rabbi in the street, he seemed to me a man coming, not from Bishopsgate or Saffron Hill [in London], but out of the remoteness of time.' As a London schoolboy with a burning interest in religion and a command of Hebrew, Hunt often crept into the Great Synagogue in Duke's Place during Sabbath services; the liturgy and the worshippers made a most favourable impression on him and left him with a lifelong 'respectful notion of Jews as a body'.[13] Hunt's contemporary, the Anglican priest Father Ignatius, an early gentile Zionist well-loved in Jewish circles, always felt 'an affection' for those who the Bible taught 'are the elect and chosen of God. They are a people, therefore, in whom I cannot but feel a profound and adoring interest.' As a schoolboy he, too, had frequently attended the Great Synagogue (and continued to visit synagogues in adulthood), and had treasured an illustrated book on Judaism. 'Whenever I met a Jewish old-clo' man, I could not forbear from taking my hat off to him, and rendering him the homage which I felt due to a representative of the aristocratic race of humanity.'[14] The identification of modern Jews with their Biblical ancestors meant that even peddlers were asked by eager Christians to arbitrate disputed passages of Scripture, especially, it seems, in the American South![15] Such phrases as 'the miracle of the preservation of the Jewish race' fell easily from the lips of Christians, and many a Jew, however lowly or non-observant, found himself fêted as 'one of God's chosen people'.[16]

A not untypical Christian response to Jewish crisis was that of a devout sympathizer who in 1854 contributed generously to the fund for Palestinian Jewry: 'What an honour to be permitted to minister in any way to the seed of Abraham, God's chosen ones!'[17] Some Christians, in their esteem for Jews, went further. J.E. Budgett Meakin, an Evangelical and orientalist who wrote sympathetically of Jews in the Near East, declared that if he 'had my choice of race it would most assuredly be that of Abraham, Isaac and Jacob', a sentiment echoed by an Australian Presbyterian minister protesting the Kishinev massacre.[18] Charlotte Elizabeth Tonna prevented herself from wearing the Jewish prayer shawl only by a nagging fear that a gentile had no right to do so; Father Ignatius owned Jewish liturgical objects including *mezuzot* affixed to doorposts and a set of *tephillin* (phylacteries); so did a dedicated Christian lay preacher and Hebraist who became learned in the Talmud and who in his role as an East End-based London policeman performed many kindnesses for immigrant Jews, with whom he conversed in serviceable Yiddish.[19] By the 1870s British gentiles with motives unconnected with marriage were pleading to be admitted to Judaism; the first known such conversion of an American had occurred in the 1840s.[20]

Frequently, Christian philosemites cited what a Beilis protest signatory, Cambridge Professor of Divinity Dr F.C. Burkitt, called 'The Debt of Christianity to Judaism'.[21] Awareness of that debt honed their sympathy. Perhaps most practising Christians of the early nineteenth century, especially Anglicans with their commitment to an Established Church – including many who fought against the persecution of Jews overseas – opposed parliamentary emancipation at home on the grounds that it would undermine the Christian state and lead to the admission of Hindus, Moslems, Parsees and pagans, all of whom would thus be able to debate and vote on matters ecclesiastical. Yet a significant number supported the measure in principle. 'I love all the seed of Abraham,' advised an Anglican cleric in 1843. 'Were I to have my will, all nations should unite in honouring the Jew; and Britain, in especial, should emancipate him from every political disqualification.'[22] 'Let us not be ungrateful to that once-distinguished nation which has been the instrument of rendering such conspicuous services to the human race,' implored a Christian newspaper in 1851.

> Think of the influence which the ancient Jewish mind has exercised over our European and Christian civilization ... Think of how ... the examples of their history, and the wisdom of their laws, have inspired, instructed and encouraged ...; how their Scriptures have been read and reverenced, more widely and deeply than any similar book or collection of books within our knowledge ... Jesus himself was a descendant of Abraham ... Let us remember, then, what we Christians owe to this people, and let us, at the same time, not forget what has been the return for it all which Christian nations have so commonly made to them or their descendants, in their outcast and despised condition,... Let us ponder upon all this; and then we may find cause, perhaps to wonder at that strange obliquity of feeling and judgment, which would now refuse to this race a free participation with us in our social and political privileges and rights;

as if, indeed, this were not eminently due to them ... in acknowledgement and return for the inestimable blessings which we have received from and through them.[23]

Anna Maria Hall, a devoutly Christian nineteenth-century British writer, wondered how Christians had the gall to despise Jews when 'We read *our* Bible, which is *their* Bible; our code of conduct is based upon *their* commandments, which are *our* commandments; our salvation is gained by the Jewish sacrifice of the lamb without spot or blemish; *our* apostles ... were Jews.'[24]

Time and again, during protests on behalf of oppressed Jews overseas, Christian philosemites replicated these points. Suggesting in 1880 that American clergymen and public figures might send a remonstrance to Bismarck regarding the rise of political antisemitism in Germany, the crusading radical New York preacher, the Reverend Henry Ward Beecher (whose daughter wrote *Uncle Tom's Cabin*) praised the progressive moral code which Jews had given to the Christian world.[25] At an Australian rally in 1881 denouncing the Russian pogroms a senior Presbyterian clergyman remarked that the world owed much to ancient Greece and Rome but a still greater obligation to the Jews, who had given it 'more important things, as they had done more than tongue could tell for the religious feeling of all humanity'.[26] At the comparable London rally Canon Farrar maintained: 'The Jews were the most trampled-upon nationality in the world. It was the nation to which humanity owed the deepest debt and on which humanity had inflicted the deepest wrong.'[27] 'As members of a Christian community we should not forget the debt of gratitude which we owe to the children of Abraham – God's chosen people,' wrote a leading Presbyterian laywoman who donated to an appeal in Australia on behalf of the survivors of Kishinev, 'for are we not indebted to them, not only for our Old Testament Scriptures, but also for our Messiah?'[28] 'We owe this persecuted people more than we can ever repay,' agreed a New York clergyman who protested at the Beilis trial.

> They gave us our religion and our sacred literature; they gave us our Sabbath and our highest ideals; they gave us our great leader ... No people has given the world, in proportion to numbers, so many great men in all departments of life. In return we persecute them, despise them, cast them out, and occasionally massacre them ...[29]

'Get rid of the Jews,' exclaimed Father Ignatius, chiding antisemitic agitators in Leeds. 'Is this your gratitude for all that you cherish as most precious in life, in death, in time, and in eternity?'[30] A Baptist minister in Swansea, denouncing the Beilis trial, declared: 'may the day soon dawn when everywhere those who call themselves servants of Jesus Christ shall cease these persecutions of the people to whom our Saviour himself belonged.'[31] 'When I think of the persecution of the Jews,' Bishop Henson told the Anglican Church Conference which condemned the Nuremberg Laws in 1935, 'I wish that we would draw the sword and fight for God's people.'[32] Over and over again, Christian philosemites made similar statements.

This brings us to the vexed question of conversionism. Since Christians regarded theirs as the true religion, it was obviously difficult if not impossible for them not to yearn, in their heart of hearts, for the ultimate conversion of Jews. And, it must at once be admitted, there were active fishers for Jewish souls in the ranks of those who demonstrated on behalf of oppressed Jewry overseas. For example, the Reverends Alexander McCaul and Baptist Noel, both of whom protested against the Damascus blood libel, were prominently associated with the (singularly ineffective) London Society for Promoting Christianity Amongst the Jews. So were, among others, the Earl of Shaftesbury (the Society's long-serving President), Lord Kinnaird, the Earl of Roden, the Reverend Hugh McNeile and two leaders of the protests in Sydney against the Russian pogroms, Archbishop Dr William Saumarez Smith and Canon Mervyn Archdall. And so was London banker Robert Cooper Lee Bevan, who like several previously named signed the 1859 petition condemning the Mortara kidnapping. He also attended the 1882 rally, at which he gave £100 for the relief of Russian Jewry. The Bishop of Stepney (Dr H.L. Paget), who had requisitioned the 1890 rally and was a Beilis protest signatory, had, notoriously, instituted a fund for the conversion of East End Jewry. In the United States, millenarians including W.E. Blackstone were associated with the missionary movement.[33]

In Britain, active conversionists tended to be Evangelicals, representatives of a movement within the Church of England which had emerged in the mid-eighteenth century. It aimed to produce an intense, deeply personal variety of Christianity in its adherents. Evangelicals, who were at the peak of their influence in the Church from between 1835 and 1860, are credited with being responsible for many social reforms in Britain, especially the abolition of slavery in the British Empire in 1833, and with being among the progenitors of 'Victorianism' in their strict religious beliefs. They emphasized the inherent sinfulness of all human beings and their damnation in the hereafter in the absence of sincere repentance, personal conversion and the conversion experience as central to religious practice, the pivotal importance of the Bible and of belief in Jesus the redeemer as necessary to salvation, and the absolute requirement of living a pious, devout Christian life in order to be saved. They are often contrasted with 'High Church' Anglicans, who emphasized the corporate, historical and Catholic features of Anglicanism and the role of the clergy (as opposed to individual believers) in obtaining salvation.[34]

Offensive and misguided as it must ordinarily seem to Jews, conversionism can perhaps be properly viewed as one particular strand of philosemitism. According to the conversionists' own lights, theirs was the ultimate act of kindness towards Jews. As the Reverend Hugh McNeile explained:

> He believed that it was scriptural truth, that every Jew dying as a Jew would be utterly lost ... It was God-like love to tell them plainly the dreadful situation in which they were placed ...[35]

Many argued that it was precisely because Jews were 'God's ancient people', a people beloved of God, that their conversion should be attempted over that of other peoples; accordingly, 'the warmest friends of the Jews' were to be found in the London Jews' Society.[36] Added to this was the millenarian belief held by many Evangelicals that in order to effect the Second Advent (or Coming) of Jews the Jews must be converted and restored to their own land.[37]

By the mid-1840s, however, a fundamental schism was emerging in the ranks of conversionists between those who believed that Jews should be converted prior to their restoration and those who insisted that such attempts were futile, since Jewry would be converted *en masse* in Zion and, moreover, would retain their distinct national characteristics based upon the ancient Covenant between their patriarch, Abraham, and God. Charlotte Elizabeth Tonna, who merits more attention from historians,[38] played a seminal role in spreading the latter viewpoint. In the widely circulated *Christian Lady's Magazine*, and elsewhere, she argued that everything the Covenant and the Mosaic Law enjoined upon the Jews, including circumcision and the ritual wearing of the prayer shawl, must continue to be practised by Jewish converts to Christianity. This brought her into conflict with those who expected converts to obliterate every trace of their former identity, and some years before her death in 1846 she resigned from the London Jews' Society together with her husband, an occasional writer on religious themes. She thus in effect conceded that, at any rate until the Restoration, Judaism constituted an alternative path to redemption, and she consequently opposed 'the erroneous plan of Gentilizing the Jews'.[39]

In 1853 she was named posthumously by a disapproving Anglican cleric as the principal villain among the 'Recordites', the strict faction within the Evangelicals which

> practically raises the Mosaic dispensation above the Christian. It is essentially a Judaizing party. The characters on which it dwells most fondly, the ordinances to which it clings most passionately, are the characters and the ordinances of Judaism. Its models of Christian life are the Jewish Patriarchs. Indeed, the religion of some members of this party seems to consist solely in love of Jews and hatred of Papists. Their favourite society is that which professes to be founded for the conversion of Israelites to Christianity, but which too often acts as a Propaganda for converting Christians to Judaism. It spends vast sums in sending emissaries over the country who diffuse Judaic views of Scripture and proclaim the spiritual inferiority of the Gentile to the Jew. Those glorious prophecies of the restoration of Israel, and the blessedness of the new Jerusalem, which have their fulfilment ... in the destinies of the Christian Church, are applied, by these propagandists to the carnal seed of Abraham, to the pawnbrokers of Monmouth Street, and the slop-sellers of St. Giles's.

Furthermore:

> the most conspicuous example of Judaizing tendencies in the party is furnished by their Sabbatarian views. In defiance of the clearest expressions of Scripture – in defiance of the universal consent of all foreign churches – Catholic and Protestant – in defiance of the express declarations of the Reformers – but in accordance with the tradition of the Scotch and English Puritans – they teach that the Lord's Day is identical with the Jewish Sabbath. Nay, they require that it should be observed with a stern severity unknown even to the Mosaic ritual.[40]

People of that ilk certainly give the lie to Barbara Tuchman's contention that to 'all the Israel-for-prophecy's sake school, the Jews ... were not a people, but a mass Error'.[41] Mrs Tonna, moreover, was conspicuously in the forefront of anti-defamation activity on behalf of Jews. Well-acquainted with Hebrew, she was one of the very few

Christians of her generation to see the inside of a synagogue let alone, as she did, occasionally join its worshippers in prayer. 'Spiritually,' she maintained, 'no Gentile can look down upon a Jew, unless from stilts of his own clumsy manufacturing.' Westminster Abbey was 'a toy of yesterday, compared with the newest, the smallest, of our Hebrew synagogues'. Calling upon 'the compilers and publishers of hymn-books' to ensure that such were not 'disgraced by ... epithets of scorn' towards Jews, she added (in anticipation of a revision approved in 1920): 'Would we might ... call on some competent authority to disconnect the name of Jew from that of Turk, Infidel, and Heretic in our prayer-books!'[42] Her knowledge of Jews, Jewish issues and of Judaism were frequently and sympathetically aired in the *Christian Lady's Magazine*, where she sometimes reproduced articles by Jews, especially *Voice of Jacob* editor Jacob Franklin, with whom she forged a strong bond of mutual respect.[43] The outlook of philosemites like her can be seen in the plea of an anonymous Christian, who in 1855 declared that non-Jews

> must cease this persecution of the covenanted people ... they must recognize the covenant which God has made. Methinks if the nations recognized that solemn covenant which reaches far into future years, the question of what is called Jewish rights would speedily be settled, and men in serious mood would in all places welcome the Jews ... So many men – grave divines even – delude themselves with the belief that the old covenant has passed away, and only the new covenant stands. But there is no greater falsehood than this beneath the sun. The covenant with Israel will abide for ever.[44]

Endorsing Mrs Tonna's proposal for an auxiliary of Christians to aid British Jews in fighting for the rights of the latters' co-religionists overseas, Shaftesbury wrote: 'All our consideration was to be bounded by the lines of their civil position in the several countries where they are to be found ... The question may be treated as the question of the Slave Trade, which was altogether distinct, in the preliminary steps, from any reference to the spiritual condition of the sufferers.'[45] This did not go as far as Mrs Tonna would have wished, but the undertaking was a generous concession from the President of the London Jews' Society.

There is no denying that some conversionists espoused the Jewish cause in order to ingratiate themselves among the potential proselytes, calculating that in showing Jews elaborate acts of kindness they might eventually entice them to Christianity. Exemplifying philosemites of this sort was a spinster of early Victorian Reading, Sarah Hooper, whose bustling philanthropy was directed at impoverished Jewish women. She kept Anglo-Jewish leaders speculating about her motives for years, until the cynics were finally vindicated when a conversionist periodical revealed that she was dispensing Christian propaganda along with handouts.[46] A less subtle form of this approach may or may not have lain behind a phrase in the Mortara protest of 1859. Essentially a liberal initiative, organized as it was by David Wire, it described the kidnapping as a 'dishonour to Christianity in the eyes of Jews'.[47] If this was meant as an affirmation of religious parity, it was an extraordinary conception for the time, although not entirely incompatible with the outlook of liberals, who stressed the need for tolerance often enough, nor perhaps alien to convinced Christians who had advocated Jewish emancipation in Britain. Wire himself declared that Jews 'must be considered children of our elder brethren in the faith, the depositories of the law and the revelation'.[48] Whoever penned the perplexing phrase in the petition (which was reminiscent of the resolution passed by the Evangelical Alliance in 1858, quoted in Chapter 2), whatever was meant by it, it must have been interpreted by conversionists, even while rejoicing that the Roman Catholic Church was calumniated, as awareness that Jews would not convert to Christianity if the latter was presented to them in a bad light.

The attitude of the average philosemitic Protestant conversionist is reflected in the words of celebrated Baptist preacher the Reverend Charles Spurgeon, who participated in protests against the Russian pogroms. 'I heartily join in your indignation that anyone should by cruelty, bribes, or oppression of any kind attempt to drive the seed of Abraham from their faith,' he assured a Jewish enquirer in 1875.

> I am sure that the great head of Christianity is angry with all such as try to lord it over the consciences of others: there is nothing in the teaching of Jesus to suggest or excuse such conduct. Yet to try to spread the truth by instruction or persuasion is most laudable, and is a part of our duty to our neighbour ... I take the liberty to beg you to search the Scriptures and see whether Jesus is not indeed the Messiah.
>
> Do not judge Christianity by the idolatrous forms of it which are so common, but ... judge by the teaching and lips of Jesus himself ... Your nation taught us at first, we cannot but honour you, and long for your restoration.[49]

The most salient point about conversionist philosemites, however, and one which is worth stressing, is that virtually all who came forward in the cause of oppressed Jewry overseas gave their support unconditionally. They championed Jews as Jews.[50] This attitude was expounded by the Bishop of Liverpool, condemning the pogroms of 1881–2:

> I cannot forget that the world owes a debt to [the Jews] which can never be repaid ... However much we may regret that their faith is not the same as ours, I am quite certain that they are the last people on earth who ought to be persecuted by Christians ... I trust ... that all Christian men in England will raise a loud cry of remonstrance, and enter a moral protest against the treatment to which so many unhappy Jews have been subjected. In that protest I desire most heartily to join.[51]

The Reverend Dr R.F. Horton, President of the Free Church Council, declared at the 1906 London rally:

> Every Christian in England trembles with indignation at the thought that the treatment of the Jew in Russia is implicitly justified by the intention of the Russian Government to change the Jew into a Christian ... in Russia there are only about 1,300 converts from Judaism ... every year ... under the tremendous pressure of this social and political persecution! ... As a Christian minister I look upon them with a sense of shame and pity that they should desert their persecuted Jewish comrades and take the sign of baptism as a means of social convenience and political freedom.[52]

During the Nazi era this philosemitic Christian principle of support for Jewry with no strings attached was reiterated by the Bishop of Rochester (Dr C.M. Chavasse), newly elected President of the Church Missions to Jews, who said that body was duty bound to champion the Jews, irrespective of its hopes for their conversion.[53] Owing to this attitude, Anglo-Jewish leaders, while ever wary, were in some circumstances prepared to tolerate the aid of conversionists as the Board of Deputies tolerated Sir Culling Eardley's in 1858–9, and even enlist it, as the Anglo-Jewish Association enlisted it in 1877. In that very year the *Jewish Chronicle*, never backward in detecting ulterior motives on the part of professed philosemites, advised that the Jewish community need have no reservations about cooperating on behalf of oppressed Jewry with the Evangelical Alliance, towards which it had once been hostile, since that body aimed to obtain justice for all regardless of creed; it had no conversionist intent.[54]

In the United States, the prominent philosemitic crusader William E. Blackstone was a firm believer in the eschatological vision bound up with the conversion and restoration of the Jews. His book, *Jesus is Coming*, first published in 1878, was translated into Yiddish and Hebrew. Yet, with a profound respect for Jews as the heirs of biblical Israel and the guardians of God's law, he did not hesitate to campaign for justice for Jews *qua* Jews. He went so far as to arrange one of the first experiments in Jewish–Christian dialogue ever to take place anywhere in the world. This was a two-day conference on the premises of a Chicago church in November 1890, at which rabbis and Protestant ministers spoke on various aspects of their respective faiths in relation to one another. In the words of its printed programme, the conference's object was 'to give information and promote a spirit of inquiry … on the basis of mutual kindness between Jews and Christians'. From the Christian side came talks on, for example, 'The Attitude of Nations and of Christian people toward the Jews', 'Israel as an evidence of the Truth of the Christian religion' and 'Israelites and Christians. Their Mutual Relation and Welfare'. A resolution was passed condemning 'all discrimination against Jews "as such"', requesting Russia to cease oppressing 'this time-honoured people', and calling upon American statesmen to use their influence with foreign rulers to achieve an end to anti-Jewish persecution.'[55]

Blackstone reported that the conference

> was a new departure as contrasted with the centuries of antipathy and ecclesiastical contention heretofore characterizing these peoples. Having the Old Testament in common, it was conceived that they could meet upon this grand fundamental rock of God's revelation to man as co-worshippers of one God. Neither Jew nor Gentile was asked to do violence to his convictions …[56]

And to quote a Christian participant, the event was

> extraordinary … neither … a theological nor a denominational debate, nor … a religious service for the evangelization of the Jews … A spirit of complete impartiality pervaded all the sessions.
> … no words of reproach for Jewish opposition to Christ and his followers were uttered … It was natural enough that [Jewish speakers] should give a hint now and then of being better pleased if no

efforts were made to convert them to Christianity, as they make none to convert Christians to Judaism.

It was quite as characteristic of this assembly that extended and indignant accounts of persecutions of Jews came from the Christian speakers.[57]

It must thus clearly be stressed that the majority of Christian philosemites were not conversionists, certainly not in the active sense. In the main even those who were associated with the London Jews' Society seem to have taken a passive approach, presumably in line with the undertaking not to proselytize given by Shaftesbury and other philosemitic practising Christians to the Board of Deputies in 1843. Strikingly, some of the most zealously Christian philosemites specifically repudiated conversionism. They came forward in the spirit of the Birmingham clergyman who in the 1840s enjoyed a 'most intimate and confidential relationship' with the local rabbi: 'the one a most determined, uncompromising Jew, and the other an equally determined, uncompromising Christian';[58] and even of the Manchester clergyman who in 1874 advanced the view that Judaism constituted an alternative road to redemption: 'I have never been able to see why the belief that saved Abraham, Moses and Elijah isn't enough to save a good Jew of today.' He wondered why Jews did not retaliate by setting up a Society for Propagating Christianity Amongst Christians: 'They might do a worse thing than convert nominal Christians by the hundreds to the thrift, charity, and Sabbath observance which are an honour to the Jewish people in the land.'[59]

During the 1854 appeal for 'famishing' Palestinian Jewry, it was noted that 'truly pious Christians' were lending support without any proselytism, on the broad principles of humanity.[60] The Reverend John Mills declared that same year:

> every man, whatever be his creed, has the right to worship God according to the dictates of his conscience. Religion is a pure matter of conscience – and conscience cannot be changed by outward force. It is formed only by belief, and belief is founded upon conviction ... we Protestants are in duty bound to proclaim this noble truth to the world, and especially in connection with the Jews.[61]

To Anglican cleric turned Theist the Reverend Charles Voysey, who condemned the pogroms and signed the Beilis protest, 'A Jew is a Jew not by reason of his religion' but by linear descent which 'dwarfs that of the proudest ancestry in Christendom. And his religion is what he is *because he is a Jew*; any other religion being impossible to him ...' Voysey expressly did not seek to proselytize.[62] On the contrary, this man who introduced Jewish melodies into his services at London's Theistic Church and was proud to have 'a grandchild who was of the seed of Abraham' proved

> something more than a friend of the Jews. He largely shared their beliefs, he was one with them in feeling. No man outside our ranks understood and appreciated Judaism better.[63]

In 1911 he issued 'A warning to Jews' against Reform Judaism; Reform left him 'horror-struck' as it posed

> a real danger to the Jewish faith, to the faith of Hebrew prophets and psalmists ... It amounts practically to a call to Jews to adopt the same views and sentiments as are held by Unitarians.[64]

Father Ignatius saw Reform Judaism as

> essentially un-Jewish in principle and utterly destructive of everything Jewish ... Jews who lightly abandon the special laws imposed upon them treat God – their Author – as if he were non-existent.
> ... The Torah acts as a barrier between the Jew and the world. But the modern Jew desires national dissolution, the end of his Jewish existence, his amalgamation as a race with the Gentile nations, an end to his unique, his marvellous history of millenniums of years.

Asked why he did not attempt to convert Jews Ignatius replied: 'They are too holy a people for me to dare to interfere with Almighty God's purposes concerning them.' When a young Jewish man came to him asking to convert, Ignatius turned him away, telling him to go instead to synagogue, lay *tephillin* and carry out all the commandments binding upon Israel. Using arguments reminiscent of Mrs Tonna over 50 years earlier, Ignatius held that 'To convert the Jews to Christianity would destroy the whole idea of Revelation, through the medium of which God has declared that the Jews are to remain a separate people. The Jews must continue to remain apart from other nations because they are the divinely chosen nation of revelation to the world.' Most of his followers in the Anglican Benedictine Order which he founded concurred.[65]

The Damascus Affair had galvanized Anglo-Jewry, aware of the need for a vehicle 'to plead their cause and attend to their own interests,' into establishing a press of its own.[66] From the first, that press attracted the unwelcome attention of stalwarts of the London Jews' Society. Yet there were always non-conversionists among the regular readership, and their numbers steadily increased. A vestry-woman who had been lent a copy of the *Jewish Chronicle* by a Jewish friend and had since persuaded her local public library to subscribe to that newspaper described its attraction:

> I read it from cover to cover, and from that time until now I have been so interested and so benefited from its contents, that in gratitude I made up my mind that others should have the same chance of reading it that I have had. Being quite ignorant of the ways and customs of Jews, I fear I thought them as something quite different from the rest of the world, but after reading your paper my idea of them is totally different ...

She hoped that the paper would become more widely available through libraries 'in order that Gentiles may read about Jews, and that they may be better understood and appreciated'.[67] An elderly Christian student of scripture testified to the paper's value in another way. He thanked a Jewish reader for replying to his query regarding Jewish fast-days, explaining that he was 'extremely anxious to follow Jewish tradition and example' and regretted that he had only recently become acquainted with the publication, 'which conveys so much sterling information on God's peculiar people'. Years earlier, while studying *The Antiquities of the Jews* by Josephus, he would have found the paper, with its frequent articles on Judaism, of 'inestimable' background use.[68]

The Jewish press had many enthusiastic correspondents of his kind. They included the celebrated Reverend John Oxlee, Rector of Molesworth, Huntingtonshire, a regular reader of the *Voice of Jacob*, who derided the aims of conversionists in three open letters to the Archbishop of Canterbury, published in 1843.[69] A particularly thankful subscriber was a Presbyterian minister and schoolmaster in Fife in the 1850s, who like many Christians was clearly delighted to learn from its columns the Jewish interpretation of scripture. 'I am perfectly satisfied that the *Jewish Chronicle* requires only to be *known* among educated, enlightened, and impartial British society to be well received and highly appreciated,' he wrote.

> Rest assured, that although 'the chosen people of God' may be calumniated by some, to whom it is a 'sport to do mischief,' yet

> there are not a few among professing Christians who pray earnestly for the welfare of the descendants of Abraham.
>
> ... the longer I read the *Jewish Chronicle* the better I become informed relative to the principles, habits, dispositions, etc., of the British Jews; and the better I become acquainted with the British Jews, the more highly do I respect *them* in particular, and the whole nation in general ...
>
> ... I would say to every Protestant Christian in the land, 'If you wish a correct and complete knowledge of modern Judaism as it exists within the bounds of the British Empire, read the London *Jewish Chronicle*.'[70]

At his own expense, he arranged for copies of the paper to be sent to a long list of academics, clerics and other people in Scotland who he thought would be interested, and he placed advertisements for the paper in several Scottish newspapers. 'The disinterested love cherished by this sincere Christian clergyman for the Jews is truly affecting,' noted a grateful *Jewish Chronicle*. 'All this kindness is *unsolicited*, and obviously emanates from the most affectionate and unselfish sympathy for our people.'[71]

Since a great deal of Christian sympathy for Jews was kindled by the emphasis on Old Testament scripture generated by the Reformation, where did this leave Roman Catholics? Anti-Catholic sentiments pervaded Victorian Britain and contrasted markedly with the goodwill of many Protestants towards Jews. Charlotte Elizabeth Tonna, for example, believed that Protestants had a two-fold purpose: 'With one hand to throw a shield over the Jew, with the other to aim a vigorous thrust at Papal Rome.'[72] When the *Voice of Jacob* was established, she was widely 'admonished for countenancing a publication that could not but be opposed to Christianity. All manner of Popish ... periodicals made their way unimpeded; but, no sooner did the first people of the earth dare to lift up their voice in a manly and generous defence of their own national character, then [sic] it became a sort of sin to name the work in public, lest anyone should be tempted 'to read it, and be judaized out of hand by its insidious doctrines.'[73] Political economist Harriet Martineau argued that Roman Catholics might be kept out of Parliament on the grounds that they were liable to proselytize and so endanger the national polity, 'but, as everybody ought to know, there can be none such [argument] in the case of a Jew. A Jew no more desires to make Gentiles Jews, than a peer desires to make all the commonalty peers.'[74]

For people of Huguenot background, who included Miss Martineau, her Unitarian divine brother James, who was involved in several pro-Jewish initiatives, and de Hochepied Larpent, who addressed the 1840 rally, the common experience of persecution often prompted, or reinforced, sympathy with Jews. At the 1890 rally London's Lord Mayor, Sir Joseph Savory, noted that his presiding presence was appropriate given his Huguenot ancestry.[75] Others of Huguenot descent were Edward Cazalet and his grandson Victor, both champions of Zionism, and the Cazenoves and Souchays, businessmen who donated to Jewish domestic charities. An explicit analogy between the plight of the Huguenots and of the Jews was sometimes drawn by philosemites during the 1930s.[76]

With their essential liberalism and insistence on the separation of Church and State, nonconformists were attracted in substantial numbers to the Jewish cause. They, too, had additional bonds. In Britain, particularly, Quakers and Jews were often perceived as akin to one another, and were accorded similar exceptional rights: for instance, to conduct their own marriages outside of the Anglican Church, a right granted uniquely and extraordinarily to both sects (but to no others) in 1836. As with other dissenting sects, they shared with Jews a basic identity with the Old Testament, and their philosemitic impulse was reinforced by their normally liberal stance in politics and their opposition to any form of religious persecution (from which they themselves had suffered). At the Damascus rally the Quaker banker Samuel Gurney expressed his 'great pleasure' in assisting 'the cause of civil and religious liberty'. He, and his firm Overend Gurney, regularly donated to Jewish domestic charities, and with rally attender (Sir) Thomas Fowell Buxton, he was a business associate of N.M. Rothschild and Sir Moses Montefiore. He also shared the compassionate, humanitarian outlook of his sect, being active in the campaign against the slave trade, in which Buxton, who had Quaker connections, played a pre-eminent part. (Sir Fowell Buxton, who addressed the 1872 rally, was the latter's grandson.)[77] Henry Richard, who followed a denunciation in the Commons of Romanian antisemitism with attendance at the 1872 rally, and who was a requisitioner of its 1882 counterpart, was the son of a Welsh Calvinistic Methodist minister. Richard was a long-serving secretary of the London Peace Society, founded by the Quaker Joseph Sturge, whose biography he wrote. Charles Gilpin MP, who also attended the 1872 rally, was Sturge's son-in-law.[78]

Some nonconformist philosemites specifically cited their own experience of religious intolerance at home and persecution abroad. Sir Joseph Pease, who spoke at the 1890 rally as the official representative of Britain's Quakers, said:

> Two hundred years ago the Society of Friends lifted up the standard of religious liberty and held it though 3000 of their members were in the gaols of England. Persecution had never effected its objects, and it would not destroy the Jews in Russia. As citizens of a country which had felt the benefit of religious liberty, they came forward ... to ask for [the Czar's] Jewish subjects the inalienable right of all people – the power to worship God according to their own conscience.[79]

Welsh-born Congregationalist the Reverend Llewelyn D. Bevan, who when a pastor in New York had spoken against German anti-semitism in 1880, also addressed Melbourne's protest at the Kishinev massacre. He wrote: 'The freedom which has been accorded to the Jews in many parts of the world, and in gaining which they owe a debt to those who themselves often suffered from injustice, would never have been secured had not both these parties, the Nonconformist ... and the Israelite, claimed that they must not be dispossessed of the common right of citizenship on grounds of religious and other opinions.'[80] Another Congregationalist, the Reverend R.F. Horton, reminded the 1906 London rally that he belonged

> to a section of the community which has not persecuted, perhaps because it has been persecuted, and has learned the horror and the absurdity of persecution by suffering severely from it ... My friend [Rev. A.A. Green], the minister of the synagogue in my neighbourhood of Hampstead, once said in my own church that he looked upon the Jews as the great nonconformist nation of the world, the great nonconformist nation of history; and I feel in sympathy with them on that account, and I feel a resolution growing in my heart that the Jew shall also enjoy those privileges of equality and justice which we enjoy here in England.[81]

The Swansea-based Baptist Reverend H.F. Mander, offering 'sympathy and prayer' to the Jews during the Beilis Affair, remarked: 'We belong to a denomination which has suffered many things at the hands of the Russian authorities.'[82]

It was upon nonconformists, especially those belonging to Calvinist-derived sects such as the Presbyterians and the Welsh Calvinistic Methodists, that the Biblical heritage of the Jews made a particular impact.[83] None testified to it more memorably than Lloyd George, raised in the Welsh chapel-going tradition:

> I was brought up in a school where I was taught far more about the history of the Jews than about the history of my own land. I could tell you all the Kings of Israel. But I doubt whether I could have named half a dozen of the Kings of England and not more of the Kings of Wales ... On five days a week in the day school, and ... in our Sunday schools, we were thoroughly versed in the history of the Hebrews.[84]

General Smuts, who belonged to the Dutch Reformed Church, praised the Bible as 'the greatest contribution to human nature, human thought and human religion', and against the spectacle of Nazi persecution he enjoined: 'Let us not forget that this book is the contribution of the Jews to mankind ... Let us remember that this extraordinary little people, so highly gifted, made this supreme contribution to the welfare of the world.'[85]

Unitarians, with their rejection of the Trinity, felt especially close to Jews. One of nineteenth-century Britain's pioneering clerical publicists on behalf of Jews, the Unitarian Reverend Henry Hawkes, was an avowed admirer of Chief Rabbi Solomon Herschell.[86] President William Taft recalled that his own lifelong regard for Jews began during his Unitarian boyhood in Cincinnati when the church pulpit was often occupied by the celebrated Rabbi Isaac Mayer Wise.[87] The *Jewish Chronicle* suggested that Joseph Chamberlain's philosemitism owed something to his Unitarian background.[88]

What of Roman Catholics? At the 1840 rally protesting the Damascus Affair a Roman Catholic speaker had been present in the person of Daniel O'Connell. The apparent role of the Roman Catholic Church in the oppression of Jewry was not central to that affair, despite the perceived machinations of the French Consul in Syria which led to Mrs Tonna to trumpet: 'Do we ask for illustrations of unchanged Popery? Look at Damascus.'[89] Things were different during the Mortara and Dreyfus Affairs, when the Roman Catholic Church seemed to be on trial, and its adherents, with a few exceptions, were well-nigh invisible in the ranks of protesters. The *Jewish Chronicle*, noting the 'numerous acts of kindness and liberality towards the Jews' by the one British Roman Catholic priest who broke ranks during the Mortara Affair, added: 'It happens so rarely that we have to record acts of kindness from Roman Catholic priests to Jews.'[90] That priest, Dr George Oliver, had condemned what he called 'that most brutal and most stupid sacrilege of parental rights'.[91] The prominent Roman Catholic layman, Sir George Bowyer, one of Jewry's staunchest pro-emancipation allies in the City of London and an occasional letter-writer to the Jewish press, who claimed always to defend Jews against their attackers, had been uneasy over the kidnapping, but did not denounce it.[92] Reports during the 1840s of the degraded status of Jews in the Rome ghetto, and the Ancona Decree of 1843, had confirmed philosemitic Protestant impressions.[93] There is no doubt that during the Mortara and Dreyfus Affairs the pro-Jewish bandwagon was lent momentum by anti-Roman Catholic passions. Those passions, fuelled by such partisans of Dreyfus as George Barlow and F.C. Conybeare, were aided by triumphant assumptions of the superiority of British justice and outright Francophobia. This prompted a remonstrance from the Archbishop of Westminster, Cardinal Vaughan, and caused an Anglican canon, while condemning the Rennes verdict, to ask: 'Has there not been a scarcely concealed delight in tracing the connection between Jesuitry in religion and untruthfulness in the Court Martial?'[94]

In Britain and other English-speaking lands in which public meetings supporting Dreyfus occurred, Roman Catholics were conspicuous by their absence. They had been placed in an invidious position, since their clerical and pro-clerical co-religionists in France were generally anti-Dreyfusard, while in Australia they might have detected in the pro-Dreyfus rhetoric of certain demonstrators a hint of that fierce sectarianism which was to bedevil Australian politics during and following the First World War. (Indeed, the fierce antipathy of Empire Loyalist committed Protestants such as Dr Alexander Leeper, the Reverend Walter Albiston, Senator Sir Robert Best and New South Wales state parliamentarian Sir Thomas Henley towards Australian Roman Catholics of Irish background, whom they regarded as disaffected agitators disloyal to Crown and Empire, contrasted markedly with their sympathy, even admiration, for Jews demonstrated on various occasions.)[95]

Nor must Roman Catholics be seen as entirely lacking in philosemitism. Most rallies on behalf of persecuted Jewry were addressed by Catholics, clerical and lay, who came forward as representatives of their Church. Perhaps this was all the more remarkable in view of the fact that Catholic clerics, in particular, who, taking their cue directly from the Vatican, were much less autonomous than their Protestant counterparts, and might have been expected to entertain misgivings about sharing a platform with clergymen not of their faith.[96] In line with papal tradition, Catholics vigorously condemned the blood libel.[97] When they came forward on behalf of Jews their support was couched in forthright adulatory language, none more stirringly than prominent Australian layman William Bede Dalley in 1881, Cardinal Manning in 1882 and 1890, and the American Cardinal Gibbons in the latter year.[98] Catholic philosemites made similar points to Protestants: Jews were commendable citizens, undeserving of persecution, and meriting special consideration from Christians. Gibbons made the point popular with anti-papist Protestant philosemites during the nineteenth century: 'it is not by coercion that men are converted, but by appeal to their consciences';[99] while the Catholic Archbishop of Sydney echoed many a Protestant cleric when he observed in 1942:

> Mark well that Abraham is called our Patriarch – our Ancestor. Anti-Semitism is incompatible with the thought and the sublime reality expressed in the text ... We Christians can have nothing to do with it. Through Christ, and in Christ, we are Abraham's spiritual descent.[100]

Gene Tunney, joining the Committee of Catholics to Fight Anti-Semitism in 1939, expressed it more simply in generalized terms: 'no one can expect the friendship of God who would persecute His children for any cause.'[101]

In 1852 a Christian reader of the *Jewish Chronicle* had advised: 'the Christian of the present day sincerely wishes to make amends for the errors of past ages',[102] and the truth of that comment was borne out not only by that newspaper's loyal readership of well-disposed and non-disputationist Christians, but by a growing number of lectures, articles, pamphlets and books by clergymen and lay activists throughout the English-speaking world depicting Jews and Judaism in a favourable light.[103] A major stumbling block to reconciliation was the perception of Jews as Christ killers, but this could be surmounted in one of two ways: expiation or (more accurately) denial. An Anglican clergyman, who in 1864 matter of factly told his audience that 'the Jews look to the Messiah as yet to come, while we look to the one already come', declared: 'If the nonconformists of the present day were unanswerable for the murder of Charles I 200 years ago, so were the Jews now living unanswerable for the death upon the Cross 1800 years ago.'[104] By contrast, the Presbyterian-turned-Baptist Reverend Madison Peters remarked in 1903:

the Jews never killed anybody. It was not their mode of punishment. And Christ would not have been crucified unless the Roman Governor had ordered it.[105]

The machinery for Jewish–Christian dialogue that was in place in most English-speaking countries by the 1940s derived from initiatives pioneered during the nineteenth century, when Christians in increasing numbers donated to synagogue building funds and attended the consecration of synagogues – in the evident spirit of followers of one God.[106] As early as 1845 a Jewish audience in the United States was told by an Episcopalian clergyman that 'I do here, in the name of Christianity, express my deep repentance for all the cruelties and wrongs that have been inflicted upon the chosen people of God by Christian hands.'[107] Some 80 years later so many American Christian ministers of various denominations participated in a tribute to Judaism held in Philadelphia under the auspices of the Fellowship of Faiths that an overflow meeting had to be held.[108] During the Nazi era the acceleration of dialogue was undoubtedly partly due to a recharged Christian empathy with the mother religion in the face of a common threat. To quote a manifesto against Nazism signed early in 1933 by 1,200 Protestant ministers across North America: 'We deplore the consequences which may ensue for the Jews and also for Christianity which tolerates this barbarous persecution.'[109] But the spectacle of unprecedented savage developments in a nation hitherto widely regarded as the most civilized in Europe also led to a reappraisal of attitudes towards Jews at home, and to a sharp pricking of the Christian conscience. This resulted in an enhanced willingness on the part of Christians of all denominations to combat what 65 leading American Catholics in a statement against antisemitism issued in 1939 termed 'this dangerous aberration in the fullness of Christian charity'.[110] It led, also, to an advancing readiness to avow responsibility for what the General Synod of the Reformed Church of America described in a denunciation of Jew-hatred made that same year as a 'record of spiritual malpractice unequalled in dealing with any other people'.[111] After the Second World War such attitudes would become virtually the rule among Christians.

8 'The Age-Long Dream': Zionist Philosemitism

The existence of 'gentile Zionism' has been extensively documented by historians.[1] George Eliot, whose pro-Zionist novel *Daniel Deronda* appeared in 1876, is the 'gentile Zionist' perhaps most familiar to a wide audience.[2] Gentiles favoured the restoration of a Jewish homeland on various grounds. Millenarian Zionists regarded the mass return and conversion of Jews as fulfilment of prophecy, a necessary prelude to the Second Advent (or Coming) of Jesus. This type of Zionism had a secure niche within the English Protestant tradition, and during the first half of the nineteenth century it was strong among Evangelical Anglicans.[3] Humanitarian Zionists – who were sometimes religiously inclined – regarded the re-establishment of a Jewish homeland, with its concomitant Jewish migration, as a realistic means of alleviating the suffering of Jews in lands of oppression. Often this was accompanied by an explicit avowal that the non-Jewish world, in supporting Zionism, was atoning for centuries of persecution. Geopolitically oriented Zionists insisted that, since Palestine was the gateway to the East, it was in Britain's strategic interests to see it in friendly, capable, and stable hands. Many gentile Zionists of whatever stamp – in fact, several strands of Zionistic motivation were often present within individuals – believed, like many Jewish Zionists, that Jews had been unfairly displaced from Palestine, and were morally, perhaps legally, entitled to repossess it. Some advocates of Jewry's return to Palestine were antisemites who saw in Zionism a way to be rid of Jews. But most were philosemites, with the interests of Jews at heart.

During the nineteenth century, Zionist expectations were raised by developments within the Turkish Empire. Keen watch was kept for the 'signs' that pointed the way, especially by millenarians and others steeped in scripture, who detected the hand of God at work. Unlike many British politicians, who, fearing the power of Russia more than that of Turkey, regretted the destruction by a British fleet of its Turkish counterpart off Navarino in 1827, Charlotte Elizabeth Tonna rejoiced:

I plainly saw that Turkey must now lie helpless before the Russian ... Devoted to the Jewish cause, I always looked upon Turkey with abhorrence ... I could not stifle a sensation of joy that a signal-gun had thus been fired for the ingathering of the scattered tribes ... I was driven to my Bible more closely than ever by this event; and the Bible which has taught me everything else, was now teaching me Millennarianism [sic] ...[4]

The Bible showed her, and other millenarians, that 'the national restoration of Israel shall be symptomatic of a shaking that will cause all earth's kingdoms to totter, the spiritual receiving of them again will be to the Gentile church as life from the dead.' The trickle of Jewish immigration into Palestine, which occurred in the decade preceding the Damascus Affair, did not escape her notice: 'The Jew is steadily setting his face towards the Zion of his love' which God gave 'to Abraham and to his literal seed for ever'. The Jew was 'the key-note in accordance with whose vibrations the whole chord must be struck'.[5] In the wake of Damascus, she declared confidently that 'God's dealings with Israel are now to become the signal whereby his work and purpose is to be declared to the rest of the world'.[6] Human agency was permissible, being 'in perfect accordance with the revealed world of God'. She therefore urged her female readers to 'aid the cause by organising an address to Queen Victoria on the subject and by collecting money towards a fund paying the travel expenses of poor Jews who wished to reach Palestine'.[7] Her novel *Judah's Lion*, serialized in the *Christian Lady's Magazine*, 1841–3, and published in book form in the latter year, 'stamps [her] as the mouthpiece of the Restoration movement'.[8] Like all kinds of Zionists, she could observe that, restored to Zion, Jews would no longer 'be a byeword [sic] and a scorn among the nations'.[9]

Mixing millenarian expectations with humanitarianism, she recognized Palestine's potential as a refuge. 'The soul of Israel's foot can know no rest till it be again planted on the mountains of Judaea,' she wrote. 'Europe *must* place some barrier against Russian aggression and extension [and] some place of refuge *must* be found for the hundreds of thousands of houseless Jews who will debark upon shores where those who love the Bible will not, cannot turn away from those who gave us the Bible.'[10] As noted in Chapter 8, she believed passionately that the ultimately restored and converted Jews would and should retain their covenanted distinctiveness. She shared this conviction with the Philadelphia Quaker, titular United States Consul in

Jerusalem and future proselyte Warder Cresson, whose relevant booklet she commended.[11]

The mainstream millenarian position, replete with citations from scripture, can be seen in the closely argued treatise on the restoration of the Jews written by the Reverend Edward Bickersteth around the time of the Damascus Affair. A stalwart of the London Jews' Society and subscriber to the *Voice of Jacob*, Bickersteth was a philosemite according to his own lights:

> Tender compassion ... is our proper feeling towards our elder brother of Israel ... Think of their past sufferings ... Think that we have been received through their rejection; by their fall salvation is come to us ...
> ... Not a shadow of doubt should remain in our minds that all Israel shall yet be saved; that they have not been so long spared, and preserved amidst ... mighty evils ... with a design full of mercy and goodness to them in the end. They shall glory in Jesus their Lord, they shall be a full blessing to the whole earth.
> Let us then help forward this to the utmost of our means and power ... Let England, Scotland, and Ireland be united in one combined effort to give to the Jews those blessings which they once conveyed to us.[12]

Some millenarians believed that Britain, too, had a divinely-ordained destiny. For the prominent British Presbyterian Dr John Cumming, lecturing in 1860, she was to be 'the Israel and Judea of Europe' with a 'sublime mission' ahead. 'God's ancient people, the Jews, were to be restored to their own land,' he rejoiced. 'Where they despised and rejected Him, they would glorify and worship him.' By thwarting Russian territorial ambitions in so crucial an area of the globe, the possession by Jews of Palestine would accord neatly with God's 'great design' for Britain.[13]

Cumming, unlike Bickersteth, but in common with many millenarians such as the Reverend Adam Cairns of Melbourne, apparently inclined towards the view propounded by Mrs Tonna that it was pointless, even improper, to convert Jews before they were restored *en masse* to Palestine.[14] Cairns set out his millenarian vision in the course of two lectures before his congregation in 1854, published as a pamphlet. Jews would be 'speedily settled as a national power, and made the cause and the object of some acts of glorious majesty and love on the part of God, without a parallel even in the past records of their own wondrous history'.[15] He told a Melbourne meeting in 1861 in support of funds for the refuge houses on Mount Zion of

> the deep interest he felt in everything concerning the Jewish nation, an interest ... which was more ardent than that which he felt for any other section of the human family ... because the Jews were a religious nation ... because they were the most marvellous nation which ever existed, and carried along with them the destinies of every other country, and ... because he learned from the Bible that they must be loved 'for the Father's sake.' (Hear, hear). Everything in the present day seemed to indicate the fulfilment of prophecy, that in the seed of Abraham all the nations of the earth shall be blessed.[16]

Cairns directed that the proceeds of his pamphlet were to go the 1854 fund for famine-stricken Palestinian Jewry. In 1881 his son-in-law, a philanthropic Victorian pastoralist whose own father, a Tasmanian politician, had also contributed to that fund, paid for the pamphlet to be reprinted in order to benefit the Russian Jewish Relief Fund. The local Jewish newspaper wished the reissued pamphlet a wide sale: 'Arguing from the Christian interpretation of the Old Testament these discourses present, in a very good light, the views held by those Christians who are not blinded by fanaticism and bigotry towards the Jews ...'[17]

South Australia's former governor, Colonel George Gawler, was influenced by prophecy, but also very much by humanitarian considerations, to advocate in a pamphlet published in 1845 the formation of Jewish agricultural colonies in Palestine. 'Every nation upon the earth which has participated in the persecutions of the Jewish people,' he wrote,

> owes to that people ... a heavy debt of retribution; and, every civilized nation, including every individual in it, be his particular creed what it may, which has received from the Jews, its principles of religion, owes to those Jews in return an unspeakably heavy debt of grateful acknowledgement. These are plain, intelligible conclusions; which no man can reject, who duly appreciates either the gross injustice of persecution, or the inestimable value of religion. If then, an opportunity is *now* before us of rendering to Jews an acceptable service, *in addition also ... to this important duty of rescuing the East from appalling degradation* – why should not the first instalment of these debts be paid? Why should not civilized

nations, *now*, come forward to contribute the comparatively very small expenses required for the formation of Jewish colonies in Palestine?[18]

Gawler believed that the establishment of such colonies was 'one of the most important political objects' of the day, and he urged Jews to take immediate advantage of any reversal of Turkey's fortunes by 'boldly' staking their claim to Palestine in the name of 'the God of Israel and his national people'.[19] The Bible showed that Jews were the 'instruments' of civilization, which they would again make 'radiate throughout the degraded East'. If they did not reclaim their 'birthright' they would lose it to gentile colonists. He found it 'revolting' that some continental Jews, instead of looking to Palestine, were advocating Jewish colonies in the New World and the Antipodes.[20]

Gawler was evidently not a millenarian. His detailed plan of colonization, like the Zionist concept of his contemporary, Colonel Charles Henry Churchill,[21] appears to have had no conversionist sting in its tail. An avid reader of the Anglo-Jewish press, he was an admirer of Montefiore's activities on behalf of persecuted Jews, and of Chief Rabbi Nathan Adler's efforts 'to inspire', as Gawler put it, 'both Jews and Christians with more liberal and unprejudiced attitudes' towards one another. During his retirement at Southsea he was frequently among the many enthusiastic gentile guests at the annual dinners of the Portsea Hebrew Philanthropic Society.[22] He offered his plan 'in all sincerity to your nation',[23] and it found favour with the *Voice of Jacob*, ever vigilant for the ulterior motive:

> We do not doubt that he is a conscientious Christian, and would trust him none the less for that, if he as constantly keep in abeyance our mutual differences of opinion in the development of his plans, as he has done in the exposition of them. In this respect [he] has manifest advantages over those who have gone before him. He proceeds on the political and humane aspects of the case, and understands both. He is neither fanatic nor visionary; for he brings to bear his experience as a colonial governor, and a colonization commissioner; and he presents business-like estimates within the apprehension and compass of those to whom he appeals.[24]

Bent on maximum impact, Gawler sent copies of the pamphlet containing his proposal to the Cabinet, other leading parliamentarians, the Lord Mayor and Corporation of the City of London, the East India Company, Britain's chief periodicals and London's clubland.

Queen Victoria and Prince Albert 'graciously' accepted copies, as did King William IV's widow, Queen Adelaide (praised by her optician, a Jew, for her generosity to Jewish charities), and the Duke of Cambridge (who in 1843 had succeeded his dead brother the Duke of Sussex as President of the Jews' Hospital). The pamphlet reportedly created considerable interest 'among the upper classes'.[25]

In 1874 Gawler's son, Colonel J.C. Gawler, Keeper of the Crown Jewels at the Tower of London, submitted his own scheme for Jewish agricultural settlements in Palestine to the Board of Deputies. 'I would call attention to the *special faculty* in the Anglo-Saxon, *far above all other races*, for receiving the Hebrew Scriptures; and the growing importance of Syria to England, if she values her existence,' he later wrote.[26] He believed in the theory that the English were descended from the ten Lost Tribes of Israel, propounded by the Anglo-Israel Association. The *Jewish Chronicle* was reluctant to look a gift horse in the mouth:

> It is not in the Jewish interest to oppose the object for which this Association contends. Let it go on and prosper. Let the powerful Anglo-Saxon race be converted to the belief that they are brethren of the Jewish people.[27]

Remembered as 'A Splendid Pro-Semite', religious writer and orientalist Elizabeth Anna Gordon, who had been a lady-in-waiting to Queen Victoria, recalled that her mistress had believed in the 'British–Israel theory' so enthusiastically that she insisted that her grandson (the future King Edward VIII) be christened David 'because it was he who was destined to lead the Jews back to Palestine'. Introduced to Zionism by Kathleen Manning, a humanitarian advocate of the cause who became Viscount Simon's second wife, Mrs Gordon bore, anonymously, virtually the entire cost of the Commission sent to East Africa by the Zionist Congress to consider the feasibility of Jewish settlement there following Joseph Chamberlain's offer of territory. Becoming a friend of *Jewish Chronicle* editor L.J. Greenberg, she contributed further substantial donations to the Zionist movement before her death in 1925. Her final years were spent in Japan, where she endeavoured to foment pro-Jewish sympathies in influential circles.[28]

The Reverend John Mills was another who advocated Jewish colonization in Palestine without expecting that in return Jews would espouse Christianity. As briefly noted in chapter 1, he was among the small group of Jews and gentiles who, in 1852, founded the

Association for Promoting Jewish Settlement in Palestine. Their aim was to establish a self-administering Jewish agricultural colony between Safed and Tiberias; livestock and equipment would be paid for by public subscription. In seeking 'Friends to this great cause', they observed that 'whilst Palestine has such high significance in the eyes of the Christians, with how much greater interest must it be regarded by the Jew? ... towards it he yet gravitates as to his natural centre'.[29] At the meeting of expatriate Welshmen which he organized in London in 1854 to raise funds for Palestinian Jewry Mills said:

> To speak my whole heart, I believe Palestine belongs to the Jews. The Almighty promised it to Abraham of old ... and have it they shall.[30]

(Donors to the appeal made such comments as: 'Though now despised and suffering ... in a little while they shall be manifested as his restored and beloved people' and 'Who can read the ninety-sixth Psalm, without feeling the honour that will be put on this loved city [Jerusalem]. Assuredly we are drawing near to the blessed day when *restored Israel* will stand on Zion's hill.'[31])

One of the earliest gentile Zionists linking humanitarian and geopolitical considerations was Edward Mitford, writing from Colombo in 1845. As a British colonial administrator in Ceylon he was conscious of Palestine's strategic importance on the overland route to India, and during an earlier stint of duty in Morocco he had become acquainted with Jews, 'a very fine' and 'extraordinary race' with the potential to be again a great nation. Their 'condition ... has long been to me a consideration of deep sympathy and absorbing interest', he explained, scoffing at the notion that a divine 'curse' was upon them and 'that to help them would be to contravene' God's purpose. The needs of oppressed Jewry and of imperial Britain would both be served with their restoration, if Britain assumed 'so noble a work of humanity' as to effect their statehood under her aegis.

> It is unworthy of a power like Great Britain, on whose vigour and integrity the peace and happiness of so many nations, and the very existence of some, depends, to allow of one of the most vital arteries of her system remaining unprotected from enemies, or at the mercy of doubtful friends ... we must have our own protection in our own hands, and we could not employ better means for securing this object, than the instrumentality of a people of sufficient abilities to act under good counsels, and united among themselves by

every tie of religion, patriotism, and nationality. The re-establishment of the Jewish nation in Palestine under British protection, would retrieve our affairs in the Levant, and place us in a commanding position from whence to check the progress of encroachment, to overawe open enemies, and if necessary to repel their advance ... it would place the management of our steam communication entirely in our own hands.

With its abundant natural resources, Palestine would achieve 'its original fertility,' and given the commercial acumen of Jews,

> this protected state might in a few years monopolise the whole import trade of Central Asia, and compete with the commerce of Russia on its own southern frontier.
>
> The advantages derivable to England from this measure are so great, that it would almost appear that my real object was to benefit my own country, instead of advocating the cause of a proscribed and harmless race; but ... the protection afforded to this people would quickly return in blessings on England, and be felt in the wretched hearts and homes of the poor manufacturers of Manchester, Birmingham, and Glasgow.

He deliberately avoided the question of conversion, but, evidently thinking of sacrifice, he felt that 'it should be made an indispensable condition of our assistance, that they should not attempt to restore their obsolete ceremonial'.[32]

Geopolitical gentile Zionism surfaced especially in the immediate wake of the Crimean War. Russia's continuing designs upon the Turkish Empire despite the Treaty of Paris (1856) worried Britain, which steadily supported Turkey in the face of a potential Russian threat to Constantinople and thence to British interests in the East. Britain also kept a wary eye upon the regional ambitions of France, which in 1860, following a massacre by Moslems of Christians in Syria, seemed set to occupy that country. Against this background a number of 'gentile Zionists' advocated the restoration of a Jewish homeland in Palestine, under British protection. The Jews' charter to Palestine 'is the oldest and most infallible extant', wrote one. 'Restore them their nationality and their country once more, and there is no power on earth that could ever take it away from them.' With their capabilities they would

> at once become one of the great powers of the world, and be a wall of defence against France on the one side and Russia on the other.

And at this day, when nationalities are starting up from their tomb of centuries, why should not the Hebrew stand up and take his place among the nations? What bond of nationality is awanting to him? What people has so glorious a past? ... He has wealth; he is the great capitalist of the world ... Syria must be occupied by a trading and commercial people; and were the Ottoman power to be displaced, that old commercial route would immediately re-open ... The Jew has dealings on every bourse of the world; and in what more skilful hands could the exchanges betwixt the East and the West be placed? ... Syria would be safe only in the hands of a brave, independent and spirited people, deeply imbued with the true sentiment of nationality, and loving freedom too dearly ever to submit to a foreign yoke. Such a people we have in the Jews.[33]

An anonymous pamphlet by 'a Christian' similarly observed:

Here is a country wanting a people, and here is a people yearning for their country. What so natural that it should return to its legitimate owners? It would be a noble mission for England to be the means of effecting it. For hundreds of years the English have been the friends of the Jews ... much of the prosperity we now enjoy has resulted from the kindness we have shown them. Year after year their importance amongst us has increased ... it would not only be a generous and a just thing, but it would be a wise thing for England, as a political necessity, to restore them to a land which is theirs by right. They would defend it to the last against all enemies; they would be to us ... a friendly and grateful nation in assisting us to maintain our foothold in the East.[34]

It was typical of these geopolitically motivated Zionists that they had no conversionist aspirations. Cheshire physician Thomas Clarke, for instance, author of an important pamphlet and several related letters to the well-disposed *Jewish Chronicle*, was concerned only with 'the political and commercial aspects' of a Jewish Palestine:

it would be foolish and presumptuous to make conversion to Christianity a necessity of the restoration ... I do not for a moment seek to infuse any conversionist themes ... Apart from longing to see it [the Jewish people] taking its recognised place once more in some form amongst the nations of the earth and to see it freed from ... the misery and degradation with which it is associated, and in which it so patiently and heroically endures ... I have no personal or selfish interest in this question.[35]

Palestine was destined to become 'commercially important' and 'a most valuable outpost to Britain'. It was 'the natural highway to Australia and China', and more crucial to Britons and Jews than to any other people. With so many Jews in need of only 'political protection' to settle in their 'inalienable birthright', did they really insist upon 'nothing short of miraculous restoration'? They were 'essentially a trading and financial people, what so natural as that they should be planted along the great highway of ancient traffic' under British protection?

> I am a Christian and an Englishman, and while I recognise with pride and enthusiasm the inheritance of these great privileges, I also recognise another, which to me is equally strong, viz. that I belong to a nation which has for many centuries been the protector and defender of the Jew. The liberties and laws of citizenship of the Jews have been more respected, and their social and political standing has been more secure in my country than in any other ... I am also most deeply sensible that the blessings bestowed upon them have a thousand-fold been repaid to us.[36]

That persistent champion of oppressed Jewry, Lord Shaftesbury, was a confirmed millenarian. His belief in the Second Advent was one of the sustaining principles of his life: 'I see everything going on in the world subordinate to this great event.'[37] In 1839, against the background of portentous events in the Near East, he held that 'In all parts of the earth this extraordinary [Jewish] people, whose name and sufferings are in every nation under heaven, think and feel as one man on the great issue of their restoration.'[38] The following year he noted that 'The very insults, misrepresentations and persecutions of the Jews at Damascus bring forward the main question.'[39] Envisaging the mass conversion of restored Jewry under the auspices of the Anglican Church and the influence of Britain, he laid his millenarian vision with some success before Lord Palmerston and *The Times*[40] and was instrumental in the establishment, in 1841, of the Anglican bishopric in Jerusalem to counter the influence of the Catholic and Eastern Orthodox Churches there. Jews were 'not less concerned than ourselves to observe the present religious aspect of Europe, and the awful advances of Popery,' he wrote.

> We must learn to behold this nation with the eyes of reverence and affection; we must honour in them the remnant of a people which produced poets like Isaiah and Joel; kings like David and Josiah;

and ministers like Joseph, Daniel and Nehemiah; but above all, as that chosen race of men, of whom the Saviour of the world came according to the flesh ... both as a Church and as a nation, we have much to hope for in the welfare of the people of Israel; ... prosperity is to be the portion of those who pray for the peace of the Holy City ...'[41]

Nevertheless, the Society for the Relief of Persecuted Jews, or the Syrian Colonization Fund, founded by Shaftesbury 'to give relief and employment to Jews, especially in the Holy Land' until they could form themselves into self-supporting colonies, was not conversionist despite assumptions to the contrary. In 1891 the Society, then under the presidency of the Earl of Aberdeen, resolved 'That it is the duty of all Christians to give practical aid to persecuted and suffering Jews, especially in the Holy Land ...' and its then Honorary Secretary, Elizabeth Anne Finn, stressed that 'Making converts has never been nor can be the work of this Society, which is limited to practical help in token of Christian sympathy to Jews, especially to sufferers at the hands of our fellow Christians.'[42]

Mrs Finn was the Reverend Alexander McCaul's daughter. Her husband, James Finn, British Consul in Jerusalem, 1845–62, describes in his memoirs several striking examples of how he aided Jews in accordance with Palmerston's directive of 1839 to the then British Vice Consul 'to afford Protection to the Jews [in Palestine] generally'.[43] The Finns sought to alleviate the indigency of Jerusalem's Jewish inhabitants, whom they regarded as exploited by Arab landlords and over-dependent on charitable donations sent by co-religionists abroad, by means of an 'Industrial Plantation' outside the city which they set up in 1852 with the help of funds raised in Britain, British India and the United States. Workers, fed a nutritious breakfast arranged by the Finns, travelled daily to the plantation to assist with pursuits ranging from land clearance to wine-making, knowing that the Consul's involvement prevented attacks by *fellaheen*. Finn regarded the venture as kindling 'the hope of cultivating the desolate soil of their own Promised Land' and 'a very small indication of the better days to come for their nation'.[44]

Both Finns were devout Christians linked to the London Jews' Society, and their motives were suspect. They were accused of helping Jews in order to make converts, indeed of making conversion a condition of aid – accusations they were at pains to deny. John Mills supported their denials. In any case, Finn considered Jewish converts to Christianity 'as still subject to the same principles of government as other Jews – being the same individuals as before their conversion and belonging to the Jewish nation'. Indeed, Finn angered some of the missionaries from the London Jews' Society by refusing them access to the worksite in order to preach. The Jews were allowed time off for afternoon prayer. 'The object of the institution was to relieve distress by means of honest industry,' he explained.

> But at the same time, the perfect freedom and religious liberty of the workpeople were respected ... if the English Consuls had authorised professed Missionaries of an English Society to come and preach and hold religious discussions, it might have savoured of attempting to convert needy people by taking undue advantage of their distress.[45]

The Zionism of diplomat and writer Laurence Oliphant, who in 1882 became the Mansion House Fund Committee's Commissioner in Brody and Lvov, perhaps owed its genesis to an acute consciousness of biblical prophecy, but took a practical, humanitarian turn. Having witnessed the plight of Romanian Jewry at first hand in 1879, he had in 1880 proposed Jewish colonization of Palestine east of the Jordan, under Turkish sovereignty and British protection.[46] He continued to advocate the cause of Zion as a refuge with its neutrality guaranteed by the powers:

> He did not pretend that any desire to fulfil prophecy was at the bottom of the scheme ... He was thoroughly convinced of the large human advantage ...
> ... there was yet growing in him a sort of dedication to the service of the race of Israel ...[47]

Although the American William Blackstone was a millenarian, his two pro-Zionist memorials (1891 and 1916) would hardly have attracted signatures from American opinion leaders of various kinds had they not been based on humanitarian concerns. The earlier memorial, for instance, declared:

> We believe this an appropriate time for all nations, and especially the Christian nations of Europe, to show kindness to Israel. A million of exiles, by their terrible sufferings, are piteously appealing to our sympathy, justice, and humanity. Let us now restore to them their land, of which they were so cruelly despoiled ...[48]

The later one, addressed to President Wilson (but never formally delivered, since Jewish American Zionists, with whom Blackstone was in constant and friendly communication, decided that it was unnecessary), declared *inter alia* that 'humanity and the Golden Rule demand speedy action'. Signed by 82 'eminent statesmen, clergymen, philanthropists, financiers, the religious and secular press', it reflected a growing conviction among influential Americans that the Jews, in recognition of past suffering, deserved a National Home.[49] Blackstone, grown old, did not canvass as energetically as he had in 1891 and this time, on Jewish advice, collected only gentile signatures and confined his activities to Los Angeles (where he was based), Chicago, New York and Ithaca. Increasing support for Jewish national aspirations is seen in President Roosevelt's acceptance, a few months after Kishinev, of the flag symbolic of the Zionist movement, 'the first time that any ruler in the world has officially accepted the Jewish flag ... it implies the highest recognition of Zionism ever accorded by any Government.'[50] It is seen, too, in the remarks of many members of the American War Congress, several of whom linked remorse for that past suffering with recognition of the Jewish contribution to civilization, and pledged their dedication to the cause in extravagantly philosemitic terms.[51] Millenarianism certainly declined by the end of the nineteenth century, although it would remain intrinsic to the world view of the Christadelphians, who have been steadfast in their support for Jews. It enjoyed a resurgence in some quarters following the Balfour Declaration of 1917. The suffragette Christabel Pankhurst was an enthusiastic and perhaps surprising recruit.[52]

Virtually all the gentile Zionists who demonstrated on behalf of persecuted Jews were motivated, it would seem, primarily if not solely by humanitarian considerations. In addition, Canadian Prime Minister Sir Wilfrid Laurier, speaking (along with two Cabinet ministers) at a big Zionist rally in Chicago in 1907, linked his fervour for the cause to the recent Russian pogroms.[53] This motivation is as true of clergy as of laymen. For instance, the Presbyterian Reverend Dr Robert Steel told Sydney's 1881 rally that he hoped some of the funds collected for Russian Jewry would be used to transfer refugees to agricultural settlements in Palestine.[54] Protesting at the pogroms of 1905, Sydney's Anglican Archdeacon J.D. Langley advocated 'a combination of the European Powers, with the view of restoring Palestine to the Jewish people, which would for ever put an end to such horrible atrocities'.[55] In Britain, a most noteworthy example was the great pre-Raphaelite painter W. Holman Hunt, who attended the London rally of 1906 to protest at the pogroms. His art had taken him to Palestine in pursuit of scriptural themes and authentic Jewish models. In 1896 owing to compassion for 'the poor oppressed Israelite', he coincided with (and perhaps narrowly anticipated) Herzl in issuing a proposal for the settlement of Jews in a Palestine purchased from Turkey. That same year, when Herzl visited London, Hunt gave him support.[56]

Major-General Sir Alfred Turner, who signed the Beilis protest manifesto in 1912, wrote that he had

> always been in the deepest sympathy with the Jewish race, admiring their wonderful tenacity of purpose, their robust vitality and vigorous growth, despite the endless persecution they have undergone at the hands of Christians from time immemorial ... extirpated either by the tide of time or cruelty of Christians, they never will be.

He believed that Jews should have refuge in a state of their own, and in 1905 'readily accepted' Israel Zangwill's invitation that he should join the Jewish Territorial Organization (ITO) – which of course did not focus exclusively upon Palestine.[57] Beilis manifesto signatory Anthony Hope also supported ITO, as did fellow writer Mrs Humphry Ward.[58] Another signatory, Sir Harry H. Johnston, had long supported the Jewish colonization of Palestine. He felt that Jews would thereby bring the region into the orbit of western civilization.[59] *Observer* editor J.L. Garvin, who also signed the manifesto, was essentially a liberal philosemite who contributed 'a practical form of Zionism' with the suggestion that the great Turkish (later Greek) city of Salonika, with its large Jewish population, be declared by international guarantee 'a free town and a free port' under Jewish administration.[60]

Also signing the Beilis manifesto were four especially stalwart gentile Zionists – the Earl of Cromer, Lord Milner, Austen Chamberlain and Arthur James (Earl) Balfour. At his death several months before the Balfour Declaration (the substance of which he had hinted at) the *Jewish Chronicle* paid tribute to Cromer, 'among the greatest of Britain's Empire-builders', who had, while British agent in Cairo, 'treated in the most generous, kindly and helpful manner' a proposal for a Jewish settlement in the El Arish peninsula, initiated by Herzl. Cromer was

> a good friend to Jews. The same thing is observable in other such British governors as Lord Milner, Lord Selborne, and Sir Harry Johnston. It springs from the imagination and the broad sympathies

which contact with various races quicken into life – as well as the realisation in more vivid form of the world position of the Jews and the sorrows that have arisen in its wake.[61]

Milner, who in 1906 protested at 'the recurrent outbursts of savagery against the Jews in Russia',[62] feared revolutionary efforts at redress, but had a firm Zionist conviction rooted in British strategic considerations. 'Milner is not a Zionist *enragé*,' a British envoy who had just spoken to him noted in 1917, 'he only hopes that the adoption of Zionism will benefit us'.[63] This is not to deny that Milner's Zionism lacked genuine humanitarian feelings for Jews. On the contrary, he had 'deepest sympathy' for attempts by Anglo-Jewry 'to obtain justice and equal treatment' for less fortunate Jews overseas, admitting that if he was a British Jew he should 'feel powerfully moved and bound to make every effort in my power to raise those of my own race and religion in other countries from the position of something approaching servitude and indignity to which in many countries they are exposed'.[64] Moreover, he disdained the assimilation of Jews who carried 'their passion for neutral tints to a point of absurdity ... by carefully covering up the traces of their own creed and race'.[65] Like Mitford over a generation earlier, he saw Jewry's need as Britain's opportunity. He asked Jews to rebuild Palestine on 'a structure of ordered liberty and moral and material civilization, worthy of both their capacities and aspirations and of the great traditions of the past', and predicted that they would 'play a very great and patriotic part' in the future of the British Empire.[66]

One of Milner's disciples, Leopold Amery, had been won over to the 'age-long dream of the Jewish people'[67] during the First World War by geopolitical considerations, for Palestine, was 'the half-way house between England and Australia, between South Africa and East Africa, and India'. However, within a short time he had broadened his view. Addressing a major Zionist meeting in 1918 he declared:

> He had since come to be interested in the movement for its own sake. He had come to sympathize with the ideals of men like Weizmann and Sokolow ... He began by regarding the problem purely from the point of view ... of Imperial security and Imperial defence ... Imperial interest demanded a buffer ... a progressive, living Community established in front of the Suez Canal, with its own resources, its own power of developing, and which would see that that region of the world should not be open to the march of aggressive militarism from Europe or anywhere else. It was only the

Jews who could create a living, prospering, developing, strong community in that country ... who had a reason within their hearts for going there.

Having spent a few days in Palestine at Allenby's military headquarters Amery had acquired a fresh perspective on the Zionist idea. 'He had imagined a bare, bleak and dusty country; he found himself in a country of waving fields of wheat ... orchards and olive groves [and] of oranges', and had been impressed by the calibre of the young Jewish colonists who came forward to join Allenby's army, which indicated 'that in spite of centuries of cooped-up city life, a Jew when he got back to his ancient soil, to the ancient agricultural conditions of his people, lived as a strong and healthy man'.[68]

Neville Chamberlain, Austen's half-brother, who chaired that major Zionist meeting, warmly welcomed the Balfour Declaration as the consummation of the work of his late father, Joseph.[69] The latter was essentially a liberal philosemite. He is on record as denouncing the oppression of Jews overseas and as early as 1876 declared his belief that the 'guarantee of freedom' lay in 'autonomy or self-government'.[70] The first British Colonial Secretary to appoint a Jew (in the person of Sir Matthew Nathan) to a colonial governship, he became famously linked with the quest for a Jewish homeland when he offered part of East Africa to the Zionists in 1903 (formally rejected two years later). During the Mandate period the *Jewish Chronicle* remembered him as 'the first Statesman, anywhere the world over, to listen sympathetically to Jewish Nationalist strivings and to give a helping hand to the Zionist movement' and 'historically the father of the Balfour Declaration'.[71]

With that Declaration and the assumption by Britain of the Palestine Mandate the Zionist movement, especially in its cultural aspects, became very widely accepted by British gentiles. Many well-known names from all sides of politics welcomed the Balfour Declaration and sent congratulatory messages to the Zionist movement or the Anglo-Jewish press on its anniversaries. All types of gentile Zionism were represented in the good wishes from sections of the press and numerous public figures following first the Declaration and ultimately the League of Nations' granting of the Palestine Mandate to Great Britain.[72] There was even the occasional outbreak of millenarian fervour: 'It ought to be apparent to everybody that the persistence of a people like the Jews during two thousand years – a fact unparalleled in history – despite every attempt to crush them, holds a meaning far deeper than that which the secular historian offers. The purposes of God are being worked out, and we can begin to see the light.'[73] More often, there was jubilation that the sufferings of the Jewish people now appeared to be at an end. 'The world ought to rejoice that the race to which it owes the idea of a spiritual life should, at last, have a footing on a land which it can call its own,' wrote a Liberal MP.[74] 'I shall welcome the day when the Jewish nation finds itself sufficiently re-established to itself claim the full rights of a self-governing and independent country,' wrote the Marquis of Ailesbury.[75] 'Die Hard' Tory E.P. Hewitt KC believed that in view of their past suffering the Jews' desire to make Palestine 'as Jewish as England is English' was 'a very natural and reasonable ambition'. He compared Britain's obligations to Jews under the terms of the Balfour Declaration with her obligations to 'Irish Loyalists'.[76] John Buchan, who succeeded Josiah Wedgwood as Chairman of the Parliamentary Pro-Palestine Committee in 1932, declared in 1934 that he saw Zionism as 'a great act of justice. It is reparation for the centuries of cruelty and wrong which have stained the record of nearly every Gentile people.'[77]

Frequently, also, there was satisfaction that what appeared to be a happy ending for the Jews would also benefit the British Empire, a development undoubtedly dear to such men as the Earl of Meath, who welcomed the Mandate as 'one of the great landmarks of history', Lord Curzon, who wished 'the Zionist cause the best of luck', and Lord Bryce, who had heartily congratulated British Zionist leaders 'on the prospect for the national home of Israel' and 'the deliverance of the country from the yoke of the barbarous Turk and by the establishment in it of a civilised Government under the Mandate accepted by Great Britain'. Citing the cultural achievement of Jews in various fields, Bryce looked forward to Palestine as a centre of intellectual life and creativity.[78] All three men had participated in rallies on behalf of oppressed Jewry.

For many people in Britain and the Dominions the Zionist movement was acceptable because it had been found to dovetail with Britain's imperial interests. They would not necessarily support Zionist demands throughout the period which saw a dilution of the spirit of the Balfour Declaration. Those that were likely to remain with the Zionist movement throughout these vicissitudes were, like Herbert Sidebotham who encapsulated both geopolitical and humanitarian Zionism,[79] likely to have a commitment which ran deeper, fixed in genuine empathy with Jewry.

The Fabian socialist and feminist Mrs Philip (Viscountess) Snowden, who like her husband, the prominent Labour politician, frequently appeared on Zionist platforms during the Mandate, recalled that her interest in Zionism was kindled

> when she was in Sunday school, when she had learnt to attach a great value to Palestine and to the people of that land ... There must be thousands of gentiles in this country who felt for Palestine a sympathy based on that same emotionalism, or religious sense ...[80]

Indeed there were throughout the English-speaking world.

Sir Mark Sykes, who saw Zionism as 'the true solution to the Eastern Question' and is credited with winning Amery to the cause, declared that 'Zionism would give the Jews of the world a higher position than they had ever held before' and that as a Christian 'he felt that in helping Zionism he was doing something to make a great amend'.[81] 'What is it, to those who do not belong to the Jewish race, that constitutes the attraction that is so irresistible when one contemplates their long and troubled history?' asked the Earl of Birkenhead (better known as F.E. Smith MP) in avowing his attachment to Zionism:

> In the first place, it is, of course because every one of us was brought up upon the Old Testament stories, because that little country of the Jews has more closely dominated the thought and the interests of the world than any other country that has ever existed ... When I look at Jewish literature I find in it some of the noblest passages ever written by human hands, and in the Psalms probably the sweetest expression of lyrical fervour that has been given to the world ... a people one of whose members could write poetry like that can never completely perish from the earth. Its resurrection is now to be witnessed in that historic setting which belongs of right, on the basis of historic claim, to the Jewish people. Throughout the ages the Jews have accomplished noble tasks ... and it is possible for them to make the future of their race even more glorious than it had been in the past.[82]

That crusading parliamentary Zionist, Josiah Wedgwood, who even learned a little Yiddish in order to address Jewish groups in the East End, described Palestine as 'the Clapham Junction of the British Empire'. He maintained that 'it is a very good bargain for England that Palestine should become a Jewish State.' Such an outcome, with a Jewish Palestine as a self-governing Dominion of the Empire, would guarantee protection to Britain's imperial 'arteries' and to the Zionist settlers. In 1929 the Seventh Dominion League was formed under his chairmanship.[83] But his enthusiasm for Zionism was not predicated on geopolitical expediency alone, nor on simple humanitarianism. Deeply conscious of the Jewish religio-ethical contribution to civilisation, he held that

> The world owed much more to Jews and to Palestine than to any other people and country ...
> ... He particularly liked those Jews who were proud of being Jews, and he found them mostly among the Zionists.
> ... It must not be forgotten ... that the amount of common culture between Englishmen and Jews is far greater than between England and any other continental nation. They share the same fundamental ideas of justice, liberty, individual enterprise, and to a large extent they have a common literature.

It behoved Britain to stand by the Jews, as Palmerston had stood by Don Pacifico. And it behoved Jews to

> Stand up for your rights now! Let us have more of the spirit of my good and gallant friend, Jabotinsky ... do not forget the countless myriads of Jews who are *still* being kicked and beaten, kicked and spat upon, tortured and murdered ... when you are a nation, when you are free, see that our fellow Jews are treated like me, that they get justice.[84]

Lloyd George, who was Prime Minister when the Declaration in the name of the then Foreign Secretary was issued in 1917 explained, half-facetiously: 'Acetone converted me to Zionism.' He 'felt a deep debt of gratitude' to 'the brilliant scientific genius' of Chaim Weizmann, who as a research scientist at Manchester University had discovered cordite, or wood alcohol, for the Allied war effort. When Weizmann was asked what honour could be bestowed on him in return,

> all he asked was to be allowed to present his case for the restoration of his people to the old country ... So the case was put before us, and when the War Cabinet began to consider the case for the Declaration, it was quite unanimously in favour.

Their receptivity 'was undoubtedly inspired by natural sympathy, admiration, and the fact that ... we had been trained even more in Hebrew history than in the history of our own country,' Lloyd George added, pointing to the deep and enduring cause of his own philosemitism, which as described in chapter 7 was embedded in the religious education he had received as a child, which left him with an almost symbiotic sense of identity with the People of the Book. This feeling was reinforced by his Welshness: he was not the first, nor the last, Welsh philosemite to avow a special affinity with Jews and the land of Israel:

> You belong to a very great race which has made the deepest impression upon the destinies of humanity ... We, the Welsh people, like you belong to a small race ... Your poets, kings and warriors, are better known to the children and adults of Wales than are the names of our own heroes!...
>
> ... You call yourselves a small nation. I belong to a small nation, and I am proud of the fact. It is an ancient race, not as old as yours ... You may say you have been oppressed and persecuted – that has been your power! You have been hammered into very fine steel, and that is why you can never be broken.[85]

To Lloyd George, the Balfour Declaration was

> not an expropriating, but an enabling clause. It is only a charter of equality for the Jews ...
>
> ... They belong to ... a race that has endured persecution which for the variety of torture – physical, material, and mental – inflicted on its victims, for the virulence and malignity with which it has been sustained, for the length of time it has lasted, and, more than all, for the fortitude and patience with which it has been suffered, is without parallel in the history of any other people.
>
> Is it too much to ask that those amongst them whose sufferings are the worst shall be able to find refuge in the land their fathers made holy by the splendour of their genius, by the loftiness of their thoughts, by the consecration of their lives, and by the inspirations of their message to mankind?[86]

Many leading Zionists said likewise, including American congressmen recommending that their government should support the Balfour Declaration.[87] Such views were also voiced by South Africa's Prime Minister, General Smuts, who had been his country's representative in the Imperial War Cabinet. In 1928, with twelve other distinguished non-Jewish South Africans including the Ministers of Justice and of Defence, the Administrator of the Transvaal, the Bishop of Pretoria, the head of the country's Methodists, and university vice-chancellors, he sent a manifesto to the South African Zionist Federation expressing willingness personally to campaign actively alongside its members for the realization of 'Jewish national aspirations'.[88] His regard for Jews was rooted in the Calvinism of his Boer inheritance. He saw the Balfour Declaration as 'a great act of historic reparation' which had righted 'The greatest most ancient wrong' and fulfilled 'the prophecies of restoration enshrined in the world's greatest poetry'. Moreover, 'we Christians, who have received from Israel not only the treasures of the noblest literature, but above all, the leadership of the Prince of Peace, are at last in a position to make some small return for those priceless blessings, and to restore Israel to the Ancient glorious Home Land.'[89]

It was no accident that during the 1920s and 1930s Britons with a special empathy for Jews, whether based on sympathy for what Jews had suffered or gratitude for what Jews had contributed to the world or (as so often) a blend of both, vigorously opposed what they perceived as the dilution by successive governments of the original terms of the Balfour Declaration. For instance, Lloyd George railed against 'a breach of national faith',[90] while Smuts, who declared that in his country all Christians 'are pro-Zionists', argued that the Declaration 'cannot now be varied unilaterally ... It represents a debt of honour which must be discharged in full at all costs.'[91]

In the United States, such gentile anger was widespread. There, 'fair weather friends' to the Zionist cause were likely to be fewer than in Mandate era Britain, where so many – Jew and non-Jew alike – tended to fix their degree of adherence to the cause in line with the policy of successive governments. During the 1930s, Franklin D. Roosevelt, Senators Borah and Robert F. Wagner and William Green, President of the American Federation of Labor, were among the gentile public figures condemning British government policy. The decade was ushered in with a pro-Zionist book written after a tour of Palestine by that steadfast friend to oppressed Jewry, the Reverend John Haynes Holmes.[92] In 1937 Green and nine other non-Jews proved themselves more Zionist than the Zionists when, as representatives of the Palestine Federation of America, an entirely non-Jewish body, they cabled the Zionist Congress in Zurich warning it not to approve Britain's plan to partition Palestine between Jews and Arabs:

> This self-betrayal of Zionist cause will alienate Christian pro-Zionists ready to support the fulfilment of the Mandate for a Jewish State on both sides of the River Jordan. As Christians we

warn the Zionist Congress that it has no right to relinquish one foot of the sacred soil of Palestine ... betraying an historical hope for which millions have bled and are now suffering ...

Signatories included the Federation's President, socialist writer Charles Edward Russell, New York Senator Royal S. Copeland, and Frederick B. Robinson, President of the City College of New York.[93]

This was, of course, issued at a time of considerable gentile Zionism throughout the English-speaking world, which demanded that the gates of Palestine be thrown open to refugees from Nazi persecution. It was the era, *par excellence*, of humanitarian gentile Zionism, for whatever other motivations might have been lurking, the perception of Palestine as a sanctuary was now the overriding one, and to most (but not all) champions of the Jewish refugees of the 1930s, the creation of a Jewish state in Palestine presented an obvious long-term solution to the problems of persecuted Jewry.

9 'The Glorious Inheritance': Conservative and Elitist Philosemitism

A surprisingly significant factor in modern philosemitism was the perception of Jews as an 'elite', a people possessing rare and valuable qualities, setting them above the general run of humanity. As already shown, there were constant references among philosemites to Jews as patriotic, law-abiding citizens practising sobriety, devoted to family life and generous to charity. But the perception of them as an 'elite' went further. It insisted on their uncommon physical vigour and disease-resistance and their extraordinary mental capacity and intellectual achievements. It dwelled on their outstanding and disproportionate achievements, and stood in awe of their 'ancient race', their 'unique' status as a surviving people of antiquity, outliving Assyrians, Babylonians, Romans, and outlasting all their persecutors. In a sense, it invested Jews with an extended version of 'chosenness.'

As discussed below, the image of Jews as an 'elite' was entertained by philosemites across the political spectrum, usually in concert with a propensity to support Jews out of one or more other and often primary motives such as liberal humanitarianism, Christian compassion, or awareness of a shared religious heritage. It was, however, likely to feature as the central philosemitic force propelling pro-Jewish political and social conservatives. For such people, the 'elitist' characteristics of Jews were likely to exert a powerful impact. Through these characteristics Jews could be seen to embody the values traditionally held dear by conservatives: an organic view of history, reverence for ancient lineage and national heritage, respect for high achievement, and stress on private enterprise, thrift and self-reliance. Conservatives, then, could empathize with and even admire Jews for being unquestionably one of the oldest continuously existing peoples in the world; for their tenacity and cohesiveness in the face of overwhelming odds, their obvious intelligence and their uncanny ability to succeed as individuals and as a group; for their contributions to society, perhaps especially the national economy; for their dogged determination to provide for their own poor and aged, shunning dependence upon general charities or state welfare schemes; for their religious and moral codes, which encouraged compliance with the law, social stability, familial cohesion and the eugenically-oriented values of hygiene and cleanliness.

To be sure, in the first half of the nineteenth century conservatives, as a rule, were among the most inveterate opponents of Jewish parliamentary emancipation, regarding such a measure as a betrayal of the existing order. And, towards a century later, the visible presence of Jews, and of others erroneously believed to be Jews, in the Russian revolutionary leadership gave rise to an unjustified identification of Jews with Bolshevism and so fed anti-Jewish prejudice in some conservatives. But there was another, sharply contrasting, side to the picture. No less than liberals, conservatives could and frequently did manifest goodwill towards a community which, while determined not to merge its religious identity in that of the majority population, aimed to play a full part in the wider society. That determination of Jews to preserve an identity based on thousands of years of history and tradition could and frequently did stir a fellowship of feeling on the part of conservatives, whose own system of values it reflected. The Jews' refusal to dissimulate by cynically and expediently taking the requisite parliamentary oath in order to obtain admission to Westminster, as many unbelievers did, earned them respect in some conservative quarters. Emancipation had its conservative champions, including a provincial newspaper which asked in 1845:

> Religious tests being abolished, why is the Jew alone excluded from parliament? ... More loyal men than the Jew do not live. They are strongly and affectionately attached to the institutions of England.
> ... If the national honour, or the credit and security of the realm were the question at issue, we should not for a single moment hesitate in saying that we would rather trust some half-hundred Jews ... than the same number of dissenters, &c., at present in the House of Commons.[1]

Moreover, the 'Anglo-Jewish gentleman' was of a type with whom gentiles of his milieu, conservatives as well as liberals, could identify. 'These wealthy and accomplished Jews are met with among our high nobility,' approvingly noted Charlotte Elizabeth Tonna, herself a Tory,

> and there is a class of educated and highly genteel men, with their families, who ... outdazzle their Gentile neighbours ... Then again,

in the walks of science, and in the paths of deep learning, at every turn you meet the accomplished Jew.[2]

Seventy years later, after the Bolshevik Revolution, first-hand experience of Jews meant that conservatives were just as likely to reject as accept the image of Jew-as-revolutionary, realizing that it did not fit the Jews with whom they came into contact. Many would have heeded, too, the anti-Bolshevik disavowals and denunciations of Anglo-Jewish leaders, and have seen that the Soviet system was as hostile to Judaism, to synagogues, Jewish schools and thus to transmission of the Jewish heritage, as it was to Christian traditions and institutions.[3]

On the European continent, the antisemitism of conservatives was often unremitting in its condemnation of Jews. More often than not, it seems fair to say, continental conservatives were relentless antisemites, whether on 'race', nationality or religious grounds. But the situation in English-speaking lands must, emphatically, not be confused with that. Nor, plainly, must philosemitism in those lands be viewed as the monopoly of liberals and progressives. The pro-Jewish public meetings and other demonstrations of solidarity which have been described in this book always included conservatives. This is true of the very first traceable public meeting, that of 1840. The conservative contingent at such meetings held under City of London auspices increased over time: by the 1870s Liberalism had ceased to be the dominant political force in the City, as its parliamentary representation showed, and the speakers and other dignitaries on the platform reflected that trend, although the core of philosemitic support overall was still supplied by liberals, and would continue to be.

British conservatives, though few of them can have realized it, were heirs to a Burkean philosemitism. In a little-known speech, Edmund Burke argued that Jews deserved support and sympathy because they were economically useful and because they were inoffensive and defenceless. For him, Britain had self-interested and above all moral imperatives to assist them whenever and wherever they were persecuted. They were, he said,

> the people whom of all others it ought to be the care of human nations to protect ... Having no fixed settlement in any part of the world, no kingdom nor country in which they have a government, a community and a system of laws, they are thrown upon the benevolence of nations and claim protection and civility from their weakness as well as from their utility. They ... could give no

well-founded jealousy to any state ... From the east to the west, from one end of the world to the other, they are scattered and connected; the links of communication, in the mercantile chain ... the conductors by which credit was transmitted through the world. Their abandoned state and their defenceless situation calls most forcibly for the protection of civilized nations ... If Britons are injured, Britons have armies and laws, the laws of nations ... to fly to for protection and justice. But the Jews have no such power and no such friend to depend on. Humanity then must become their protector and ally.[4]

Those conservatives who, almost certainly in unwitting echo of Burke, answered the humanitarian call, typically made the Jewish contribution to society their focus, often reflecting an 'elitist' outlook. At the 1840 Damascus rally the banker John Masterman, who was elected the following year as Conservative MP for the City of London, identified Jews as 'a most influential and respectable class of persons' whose wealth benefited the nation in both commerce and philanthropy. His fellow banker and Conservative, Matthias Wolverley Attwood, declared that it was an 'honour' and a 'privilege' as well as a 'duty' to defend the Jews' religion from obloquy.[5] Their party leader, Sir Robert Peel, so solicitous of the welfare of Damascus Jewry and long since won over to the cause of Jewish parliamentary emancipation, lauded the part played by Jewish entrepreneurs, while the anti-democrat Sir Charles Nicholson, a supporter of state aid to Judaism in New South Wales who chaired a meeting in Sydney in 1854 to raise funds for the relief of Palestinian Jewry, declared: 'They belonged to a people from whom we have derived, in one form or another, all that was good or glorious – all that had raised Great Britain to the high and honourable position she now holds among the nations of the earth.'[6]

Proposing a Jewish fellow-Conservative as Southampton's Mayor in 1865, the President of the town Chamber of Commerce described Jews as 'a suffering people' who deserved support, being 'amongst the most industrious, the most wealthy, and the most useful in the world'.[7] Conservative MP R.N. Fowler, who is credited with engineering the City's decisive swing to the Tories about 1870, told the 1872 Mansion House rally of his 'sorrow and shame'[8] at centuries of persecution towards a people to whom so much was owed, and at the 1890 Guildhall rally he paid tribute to the economic benefits which successive generations of Jewish financiers and merchants had brought to the City of London.[9] At the 1882 rally Conservative MP J.G. Hubbard reminded Russia of the advantages of toleration: 'the foundations of English commerce and industry were laid partly by Jews'.[10]

Leopold Maxse ascribed Dreyfus's unpopularity among certain brother officers to the fact that he was 'a Jew and an industrious man',[11] perhaps a fixed linkage in Maxse's mind. At Adelaide's 1905 rally a conservatively inclined businessman observed that Jews had a special claim upon gentile 'reverence and sympathy' because they were in the forefront of human achievement, producing 'leaders of intellect', industry and statecraft.[12] The imperial administrator Lord Milner, a former Governor of both Cape Colony and the Transvaal, was, as we have seen, a dedicated Zionist. A close friend of Claude G. Montefiore, founder of Liberal Judaism in Britain, Milner had acknowledged Yiddish as a European tongue when elements within South Africa were attempting to discriminate against Eastern European intending immigrants by use of a language test; he mentioned at the 1906 London rally the significant economic contribution of Jews to the Empire.[13]

The eminent barrister E.P. Hewitt KC, an interwar crusading Zionist and an extreme rightwing Conservative, admired Jews because, despite 'many centuries of cruel persecution', they 'with extraordinary tenacity and patience', have retained their identity'.[14] Lord Hailsham, Conservative Lord Chancellor and father of the pro-Jewish Quintin Hogg MP, remarked in 1931 that Jewish ancestry involved 'the glorious inheritance of tradition'.[15] The following year, the newly elected Conservative MP Henry Procter, a long-time student of Hebrew, extolled Jews for their 'intellectuality, benevolence, sobriety and industry', and attributed antisemitism to 'sheer envy of the high attainments which redounded so much to their credit'. A convinced Zionist, Procter nevertheless believed 'that it will be a great loss to the world if the Jewish contribution is confined solely to the Judaean Hills. They possess gifts which no other people have got.'[16]

Similar considerations almost certainly weighed with other Conservative and imperialistic philosemites, including Leopold Amery as well as Sir James Barrett and (Sir) Charles Merrett, two of Australia's most active rightwing Empire loyalists during the interwar period. Barrett and Merrett supported Jewish refugee immigration, a cause championed by the conservative *Sydney Morning Herald* apparently more ardently than by virtually every other Australian newspaper.[17] The *Herald* had demonstrated its goodwill since colonial times, when it praised Jews' 'fortitude and constancy' to their ancestral tradition in the face of persecution, and condemned their treatment by 'the prejudiced and superstitious'. It invoked a common theme when it declared: 'What an enormous chasm would be made in history were the Jewish element withdrawn!' And it appeared to endorse Disraeli's conception of Jews as 'the very aristocracy of intellect'.[18]

Some Conservatives and imperialists were undoubtedly drawn to a pro-Jewish position because they admired 'the wonderful career of Disraeli', to quote the robustly imperialistic, rightwing *Daily Mail* in 1934.[19] Anglican convert though he was, the creator of One Nation Toryism and hero of the Congress of Berlin was in his mind very much a Jew, and few considered him anything else: 'he was never ashamed of his race', recalled that same newspaper approvingly.[20] It seems inconceivable that at least a proportion of those who esteemed him in his lifetime or honoured his memory – for instance, through the enormously popular Primrose League – failed to imbue empathy for the people from whom he sprang. His devoted Tory Private Secretary, Lord Rowton (Montagu Corry), owed a strong personal attachment to the Jewish cause to that personal association. Rowton was a requisitioner of the 1890 Guildhall rally, and in 1902 one of the comfortable club-style hostels he established for London's needy opened in Jewish Whitechapel. He planned the enterprise in deliberate consultation with Chief Rabbi Herman Adler, a friend with whom he 'discussed Jewish matters with considerable knowledge and sympathy'.[21] Another requisitioner of the 1890 meeting, Conservative MP Howard Vincent, was an ardent advocate of Imperial Federation who sat on the Grand Council of the Primrose League.[22] Perhaps empathy for Disraeli led the Tory Lord Glenesk, during the 1870s, to tackle a powerful Russian statesman regarding the blood libel; Glenesk, who addressed the 1906 rally, was 'perfectly dumbfounded' to learn that his target genuinely believed that Jews commit ritual murder, and pondered dejectedly on how entrenched, therefore, anti-Jewish superstition must be among the Czar's backward subjects.[23]

For contemporary and later Tories Disraeli was the saviour of his party and architect of Empire, an icon of imperialism, 'the first' to instil in Britons 'a sense of imperial pride', as Hailsham remarked in 1931.[24] This might have informed the philosemitic stance of the Earl of Meath, Sir John Colomb and the future Lord Curzon, not to mention Queen Victoria, with her concern for Russian Jewry (and for Dreyfus) – a concern shared by her son, King Edward VII, who in 1908 made discreet overtures to the Czar on behalf of the latter's

Jewish subjects.[25] Disraeli's services to the Empire were, naturally enough, appreciated by 'overseas Britons', especially Australians grateful that by obtaining the Suez Canal for Britain and by neutralizing the power of Turkey he had secured their country's lifeline to the Motherland. Such considerations no doubt weighed with Australian conservative supporters of the Jewish cause. Sir George Reid, who attended Sydney's 1881 protest meeting, wrote that before Disraeli's resolute handling of the Eastern Question in 1878 'I never looked upon him as quite an Englishman,' but that thereafter 'few could be more ardent admirers than I was ... I could not think of any man who was a truer Englishman.'[26] (Sir) Patrick Jennings, a future Premier of New South Wales who contributed to the Russian-Jewish relief fund opened at that 1881 meeting, had in 1878 spoken at a rally in Sydney praising Disraeli's international statesmanship.[27] Sir Francis Newdegate, successively Governor of Tasmania and Western Australia, a pro-Zionist who was attracted to Jewish ritual and forged strong bonds with Jews in the states he served, in 1920 cited Disraeli as an exemplar of Jewish loyalty to Britain and the Empire.[28]

Disraeli became, also, a symbol of those whom the Nazis were persecuting, a reminder of the Jewish genius which they spurned and outlawed. Leopold Amery remarked as soon as they seized power that the statesman whose 'memory ... was ever fresh' in British minds would be under the Nazis utterly incapable of holding office.[29] Former Conservative MP Sir Reginald Mitchell Banks, who in 1937, when a county court judge, praised Jewry's intellectual achievements and expressed sympathy for their persecution, cited Disraeli as one of the 'valiant and brilliant sons of Israel' who had enriched British society.[30]

In Australia a similar iconic function was served by the greatly admired Jewish First World War hero, General Sir John Monash, Commander-in-Chief of the Australian armies in France, and perhaps the first Jew to serve as a general since Roman times. Indeed, between 1927 and 1931 extreme rightwingers implored Monash to assume control of Australia in a military dictatorship to rescue the country from the debilitating effects of machine politics, labour unrest and the threat of Communism. His state funeral procession in Melbourne in 1931 attracted up to 300,000 mourners lining the route:

> The funeral was the most impressive and largely attended Australia had known. If the King had died he could not have been shown more respect ...

Never, perhaps, had Melbourne seen so many flags, at half-mast ... The funeral had been broadcast. Services and ceremonies were held all over Australia ... at the University of Sydney hundreds of people stood bareheaded as Chopin's funeral march rang out from the war memorial carillon ... The *Age*'s special writer found a Kipling association: Monash had 'acquired an extraordinary Imperial prestige without favour and without fawning ... had walked with Kings, nor lost the common touch.'[31]

People with a fundamental belief in human inequality were likely to be especially receptive to the idea of Jews as an 'elite'. Sir Francis Galton, who, liberal though he essentially was, advanced in 1869 the theory of differences in human intellectual ability, regarded them as such. Their demonstrable disproportionate presence in many fields of intellectual endeavour suited in many ways the concept of striving to improve average natural ability that lay at the heart of the science of eugenics which he founded in 1883. He recognized Jews' 'high intellectual' prowess and admired their 'fitness', which he interpreted as an adaptation to the rigours of centuries of persecution, and he commended their predilection to early marriage and their fecundity.[32] He died in 1911 and so was not among the eminent signatories to the Beilis protest. His disciple, Karl Pearson, was, and went on to advocate Jewish colonization of Palestine.[33] To that pre-eminent liberal thinker of the nineteenth century, John Stuart Mill, 'the Jews, instead of being stationary like other Asiatics, were, next to the Greeks, the most progressive people of antiquity, and, jointly with them, have been the starting point and main propelling agency of modern cultivation.'[34] The conviction that Jews were, for various reasons, an 'elite' people, was certainly not confined to conservatives.

Medical science abetted that conviction, with the frequently noted Jewish tendency to longevity and comparative resistance to serious diseases such as cholera, measles, scarlet fever and smallpox. Some gentile authorities attributed this tendency to the Judaic rituals of purification and cleanliness (a clear contrast to antisemitic notions of the 'dirty' Jew) and, especially, to the Jewish dietary laws. For example, a nineteenth-century Australian physician, more familiar with Jews and their habits than most, concluded that the healthful consequences of their traditional lifestyle was 'an ever living witness for the Almighty of the truth of His Holy Word'.[35] The distinguished pioneering British physician and medical writer Sir Benjamin Richardson became so convinced of the connection between 'the vitality of the Jews' and the 'Mosaic sanitary code' that in order to eradicate certain diseases he recommended the introduction generally of a *kashrut*-type system of food selection and inspection. Richardson, an amateur man of letters who moved in literary circles and took a deep interest in Jewish history, became a close friend of Chief Rabbi Adler. He developed a warm attachment to Anglo-Jewry. On a number of occasions he presided over literary meetings at Jews' College. He supported the London Jews' Hospital and Orphan Asylum, and occasionally spoke at communal functions. His admiration for the Maccabean leader Simeon Bar Kochba, who made a desperate ill-fated stand against the Roman occupiers of Judaea, found expression in a novel, *The Son of a Star*, and at his death in 1896 he had begun work on another, based on the life of the great medieval Jewish philosopher, Maimonides.[36]

Richardson's contemporary, the well-known British historian W.E.H. Lecky, accepted the medically and eugenically-based notion of Jews as an elite. He wrote of 'the physiological force and tenacity' of the Jews.

> The physical characteristics of the race are very remarkable and they are especially displayed among the Eastern [Russo-Polish] Jews who still maintain scrupulously amid poverty and persecution the religious observances of their ancestors. It is now clearly shown that the Levitical code was in high degree hygienic, and even anticipates some of the discoveries of modern physiology ... They have been as a rule singularly free from the kinds of vice that do most to enfeeble and corrode a race.

Noting that Jews 'have at all times been distinguished for their love of learning', Lecky continued: 'it is an undoubted fact that Jewish families and families mixed with Jewish blood have produced an amount and variety of ability that far exceed the average of men. The ability goes rather with the race than with the religion.'[37]

The idea that Jews constitute an intellectual 'elite' was already becoming commonplace by the mid-nineteenth century, when a New York newspaper, deploring the House of Lords' resistance to according them parliamentary emancipation, described them as 'brilliant in brain' and a reviewer in a London journal acknowledged their 'extraordinary faculties' and 'the remarkable proportion of their great men in relation to their numbers'.[38] The image proved especially powerful and enduring, the source of much goodwill towards Jews, whom it endowed with a sort of mystique, especially when combined with the consideration that, in the words of a pro-emancipation Portsmouth town councillor explaining why they merited 'every respect', they 'are the most ancient nation in the world'.[39]

Examples of this line of thought abound. For instance, the Liberal statesman Robert Lowe (Lord Sherbrooke) argued during his Sydney career in the 1840s that state aid to Judaism was justified because Jews had been a great nation 'before the most prized records of ancient history had obtained an existence'.[40] Celebrated American poet William Cullen Bryant, in the New York newspaper that he edited, praised 'the grandeurs of the Jewish race', 'that superiority of intellect which has survived all persecution', and marvelled at 'how many of the great events which mark the progress of the age or minister to its improvements, or elevate its tastes, may be traced to the wonderful workings of the soul of the Hebrew, and the supremacy of that spiritual nature which gave mankind its noblest religion, its noblest laws, and some of its noblest poesy and music.'[41] George William Curtis, editor of *Harper's Weekly*, reflected ashamedly on how much was owed to 'the Jewish genius,' 'to a people whose name is so constantly used as a word of reproach'.[42] The same considerations led North Carolina Senator Zebulon B. Vance to state in his much-circulated philosemitic lecture: 'The Jew is beyond doubt the most remarkable man of this world – past or present.'[43]

A Philadelphia newspaper, deploring in 1863 orders by General Grant and by a general in the west banning Jews from their lines, dwelt at length on this theme, noting, *inter alia*:

> the Jews, whatever they undertake, carry out further and with greater earnestness and success than any other equal body of people on earth – they have ever since the beginning of their nationality. In the history of the world's civilisation and advancement, Jews have ever been the leaders in every branch of progress, in ancient and modern times ... They have for ages been the great capitalists of the civilised world, and they have pushed their researches further into the laws of every subject than any other people.[44]

The Jew, observed a wellwisher in 1861, 'traces back the line of his ancestry into ages that long preceded the rise of the oldest monarchy now on the earth'.[45] A Texan legislator in 1872 reminded a colleague who had derided Jews of all that the world owed to a people whose greatness was rooted in antiquity:

> Oppressed ... their tenacious life yet breaks out through almost all

the channels of human activities in all the world ... Scattered and divided, their heroism and their genius have not forsaken them ... They can be felt in every avenue of human influence.[46]

That same year a British judge admonished in similar vein a defendant who had used 'Jew' as a term of opprobrium.[47] An Australian former politician told Melbourne's protest meeting in 1881 that continental European antisemitism was driven by jealousy of Jews, since they were in the forefront of so many fields of human endeavour, a sentiment shared by the city's Anglican Dean.[48] At Sydney's equivalent protest, a prominent politician spoke of a 'richly gifted people', and another, giving examples, praised 'a people that in all ages had been one of the noblest in the world ... of great intelligence'.[49] Canons Fleming and Farrar went beyond straightforward 'Christian philosemitism' when, respectively, they stated in 1882:

> Whether you look at their genius, or their antiquity, or the legacy they have given to the world, or their industry and enterprise ... [Jews] are of all people under the sun the last that should be despised, scorned, or insulted ...

and

> ... The Jews have always had a talent for succeeding ... All history has proved that they are a race of intense physical vitality and splendid achievements ... the Jews are exceptionally gifted ... In England they are a comparatively small community, yet they have acquired an influence entirely out of proportion to their numbers ... all Europe might profit by the moral and intellectual qualities of Israelites.[50]

At the 1890 London Guildhall rally the Duke of Westminster observed: 'This ancient Jewish race is remarkable for its intelligence and distinguished by its many great qualities ... it has a way of making its way to the front.'[51] At a civic protest meeting in New Orleans in 1903 protesting the Kishinev pogrom the President of Tulane University declared that

> In order to develop the moujik [peasant], the Russian feels it necessary to oppress the Jew ... the Jew has ten times the gifts of the moujik ... I have seen him grow eminent in every field of life, preeminent in every art, unweakened in vitality, either intellectual or physical or racial – one of the greatest forces to be reckoned with in the civilization of the world.[52]

'It may well be believed,' wrote an American clergymen protesting at the same atrocity,

> that Jews outstrip the people among whom they live ... They are of a race that bred Heine, Disraeli, and Auerbach, Zangwill, and Maimonides, Mendelssohn, Rubinstein, Neander, and Heschel, and Ricardo. From what race of equal numbers on the earth can be duplicated the list of poets, historians, statesmen, philanthropists, scientists, philosophers that make the illustrious roll of those who since [the] days of Solomon and David have displayed the intellectual greatness of Abraham's descendants?[53]

An Australian Methodist minister and veteran philosemite castigated in 1905 Russia's 'long continued and infamous treatment of the race which gave to the world in every century those who, in every department of human activity, have stood foremost among men'.[54]

Liberal MP Thomas Burt, a requisitioner of the 1890 Guildhall rally, when introducing in 1909 a lecture celebrating Jewish political emancipation by another, also non-Jewish, Liberal MP, voiced the by that time well-entrenched view that 'There was no more gifted race.'[55] A Swansea newspaper, deploring in 1911 rioting against Jewish shopkeepers in the South Wales valleys and describing the persecution of Jews as 'the saddest thing in history', noted 'the brain-power of the Jews' and the 'dazzling galaxy' of achievers they had produced.[56] Immediately following the First World War a prominent Progressive (soon-to-turn Republican) Congressman explained why he supported the 'long-delayed justice' of a Jewish National Home:

> For more than twenty centuries, the Jew has been persecuted because he feared the wrath of God more than that of man and loved truth more than life ...If patient suffering ennobles, the Jew has no peer, and has earned the chosen vessel of national heritage.
>
> Back through all the ages, along the path of civilization the Jew has shed a continuous light. When barbaric darkness settled over the world, the Jew retained his former civilization ...
>
> When kings could not write their names, and the monks of the West were spelling out their litanies, the Jews were lecturing on scientific, political and ethical subjects. The Jewish doctors were studying natural laws and laying the foundation of our present system of medicine. Their universities were unrivalled and the revival of learning is due to the influence of the Jew more than any other cause.[57]

Around the same time the pro-Zionist American social philosopher Thorstein Veblen (of Norwegian descent) was writing at length of

> that massive endowment of spiritual and intellectual capacities of which [Jews] have given evidence throughout their troubled history ...
>
> It is a fact which must strike any dispassionate observer that the Jewish people have contributed much more than an even share to the intellectual life of modern Europe ... It is not only that men of Jewish extraction continue to supply more than a proportionate quota to the rank and file engaged in scientific and scholarly work, but a disproportionate number of the men to whom modern science and scholarship look for guidance and leadership are of the same derivation ...
>
> The cultural heritage of the Jewish people is large and rich, and it is of ancient and honorable lineage.[58]

During the Nazi era there were innumerable references to the Jews as an 'elite' element in the populations of both Germany and Britain. The High Sheriff of Leicester, in a representative speech, referred to 'that noble race' and invoked 'the debt Britain owes to that heroic people', who had materially assisted 'the commercial supremacy and leadership' of the Empire.[59]

So ingrained were certain attitudes that it did not take a reactionary to make invidious distinctions between Jews and other 'races', complimentary to the former. (Sir) Walter Besant, for many years Secretary of the Palestine Exploration Fund and a requisitioner of the 1890 Guildhall rally, wrote:

> Poet, lawyer, painter, actor, statesman, physician, musician – there is not a branch of learning, art, or science, in which the Jew is not in the front rank. The thousand years of oppression have left no mark upon his mighty spirit ... Other races have been persecuted and despised. What have they done? Nothing! Parsee, Czech, Basque, Wend, Celt, Cagot [a people in the Western Pyrenees] – what have they done? Nothing! Nothing![60]

Following Kishinev, a distinguished speaker at a protest meeting in St Louis condemned 'the savage passions which the uncivilized Russian possesses in common with the Chinaman, the Kurd and the Apache', while a Kentucky newspaper denied any analogy between Russia's treatment of Jews and the American South's treatment of blacks:

The cases are so dissimilar that it is hardly necessary to argue the point. In nearly all cases where lynchings take place it is an expiation for some terrible crime; the Jews in Russia were murdered for no reason other than they were frugal and industrious among a sodden and idle peasantry, who were jealous of their prosperity.[61]

As mentioned in chapter 6, most Australian philosemites approved of the White Australia policy which, engendered in the 1880s, did not start to crumble until the 1960s. Lloyd George declared in 1933 that every German Jew-baiter was acknowledging his own 'inferiority' to a cleverer people: since 'he cannot fight the Jew on equal terms ... he is going to beat Jewish brains ... with a bludgeon.'[62] Bertrand Russell, convinced of 'a difference of average innate capacity' between Jews and non-Jews, concurred: 'Jews are able, and because they are able, gentile contempt for them is tinged with fear. If they were as unintelligent as the gypsies, they would be as little hated.'[63] The Bishop of Durham agreed that Jews were victimized because of their 'greater intelligence' than other Germans.[64]

Reinforcing such attitudes, and one of the most potent forces for philosemitism during the interwar period (and subsequently) was the unique status enjoyed by Albert Einstein as the 'world's cleverest man' and greatest scientist of the century. The plight of Einstein and other Jewish intellectuals during the Nazi years drew, as indicated in chapter 5, deep sympathy from many quarters; this was especially true of the United States, where science and university-based learning were highly respected.[65] The reputations of Einstein, Freud and others also helped to form and solidify the image of Jews as uniquely gifted at many intellectual pursuits such as theoretical science, mathematics and music. It has led to many attempts to explain the unquestionably gross over-representation of Jews among Nobel Prize winners and other leading modern intellectuals, for example by C.P. (Lord) Snow, who in 1960 wrote memorably that 'the Jews, who have not been lucky in much, have obviously been lucky in their genes' and offered a controversial explanation for their domination of many intellectual fields.[66]

'Elitist' philosemitism can be seen, too, underpinning the Zionism of gentiles whose advocacy of a Palestine repopulated and redeveloped by Jews had political and economic considerations. It occurred in the *Spectator* during 1845, which observed that the Jews, with their 'superior intelligence, industry, and wealth' would teach the native Arabs 'steady and industrious habits' and be 'in every way' an asset to the region.[67] And it occurred in the following passage written in 1861:

[The] Hebrew ... traces back the line of his ancestry into ages that long preceded the rise of the oldest monarchy now on the earth. His fathers were powerful princes, governing flourishing kingdoms, and ruling over a polished and civilised people, well acquainted with literature and the arts ... He has wealth; he is the great capitalist of the world. For his vast wealth he would find ample room in building roads, laying down railways, rebuilding his ancient cities, and developing the ... resources of his land. To any other people such a task would be impossible. To the Jew it would be easy ... In fine Syria would be safe only in the hands of a brave, independent and spirited people ... Such a people we have in the Jews.[68]

There are signs of it, too, in the comments of some British travellers returning from Palestine during the Mandate. One, for instance, contrasted the 'progressive intellect' of the Jewish pioneers there with the 'stationary intellect' of the Arab population.[69] Another, disgusted by 'the dirty, inefficient and greedy *baksheesh*-hunters' who seemed to be ubiquitous, seeing Arabs as 'shiftless, shambling creatures ready to collapse at the first hint of adversity', and seeing the Jews as 'industrious, enterprising and adult ... superior in energy, talent and industry', returned full of burgeoning 'rage' towards pro-Arab fellow-countrymen. When he tackled some of them, saying that the Arabs 'seemed a lot of lazy and incompetent louts', he was 'instantly subjected to recitals of the oppressions the Arabs had had to bear under Turkish misrule. No doubt they have, but the Jews have suffered the extremes of persecution ... yet they have maintained their spirit and their fortitude, and Israel, under their cultivation, blossomed in the past, as it is beginning to blossom in the present, like a rose.'[70]

While only rarely discussed or examined, elite philosemitism was an important element in winning sympathy for Jews, a factor which has been seriously underestimated in accounts of Jewish–Gentile relations. It was especially important in those societies within the English-speaking world, particularly the United States, which placed emphasis on individual achievement, regarded the individual achiever as the prime mover of society, and created institutions, especially in the field of education, which deliberately facilitated upward social mobility and individual achievement. In these societies the very qualities of ability and achievement which made the Jew so hated and feared in continental Europe made him often widely admired.

Epilogue

10 'The Jewish Emergence from Powerlessness': Philosemitism in the Contemporary World, 1945 to the Present

The nature and importance of philosemitism changed fundamentally after the Second World War, such that only with difficulty can a direct link always be seen with the manifestations of philosemitism from the century after 1840 which are discussed in this book. To state the matter briefly, since 1945, largely because of the Holocaust, the Western world has been transformed from a place where antisemitism was apparently the norm and philosemitism the exception to one in which philosemitism is the norm and antisemitism the exception. Indeed, antisemitism in the mainstream has declined to such an extent that it has virtually disappeared, or may well be seen as on the way to disappearance within a generation or two. Alongside this decline in antisemitism has come another, probably related, change: an obvious increase in the power and ability of the Jewish people to influence relevant events, a change most centrally illustrated by the creation of the State of Israel in 1948. Indeed, many observers have seen the formation of the Jewish state as 'the Jewish emergence from powerlessness', as Yehuda Bauer put it.[1] In the Diaspora, direct and apparently successful attempts by a fully legitimate 'Jewish lobby' to influence governments in order to secure Jewish interests, especially the security of Israel, have become ubiquitous in all countries with a significant Jewish population, the United States in particular.

Together, these changes have fundamentally altered the circumstances in which any demonstrations of support for, or admiration of, the Jewish people occur, especially in response to antisemitism. What might be termed the 'balance of power' between Jews and non-Jews has altered fundamentally, so that Jews are far more advantageously placed than in the past. They rely far less than before 1945 upon salient support from influential non-Jews to achieve their goals or defeat their enemies, and far more upon their own resources. The central focus of Jewish concern and indeed of Jewish identity during the past 50 years, the maintenance of the State of Israel in security, is itself the most important manifestation of the fundamental change which has occurred in this 'balance of power'. While most Jews and influential Jewish groups of course welcome the support of non-Jews, since the Holocaust and the re-establishment of Israel there is a widespread sense that reliance on powerful non-Jewish friends is itself demeaning and a relic of the days of the ghetto and of Jewish powerlessness. Non-Jewish supporters and admirers of the Jews may, in the decades since 1945, paradoxically be less welcome than in the past, at the very time when they are even more numerous than before the Second World War, and often motivated by sincere feelings of remorse for the antisemitism of previous generations, especially the Holocaust.

Other fundamental changes have affected the nature of philosemitism in the postwar world. Increasingly since 1945 there has occurred what might be termed the 'normalization' of Jewish history and of the Jewish experience, such that post-exilic Jewish history is now seen as an integral and legitimate part of Western history, and the Jews as a legitimate component of the mainstream of Western humanity rather than outside of it. This normalization has been caused by many factors. There has occurred an evolution in the nature of historiography from an emphasis on 'kings, dates, and battles' and other aspects of 'High Politics', which naturally excluded the Jewish experience until very recently, to a more all-embracing social history. Guilt over the Holocaust and other varieties of antisemitism, the success, since emancipation, of so many Jews in so many fields, and the presence of a disproportionate number of Jews in academia and among the intelligentsia, especially in the United States, have also contributed to the legitimation of the Jewish experience. The virulence of antisemitism and the treatment of Jews in a particular society is increasingly seen as (to use a phrase often employed) a 'litmus test' of the stability of that society and, by definition, of the health of a society's democratic institutions, and have, for these reasons, attracted the attention of more and more historians. Another important area of the 'normalization' of the Jewish presence is religious: since the Second World War Judaism as a religion has increasingly been seen as just another Western faith, dissimilar to Christianity only because it is older, and the ancestral religion of the other Western faiths. Almost without exception, Judaism's rejection of the divinity of Jesus is no longer seen as execrable, but as irrelevant: the traditional Jewish position, that God granted His revelation to the Jewish people at Mount Sinai, and that this revelation, and God's election of the Jewish people, has not been negated by the life of Jesus, is now almost universally accepted in the Christian mainstream. Since the Second World War, and despite their very small numbers, Jews have increasingly been regarded as fully equal to the larger religious sects of the majority.

In the United States this equality was suggested most famously in Will Herberg's 1955 study of American religion in the 1950s, *Protestant–Catholic–Jew: An Essay in American Religious Sociology* (New York, 1955). To this day, there are certainly millions of Americans who believe that Jews are far more numerous than they actually are (about 2.5 per cent of the American population) and somehow fully equal in size to the vastly larger Protestant and Catholic communities. This numerical equality is also implied in the titles of interfaith groups such as the Council of Christians and Jews. Many civic occasions in contemporary America begin, as a matter of course, with a benediction recited by a Protestant minister, a Catholic priest and a rabbi, and there are few public ceremonials which would exclude a rabbi as speaking on behalf of a faith which is insignificant or marginal, let alone illegitimate. In Britain, where Jews today comprise only 0.6 per cent of the population, the Chief Rabbi of the day has, for the past 30 years or so, possibly been the most visible and widely interviewed non-Anglican theologian in Britain. The two most recent British Chief Rabbis, Immanuel Jakobovits and Jonathan Sacks, have been interviewed by the press and media certainly nearly as frequently as the Archbishop of Westminster, the spiritual leader of Britain's much larger Catholic community. Margaret Thatcher, Britain's arch-Conservative Prime Minister from 1979 until 1990, was well known to have been particularly friendly to Rabbi Jakobovits, an avowed conservative whose views were frequently contrasted with the 'wet' left-liberalism and semi-Marxism of many Church of England leaders. Mrs Thatcher gave a life peerage to Jakobovits in 1987 and in other ways showed her sympathy for the Jewish community. By the mid-1980s her Cabinet had five Jews in it simultaneously, leading Harold Macmillan, before his death in 1986, to make the famous witticism that it contained 'more old Estonians than old Etonians'.

Unrelated to these factors are a number of others which have also altered the situation immeasurably since the time before the Second

World War. Since 1945 Jewish self-defence and anti-defamation groups have mushroomed, become far more visible and outspoken than before the war, and have generally achieved an immediate and direct access to government leaders. This has been a hallmark of Jewish politics during the postwar era, especially in the United States, where the so-called 'Jewish lobby' has emerged as among the most powerful in Washington. Effective Jewish lobbying groups have also emerged in most other Western nations with significant Jewish populations. Secondly, the period since about 1960 may be sharply distinguished from any previous time – including the early postwar years – in that virtually every Western nation has enacted legislation forbidding discrimination against Jews (and other minorities) in areas such as employment, the provision of public services, the sale and rental of housing, and the like. Almost as often, most countries have made racist incitement illegal. Some countries have gone further, outlawing so-called 'Holocaust denial' propaganda spread by neo-Nazi and antisemitic groups, and have made membership in such groups virtually illegal. Such laws, it should be realized, are quite new: no such laws existed at the national level in the United States, Britain, Australia or Canada before the mid-1960s. The American law prohibiting discrimination against religious minorities in employment and the provision of public services was enacted by New York State only in 1945. Similar legislation at a national level in the United States had to wait until the passage of the Civil Rights Act of 1964. Great Britain passed similar legislation only in 1966.

In addition to all of this, other broader trends have facilitated the decline of antisemitism. Demographically, since 1948 the Jewish people have increasingly lived in numbers in only two places, the State of Israel and the 'New Diaspora' of the West, especially the United States. The demographic effects of the Holocaust on European Jewry, the emigration of most of the survivors to Israel or the West, and the flight of virtually all Afro-Asian Jews to Israel, have had the inadvertent and unintentional effect of sharply decreasing the number of Jews who lived in countries and regimes where they were persecuted or likely to be persecuted. After the early 1950s, only one substantial group of Jews continued to live in a society which engendered antisemitism as a matter of course, the 2.5 million Jews of the Soviet Union. By 1991 the Soviet Union had ceased to exist and its Jews were free to emigrate or to live, for the first time in a thousand years, in freedom in Russia and the other Soviet successor states. By the end of the twentieth century not more than 25,000 Jews, far less than 1 per cent of the world's Jewish population, lived in such countries as Iran and Syria which could be termed antisemitic. One hundred years earlier, the majority of the world's Jews had lived in countries like Russia, Romania and Turkey where they were officially persecuted as a matter of policy, while most of the rest lived in countries (like Germany) with minor but vexing antisemitic restrictions or in countries (like France) where antisemitic movements were rife. At that time the Jews knew genuine freedom perhaps only in the English-speaking world, and even here nativist and socialist antisemitic barriers, especially in the social sphere, were frequently encountered, whatever the genuine traditions of democracy and toleration of those societies.

As well, Jews experienced another drastic change in the decades since 1945: the virtual disappearance of the Jewish working class and the movement into the upper middle classes of virtually the entire Jewish people, certainly of the majority. And while Jewish entrepreneurial abilities continued as before, with Jews, if anything, perhaps more overrepresented in the economic elites of the Western world than previously, this largely occurred in capitalist societies where Jewish wealth and business acumen attracted little attention or hostility, or even notice.

Standing behind everything, it could be argued, has been the impact of the Holocaust upon the permissibility of subsequent antisemitism in deed or word. Once the Holocaust became internalized among the intelligentsia and later among the general public, the explicit enunciation of antisemitism in virtually any form became one of the most unbreakable of contemporary taboos. Negative stereotypic depictions of Jews, of the kind formerly commonplace in popular fiction like detective stories, simply vanished by the 1950s.[2] By the 1980s the Holocaust itself had become one of the most infamous events in modern history, an evil without parallel and without explanation, the subject of a thousand books and documentaries, and even more fascinating in its evil, perhaps, to today's students than in the past. The centrality of the Holocaust in Western consciousness did not begin at once, a fact which has been widely noted. For the past 15 years or so after the end of the war, very little was written about the Holocaust, and its singularity and centrality appears not to have penetrated into the consciousness of, for instance, most non-Jewish Englishmen until long afterwards. Indeed, as late as the early 1960s many well-informed Englishmen often likened Auschwitz to the firebombings of Dresden in early 1945 by the Royal Air Force, an analogy which today might well only be drawn by neo-Nazis. Into the 1970s or even later, Auschwitz was frequently linked with the atomic bombing of Hiroshima as twin symbols of the limits of modern evil.[3] Again, fewer people would wish to make such a comparison today: the scale of destruction in the Nazi extermination camps was vastly greater than the atomic bombing of Hiroshima, which, as controversial as it was, was carried out explicitly to shorten the war against Japan. Since Japan surrendered within a few weeks of the Hiroshima and Nagasaki bombings, the aim of the Americans was achieved; indeed, probably hundreds of thousands of lives which would have been lost in an Allied invasion of Japan in the absence of a quick surrender were thereby saved. As well, while Auschwitz and the other extermination camps functioned as part of an attempt by the Nazis to achieve a racially-based totalitarian empire throughout Europe, Hiroshima and Nagasaki were bombed in order to overthrow Japanese fascism, bring democracy to that country and liberate the millions of Asians enslaved by Japanese expansionism. Only in the 1980s, perhaps, did the Holocaust become so central a part of Western consciousness.

The effects of all of these profound changes have been to alter the nature of philosemitism, from a viewpoint and an emotion by which the strong benefited the weak, to a stance between equals, or at least between groups which are more equal than in the past. Since 1945, too, rather than always welcoming the assistance and help of sympathetic non-Jewish supporters, Jews often mistrust such support and more often regard it as patronizing if not the product of post-Holocaust gentile guilt. The creation of the State of Israel and its increasing centrality to most Jews has also affected the sources of philosemitism. While before 1939 the ideological sources of philosemitism in the English-speaking world have always been surprisingly varied, by and large most liberals were more sympathetic to the plight of the Jews, and opposed to the oppression of the Jews on religious, cultural and nationalistic grounds, than were conservatives. The creation of Israel, and its maintenance as a pro-American, pro-Western bastion, its enemies being revolutionary terrorists and Marxist regimes, has altered this to a considerable degree, as has the perception of successive Israeli governments as oppressors of the Palestinians. After 1967, and certainly until the collapse of Communism in the late 1980s and the Oslo Accords of 1993, Israeli policy and even the existence of the State of Israel became the targets of the extreme left throughout the Western world, while Israel was most likely to be supported by moderate, old-fashioned social democrats or by mainstream conservatives.[4] Increasingly, too, a source of support for the State of Israel has emerged which most Jews – wrongly – regard as entirely novel and which many Jews mistrust: fundamentalist Protestants, especially in the United States, who see in the reemergence of Israel signs of the fulfilment of Biblical prophecy.[5]

Because so much has changed during the past half-century, ironically one can probably identify fewer areas of philosemitic activity in the English-speaking world than in the century before the Second World War, although there is much less antisemitic hostility to Jews than ever before. Indeed, one can point with assurance to only a handful of areas in which philosemitic support for Jews by non-Jews has continued in the old manner.

One such area has been in the field of interfaith activities, although even here there are significant and even fundamental changes in the nature of the relationship between Jews and non-Jews. The Second World War and postwar years saw the formal initiation of bodies dedicated to producing better relations between Jews and Christians. In Britain, as mentioned in chapter 5, the Council of Christians and Jews was formally initiated early in 1942.[6] The obvious immediate background to the group's formation was the Holocaust. By early 1942, it was widely known in the West that the Nazis had carried out horrendous massacres, of a kind probably unprecedented in modern history, in the course of their invasion of the Soviet Union, which began in June 1941. (The gas chambers, and the systematic attempt to exterminate European Jewry, which commenced at that time, were not known in the West until October–December 1942.) The 'Nazi attack on Jewry' was specifically cited in the resolutions of 20 March 1942 forming the Council.[7] Both Christian and Jewish leaders were, at first, for the most part extremely wary of the new venture, fearing that the Council would compromise their beliefs. Orthodox Jewish leaders were (and often are) especially hostile to interfaith dialogue of anything more than a superficial kind. The Christian members of the Council repeatedly lobbied the British government to do more to assist Jewish victims of Nazi persecution, although there was virtually nothing that the British government could do.[8] On the future of Palestine, the initial attitude of the Council was to favour greater generosity towards the admission of Jewish 'displaced persons' after the end of the war. In September 1947, the Council expressed its 'profound dismay' at the harsh treatment by the Attlee government of the *Exodus* refugees, who were returned to refugee camps in Germany after being refused entry to Palestine.[9]

With Israeli independence secured in 1948, however, the attitude of the Christian churches associated with the Council changed, becoming progressively more uneasy and eventually more hostile. Some disquiet was expressed from the first days of Israel's existence about the failure to create an internationalized Jerusalem or to safeguard the Christian holy places.[10] After the 1967 War, many Protestant Churches took a public stance against Israel's occupation of the West Bank and its handling of the Palestinian question, which many Jews took to be one-sided, if not worse. The Council of Christians and Jews found itself criticized by many Jews for being insufficiently supportive of Israel and also attacked by many Christians for being insufficiently hostile.[11] From the 1970s, many Protestant Churches and church groups produced reports and statements specifically critical of Israeli policy, in ways and with a rhetoric which many Jews regarded as unfair. This movement among some church groups to an anti-Israel stance may have to a limited extent been occasioned by old-style theological antisemitism, but certainly to a greater degree by a number of other factors. Many Western Churches had branches and members in the Middle East, including the West Bank and Israel itself, and naturally represented their perspective, often one bitterly hostile to Israeli occupation (but also sometimes to Islamic fundamentalism.) More importantly, the Protestant Churches had come, from the 1960s until the 1990s, to be dominated by leftist champions of the Third World, often thinly disguised Marxists who were invariably hostile to the West, to the United States, American military involvement, 'neo-colonialism' and capitalism, and who were as outspoken in their condemnation of the West as they were mute on the evils of Communism. This ideology became particularly dominant in international church bodies such as the World Council of Churches, but also within components of the leadership elements of many churches.[12] By the 1980s Israel came to be seen as one of the major targets of the international left, including the clerical left. A pro-American Western bastion in the Third World, to some on the far left it came to be seen as an illegitimate pariah state not much different from South Africa.[13] British Jews and supporters of Israel were compelled, in the 1980s, to deal with a stream of hostile reports and statements from church sources on Israel which they regarded as extremely one-sided, for instance the Christian Aid video *Palestine: Much Promised Land* (1988) and the British Council of Churches' *Impressions of Intifada* (1989).[14] Similar statements have been issued from Protestant church groups around the world.[15] In contrast to left-leaning Christians, the most pro-Zionist component of Western Protestantism was often the 'Christian Right', the vocal Protestant fundamentalists, especially the so-called 'Moral Majority', in the United States. One 1995 survey found that 'after American Jews, the strongest supporters of Israel in the United States are white evangelical Protestants'.[16] About 250,000 American Evangelical Protestants visit Israel every year, more than the total number of American Jews who visit Israel.[17] The Roman Catholic Church was moving in the opposite direction. Before the Second World War it was unquestionably more antisemitic than were most Protestant Churches, especially those in the English-speaking world. As this book has shown, many Protestants and secular liberals were hostile to Catholicism in part *because* of its strong association with antisemitism, seen as a barbaric relic of Catholic medievalism. In Europe from 1870 until the Second World War, the Catholic Church was often closely associated with ultra-conservative 'integral nationalist' movements which were strongly antisemitic. During the Second World War, the failure of Pope Pius XII publicly to condemn the Holocaust is notorious, while such regimes as Horthy's in Hungary and Tiso's in Slovakia were both Catholic clericalist and close allies of Hitler. (On the other hand, it must also in fairness be noted that the Catholic Church deeply mistrusted Nazi Germany and in no way supported Nazi genocide; the suffering of Catholic Poles under Nazism was second only to the suffering of the Jews, and the important left-of-centre Christian Democratic movement, closely associated with the Catholic church, emerged at this time throughout Western Europe.) After the Second World War, the Vatican apparently acted as the provider of a secret 'underground railway' which allowed hundreds of Nazi war criminals to escape justice and flee to safety in Latin America and other predominantly Catholic countries. Even in the English-speaking world, Catholics were often long regarded with suspicion by Jews, who feared that their bitter hostility to Communism often had an antisemitic edge.

With the coming of the Second Vatican Council in the early 1960s, all this was to change dramatically. The most important step in this evolution of contemporary Catholic attitudes was the publication of *Nostra Aetate*, a 1965 Papal encyclical which stressed the Catholic Church's origins in Judaism. In particular, it explicitly noted that 'the Jews remain very near to God', a near-total reversal of Catholicism's traditional view that in rejecting the divinity of Jesus, the Jews had abandoned God and were no longer His Chosen People. In 1974,

1985 and 1988 came three important church guidelines on presenting the Jews and Judaism to Catholics in statements and educational material. In 1980 Pope John Paul II stated explicitly that the ancient Covenant between God and the Jews 'had never been revoked'.[18] While the evolution of the Church's attitude to the Jews began well before Pope John Paul II assumed office in 1978, it has obviously been highly significant to recent developments that John Paul, the first non-Italian pope in centuries, was a Pole with Jewish friends in pre-Holocaust Poland and an anti-Nazi resistance fighter during the war. At the end of the twentieth century, Jewish–Catholic relations were arguably better than they had been since Christianity became the official religion of the Roman Empire under Constantine. Contemporary Catholics appear to be attracted to Jews and Judaism for much the same reason as some Protestants were in the past: today's Jews represent a living link with the Bible at a time when the authenticity of orthodox religious belief is under sustained threat from secularism. In addition, Catholics appear to be genuinely ashamed and remorseful over the role which the Catholic Church played in fomenting antisemitism down the ages and over its silence during the Holocaust.

Yet problems obviously remain. By the 1990s American Catholic textbooks were purged of most, but not all, gratuitously negative references to Biblical Judaism.[19] The issue of a Carmelite convent at Auschwitz was unresolved for years. The most important issue of contention, however, probably remained Israel. The Vatican established diplomatic relations with Israel only in the late 1990s and certainly has never recognized Israeli sovereignty over the whole of Jerusalem. (For decades the Vatican officially supported the internationalization of Jerusalem.) A significant proportion of Palestinians (and Lebanese) are Eastern Christians whose Churches are in communion with Rome. Despite making innumerable trips around the world, the present Pope has never visited Israel and its Christian holy places, in curious and vexing contrast to his undoubted philosemitism, and in contrast to his predecessor, Pope Paul VI, who visited Israel in January 1964 (before the Six Day War and its gains for Israel). Nevertheless, Catholic–Jewish relations are probably better now than those between Protestants and Jews, especially those mainstream and left-of-centre Protestant sects with an anti-Western political agenda, one which has, since 1967, almost inevitably been anti-Israel. The sphere of interfaith activities well illustrates the evolution of philosemitism in the recent past. Before the Second

World War, the actively philosemitic cleric or religious leader was the exception, one welcomed by most Jews (despite suspicions about conversionists) for the influence he could bring to bear on Western national 'Establishments' to ameliorate conditions for Jews in oppressive, antisemitic regimes. Today, Jews have considerably more power than in the past and a greater ability to influence events. They are not consciously reliant on the support of non-Jews. Nevertheless, there is today considerably more Christian philosemitism than in past generations. When there is hostility to Jews, this characteristically takes the form of mistrust of the exercise of Jewish national power in the State of Israel, by Christian groups which perceive that exercise as oppressive to the Palestinians. The situation of Jews and Christians today illustrates how fundamentally relations between the two have changed since 1945.

Another notable area of postwar philosemitism has been support by non-Jews for the State of Israel, especially when Israel's existence appears to have been directly threatened by the Arabs. This book has indicated the long history of Zionist philosemitism and the importance of gentile Zionists in helping to make the Zionist dream a reality. Zionist philosemitism was at least as important to the establishment of the State of Israel in 1947–8 than at any time before, especially the crucial support given by President Harry S. Truman to the creation of Israel.[20] Truman was at least as sympathetic to the Jewish people as was his predecessor Franklin D. Roosevelt. In Britain, opposition to the postwar Labour government's pro-Arab policy came from both Conservative Zionists like Winston Churchill and from Labour Zionists like Richard Crossman. In Australia, surprisingly, crucial support for the creation of Israel was provided by Foreign Minister Dr H.V. Evatt, who was chairman of the UN Ad Hoc Committee which decided, in 1947, on partition of the Palestine Mandate, thus leading to the creation of the Jewish State. Evatt was apparently motivated by sympathy for Jewish suffering in the Holocaust and by effective Zionist lobbying.[21] Even before the birth of Israel in May 1948, American public opinion had hardened in support of the state's creation. While Americans holding 'no opinion' about the future of Palestine had made up one-half of the population at the beginning of 1948, by March of that year a public opinion survey asking 'If Jews independently set up a Jewish state [in Palestine] should the United States support them?', found that 50 per cent of Protestants and 44 per cent of Catholics answered 'Yes', compared with only 10 per cent of Protestants and 14 per cent of

Catholics who said 'No'.[22] This clear majority for the Zionist goal at a time when very considerable amounts of social antisemitism continued to exist in the United States is very significant and presaged the continuing support given to Israel by Americans at most junctures since 1948, especially after the early 1970s.

Nevertheless, it is apparent that support by non-Jews for Israel peaked in 1967 at the time of the Six Day War. In June 1967, five Arab armies attacked Israel with the explicit aim of destroying the Jewish state. It seemed to many, just before Israel's extraordinary victory, that a second Holocaust was at hand, and what might be described as a wave of popular philosemitism swept the Western world. At this time literally thousands of non-Jews attended rallies, contributed to Israeli causes, donated blood and even volunteered to serve in the Israeli armies. In Britain, 100 non-Jews were among 500 volunteers assembling in London in early June 1967, before the war began, to leave for Israel where they were to perform civilian jobs vacated by Israelis called up to military service.[23] A non-Jewish body representing 3,000 British ex-servicemen also volunteered to fight for Israel at this time.[24] Innumerable well-known non-Jewish British figures in cultural life signed petitions in support of Israel, ranging from Anglo-Catholic commentator Malcolm Muggeridge to Roger Moore and even Vanessa Redgrave (later more renowned for her outspoken support of the PLO).[25] A public opinion poll taken at this time found that 46 per cent of Britons supported Israel, only 4 per cent 'Egypt and other countries', while 19 per cent actually wanted Britain to fight in support of Israel.[26] By mid-June 1,230 non-Jews had registered to do voluntary work in Israel while the war was raging, including 'a number of middle-aged farmers, mainly from Essex and Scotland', who 'volunteered to help in Israel's harvest'.[27] Similar scenes of popular philosemitism were seen around the world, even in Germany: for instance, 2,500 people attended a pro-Israel rally in Frankfurt.[28] Editorial commentary around the Western world was almost – but not quite – unanimous in support of Israel, ranging in sophistication from the British church press to crude tabloids. While the *Church Times*, the weekly Anglican newspaper, expressed the gratitude of 'the whole Christian world' to 'the brilliance of Israel's generals and the courage of her soldiers' for minimizing damage to Jerusalem during the war, in Brisbane, Queensland, the gutter tabloid *Sunday Truth* produced an editorial entitled 'Full Dues to the Jews' which opined:

whether you like Jews or you don't like Jews, you have got to really dip your lids at their fantastic military achievement last week ... Allah had been called to stand by for the annihilation of the entire Jewish race. And look what happened. In four short days the Jews took on everybody at once and belted the living daylights out of them.[29]

This mood was, of course, too good to last. Even in 1967, a significant part of the mainstream left in the West had already expressed reservations about the fact that so many Arabs had come under Israeli occupation, while the problem of the Palestinian refugees had in no sense been resolved by the Six Day War.[30] At the same time, most of the Marxist left turned fiercely against Israel, with the Soviet Union and all of its satellites except Romania severing diplomatic relations. Mainstream enthusiasm for Israel, however, continued, although it was gradually dented by the 1973 Yom Kippur War (with its accompanying Arab oil embargo of the West) and, in particular, by the very controversial 1982 Lebanon war, in which most mainstream media and opinion-makers turned unreservedly against Israel.

Nevertheless, in the United States at any rate, the position of Israel in the esteem of millions of Americans actually increased steadily from the 1970s onwards. Increasingly, Israel was portrayed as a reliable American ally and security asset in the Middle East, one of America's firmest allies in the world. Largely as a result, American public opinion appeared to consolidate in Israel's favour at a time when elite opinion often declined, at least compared with its apogee in 1967.[31] Assiduous support for Israel by the universally respected (and feared) 'Jewish lobby' in America also helped to explain the extraordinary levels of support for Israel by successive American presidents and in Congress, but this factor alone is probably insufficient to explain the remarkably high support for Israel in Washington, DC, approaching unanimity. Logically, if the 'Jewish vote' is perceived as important to the electoral success of a Congressman, this will help to account for the support of legislators from states with large Jewish populations, like New York or New Jersey. However, it will not explain the degree of support, often as firm (or firmer) for Israel by Congressmen from states where there are virtually no Jews, and the 'Jewish vote' cannot possibly influence the outcome of elections. Some realists have tried to explain this largely in terms of Jewish financial contributions to favoured candidates, but this is obviously not the full story.[32] Many conservatives, especially fundamentalist

Christians associated with the 'Moral Majority', not merely support Israel in general but overtly side with Likud and their maximalist demands for Jewish control over as much of the West Bank as is possible. (A recent example of this is the former Speaker of the US House of Representatives, Newt Gingrich, an extreme conservative from Georgia.) American liberals (except on the extreme left) continue to support Israel, albeit perhaps in a more muted way than a generation ago, as obviously preferable to the violently anti-American radical regimes of the area. Overt Congressional criticism of Israel, except on rare occasions, is also seldom heard, and appears to be based in perceptions of both mutual interest and shared ideals. The importance of the Holocaust as the universal symbol of evil, now universally internalized, is obviously extremely important.

For all of these reasons, the historical typology of philosemitism analysed in this book needs to be modified in the light of the experience of the postwar world. All the strands described still exist and can still be readily identified without too much difficulty. Nevertheless, they exist today in a vastly different situation from that before the Second World War, one in which the Jewish people are much more powerful than formerly, their experience and history much more normal and less marginal, and, above all, antisemitism is weaker. Indeed, it may be possible realistically to speak of the twenty-first century as the time when antisemitism may effectively disappear as a phenomenon of any more than curiosity value, a situation which, indeed, may well already exist today. There are historical precedents for the disappearance of once virulent forms of religious and ethnic hostility. In particular, anti-Catholicism has virtually disappeared in the English-speaking world (with the obvious exception of Northern Ireland). Yet during the nineteenth century, anti-Catholicism in Protestant countries was probably as important and pervasive as antisemitism. The American 'Know-Nothing' party of the 1850s, organized as a virulently anti-Catholic movement to oppose Irish immigration, won important elections in several states. (In contrast, no specifically antisemitic party of importance was ever established in the United States.) In Britain, centuries of Protestant hostility to Catholicism included the campaign by Lord John Russell against so-called 'Papal Aggression' in 1850 and also underpinned much of the support for Ulster and for Unionism after the mid-1880s.[33] In Australia the 'sectarian struggle' between Protestants (especially Scottish-origin Presbyterians) and Irish Catholics was a major feature of politics into the 1970s. Even in Wilhelmine Germany, Bismarck's

Kulturkampf was aimed at Catholics, not Jews. Despite all of this, anti-Catholicism is so forgotten today in the English-speaking world that few realize it ever existed, and it has probably attracted much less examination by recent historians than antisemitism, although it was arguably far more important. The decline of anti-Catholicism, so that today the latter is literally forgotten, may well be paralleled in the next generation by a similar decline in antisemitism, something which indeed has already happened to a considerable extent. The two cases are not exactly similar, of course, and the memory of the Holocaust and its central place in Western consciousness will probably always ensure that the historical legacy of hostility to Jews continues to be remembered. Nevertheless, if antisemitism does vanish as a force of any consequence, it is more important than ever that the non-Jewish friends and partisans of the Jewish people, who sustained and supported the Jews in times of peril and adversity, be remembered and their beliefs and achievements recorded for all to know.

Notes

1 'BARBARISM AND BIGOTRY'

1. Figures derived from Arthur Ruppin, *The Jewish Fate and Future* (London: 1940), Table 1, p. 29. Ruppin's figures are for 1850.
2. Ibid.
3. Ibid.
4. On the emancipation of the Jews, see Jacob Katz, *Out of the Ghetto: The Social Background of Jewish Emancipation, 1770–1870* (New York: 1978).
5. See M.C.N. Salbstein, *The Emancipation of the Jews in Britain: The Question of the Admission of the Jews to Parliament, 1828–1860* (London: 1982).
6. See Jonathan Sarna, 'The Impact of the American Revolution on American Jews', in idem., ed., *The American Jewish Experience* (New York: 1986); Eli Faber, *A Time for Planting: The First Migration 1654–1820* (Baltimore: 1992) and Hasia R. Diner, *A Time for Gathering: The Second Migration 1820–1880* (Baltimore: 1992; vols. 1 and 2 of *The Jewish People in America* series). Recent works on American anti-semitism which, in our view, overstate its volume and importance include Leonard Dinnerstein, *Antisemitism in America* (New York: 1994), and Frederic Cople Jaher, *A Scapegoat in the Wilderness: The Origins and Rise of Anti-Semitism in America* (Cambridge, Mass.: 1994). On Australia, see Israel Getzler, *Neither Toleration nor Favour: The Australian Chapter of Jewish Emancipation* (Melbourne: 1970); Hilary L. Rubinstein, *The Jews in Australia: A Thematic History. Volume One: 1788–1945* (Melbourne: 1991), pp. 3–24, 471–8.
7. See W.D. Rubinstein, *A History of the Jews in the English-Speaking World: Great Britain* (London: 1996), pp. 1-27.
8. For a comprehensive account of events see Jonathan Frankel, *The Damascus Affair: 'Ritual Murder', Politics, and the Jews in 1840* (Cambridge: 1997). The Jewish population of Damascus is believed to have been about 5,000; the total Syrian population was perhaps 100,000. Ibid., p. 32.
9. See ibid., pp. 69–72 for an overview of the Rhodes case.
10. Ibid., pp. 145–6, 207–11 quotation at p. 144. In addition to the press comment cited by Frankel, see *Chambers' Edinburgh Journal*, 4 July 1840, which called the blood libel and arrest a 'barbarous atrocity'; *Protestant Magazine*, 1 June 1840; *Morning Post*, 23 August 1843, quoted in *Voice of Jacob*, 1 September 1843.
11. For a survey of the religious polemics surrounding the allegation, see Frankel, op. cit., pp. 262–9. The British businessman and banker referred to, E. Kilbee, who transmitted charitable donations (*chalukhah*) collected by European Jewry for the benefit of Jews in

Palestine, had alerted a Jewish contact in Amsterdam about developments in Damascus in a letter received on 18 March. See ibid., pp. 66, 75, 84, 201, 299.
12. *The Times* of 25 June 1840 went so far as to observe that if it was indeed true that Jews made use of Christian blood, 'the Jewish religion must at once disappear off the face of the earth'. This came in reaction to the allegations of a Romanian Jewish apostate, first made in 1803, which appeared in *The Times* on the same day. These remarks should be seen in context amid general goodwill towards Jews in the paper's editorials and its correspondence columns.
13. Frankel, op. cit., pp. 211–12; *Christian Observer*, November 1840, pp. 702–2; *Protestant Magazine*, 1 June 1840; *Tablet*, 6 June 1840. The (anonymous) editor of the *Protestant Magazine*, Charlotte Elizabeth Tonna, had earlier declared in the *Christian Lady's Magazine* (January 1840, p. 89) that Protestants had a two-fold purpose: 'With one hand to throw a shield over the Jew, with the other to aim a vigorous thrust at Papal Rome.' A few Christian leaders, such as 'A Minister of the Established Church' writing in *The Times* (26 August 1840), supported the allegations, while the occurrences at Damascus and Rhodes were ignored by some religious journals.
14. See W.T. Gidney, *The History of the London Society for Promoting Christianity Amongst the Jews, from 1809 to 1908* (London: 1908); Mel Scult, 'English Missions to the Jews – Conversion in the Age of Emancipation,' *Jewish Social Studies*, vol. 35 (1973), pp. 3–17. The *Jewish Chronicle*, 22 February 1850, in a scathing attack upon McCaul, called the Hebrew College 'the Conversion College – the school for educating conversion missionaries'.
15. Alexander McCaul, *Reasons for Believing that the Charge lately Revived against the Jewish People is a baseless Falsehood* (London: 1840); *The Times*, 15 July 1840.
16. *The British Magazine, and Monthly Register of Religious and Ecclesiastical Information*, 1 August 1840.
17. Frankel, op. cit., p. 126 et seq. Ten years later Palmerston ordered a blockade of the Greek coast in support of the compensation claim of the pillaged, Athens-based, Jewish moneylender Don Pacifico, who claimed British citizenship since he had been born in Gibraltar. *Times*, 26 June 1850; *Jewish Chronicle*, 5 November 1903.
18. Frankel, op. cit., pp. 194–6.
19. See Louis Loewe, ed., *Diaries of Sir Moses and Lady Montefiore*, 2 vols. (London: 1890); *Voice of Jacob*, 29 October 1841.
20. For discrimination against Jews in the City of London and its gradual erosion, see David Kynaston, *The City of London, Volume 1: A World of its Own, 1815–1890* (London: 1994), pp. 20–1, 23, 53–4, 62, 92, 252–3, 270; *Voice of Jacob*, 26 May 1843; *Jewish Chronicle*, 8 January 1847; *Douglas Jerrold's Weekly Newspaper* (n.d.), quoted ibid., 16 July 1847. The change was partly ascribed to the influence with the urban middle class of the philosemitic Duke of Sussex. See also W.D. Rubinstein, *A History of the Jews in the English-Speaking World: Great Britain* (London: 1996), pp. 54–5, 74–6.

21. See, for example, Hereford Town Council meeting, ibid., 14 March 1851; Norwich Town Council petition, ibid., 28 April 1853; text of petition from Lord Mayor, Alderman and Common Council of the City of London, ibid., 11 March 1853.
22. For Salomons, see *Dictionary of National Biography*, vol. 17 (London: 1909), pp. 700–1; *Jewish Chronicle*, 18 October 1844. See Hans W. Spiegel, 'An Early English Intervention on Behalf of Foreign Jewry', *Proceedings of the American Jewish Historical Society*, vol. 35 (1939), pp. 213–17, for British government initiatives in the 1740s regarding the threatened expulsion of Jews from Bohemia and Moravia.
23. David Salomons, *An Account of the Recent Persecution of the Jews at Damascus* (London: 1840). Pieritz's findings are itemized in Frankel, op. cit., p. 40.
24. Cf. ibid., p. 225, which claims that 'a broad, interdenominational character' was lacking at the meeting.
25. *The Times*, 4 July 1840; *Jewish Chronicle*, 23 October 1874. Some of those mentioned as attending cannot be precisely identified. For example, the 'Mr. Dent' named in *The Times* report might have been the publisher Joseph Dent, but was in all likelihood the merchant banker Thomas Dent. 'Mr Took' was presumably either the noted economist and free trade advocate Thomas Tooke, or his younger brother, solicitor William Tooke F.R.S., a former Reformer MP; both were prominent in the City.
26. *The Times*, 4 July 1840; *Hansard*, vol. 54 (May–June 1840), 22 June 1840.
27. *The Times*, 4 July 1840. On the envoy's responses see ibid., 24 July 1840; Frankel, op. cit., p. 224.
28. *The Times*, 21 July 1840; Frankel, op. cit., p. 225.
29. Isaac Marcus Jost (editor) in *Israelitische Annalen*, 24 July 1840, and article in *Allgemeine Zeitung des Judentums*, 1 August 1840; both quoted in Frankel, op. cit., p. 253.
30. *Persecution of the Jews in the East. Containing the Proceedings of a Meeting held at the Synagogue Mikveh Israel, Philadelphia ... 27th of August, 1840* (Philadelphia: 1840), pp. 20–3.
31. Joseph L. Blau and Salo W. Baron, eds., *The Jews of the United States: A Documentary History*, vol. 3 (New York: 1963), pp. 940, 942–3; Frankel, op. cit., p. 224.
32. Ibid., pp. 212–13; Blau and Baron, op. cit., pp. 926–32; *Persecution of the Jews in the East*, pp. 27–30. The ensuing enhanced awareness of Jewish sufferings overseas led to an invitation by Yale University to a New York Jewish minister to address the student body on the 'Past, Present and Future of the Jews', a breakthrough hailed by the New Haven press. See *Voice of Jacob*, 13 February 1846.
33. For example, Franz Kobler, *The Vision Was There: A History of the British Movement for the Restoration of the Jews to Palestine*, London, 1956; Barbara W. Tuchman, *Bible and Sword: How the British came to Palestine* (New York, 1956); Mayir Vereté, 'The Restoration of the Jews in English Protestant Thought, 1790–1840', *Middle Eastern Studies*, vol. 8, no. 1 (January 1972), pp. 3–50; Michael Polowetzky,

Jerusalem Recovered: Victorian Intellectuals and the Birth of Modern Zionism (Westport, Ct.: 1997).
34. Ashley's diary entry for 24 August 1840, quoted in Frankel, op. cit., p. 303.
35. Edward Bickersteth, *The Restoration of the Jews to Their Own Land in Connection With Their Future Conversion and the Final Blessedness of Our Earth* (London: 1840, and 2nd edn, enl., 1841). Bickersteth was Rector of Watton, Herts.
36. *The Destiny of the Jews, and their connexion with the Gentile Nations, viewed practically, in a course of lectures delivered at St. Bride's Church, Liverpool. By several Clergymen of the Church of England* (London: 1841), pp. 298, 310, quoted in Frankel, op. cit., p. 300.
37. *The Times*, 17 August 1840. According to Kobler, op. cit., p. 61, followed by Tuchman, op. cit., p. 195, the full text of the memorial is given in *The Times*, 9 March 1840, but we find only brief mention there.
38. *Voice of Jacob*, 18 August 1843; *Ipswich Express*, 22 August 1843.
39. *Voice of Jacob*, 1 September 1843.
40. Quoted ibid., cf. *Royal Gazette and Jamaica Standard*, 4 October 1843.
41. Quotation from *Protestant Magazine*, 1 September 1843; cf. ibid., 1 December 1843. Charlotte Elizabeth edited the *Protestant Magazine* anonymously, presumably in view of her sex. Hilary L. Rubinstein, 'A Pioneering Philosemite: Charlotte Elizabeth Tonna (1790–1846)', in *A Portion of Praise: A Festschrift to Honour John S. Levi* (Melbourne: 1997), pp. 215–36. For her writings in general, see *The Works of Charlotte Elizabeth*, 7th edn, 2 vols. (New York: 1849), with an Introduction by Harriet Beecher Stowe; entry by Joseph Kestner in *Victorian Britain: an Encyclopedia* (Chicago: 1988), p. 594.
42. *Voice of Jacob*, 29 September 1843. O'Connell's 'Kinsman and intimate friend', William John O'Connell, was also a philosemite. *Jewish Chronicle*, 7 November 1856.
43. *The Times*, 14 July 1843. The *ukase* was dated 20 April in the Julian calendar.
44. *Morning Herald*, 8, 13, 20 December 1843, 5 January 1844; *The Times*, 18 December 1843, cf. 16 February 1844.
45. *Britannia*, n.d., quoted in *Christian Lady's Magazine*, March 1844, p. 265.
46. Ibid., January 1844, pp. 66–76. this periodical also reproduced Grace Aguilar's pertinent poem, 'The Hebrew's Appeal.' Ibid., February 1844, pp. 163–5; cf. ibid., March 1844, pp. 259–65, October 1844, pp. 303–4.
47. *Guernsey Star*, n.d., quoted in *Voice of Jacob*, 1 March 1844.
48. *Morning Herald*, 20 December 1843.
49. *Voice of Jacob*, 29 September 1843; 22 March 1844.
50. Ibid., 15 September 1843.
51. *Voice of Jacob*, 22 December 1843; see also 'Duties of the "Friends of Israel"', ibid., 14 April 1843; *Christian Lady's Magazine*, March 1844, pp. 259–61,
52. *Voice of Jacob*, 6 September 1844; for the relationship between Franklin and Mrs. Tonna see Rubinstein, 'A Pioneering Philosemite: Charlotte Elizabeth', pp. 218 et seq.

53. Quoted in *Christian Lady's Magazine*, March 1844, pp. 259–61.
54. Ibid., p. 265. Her readers were by no means entirely female, but she assumed that those who were would influence their menfolk. The periodical had a wide circulation, reaching Queen Victoria and many prominent persons. See Charlotte Elizabeth Tonna, *Personal Reminiscences*, 3rd edn (London: 1847), pp. 46–7; W.J. Conybeare, 'Church Parties', in his *Essays Ecclesiastical and Social* (London: 1855), pp. 81–3. That essay first appeared in 1853 in the *Edinburgh Review* and passed through many editions.
55. Tonna, *Personal Reminiscences*, p. 410; *Voice of Jacob*, 31 July 1846.
56. Ashley to C.E. Tonna, 9 May 1843, in *Jewish Chronicle*, 8 May 1908.
57. *Christian Lady's Magazine*, May 1844, p. 265.
58. Ibid., October 1844, pp. 299–300.
59. *Voice of Jacob*, 22 March 1844; see also *Jewish Chronicle*, 19 October 1877.
60. *Voice of Jacob*, 15 November 1844.
61. William Willshire to Judah Guedalla, 28 September 1844, quoted ibid.
62. *Christian Lady's Magazine*, December 1844, pp. 527, 543.
63. *Voice of Jacob*, 15 November, 20 December 1844, 31 January 1845, 3 January 1846.
64. The Jewish press throughout the nineteenth century regularly published lists of donors to Jewish domestic causes.
65. *Jewish Chronicle*, 16, 23 June, 25 August 1854.
66. 'A Poor Cripple', who gave sixpence, might or might not have been Jewish.
67. For donors' lists, see ibid., 16 June, 10 August, 8 September 1854. There was some evident overlap with Mogador fund donors recruited by Mrs. Tonna.
68. For the Association's executive and aims, see ibid., 24 December 1852.
69. Ieuan Glan Alarch (pseud., i.e. John Mills), *Iuddewon Prydain* (Llanidloes: 1852); John Mills, *The British Jews: Their Religion, Ceremonies, Social Conditions, Domestic Habits, Literature, Political Statistics*, etc. (London: 1862, c. 1853), p. v. This remarkably useful and objective work drew almost exclusively on Jewish sources. See also Richard Mills and N. Cynhafel Jones, *Buchdraeth y Parch. John Mills* (Aberdare: 1881), Chapters 6, 7, 8.
70. *Jewish Chronicle*, 30 March, 6 July, 21 December 1855.
71. Ibid., 28 July 1854.
72. Ibid., 2 March 1855: this list also includes Jamaica; *Sydney Morning Herald*, 19 September 1854; L.M. Goldman, *The Jews in Victoria in the Nineteenth Century* (Melbourne: 1954), p. 112; *Argus* (Melbourne), 21 August 1854; M.Z. Forbes, 'Palestine Appeals in the Fifties and Sixties', *Australian Jewish Historical Society Journal*, vol. 3, part 7 (1952), pp. 319–20.
73. *Sydney Morning Herald*, 5 March 1861; *Argus*, 31 December 1861; Israel Klausner, 'Haym Zvee Sneersohn's Australian Mission', *Herzl Year Book*, vol. 6 (1964–65), pp. 25–51; *Jewish Chronicle*, 20 October, 3 November, 22 December 1865, 5 January, 27 April, 18 May 1866. South African donors towards the relief of Jews at Rawa, Poland, following a

'calamitous fire' included many gentiles. Ibid., 6 September, 8 November 1861.
74. Letter from David Hatchwell, Gibraltar, ibid., 18 November 1859. Other Tangier Jews placed themselves under Spanish protection. For members of the relief committee see ibid., 23 December 1859.
75. Resolutions, London Committee of Deputies of British Jews under presidency of Sir Moses Montefiore, 7 November 1859, in ibid., 2 December 1859.
76. Ibid., 9, 23 December 1859; see, for example, *Kent Herald*, quoted ibid.
77. Ibid., 23 December 1859.
78. Ibid.; for lists of donors, see ibid., 9, 23 December 1859.

2 'THE SYMPATHIES OF ALL GOOD MEN'

1. For a general description of the Mortara Affair see Bertram W. Korn, *The American Reaction to the Mortara Case* (Cincinnati: The American Jewish Archives, 1957), pp. 3–20; David I. Kertzer, *The Kidnapping of Edgardo Mortara* (New York: 1997).
2. Ibid., pp. 5–6, 12–13; *Jewish Chronicle*, 13 August 1858.
3. See, for example, ibid., 12 November 1858, 28 January 1859.
4. Letter from 'Another Christian', ibid., 12 November 1858.
5. *Daily Telegraph*, n.d., quoted ibid.
6. Ibid., 17 September, 29 December 1858. The paper later claimed to have 'misinterpreted the silence of the Roman Catholic laity', who were muzzled: 'this crime is just as much abhorred by the overwhelming majority of intelligent Roman Catholics, as by all Protestants.' Ibid., 4 March 1859.
7. George Oliver to Alexander Alexander, 24 September 1858, in ibid., 15 October 1858. Sir George Bowyer, a Roman Catholic supporter of Jewish parliamentary emancipation and a regular reader of the Jewish press, could 'never think' of the Mortara Affair 'without much pain, though there is a good deal to be said on both sides.' *Jewish Chronicle*, 25 February 1876. See also Josef L. Althotz, 'A Note on the English Catholic Reaction to the Mortara Case', *Jewish Social Studies*, vol. 23 (1961), pp. 111–18.
8. Ibid., 26 November 1858.
9. Eardley to Montefiore, 30 October 1858, in ibid.
10. Ibid., and Montefiore to Eardley, 3 November, in ibid., 26 November 1858.
11. Eardley to Montefiore, 24 December 1858, in ibid., 28 December 1858.
12. Ibid., 12 November, 19 December 1858.
13. Ibid., 3 December 1858. See Malmesbury's replies, through Edmund Hammond, to the Protestant Association, Scottish Reformation Society, and Shaftesbury, ibid., 30 November, 3 December, 24 December 1858. For the Jewish community's attitude to Eardley see ibid., 29 May 1863.
14. Shaftesbury to Malmesbury, 11 December 1858, in ibid., 24 December 1858.

15. Ibid., 10 December 1858.
16. Ibid., 11 February 1859.
17. *The Times*, 19 October 1859.
18. Ibid. *Jewish Chronicle*, 11 November 1859.
19. An analysis, ibid., 28 October 1859, put the number of signatories given in *The Times* as 454 (459 in the reckoning of the present authors) and described them thus: '26 peers ... 20 bishops; 34 Members of Parliament; 68 Mayors ... 11 Provosts ... 42 magistrates and other Persons of eminence; 117 ministers of Protestant denominations ... the secretaries of all religious societies; 10 banking firms ... 123 others representing all professions and the higher middle classes of the realm.' Sir Culling Eardley, on 7 November, reported '79 mayors and provosts, 27 dukes and peers, 22 bishops and archbishops, 36 members of parliament, and a large number of the clergy and laity.' Ibid., 11 November 1859. The Duke of Wellington was the son of the victor of Waterloo, who died in 1852.
20. *The Times*, 19 October 1859; *Jewish Chronicle*, 28 October 1859.
21. *The Times*, 19 October 1859.
22. *Jewish Chronicle*, 4 November 1859; Smith to the Bishop of London, 15 November 1859, in ibid., 25 November 1859.
23. Ibid., 22 July 1859. Montefiore's popularity in the general community was sufficient for a cigarette manufacturer to feature him in its advertisements, and his funeral procession through Ramsgate in 1884 attracted a geat throng of gentile mourners. See Anne and Roger Cowen, *British Jews through Victorian Eyes* (Oxford: 1986), pp. 74, 77.
24. *Jewish Chronicle*, 11 November 1859. At the time there were two major-generals named Alexander: Robert and (Sir) James. The relevant one resided in Blackheath. On Fowler's philosemitism, see H.L. Malchow, *Gentlemen Capitalists: The Social and Political World of the Victorian Businessman* (Stanford, Ca.: 1992), pp. 179–80.
25. *Jewish Chronicle*, 11 November, 1859.
26. Ibid., 29 November 1859.
27. Ibid., 18 November, 1859. The printed list did not specify *Scottish Reformation Society*.
28. Ibid., 5 January 1879; Romania became an independent kingdom in 1881.
29. Prince Charles to Montefiore, 18/30 August 1867, quoted ibid., 12 September 1913.
30. Ibid., 23 February, 19, 26 April 1872.
31. Ibid., 26 April 1872.
32. *Daily Telegraph*, 15 May 1872, quoted ibid., 17 May 1872. For a synopsis of institutionalized Romanian antisemitism, see ibid., 24 July 1874.
33. Ibid., 26 April 1872, 2 July 1897 (article on Sir John Simon).
34. Hiam Guedalla, *The Roumanian Government and the Jews* (London: 1872); cited in *Jewish Chronicle*, 17 May 1872. Guedalla was Montefiore's nephew by marriage.
35. Ibid., 24 May 1872.
36. Ibid., 27 July 1897 recalled the Lord Mayor as Alderman Hubbard.
37. *The Times*, 31 May 1872; *Jewish Chronicle*, 31 May 1872.

Notes 211

38. Ibid.
39. Ibid. See also ibid., 14 June 1872; *The Times*, 31 May 1872.
40. *Jewish Chronicle*, 7 June, 31 May 1872. Lord Houghton, formerly Richard Monckton Milnes MP, was a poet and writer of some note.
41. See ibid., 24 May, 7, 28 June 1872; *The Times*, 18 June 1872; Lloyd P. Gartner, 'Rumania, America, and World Jewry: Consul Peixotto in Bucharest, 1870–1876', *American Jewish Historical Quarterly*, vol. 58 (1968), pp. 25–117. On 22 May 1872 the German Parliament received a petition regarding Romanian Jewry, *Jewish Chronicle*, 24 May 1872.
42. Ibid., 19 January 1877. The London *Evening News*, 5 August 1877, drawing attention to the continued suffering of *Russian* Jewry, hoped that at the peace settlement they would 'not be forgotten'.

3 'THE IMPERISHABLE PEOPLE'

1. See I. Michael Aronson, *Troubled Waters: The Origins of the 1881 Anti-Jewish Pogroms in Russia* (Pittsburgh: 1991); John D. Klier and Shlomo Lambroza, eds., *Pogroms: Anti-Jewish Violence in Modern Russian History* (Cambridge: 1992); Heinz-Dietrich Löwe, *The Tsars and the Jews: Reform, Reaction, and Anti-Semitism in Imperial Russia, 1772–1917* (Chur, Switzerland: 1993).
2. Ibid., p. 66.
3. Ibid., pp. 65–6.; Klier and Lambroza, op. cit., p. 41.
4. 'The Times and the Jews', *Jewish Chronicle*, 4 January 1935. Editorial, *Illustrated London News*, 21 January 1882, typifies general press sympathy.
5. *The Times*, 23 January 1882; *Outrages Upon the Jews in Russia. Report of the Public Meeting at the Mansion House on Wednesday, February 1st, 1882* (London: 1882), p. 3. The latter pamphlet was issued by the AJA.
6. *The Times*, 2 February 1882.
7. *Jewish Chronicle*, 25 November 1859, 5 October 1877, 4 January 1907.
8. Ibid., 2 December 1921. Soulsby attended the 1906 rally: *The Times*, 9 January 1906.
9. 'Browning and the Jews', ibid., 25 February 1921; L.V. Rosenbaum, 'The Jewish Traits of Robert Browning', ibid., *Supplement*, 29 August 1924; R. Ackerman, 'Browning's "Holy Cross Day"', ibid., *Supplement*, 30 April 1929; Judith Berlin-Liberman, *Robert Browning and Hebraism* (Jerusalem: 1934). For Swinburne, see *Jewish Chronicle*, 16 April 1909; L.M. Findlay, ed., *Swinburne: Selected Poems* (Manchester: 1982), p. 228. For Reade, see *South Wales Daily News*, 25 January 1882. It is not known whether Swinburne or Reade attended the rally.
10. *The Times*, 2 February 1882; *Outrages*, pp. 6–7.
11. *The Times*, 2 February 1882.
12. Ibid. *Outrages*, p. 17; Manning's 'passionate eloquence' that day was recalled by the *Jewish Chronicle*, 4 February 1938.
13. *The Times*, 2 February 1882.
14. Ibid., 15, 21 February 1882; *Swansea Journal*, 11 March 1882.
15. *The Times* 2, 23 February, 25 March, 22 June 1882.

16. Full list in *Outrages*, p. 29.
17. See, for example, *The Times*, 2, 7 February 1882; *Cardiff Times*, 4 March 1882; *Merthyr Express*, 11 March 1882.
18. *Swansea Journal*, 1 April 1882; *The Times*, 3, 18 February 1882; *Jewish Herald* (Melbourne), 5 May 1882.
19. *The Times*, 18, 27 February 1882; *Jewish Chronicle*, 25 October 1895.
20. See, for instance, *South Wales Daily News*, 16 January 1882; *Aberystwyth Observer*, 28 January 1882; *Aberdare Times*, 11 February 1882. Among journals highlighting the precarious status of Jews on the continent and positive contributions Jews had made were *Nineteenth Century*, 1881, pp. 813–29; *Contemporary Review*, 1881, pp. 365–84; *Temple Bar*, Vol. 65, 1882, pp. 31–7. See especially [Charlotte Dampster], 'Persecution of the Jews', *Edinburgh Review*, Vol. 157 (1883), pp. 291–320.
21. Codicil to will dated 2 April 1883, *Jewish Chronicle*, 17 February, 13 October 1899.
22. See Hilary L. Rubinstein, '"A Noble Sight to See": Philo-Semitic Responses in Late Nineteenth and Early Twentieth Century Australia to Jewish Crises Overseas', *Australian Jewish Historical Society Journal*, vol. 13, part 3 (1996), pp. 424–62.
23. Ibid., pp. 432–2.
24. Ibid., pp. 432–4.
25. Ibid., pp. 430, 434–7. Bendigo was at that time known as Sandhurst.
26. *New York Times*, 2 February 1882. A letter from Judge John R. Brady was also read out. Grant's interest in the meeting was mentioned by the Reverend Newman. According to Jacob Rader Marcus, *United States Jewry 1776–1985, Volume III: The Germanic Period, Part 2* (Detroit: 1993), p. 50, Grant 'served as a sponsor of an anti-Russian protest meeting after the pogroms of 1881.' Fish (1808–93) should not be confused with his philosemitic son and namesake, mentioned in Chapter 5.
27. *New York Times*, 7 June 1882.
28. Ibid., 16 February 1883.
29. Ibid., 5 March 1883.
30. Ibid., 3 May 1882. For the joint resolution passed by Congress on 6 March 1882, see Louis Greenberg, *The Jews in Russia: The Struggle for Emancipation*, 2 vols in one (New Haven: 1965), pp. 60–1.
31. See, for example, *New York Times*, 5–24 March 1882. The US Evangelical Alliance protested the persecution of Russian Jewry and resolved to memorialize the Russian government. *The Times*, 2 February 1882. Americans also spoke out against the antisemitic movement in Germany. See, for instance, the pleas of the Reverend Henry Ward Beecher, and other Christian clergymen, *New York Times*, 20, 27 December 1880.
32. MPs among the requisitioners ranged from 'advanced Liberals' like Mark Oldroyd to rightwing Tories like Edwin De Lisle. *The Times*, 11 December 1890; cf. 'Our Home Letter', *Jewish Herald* (Melbourne), 2 January 1891. For Leighton see *Jewish Chronicle*, 31 January 1896; for Price Hughes' part-Jewish ancestry and philosemitic attitude, see Dorothea Price Hughes, *The Life of Hugh Price Hughes* (London:

1904). Empire Day was officially celebrated each 24 May (Queen Victoria's birthday) from 1904.
33. 'Our Home Letter', *Jewish Herald* (Melbourne), 30 January 1891. The speakers are depicted in the *Graphic* and the *Illustrated London News*, both 20 December 1890. There were persistent rumours that Booth's mother was Jewish. He declared cryptically that he was 'a Jew in the spirit if not in the flesh'. *Jewish Chronicle*, 23 August 1912.
34. *The Times*, 11 December 1890.
35. *Jewish Herald*, 2 January 1891; *The Times*, 6, 10, 11 December 1890.
36. Cardinal Manning to Sir John Simon, 8 December 1890; *The Times*, 10 December 1890, evidently quoting from *The Persecution of the Jews in Russia*, published by the London-based Russo-Jewish Committee on 20 November. See *Jewish Herald*, 30 January 1890.
37. Petition dated 10 December 1890, *Jewish Chronicle*, 9 January 1891.
38. *The Times*, 11 December 1890. Baroness Burdett-Coutts's husband, an American-born Conservative MP, had been willing to replace Pease. *Jewish Herald*, 30 January 1890.
39. Ambassador Sir Robert Morier was ambivalent towards Jews. See Moshe Perlmann, 'The British Embassy in St. Petersburg on Russian Jewry, 1890–92', *Proceedings of the American Academy for Jewish Research*, vol. 48 (1981), pp. 297–323; quotation at p. 304.
40. *Jewish Chronicle*, 2 January 1891.
41. Pearlman, op. cit., p. 304; *Jewish Herald*, 30 January 1891; *Jewish Chronicle*, 13 February 1891. For text of petition (dated 10 December 1890) and covering letter (dated 24 December 1890) see ibid., 9 January 1891.
42. Ibid., 13 February 1891; *Novoe Vremya*, 14 December 1890, quoted *The Times*, 15 December 1890; cf. Olga Novikoff, ibid., 10 December 1890; Eliot to Marquis of Salisbury, 25 December 1890, 12 February 1891, Pearlman, op. cit., pp. 315, 318–21; cf. editorial, *New York Times*, 19 December 1890.
43. Oswald John Simon, letter, *The Times*, 24 October 1896.
44. *Jewish Chronicle*, 23 January, 6 February 1890. For the Manchester and Birmingham meetings, see ibid., 16, 23 January, 27 February 1891. The impetus for the latter's requisition came from a number of prominent Christian clergy of all denominations. Ibid., 2 January 1891.
45. *The Times*, 3 November 1890.
46. See Ellen Dysart, 'Tsar v. Jew', *Nineteenth Century*, vol. 29, 1891, pp. 969–78 (the Countess of Dysart was Jewish); C.B. Roylance-Kent, 'The Persecuted Russian Jews', *National Review*, vol. 17 (1891), pp. 828–37; C.H.H. Wright, 'Some Great Jewish Rabbis', *Nineteenth Century*, vol. 31 (1892), pp. 905–24; see also *Jewish Chronicle*, 6 February 1891, for excerpt from *Quarterly Review*; Hall Caine, *The Scapegoat* (London: 1891).
47. *New York Times*, 6 March 1891; Cyrus Hamlin, 'International Aid for the Jews', *Our Day*, vol. 8, 1891, pp. 1–8; Anita Libman Lebeson, 'Zionism Comes to Chicago', in Isidore S. Meyer, ed., *Early History of Zionism in America* (New York: 1958), pp. 155–72. Marnin Feinstein, *American Zionism, 1884–1904* (New York: 1965), pp. 56–79. David D.

Brodeur, 'Christians in the Zionist Camp: Blackstone and Hechler', *Faith and Thought*, vol. 100 (1972), pp. 290–1. Blackstone is sometimes incorrectly described as a clergyman, for example in Harold Berman, 'An Early Christian Jewish Nationalist', *Jewish Chronicle Supplement*, 30 March 1928. See particularly Yaakov Ariel's outstanding chapter on Blackstone in his *On Behalf of Israel: American Fundamentalist Attitudes Toward Jews, Judaism, and Zionism, 1865–1945* (Brooklyn: 1991), pp. 55–96, and ibid., pp. 30–4, for Dwight L. Moody's ambivalence regarding Jews.

48. *Jewish Chronicle*, 2 January 1891. Gibbons and other prominent Americans had earlier given their views on antisemitism in a questionnaire prepared by a Jewish journal. *American Hebrew*, 4 April 1890, summarized in *New York Times*, 5 April 1890. For views of explorer, author and journalist George Kennan and ex-Commissioner for Immigration John B. Weber, see ibid., 6 February 1891, 10, 17 May 1893. See also note 60, *infra*.

49. Harold Frederic, *The New Exodus: A Study of Israel in Russia* (London: 1892); M. Bourchier Sanford, 'In Favour of the Jews', *North American Review*, vol. 152 (1891), pp. 126–8; W.E.H. Lecky, 'Israel Among the Nations', *Forum*, vol. 16 (1893), pp. 442–5; Felix L. Oswald, 'The Mask of Anti-Semitism', *Open Court*, vol. 7 (1893), pp. 397–8. See also Louise A. Mayo, *The Ambivalent Image: Nineteenth-Century America;s Perception of the Jew* (Cranbury, N.J.: 1988); Gary Dean Best, *To Free A People: American Jewish Leaders and the Jewish Problem in Eastern Europe, 1890–1914* (Westport, Conn.: 1982).

50. *The Scotsman*, 25 May 1903. On Kishinev, see Shlomo Lambroza, 'The Pogroms of 1903–1906,' in Klier and Lambroza, op. cit., pp. 195–211.

51. *The Times*, 6 June 1903; Michael Davitt, *Within the Pale: the True Story of Anti-Semitic Persecutions in Russia* (London: 1903).

52. Letter, *The Times*, 9 June 1903; in fact there had over the centuries been several papal decrees against the blood libel. See *Tablet*, quoted in *Jewish Chronicle*, 19 June 1903, regarding Rumbold's proposal. In 1936 Rumbold was Vice-Chairman of the Peel Commission which proposed the first partition of Palestine between Jews and Arabs. Its report said, *inter alia*: 'It is impossible ... for any unprejudiced observer to see the National Home and not to wish it well. It has meant so much for the relief of unmerited suffering. It displays so much energy and enterprise and devotion to a common cause.' Quoted ibid., 28 December 1973.

53. See *The Times*, 18, 20 May, 6, 26 June 1903; letters from Sir John Blunt, ibid., reproduced *Jewish Chronicle*, 10 July 1903; Kathleen Manning (later Viscountess Simon), ibid., 5 June, 3 July, 21 August, 2, 16 October 1903; Robert P. Yates (British Israelite, Birmingham), ibid., 17 July 1903; talk by Herbert Burrows, President, United Garment Workers' Union, ibid., 30 October 1903; and letter from him, ibid., 5 June 1903. Non-Jewish artists donated pictures for auction for the fund. Ibid.

54. Ibid., 26 June 1903.

55. *Jewish Chronicle*, editorials, 29 May, 3 July 1903. Some Jews such as

Herbert Bentwich (ibid., 12 June 1903) and the Reverend A.A. Green (*The Times*, 2 June 1903) denounced Samuel's decision, accusing him of not daring to call a meeting on behalf of fellow-Jews. Samuel, later Viscount Bearsted, was founder of Shell Oil; did he, perhaps, have business interests in Russia?

56. Details in Rubinstein, "'A Noble Sight to See'", pp. 425, 427, 436–9. These Australian meetings put Samuel on the defensive. See *Jewish Chronicle*, 3, 17 July 1903. For Christian sympathy in Jamaica, see ibid. A meeting under Jewish auspices attended by about 1,000 people took place in Cape Town, ibid., 10 July 1903. Public demonstrations of sympathy occurred elsewhere in the Western world: for a great protest organised by the University of Paris, involving noted intellectuals, and a leftist-inspired public meeting in France, see ibid., 22 May, 3 July 1903, *The Times*, 27 June 1903.

57. Cyrus Adler, ed., *The Voice of America on Kishineff*, Philadelphia: Jewish Publication Society of America, 1904; see also Philip Ernest Schoenberg, 'The American Reaction to the Kishinev Pogrom of 1903,' *American Jewish Historical Quarterly*, vol. 63 (1974), p. 269.

58. Adler, op. cit., pp. 116–36. Several subsidiary protest meetings were held in the city.

59. Ibid., p. 80.

60. Ibid., pp. 467–81; *Jewish Chronicle*, 26 June, 3, 10, 17 July 1903, *Times*, 20 May 1910, 9, 26, 30 June 1903. Secretary of State John Hay donated $200 to the relief fund; ibid., 29 May 1903. See also address by the Baptist Reverend George C. Lorrimer, *New York Times*, 8 June 1903; W.C. Stiles, *Out of Kishineff: The Duty of the American People to the Russian Jew* (New York: 1903); Samuel Harden Church, *Russian Persecution of the Jews* (Pittsburgh, Pa.: 1903); Stuart E. Knee, 'The Diplomacy of Neutrality: Theodore Roosevelt and the Russian Pogroms of 1903–1906', *Presidential Studies Quarterly*, vol. 19 (1989), pp. 71–8; Kenton J. Clymer, 'Anti-Semitism in the Late Nineteenth Century: The Case of John Hay', *American Jewish Historical Quarterly*, vol. 60 (1971), pp. 344–54; for a laudatory Jewish account, see Joseph Krauskopf, *Secretary Hay and the Roumanian Jews. A Sunday Lecture Before the Reform Congregation Keneseth Israel ... Philadelphia, Pa.* (Philadelphia: 1902). John B. Weber, 'The Kishineff Massacre and its Bearing upon the Question of Jewish Immigration into the United States', *Collier's Weekly*, 6 June 1903, pp. 8–10; Alexander Hume Ford, 'America's Debt to the Russian Jew', ibid., p. 10. The latter article praised 'Americanized' Russo-Jewish merchants for enabling the United States to establish a commercial foothold in the Czarist Empire.

61. Lambroza, op. cit., pp. 226–31.

62. The reasons for the Aliens Act as well as the extent to which it may reasonably be termed antisemitic are debatable. Before 1905 Britain had *no* restrictions of any kind on immigrant settlement. Such restrictions were obviously inevitable, especially after the beginnings of the 'Welfare State' a few years later. It is generally believed that the Aliens Act decreased Russian Jewish migration to Britain by about one-third down to 1914, although other factors (such as greatly increased 'chain

migration' to the United States) were significant. The most balanced accounts of the Aliens Act include John A, Garrard, *The English and Immigration, 1880–1910* (Oxford: 1971), and Eugene C. Black, *The Social Politics of Anglo-Jewry, 1880–1920* (London: 1988). See also W.D. Rubinstein, *A History of the Jews in the English-Speaking World: Great Britain* (London: 1996), pp. 153–9.

63. *The Times*, 9 January 1906; *Jewish Herald*, 20 December 1905; *Massacre of Jews in Russia. Report on the Protest Meeting at Queen's Hall, January 8th, 1906* (London: 1906).
64. Ibid., pp. 9–38.
65. *Jewish Herald*, 17 November, 1, 15 December 1905; Rubinstein, "'A Noble Sight to See'", pp. 443–50.
66. Ibid.
67. *Jewish Herald*, 1 December 1905. In the Australian context a Liberal denotes a political conservative. At Adelaide's Kishinev protest O'Reily explained his lifelong philosemitism. Ibid., 19 June 1903.
68. *Jewish Herald*, 12 January 1906.
69. *New York Times*, 13 November 1905.
70. Ibid., 27 November, 19 December 1905.
71. Ibid., 13, 16, 27 November 1905. The Reverend Dr Madison Peters, originally a Presbyterian, was a prolific author whose other philosemitic books include *The Jew as Patriot* (1902), *The Jews in America* (1905), *Haym Solomon* (1911), *The Jews who Stood by Washington* (1915).
72. *New York Times*, 12 November 1905; cf. ibid., 16 November 1905.
73. Ibid., 12 April 1906.
74. Ibid., 23, 27 June 1903: see also ibid., 5 December 1905, 21 June 1906.
75. Ibid., 29 April 1906; Roosevelt's medal was presented by Dr Cyrus Adler on behalf of the executive committee in charge of celebrating the 250th anniversary of the settlement of Jews in the United States. For Roosevelt's philosemitism and high standing with Jewry see *Jewish Chronicle*, 2 October 1903, 12 March 1909, 20 May 1910.

4 'AN UNSPEAKABLE INJUSTICE'

1. For an admirably balanced analysis, see Albert S. Lindemann, *The Jew Accused. Three Anti-Semitic Affairs (Dreyfus, Beilis, Frank) 1894–1915* (Cambridge: 1991).
2. Ibid., pp. 94–128. A useful recent history of the Dreyfus Affair in the context of wider French society is Eric Cahan, *The Dreyfus Affair in French Society and Politics* (London: 1994). For international reaction to the verdict see *The Times*, 11 September 1899; *Jewish Chronicle*, 15 September 1899.
3. Lindemann, op. cit., pp. 94–7.
4. Ibid., pp. 109–18, 120, 121.
5. *The Times*, 31 January, 16 March 1898; *Jewish Chronicle*, 2 June 1899.
6. George Barlow, *The History of the Dreyfus Case* (London: 1898); *The Times*, 26 December 1898.

Notes 217

7. See especially L.J. Maxse, 'M. Cavaignac's Vindication of Captain Dreyfus', *National Review*, vol. 31, August 1898, pp. 814–34; idem., 'Russia and Captain Dreyfus', ibid., vol. 32, November 1898, pp. 357–73; F.C. Conybeare, 'French Military Justice', ibid., pp. 337–56; L.J. Maxse, 'Some International Aspects of the Dreyfus Case', ibid., vol. 32, January 1899; Godfrey Lushington, 'The Conspiracy Against Dreyfus', ibid. pp. 1–64; idem., 'The Verdict at Rennes', ibid., October 1899, pp. 179–202; idem., 'The Dreyfus Case: An Examination of the Facts and the Evidence', *The Times*, 13 October 1898. A pro-Jewish anonymous account of the Affair appeared ibid., 27 June 1898. The *Jewish Chronicle*, 2 June 1899, praised the roles of Barlow, Christie Murray, Lushington, Maxse and, above all, Conybeare. Maxse later wrote: 'The *National Review* is violently assailed by the Jewish Press for expressing distrust of Jews, but it is not Jews *qua* Jews who provoke our uneasiness, but Jews of Germanic origin, most of whom were decidely pro-German before the war. They are not suitable confidants of responsible statesmen.' Quoted ibid., 7 September 1917.
8. Joseph Prag, 'The Influence of the English Press on the Dreyfus Case', ibid., 23 June 1899; Emily Crawford's response, ibid., 21 July 1899. Mrs. Crawford was a confirmed leftwinger. See Anne Sebba, *Battling for News: The Rise of the Woman Reporter* (London: 1994), pp. 20–2.
9. Ibid., 15 September 1899.
10. 'London Letter', *South Wales Daily News*, 11 September 1899; *Spectator*, quoted in *Jewish Chronicle*, 15 September 1899. *The Times*, 14 September 1899, reported that virtually all of its 'enormous' correspondence on the subject was pro-Dreyfus.
11. *Jewish Chronicle*, 22 September 1899; *South Wales Daily News*, 14, 19 September 1899; *The Times*, 11, 14, 15, 22 September, 3 November 1899. A resolution was signed by 25 representatives of the Congregational Churches of Great Britain (including an Australian) who had just arrived in Boston, Massachusetts, to attend a conference. *New York Times*, 11 September 1899.
12. Alderman W.D. Stephens, *The Times*, 12 September 1899.
13. Ibid., 12, 13, 15, 16 September 1899; *South Wales Daily News*, 14, 15 September 1899; *Age* (Melbourne), 18 September 1899; Abernant Dinas Brick and Cement Co., Glyn-Neath, *Swansea Journal*, 16 September 1899. The boycott movement, evident in many countries, subsided once Dreyfus was pardoned and released.
14. *Jewish Chronicle*, 15 September 1899.
15. *Daily Chronicle*, n.d., quoted ibid., 22 September 1899.
16. In mid-1899 the *New York Journal* printed messages of sympathy for Dreyfus from well-known Britons and Americans: see *Jewish Chronicle*, 7 July 1899. Queen Victoria, who followed the case attentively, received telegrams asking her to intercede: *South Wales Daily News*, 14 September 1899.
17. *The Times*, 14 September 1899; *Jewish Chronicle*, 13 October, 1 December 1899; 24 July 1903; Nellie Melba to Mme. Dreyfus, in Louis Snyder, *The Dreyfus Case: A Documentary History* (New Brunswick, N.J.: 1973), pp. 362–3.

18. Robert Speaight, *The Life of Hilaire Belloc*, London, 1957, p. 97.
19. *The Times*, 11, 13, 15, 18, 29, 21 September 1899. The Lord Mayor of Sheffield denounced French justice and announced his readiness to sign an address of sympathy to Dreyfus. Ibid., 13 September 1899.
20. *Daily Chronicle*, 11, 18 September 1899; report in Melbourne *Age*, 22 September 1899.
21. East London Christian Evidence Association and Protestant Forward Movement, *The Times*, 19 September 1899.
22. *Daily Telegraph*, 18 September 1899; *Jewish Chronicle*, 22 September 1899.
23. *The Times*, 18 September 1899.
24. Ibid.
25. *Jewish Chronicle*, 22 September 1899; cf. Ronald K. Huch, 'British Reaction to the Dreyfus Affair', *Social Science*, vol. 50, no. 1 (1975), pp. 22-8, which (p. 26), following a jaundiced *The Times* report of 18 September, claims that 'There was little said about anti-Semitism.'
26. *Jewish Chronicle*, 7 July 1899, citing *New York Journal*, n.d. See reports by, among others, Harold Frederic and Walter Littlefield, *New York Times*, 23 January, 22 May, 21 August 1898.
27. Ibid., 13 September 1899, and 11-18 September for comprehensive reportage; see also *The Times*, 11, 12 September 1899: see *New York Times*, 11 September 1899.
28. *The Times*, 13 September 1899.
29. Ibid., editorial, 15 September 1899; cf. editorial, 11 September 1899.
30. *The Times*, 11 September 1899.
31. *New York Times*, 13 September 1899.
32. Ibid., 14 September 1899.
33. Ibid.
34. Laffin Agency Report. *The Times*, 11 September 1899; see also Egal Feldman, *The Dreyfus Affair and the American Conscience, 1895-1906* (Detroit: 1980).
35. *Argus*, 12, 13 September 1899.
36. *Age*, 20 September 1899.
37. *Argus*, 20, 25 September 1899. See also Hilary L. Rubinstein, '"A Disgrace to Christendom": Australian Reactions to the Dreyfus Affair', *Australian Jewish Historical Society Journal*, vol. 12, part 3 (1994), pp. 467-83; Colin Thornton-Smith, 'Reactions of the Australian Catholic Press to the Dreyfus Case', ibid., vol. 14, part 5 (1997), pp. 57-92.
38. *Sydney Morning Herald*, 14 September 1899. See also ibid., 16 September 1899. At a dramatic event in Auckland one of the performers tore the French flag to pieces to 'a storm of applause'. *Bendigo Advertiser*, 14 September 1899.
39. *The Times*, 12 September 1899; text of telegram from the citizens of Johannesburg, 'irrespective of nationality and creed', to Mme Dreyfus, asserting 'The residents of the South African Republic ally themselves with all the world on the side of Captain Dreyfus', *South Wales Daily News*, 19 September 1899; *Jewish Chronicle*, 22 September 1899.
40. See Lindemann, op. cit., pp. 177-93; Maurice Samuel, *Blood*

Accusation: The Strange History of the Beilis Case (Philadelphia: 1966); Ezekiel Leikin, *The Beilis Transcripts: the Anti-Semitic Trial that Shook the World*, Northvale, N.J., 1993; 'The Beilis Affair', *American Jewish Year Book 5675* (Philadelphia: 1914), pp. 19–89.
41. Ibid., pp. 76–9; cf. pp. 34–7, 62–4.
42. Ibid., pp. 70–6. The French signatories included Aimé Pallière, the priest who later converted to Judaism.
43. *The Times*, 6 May 1912, reprinted in *Jewish Chronicle*, 13 May 1912 and 22 August 1913. John Galsworthy, Rev. Charles Voysey, Sir Gilbert Murray and Dr W.H. Gaskell signed following initial publication. For Voysey's earlier condemnation of Russian antisemitism see ibid., 22 September 1911. See also chapter 6, notes 21 and 77.
44. *New York Times*, 27 October 1913. There were Jewish signatories to the British petition: Arthur Pinero and H.L.W. Lawson MP. The Russian, German and French signatories included women.
45. *Jewish Chronicle*, 5 April 1912.
46. *Sydney Morning Herald*, 20 October 1913. See *Jewish Chronicle*, 31 October–14 November 1913 for samples of press opinion.
47. *The Times*, 29 October 1913.
48. See *Jewish Chronicle*, 28 November 1913, commenting on Thurston's article in *The Month*, November 1913; Herbert Thurston, *Anti-Semitism and the Charge of Ritual Murder* [n.p., n.d.], reprinted from *The Month*, June 1898. For Bourne and the Roman Catholic press, see *Jewish Chronicle*, 31 October 1913.
49. *The Times*, 29 October 1913; ibid., 31 October 1913.
50. Ibid.
51. *Westminster Gazette*, n.d., quoted ibid., 7 November 1913.
52. Lucien Wolf, ed., *The Legal Sufferings of the Jews in Russia* (London: 1912).
53. *The Times*, 29 October 1913; *Jewish Chronicle*, 31 October, 7 November 1913. Liberal Russian newspapers praised the meeting.
54. *New York Times*, 3 November 1913; *Jewish Chronicle*, 31 October, 14, 21 November 1913.
55. *American Jewish Year Book 5675*, pp. 79–82.
56. Ibid. An incomplete list of signatories appears in *New York Times*, 7 November 1913. Curiously, Cardinal Gibbons' name is not among the signatories, but he was entirely sympathetic to the cause. Ibid., 28 October 1913.
57. Ibid., 30 October 1913; cf. 14, 27 October 1913.
58. Letter from Louis N. Hammerling, President, American Association of Foreign Language Newspapers Inc., ibid., 16 October 1913.
59. Ibid., 14, 15 October 1913; *Jewish Chronicle*, 7 November 1913.
60. Ibid., 23 October, 7 November 1913.
61. Ibid., 20, 22, 24 October 1913.
62. *Jewish Chronicle*, 31 October 1913.
63. See Lindemann, op. cit., pp. 235–72; Harry Golden, *A Little Girl is Dead* (Cleveland: 1965); Leonard Dinnerstein, *The Leo Frank Case* (New York: 1968).
64. Lindemann, op. cit., p. 251; Arthur Train, 'Did Leo Frank get Justice?',

Everybody's, vol. 32, March 1915, p. 317; *New York Times*, 28 November 1914, 26 May 1915.
65. Bernard Postal, 'Jews in the Ku Klux Klan', *Jewish Tribune*, 14 September 1928; Harry L. Golden, 'Jew and Gentile in the New South', *Commentary*, vol. 20 (November 1955), pp. 403–12; Walter Nugent, *The Tolerant Populists* (Chicago: 1963); Norman Pollack, 'The Myth of Populist Anti-Semitism', *American Historical Review*, vol. 68 (October 1962), pp. 76–80.
66. Walter White, *Rope and Faggot: A Biography of Judge Lynch* (New York: 1929), pp. 199–200; Robert L. Zangrado, *The NAACP Crusade Against Lynching, 1909–1950* (Philadelphia: 1980), pp. 4–8.
67. Train, op. cit., p. 314.
68. *New York Times*, 28 November 1914.
69. Train, op. cit., p. 317.
70. Lindemann, op. cit., pp. 235–6, 242–4; C.P. Connolly, 'The Frank Case,' *Collier's Weekly*, 19, 24, December 1914.
71. Dinnerstein, op. cit., pp. 74–5.
72. Train, op. cit., p. 317; 'Atlanta and the Frank Case', *New York Times*, 13 December 1914.
73. *Atlanta Journal*, 10 March 1914.
74. *New York Times*, 19 March 1914.
75. Ibid.
76. *The Atlanta Georgian*, quoted in *Kansas City Star*, 17 January 1915.
77. [Anon.], 'A Dozen Reasons Why I Believe Conley Slew the Little Phagan Girl', *New York Times*, 28 November 1914. This writer was clearly a Christian – and contemptuously anti-Black, as were many of Frank's outspoken supporters.
78. David Robinson, ibid., 14 December 1914.
79. 'Atlanta and the Frank Case', ibid., 13 December 1914; see also ibid., 18 December 1914, commending Dr Rebecca Brannon's article 'Another Joseph, Unjustly Accused – Negro Conley the Real Murderer', excerpted from the *Atlanta Saturday Night*.
80. *New York Times*, 21 May 1915.
81. Ibid., 21, 22, 25, 28 May, 6 June 1915.
82. *Atlanta Journal*, 24 May 1915, previewed in *New York Times*, 23 May 1915.
83. Ibid., 25, 26 May, 14, 15 June 1915.
84. Ibid., 19 May 1915.
85. Ibid., 26 March, 1 April, 28 December 1914; 4 January, 1 May 1915. For Ford's remorse concerning antisemitism in his newspaper, see his statement to Louis Marshall, 30 June 1927, *American Jewish Year Book 5688* (Philadelphia: 1927), pp. 386–7. For Edison's possible influence on Ford's decision to drop the antisemitic series from his newspaper, see A. Lee, *Henry Ford and the Jews* (New York: 1980), pp. 155–6, quoted in Gould, op. cit., pp. 281–2.
86. *Baltimore Sun*, 19, 23 November 1914; C.P. Connolly, op. cit.; A.B. Macdonald, 'Has Georgia Condemned an Innocent Man to Die?', *Kansas City Star*, 17 January 1917; Train, op. cit., Connolly and Train were lawyers.

87. *New York Times*, 24 May 1917.
88. Ibid., 4 June, 18 May 1915.
89. Ibid., 8, 14, 17, 18, 23, 24 May 1915.
90. Ibid., 30 May 1915.
91. Dinnerstein, op. cit., p. 118; *New York Times*, 18, 30 May, 4 June 1915. This list of governors may be incomplete.
92. Ibid., 18, 25, 26, 30 May 1915. The Governor-elect received volumes of mail in the same vein. Ibid., 29 April 1915. Forms were printed by newspapers in Boston, Cincinnati, Detroit, Los Angeles (several), Louisville, and Omaha. Dinnerstein, op. cit., p. 118.
93. Ibid., pp. 118–9; *New York Times*, 18, 24, 30 May 1915.
94. *New York Times*, 27 December 1914, 30 May, 28 April, 1 January 1915.
95. Ibid., 8, 13, 23, 24, 26, 28, 30 May, 4 June 1915. New York's total Jewish population was 975,000, Chicago's 200,000. *American Jewish Year Book 5675*, pp. 353, 354.
96. *New York Times*, 28, 30 May 1915.
97. Ibid., 19 May 1915; Madison C. Peters, ibid., 24 May 1915. Frank's lynching was widely condemned in Georgia. Ibid., 18 August 1915. In 1919 at a mass meeting in Atlanta protesting the pogroms of Eastern Europe, District Attorney Hooper Alexander recalled Georgia's shame over the lynching, ibid., 11 June 1919.

5 'THE INMOST HEART OF HELL'

1. *Jewish Chronicle*, 23 May, 18 July 1919.
2. Ibid., 27 June 1919. Edwards had participated in Cardiff's 1913 Beilis protest meeting.
3. Ibid., 4 July 1919.
4. Ibid., and 6 December 1918; *The Times*, 23 November 1925. Signatories included Sir Muirhead Bone and George Bernard Shaw. See Rubinstein, *A History of the Jews in the English-Speaking World: Great Britain*, p. 296.
5. *Jewish Chronicle*, 4 July 1919.
6. Ibid. Brailsford's eyewitness account of Polish antisemitism, in 'Poland as Barrier,' *New Republic*, 30 March 1919, helped to stir outrage in the United States. *New York Times*, 27 May 1919.
7. *Jewish Chronicle*, 11 April, 27 June, 4 July 1919. Parmoor, father of Sir Stafford Cripps, was one of several prominent non-Jews who supported the formation, on a Jewish initiative, of a League of Religions for Promoting Universal Peace. Ibid., 23 May 1919. For an 8,000-strong demonstration at the Royal Albert Hall against Russian persecution of religion, convened by the Christian Protest Committee and addressed by prominent non-Jews and the Chief Rabbi, see ibid., 27 December 1929.
8. Ibid., 30 May 1919.
9. Ibid., 28 November 1919, and 4 July 1919 for a meeting at Baltimore; *New York Times*, 11 June 1919 for a meeting in Atlanta.
10. *Jewish Chronicle*, 9 February 1917, 31 January 1919, 28 November 1919;

New York Times, 23 May, 23 October 1919. For protests by gentiles in France and elsewhere see ibid., 6 October 1919, *Jewish Chronicle*, 6 December 1918, 30 May, 12, 26 September 1919; *American Jewish Year Book 5682* ... (Philadelphia: 1921), p. 115.
11. *Jewish Chronicle*, 9 February 1917. A lecture Taft gave in January 1917 to the National Geographic Society on 'The Progressive World Struggle of the Jews for Civil Liberty: Will this War Help?' had to be delivered twice owing to demand.
12. Speech, Chicago, quoted ibid., 4 February 1921.
13. Ibid.
14. Ibid., 24 May 1929.
15. *American Jewish Year Book 5682*, p. 117. Text in *America and the Jews* (London: 1921), pp. 7–8. This pamphlet was issued by the British Board of Deputies.
16. *Jewish Chronicle*, 4 January 1921; *America and the Jews*, p. 3.
17. List (118 out of total 121 names), ibid., pp. 8–12. Holmes, for example, a celebrated New York clergyman who became close to Rabbi Stephen S. Wise, had been prominent in the Kishinev protest; he would also champion Zionism and protest Nazi antisemitism. See also Egal Feldman, *Dual Destinies: the Jewish Encounter with Protestant America* (Urbana, Ill.: 1990), pp. 126–7. For other initiatives against domestic antisemitism in 1921, including a joint resolution by the Wisconsin Legislature, see *American Jewish Year Book 5682*, p. 118.
18. *Jewish Chronicle*, 18 June 1937. James Hall, Labour MP for Whitechapel, addressed this essentially Jewish meeting.
19. Ibid., 11 February 1938.
20. *American Jewish Year Book 5699*, vol. 40, 1938–9 (Philadelphia: 1938), pp. 100–2.
21. Ibid.
22. *The Times*, 28 June 1933; *Jewish Chronicle*, 30 June 1933. For Lang on rescuing Europe's Jews, see ibid., 5 March 1943. On this topic see Rubinstein, *A History of the Jews in the English-Speaking World: Great Britain*, pp. 280–363, and idem., *The Myth of Rescue: Why the Democracies Could Not Have Saved More Jews from the Nazis* (London: 1997).
23. Ibid., 30 June 1933. Gilbert Murray had been due to chair the meeting but was indisposed. For Steed on Nazi antisemitism see Wickham Steed, *Hitler, Whence and Whither?* (London: 1933).
24. Ibid., 7 July 1933.
25. *The Times*, 3 May 1933; *Jewish Chronicle*, 12 May 1933. T.J. O'Connor (1891–1940) should not be confused with T.P. O'Connor (1848-1929), a Beilis protest signatory who seems to have been close to the Jewish community.
26. *The Times*, 28 June 1933; *Jewish Chronicle*, 30 June 1933.
27. Ibid., 19 May 1933.
28. Ibid., 5 May 1933.
29. Ibid., 12 May 1933, 8 June 1934; *New Tredegar, Bargoed and Caerphilly Journal*, 13 May 1933; see also Lansbury in *The Times*, 19 December 1938; W.D. Rubinstein, 'The Anti-Jewish Riots of 1911 in South

Wales: a Re-Examination', *Welsh History Review*, vol. 18, no. 4 (1997), pp. 667–9.
30. *Jewish Chronicle*, 14 April 1933. See John Buchan, 'Russia and the Jews', *Spectator*, 18 November 1905; Gertrude Himmelfarb, 'John Buchan: An Untimely Appreciation', *Encounter* (September 1960), pp. 46–53; Janet Adam Smith, *John Buchan: A Biography* (London: 1965), pp. 124–7, 154–7, 283–4, 316–7, 426–7. For Locker-Lampson, Elmley and Sueter on improving opportunities for Jewish refugees to acquire British citizenship, see ibid., 28 July 1933; that measure was also backed by MPs Patrick Hannon, Holford Knight, W.J. Stewart and Sir Wilfred Sugden.
31. Ibid., 7 April 1933.
32. Ibid.
33. Tribute by S. Phillips, ibid., 16 December 1938. See also H. Henson, *Retrospect of an Unimportant Life: Vol. 1, 1920–1939* (Oxford: 1943). Also notable was the Archbishop of York, Dr Cyril Garbett (formerly Bishop of Winchester) and the Bishop of Chichester, Dr George Bell: the latter was especially outspoken on behalf of non-Aryan Christians. In contrast to general clerical sympathy for persecuted Jewry, the Bishop of Gloucester was an apologist for Nazi Germany. See, for example, *Church Times*, 24 March 1939, citing his article in the *Church of England Newspaper* (n.d.).
34. *The Yellow Spot: the outlawing of half a million human beings ...* (London: 1936), pp. 5–8.
35. *Church Times*, 30 December 1938.
36. *Jewish Chronicle*, 1 September 1933.
37. Ibid., 7 April 1933.
38. *The Times*, 19 November 1938.
39. *Jewish Chronicle*, 9 June 1933.
40. Ibid., 7 April 1933.
41. Quoted ibid.
42. Ibid., 16 June 1933.
43. Letter, *Time and Tide*, 25 November 1933; advertisement, ibid., 10 February 1934. For forthright denunciations by Barker and Deedes of Nazi antisemitism, see *Jewish Chronicle*, 15 November 1935.
44. *Church Times*, 29 October 1933.
45. *Jewish Chronicle*, 18 October 1933. Other speakers were the organizer, Charles Cooley, and Maude Royden. With Sylvia Pankhurst, Canon Donaldson, Lords Marley and Strabolgi and other prominent gentiles, Maude Royden sent a message of support to a protest meeting against Mosleyite harassment of Jews, organized by the New World Fellowship and chaired by William W. Holroyd. Ibid., 6 July 1934.
46. Ronald W. Clark, *Einstein: The Life and Times* (London: 1973), pp. 398–416; *Jewish Chronicle*, 1 November 1935; cf. Locker-Lampson on Einstein, ibid., 28 July, 22 December 1933, and George Bernard Shaw's adulation of Einstein, ibid., 31 October 1930.
47. Ibid., 1 April, 2 June 1933; see also Rubinstein, *A History of the Jews in the English-Speaking World: Great Britain*, London, p. 499. On Haldane see note 50 *infra*.

48. Letter by W.H. Beveridge, *Jewish Chronicle*, 16 December 1938.
49. *The Times*, 26 April 1933.
50. Ibid., 12 May 1933; *Jewish Chronicle*, 26 May 1933. John Burden Sanderson Haldane should not be confused with his father and fellow philosemite, noted physiologist James Scott Haldane (1860–1936). The author Naomi Mitchison, J.B.S. Haldane's sister, also deplored Nazi antisemitism. His wife was Secretary of the Friends of the Library of the Burned Books, whose members included George Catlin, H.G. Wells, Margot Asquith, Wickham Steed and Haldane himself. *Time and Tide*, 14 April 1934.
51. *Jewish Chronicle*, 31 March, 7 April 1933, 1 April 1938. See also ibid., 7 July 1933 for Swaffer at a Jewish protest meeting in London.
52. Ibid., 25 October 1935. Vyvyan Adams MP, a scheduled speaker, was unavoidably absent; his wife attended in his stead. The World Non-Sectarian Anti-Nazi Council to Champion Human Rights had been set up in 1934 by the International Boycott Conference representing 12 countries. Ibid., 30 November 1934. For press extracts condemning the Nuremberg Laws, see ibid., 20, 27 September 1935.
53. Ibid., 8, 15, 22 July 1938.
54. Ibid., 24 June 1938; *Time and Tide*, the 'staunch Conservative' Duchess of Atholl's warnings regarding Nazism, 8 August 1936, 25 February, 11 March 1939. See also Margot Asquith, letter, *The Times*, 14 November 1938.
55. *Jewish Chronicle*, 10 June 1938; cf. 22 July 1938.
56. Ibid., 1 April 1938, 27 August 1943; *Time and Tide*, 31 December 1938.
57. *Time and Tide* (Supplement), 26 November 1938.
58. *The Times*, 14, 17 November 1938; *Jewish Chronicle*, 18 November, 2 December 1938; see text of petition of 23 self-described 'ordinary people' of Bradford, in Tony Kushner, *The Holocaust and the Liberal Imagination: a Social and Cultural History* (Oxford: 1994), p. 49. (Bradford held public protest meetings in 1933 and 1938.)
59. *Jewish Chronicle*, 18, 25 December 1938; see also Appeal for Amnesty for Germany's Political Prisoners [including Jews], ibid., 21 October 1938. For Thomas see *Who's Who in Wales* (Cardiff: 1934).
60. *The Times*, 12 November 1938.
61. Ibid., 15 November 1938.
62. *Jewish Chronicle*, 18 November 1938.
63. Ibid., 2 June 1939.
64. Ibid., 18 November, 1938.
65. *The Times*, 18 November 1938.
66. Cited in *Jewish Chronicle*, 25 November 1938.
67. *Time and Tide*, 26 November 1938.
68. *The Times*, 17 November 1938.
69. Ibid., and see ibid., 19 November 1938 for resolutions at Glasgow University and Bedford College for Women, University of London.
70. *Jewish Chronicle*, 9 December 1938. It has recently come to light that Amery's mother was Jewish. See William D. Rubinstein, 'The Secret of Leopold Amery', *History Today*, February 1999, pp. 17–23.
71. *The Times*, 19 November 1938.

72. *Jewish Chronicle*, 4 November, 2 December 1938.
73. *Daily Herald*, quoted with other newspapers in *Jewish Chronicle*, 18 November 1938.
74. *The Times* editorials, 11, 17 November 1938; cf. *Church Times*, 13 January 1939, quoted in note 88, *infra*.
75. *Jewish Chronicle*, 7 July 1933; *Time and Tide*, 31 December 1938; *The Times*, 15 July 1938.
76. Quoted in *Jewish Chronicle*, 6 May 1938.
77. Ibid., 21 May 1943.
78. *The Times*, 12 November 1938.
79. *Jewish Chronicle*, 18 November 1938.
80. Ibid., 16 December 1938.
81. *Time and Tide*, 10 December 1938: most of the 25 signatories were non-Jews.
82. Ibid., 17 August 1940.
83. Letter to Neville Laski, Chairman, British Board of Deputies, *Times*, 19 December 1938. Another example of gentile countering of anti-semitism from a very different source was Elizabeth A. Allen (General Secretary of the National Council for Civil Liberties), *It Shall Not Happen Here: anti-semitism, Fascists and civil liberty* (London: 1943). See also speech of Lord Snell, Chairman of London County Council, on 'The Moral Debasement of Anti-Semitism', *Jewish Chronicle*, 25 February 1938.
84. A.L. Easterman, ibid., 25 December 1942. Lord Simon, formerly Sir John Simon, was not Jewish: he should not be confused with his nineteenth-century Jewish namesake. Lady Simon, formerly Mrs Kathleen Manning, was an ardent gentile Zionist.
85. Sir John Squire, 'The Jews' Christmas 1942', *Jewish Chronicle*, 1 January 1943, first published in *Daily Express* during the final week of 1942.
86. *Jewish Chronicle*, 11, 18, 25 December 1942. Whale (1896–1997) had a most distinguished career ahead of him.
87. See speeches, House of Lords, ibid., 25 December 1942.
88. Ibid., 11, 25 December 1942.
89. Ibid., 19 March 1943; cf. *Church Times*, 13 January 1939, in an unattributed review of Dorothy Frances Buxton, *The Economics of the Refugee Problem* (London: 1939): 'there is no one sovereign remedy. But that is not an excuse for doing nothing; it is rather a powerful argument for immediate and persistent activity.'
90. See, for instance, *Time and Tide*, 26 December 1942, 1 April 1944; *Jewish Chronicle*, 25 December 1942, 1, 15, 29 January, 5, 12 February, 5, 19 March 1943; 21 January, 23 June 1944. Malcolm was former High Commissioner for Refugees.
91. National Committee for Rescue from Nazi Terror, *Continuing Terror: How to Help Rescue Hitler's Victims – a Survey and a Programme* (London: 1944), p. 19.
92. *Jewish Chronicle*, 12 February 1943.
93. See note 91 *supra*.
94. *Continuing Terror*, p. 20.
95. *The Times*, 16 February 1943.

96. *Continuing Terror*, pp. 21–2.
97. See Rubinstein, *The Myth of Rescue*. A statement in 1943 by the Churches' Peace Aims Group declared that no world settlement which failed to give reasonable security and freedom to religious, cultural, and other minorities, and especially the Jewish people, would be said to have succeeded. Signatories included the Archbishops of Canterbury and York, the Bishop of Chichester, the Moderator of the Church of Scotland, Nonconformist leaders, the Master of Balliol, Sir John Hope Simpson and R.H. Tawney. *Jewish Chronicle*, 27 August 1943.
98. Ibid., 31 March 1933.
99. Ibid., 12 May 1933.
100. Ibid., 9 June 1933.
101. Ibid. Several were signatories to the 1921 petition.
102. Some press comments are given ibid., 18 November 1938; *Age* (Melbourne), 21 November 1938.
103. Ibid., 7 September 1934. Pierre van Paassen and James Waterman Wise, eds., *Nazism: An Assault on Civilization* (New York: 1934).
104. Dorothy Thompson, *Refugees: Anarchy or Organization?* (New York: 1938).
105. *Jewish Chronicle*, 23 September 1938.
106. Ibid., 2 July 1937. For Lewis's hatred of racism towards Jews and blacks see Mark Schorer, *Sinclair Lewis: an American Life* (New York: 1961), pp. 305, 730, quoted in Gould, op. cit., pp. 317–18.
107. Ibid., 13 July 1934.
108. Ibid., 19 March 1937.
109. See, for example, ibid., 25 October, 8 November 1935, 11 July 1937, 6 May 1938, 7 July 1939.
110. Ibid., 25 November 1938; see also *American Jewish Year Book 5699*, pp. 91 *et seq*.
111. *Argus* (Melbourne), 22 November 1938.
112. *Jewish Chronicle*, 6 May 1938.
113. *The Times*, 16 November 1938; *Argus* (Melbourne), 16 November 1938; *Jewish Chronicle*, 25 November 1938.
114. See, for example, *The American War Congress and Zionism: Statements by Members of the American War Congress on the Jewish National Movement* (New York: 1919); *Jewish Chronicle*, 7 March 1919, 2 February 1923, 6 March 1931, 1 July 1932.
115. See ibid., 21 October 1938 for the Lodge–Fish resolution and the terms of the America-British Mandate of 1924 which safeguarded the rights of United States citizens in Palestine. Fish (1849–1936) should not be confused with his father, who is mentioned in chapter 3.
116. Ibid., 1 July 1932.
117. Ibid., 4 November 1938.
118. Ibid., 28 October 1938; *Church Times*, 6 January 1939.
119. *Jewish Chronicle*, 14 October 1938. New York attorney Thomas E. Dewey, Republican presidential candidate in 1944 and 1948, soon-to-be-Governor of New York, also signed, probably with an eye to the Jewish vote.
120. *Age* (Melbourne), 21 November 1938.

121. *Jewish Chronicle*, 2 June 1939.
122. Ibid., 11 December 1942.
123. Ibid., 12 March 1943.
124. Ibid.
125. Ibid.
126. Ibid., 4 February 1944. For Murphy's denunciation of antisemitism when Governor of Michigan, see ibid., 24 December 1937. Such activities contradict the curious statement in Feldman, *Dual Destinies*, p. 193: 'As the Nazi noose tightened around the fate of Europe's Jews, American Jews found themselves desperately alone, surrounded by a noncaring Gentile world.'
127. Ibid., 12 March 1943, 27 August 1943. Van Paassen, with Rabbi Stephen S. Wise's son, had co-edited a book on the evils of Nazism: see note 103 *supra*. On a visit to Atlanta in 1922 he had explored the official court documentation on the Leo Frank Affair, uncovering suppressed material underlining Frank's innocence. Pierre van Paassen, *To Number Our Days* (New York: 1964), pp. 19–64. Notable British advocates of a Jewish army were Labour MP Seymour Cocks and Conservative MPs Ian Hannah and Oliver Locker-Lampson.
128. See, for example, denunciations by Canadian church groups, *Jewish Chronicle*, 13 May, 17 June 1938.
129. *The Times*, 22 November 1938.
130. Ibid., 17, 22 November 1938.
131. On the pervasively widespread nature of antisemitism in interwar Quebec, see Esther Delisle, *The Traitor and the Jew: Anti-Semitism and the Delirium of Right-wing Nationalism in French Canada From 1929–1939*, (Montreal: 1993), and Irving Abella, 'Anti-Semitism in Canada in the Interwar Years', in Moses Rischin, ed., *The Jews of North America* (Detroit: 1987).
132. Ibid., 22 November 1938. Several months earlier, 10,000 people had attended a demonstration in Montreal against antisemitism, addressed by the local Bishop, John C. Farthing. Ibid., 8 July 1938. For a survey of Canadian church attitudes towards Nazi antisemitism see Marilyn F. Nefsky, 'The Shadow of Evil: Nazism and Canadian Protestantism', in Alan Davies, ed., *Antisemitism in Canada: History and Interpretations* (Waterloo, Ontario: 1992), pp. 197–225.
133. *Argus*, 28 April 1933.
134. *Sydney Morning Herald*, 19 May 1933. The Legislative Council is the state upper house, traditionally conservatively inclined. See also W.D. Rubinstein, 'The Attitude of the Australian Jewish Community and of Non-Jewish Opinion Leaders to the Rise of Nazi Anti-Semitism in 1933', *Australian Jewish Historical Society Journal*, vol. 12, part 1 (1993), pp. 101–14; *Hebrew Standard* (Sydney), 19 May 1933; *Jewish Chronicle*, 21 July 1933, 4 November 1938; *Argus*, 18 November 1938.
135. *Jewish Chronicle*, 28 July 1933; *Adelaide Advertiser*, 5 October 1933; *Jewish Weekly News* (Melbourne), 25 January 1935; S.M. Bruce to J.A. Lyons (Australian Prime Minister), 21 November 1938, quoted in Michael Blakeney, *Australia and the Jewish Refugees 1933–1948* (Sydney: 1985), pp. 141–2.

136. *Jewish Chronicle*, 13 May, 8 July, 26 August, 21 October 1938; *Sydney Morning Herald*, 4 February 1940; *Australians and Jewish Settlement in the Kimberleys ... a collection of Articles from the Australian Press* (Sydney: 1940); Solomon Stedman, *A Jewish Settlement in Kimberley* (Sydney: 1940). Cramsie also suggested an alternative settlement of 100,000 refugees on Melville Island. *Sydney Morning Herald*, 2 December 1938. For the Kimberley scheme and further references regarding support, see Hilary L. Rubinstein, *The Jews in Australia: a Thematic History. Volume 1: 1788–1945* (Melbourne: 1991), pp. 180–96, 506–11. For Australia's comparatively generous refugee intake see W.D. Rubinstein, 'Australia and the Refugee Jews of Europe, 1933–1954: a Dissenting View', *Australian Jewish Historical Society Journal*, vol. 10, part 6 (1989), pp. 500–23.
137. *West Australian*, 6 September 1939.
138. *Argus*, 1 December 1939 (46 signatories); *Sydney Morning Herald*, 19 April 1940 (55 signatories). There were a few Jewish signatories. The Jewish community was split on the scheme, with Zionists in general vehemently opposed.
139. *Australian Jewish Forum*, October 1944, p. 3
140. See Hilary L. Rubinstein, 'Critchley Parker (1911–42): Australian Martyr for Jewish Refugees', *Australian Jewish Historical Society Journal*, vol. 11, part 1 (1990), pp. 56–68.
141. *Hebrew Standard*, 19 November 1942. Lord Mayor Stanley Sadler Crick and Harrison had signed their state's Kimberley manifesto. *Sydney Morning Herald*, 19 April 1940.
142. Max Freilich, *Zion in Our Time: Memoirs of an Australian Zionist* (Sydney: 1967), pp. 94–5, 113.
143. *Hebrew Standard*, 16 September 1943.
144. *Jewish Chronicle*, 10 December 1926, 4 March 1927; see also 6 April 1928, 10 October 1930; Barry Kraut, 'Towards the Establishment of the National Council of Christians and Jews: The Tenuous Road to Religious Goodwill in the 1920s', *American Jewish History*, vol. 77 (1988), pp. 390–1; Lance J. Sussman, 'Toward Better Understanding: The Rise of the Interfaith Movement in America and the Role of Rabbi Isaac Landman', *American Jewish Archives*, vol. 34 (April 1982), pp. 41–58.
145. *American Jewish Year Book 5683*, p. 118.
146. *Jewish Chronicle*, 8 June 1923, 3 September 1926, 6 May, 30 December 1927, 6 April, 10 August 1928, 4 January, 27 December 1929, 8 March 1935, 10 September 1937. In 1937 Manning published an appeal to Nazi leaders to cease persecuting Jews. Ibid., 24 December 1937.
147. *Jewish Chronicle*, 19, 26 October 1928.
148. Feldman, *Dual Destinies*, pp. 198–201; Robert Anderson, 'Protestants and Jews in the Twentieth Century: Some Aspects and Some Prospects', in *A Portion of Praise*, p. 184; cf. *Jewish Chronicle*, 6 March 1931, 1 July 1932.
149. Ibid., 8 April 1938.
150. Ibid., 16 June, 7 July 1939. See also ibid., for resolution of Catholic Press Association. Wagner (1910–91), Mayor of New York, 1953–65,

should not be confused with his father and namesake, the demonstrably pro-Zionist anti-Fascist Senator Robert F. Wagner (1877–1953).
151. Ibid., 16 June, 7 July 1939: reports of the Sons of Italy, the General Synod of the Reformed Church in America and the Federal Council of Churches of Christ. There was also a U.S. Council Against Intolerance. See also Johan M. Snoek, *The Grey Book: A Collection of Protests Against Anti-Semitism and the Persecution of Jews Issued by Non-Roman Catholic Churches and Church Leaders during Hitlers [sic] Rule* (Assen: 1969).
152. Sidney Dark, *The Jew To-Day* (London: 1933) (with endorsement on dust cover by Chaim Weizmann); Sidney Dark and Herbert Sidebotham, *The Folly of Anti-Semitism* (London: 1939). Sidebotham wrote his political column as 'Scrutator'; he authored *England and Palestine: Essays towards the Restoration of the Jewish State* (London: 1918); *The Future of Palestine* (London: 1922); *British Policy and the Palestine Mandate: Our Proud Privilege* (London: 1929); *British Interests in Palestine* (London: 1934), and *Great Britain and Palestine* (London: 1937). See David Carrington, 'A non-Jew's contribution to Zionism', *Jewish Chronicle*, 19 May 1950; Harry Sacher, 'Herbert Sidebotham', in idem., *Zionist Portraits and Other Essays* (London: 1959), pp. 107–10.
153. See, for instance, the following books by James Parkes: *The Jew and his Neighbour* (London: 1930); *The Jewish Problem in the Modern World* (London: 1939); *An Enemy of the People: Antisemitism* (Harmondsworth: 1945), and *Voyage of Discoveries* (London: 1969), especially chapter 6. See also Marcus Braybrooke, *Children of One God: A History of the Council of Christians and Jews* (London: 1991); William W. Simpson, 'Jewish–Christian Cooperation in Great Britain', *Contemporary Jewish Record*, vol. 7, no. 6 (1944), pp. 641–5; idem., 'Jewish-Christian Relations Since the Inception of the Council of Christians and Jews,' *Jewish Historical Society of England Transactions* (London: 1984). See also Richard Jones, *The A.B.C. of Jew-Baiting: an Address ... April 23, 1939* [Pontypridd: 1939] as an example of Christian clerical philosemitism.
154. See, in particular, B. Burgoyne Chapman, T*he Complete Anti-Semite*, 2nd edn, rev. (Sydney: 1945), to which Professor Walter Murdoch contributed a preface.
155. Israel Porush, 'The New South Wales Council of Christians and Jews (1943–1948)', *Australian Jewish Historical Society Journal*, vol. 6, part 4 (1968), pp. 181–95; *Jewish Chronicle*, 8 March 1935, 17 June 1938 (speech of the Bishop of Johannesburg).

6 'THE SPIRIT OF THE AGE'

1. *Jewish Chronicle*, 2 December 1938.
2. Thomas Babington Macaulay, 'Civil Disabilities of the Jews', *Edinburgh Review* (January 1831), reprinted in idem., *Critical and Historical Essays Contributed to the Edinburgh Review* (London: 1843), vol. 1, pp. 295–310; cf., for example, G.S. Venables, 'The Admission of the

Jews into Parliament', *Tait's Edinburgh Magazine*, vol. 17 (July 1850), pp. 427-33; Harriet Martineau, quoted in *Jewish Chronicle*, 1 March 1850; Lord John Russell, ibid., 24 July 1846; *Bristol Gazette*, 17 February 1853, quoted ibid., 25 February 1853.
3. Israel Getzler, *Neither Toleration Nor Favour: The Australian Chapter of Jewish Emancipation* (Melbourne: 1970); *Royal Gazette* (Kingston, Jamaica), 24 October 1843, quoted in *Voice of Jacob*, 8 December 1843; President John Tyler, ibid., 20 June 1845; *Jewish Chronicle*, 5 February 1858, 29 December 1897; Sheldon J. Godfrey and Judith C. Godfrey, *Search Out the Land: The Jews and the Growth of Equality in British Colonial America 1740-1867* (Montreal: 1995).
4. Hans Kohn, *The Idea of Nationalism: A Study in Its Origins and Background* (New York: 1967); idem., *American Nationalism: An Interpretive Essay* (New York: 1957).
5. *Jewish Chronicle*, 8 January 1847, 6 October 1865.
6. *Voice of Jacob*, 26 May 1843. See also David Kynaston, *The City of London. Volume One: A World of Its Own 1815-1890* (London: 1994).
7. *Jewish Chronicle*, 6 April 1855, 4, 11 December 1874; Sir William Soulsby, 'The Jew in Civic Life,' ibid., 2 December 1921, citing Reginald R. Sharpe, *London and the Kingdom* (London: 1895); *Voice of Jacob*, 26 May 1873; Charles Kensington Salaman, *The Jews As They Are* (London: 1882), pp. 64-82. Polly Pinsker, 'English Opinion and Jewish Emancipation (1830-1860)', *Jewish Social Studies*, vol. 14 (1952), pp. 51-94. Salomons became an alderman in 1847 following his third election to the post. He was first elected to Parliament (for Greenwich) in 1851.
8. *Jewish Chronicle*, 13 May 1842; see also ibid., 5 March 1847, 14 December 1860; *Illustrated London News*, 6 November 1858.
9. *Stock Exchange Journal*, 24 September 1845, quoted in *Jewish Chronicle*, 6 October 1845; see also ibid., 15 April 1864, text of petition to the House of Commons from the Lord Mayor, Aldermen and Common Council of the City of London, ibid., 11 March 1853; speech of James Thompson, Treasurer of Portsoken Liberal Committee, Portsoken Ward, *Voice of Jacob*, 15 August 1845; 'Rise and Progress of British Industry', *Wade's London Review*, n.d., cited ibid., 20 June 1845; William Thornborrow, letter, ibid., 11 September 1846; idem., *Advocacy of Jewish Freedom* (London: 1847). Thornborrow was Chairman of the Liberal Committee of Cornhill ward. Rothschild was elected MP for the City in 1847, 1849, 1852, and 1857, finally taking his seat in 1858.
10. *An Appeal to Popular Prejudices in Favour of the Jews* (London: 1796), extracted, with commentary, in *Jewish Chronicle*, 13 March 1863; cf. *Westminster Review*, vol. 10 (1869), pp. 435-43.
11. *Jewish Chronicle*, 5 June 1874.
12. Were there perhaps two visits? According to *Voice of Jacob*, 26 May 1843, the visit occurred in 1806, when Sussex was accompanied by the Dukes of Clarence (afterwards King William IV) and Kent (father of Queen Victoria). However, when he visited on 14 April 1809, he was accompanied by the Dukes of Cumberland and Cambridge (also a philosemite). See David Katz, *The Jews in the History of England*

1485–1850 (Oxford: 1994), pp. 373, 374n.
13. *Voice of Jacob*, 24 June 1842, 28 April, 4, 12, 26 May, 24 June 1843, 4 October 1844. Unlike 'The late Duke of Sussex', ibid., 26 May 1843, which dates his patronage (under Goldsmid's influence) of the Jews' Hospital to 1817, James Picciotto, *Sketches of Anglo-Jewish History* (London: 1875, repr. 1956), p. 277, dates it to 1813, claiming Sussex was persuaded by Joshua van Oven to accept the post. See also A. Barnett, 'Sussex Hall: The First Anglo-Jewish Venture in Popular Education', *Transactions of the Jewish Historical Society of England*, vol. 19 (1960), pp. 65–79.
14. See, for instance, *Freemason's Quarterly*, n.d., cited in *Voice of Jacob*, 27 October 1843; ibid., 14 September 1844; Dudley Wright, 'Early English Jewish Masons', *Jewish Chronicle Supplement*, 27 March 1925; Frederic, op. cit., pp. 178–9; Rubinstein, *The Jews in Australia: A Thematic History*, vol. 1, pp. 19–21.
15. *Voice of Jacob*, 24 June 1842, 26 May 1843.
16. Ibid.
17. Ibid., 23 June 1843; *Jewish Chronicle*, 12 July 1850, 16 April 1851.
18. For instance, both John Abel Smith and Samuel Gurney regularly contributed to Jewish charities, as did, with remarkable generosity, Smith, Payne and Co. and Overend Gurney and Co., the companies with which they were respectively associated. Some attenders at the rallies, including MPs Kirkman Hodgson and Mortara protest signatory William Roupell, made single or occasional donations. Founders of firms which acquired household names, such as Colman's mustard and Rimmel's cosmetics, also appeared in donors' lists. One of the partners of Debenham, Storr, and Sons, auctioneers, who appears in donors' lists, made bequests to Jewish charities and individuals. Ibid., 22 April 1864. For donors' lists, see ibid., May–July each year.
19. *Voice of Jacob*, 24 June 1842; cf. David Wire, ibid., 13 May 1842; Charles Pearson, *Jewish Chronicle*, 22 February 1856.
20. *Voice of Jacob*, 17, 24 December 1841, 28 January, 9 December 1842; *Jewish Chronicle*, 15 May, 25 December 1846. See also, for example, ibid., 30 May 1851 (Manchester dinner in aid of the building fund of the New Jews' School, Cheetham Hill), 13 December 1850, 9 February 1855, 17 December 1858.
21. Maria Edgeworth, *Harrington* (London: 1817), quoted in R. Papperovitch, 'Jews in the Novels of Maria Edgeworth', *Jewish Chronicle Supplement*, March 1934, p. v. Dramatists, essayists, novelists and poets attempting to allay anti-Jewish prejudice included Robert Browning, Richard Cumberland, Thomas de Quincey, George Eliot, William Hazlitt, Tobias Smollett and Thomas Wade. Samuel Taylor Coleridge, an intimate friend of the Montefiore family, was also sympathetic. For Smollett's little-known impact upon Cumberland, see M.J. Landa, 'Sir Walter Scott's 100th Jahrzeit', *Jewish Chronicle*, 16 September 1932. See also idem., 'The Jewish Confessions of de Quincey', *Jewish Chronicle Supplement*, February 1930, pp. v–vi; idem., 'Hazlitt's Defence of the Jews', ibid., September 1930, pp. ii–iii; A. Cohen, 'English Essayists and the Jews', ibid., 26 January 1923; idem.,

'Some Precursors of Anglo-Jewish Emancipation', ibid., March 1930, pp. v–vi; Maurice Edelman, 'A Study in Loyalties: A Tribute to the Memory of John Galsworthy', ibid., January 1934, pp. v–vi; 'Friends and Vindicators of the Jews', *Jewish Chronicle*, 15 May 1874, and articles ibid., 27 April 1917, 1 August 1919, 17 August 1923, 10 January 1930. Conan Doyle, who like Galsworthy signed the Beilis protest, campaigned strenuously for the release of 'this poor Jew' Oscar Slater, gaoled in 1912 for a murder in Glasgow, whose innocence he upheld, ibid., 9 September, 2 December 1927.

22. A Jewish guest at a banquet in Birmingham, *Voice of Jacob*, 18 August 1843.
23. Ibid., 24 June 1842; *Jewish Chronicle*, 16 May 1851, 24 November, 8 December 1854. Stuart was a son of the Marquis of Bute and a relative of Baroness Burdett-Coutts.
24. *Weekly Dispatch*, ca. 26 March 1854, quoted ibid., 31 March 1854 (emphasis in original); see also extract from the same newspaper, ibid., 16 July 1847, and ibid., 21 June 1850, 1, 8 August 1851, 17 February, 11, 18 March, 6 May 1853, for a sample of other philosemitic press extracts.
25. Ibid., 11 January 1850.
26. Ibid., 8 January 1847.
27. See, for instance, Dr John B. Melsom (a Mortara protest signatory), *Birmingham Journal*, 12 August 1843, quoted in *Voice of Jacob*, 1 September 1843; Portsmouth town council meeting, *Hampshire Independent*, 10 February 1844, quoted ibid., 16 July 1844; anon., *The Mysteries of London*, quoted in *Jewish Chronicle*, 19 March 1847; *Weekly Dispatch*, n.d., quoted ibid., 16 July 1847; Councillor J. Aikin, Liverpool, ibid., 25 December 1847; letter from 'S.R.', an Irish Roman Catholic, ibid., 8 March 1850; press extracts, ibid., 14 July 1854; letter from 'A Gentile Reader,' ibid., 15 June 1855; extracts by William Gilbert, ibid., 1, 8, 15 July 1864; Kathleen Manning, ibid., 12 June 1903; George R. Sims, ibid., 22 February 1907; Margaret McMillan, ibid., 27 December 1907; Sir Humphry Rolleston, ibid., 30 November 1923; Sir Alexander Porter, ibid., 29 November 1912; Sir Leo Chiozza Money, ibid., 6 November 1925.
28. Alderman Daniel Howard, *Voice of Jacob*, 16 February 1844.
29. Jewish eyewitness, quoted ibid., 18 August 1843; cf. *Birmingham Journal*, 12 August 1843, quoted ibid., 1 September 1843.
30. David Barnett, *Jewish Chronicle*, 15 May 1846.
31. *Hampshire Independent*, n.d., quoted in *Voice of Jacob*, 23 March 1844.
32. Ibid., 24 November 1843; letter from Emanuel Emanuel, ibid., 23 March 1844; cf. ibid., 5 November 1858.
33. Ibid., 10 April 1846, regarding Isaac M. Emanuel. A branch of the family became well-respected in Australian political and pastoral circles.
34. *Jewish Chronicle*, 4 July 1851. Ironically, Salomons' opponent was Alderman Wire, who had been tempted to stand on the grounds that, if elected, Salomons would not be able to take his seat.
35. Ibid., 28 April 1853.

Notes 233

36. Ibid., 22 November 1861. It was only partially completed at his death.
37. *Cumberland Times*, n.d., quoted in *Voice of Jacob*, 24 April 1846.
38. *Morning Chronicle* (Sydney), n.d., quoted ibid., 19 July 1844. See also ibid., 28 October 1842, regarding Jews in the Indian Army.
39. H.N. Brailsford, *The Fruits of Our Russian Alliance* (Letchworth, Herts.: *ca.* 1912), p. 27; cf. *Daily Telegraph*, 11 March 1864: 'A country's progress is tested by the consideration and justice with which it treats these patient citizens.'
40. Message to public meeting to protest Polish antisemitism, *Jewish Chronicle*, 18 June 1937.
41. *The Times*, 4 July 1840.
42. *Jewish Chronicle*, 31 May 1872.
43. *Outrages Upon the Jews in Russia*, p. 22; *The Times*, 18 February 1882.
44. Ibid., 11 December 1890.
45. Adler, op. cit., p. 113.
46. *Hansard*, 10 July 1905, pp. 154–5; cf. his letter to Lord Rothschild, 26 December 1905, *The Times*, 9 January 1906; for Meredith see *Jewish Chronicle*, 28 May 1909.
47. *The Times*, 6 May 1912.
48. *Jewish Chronicle*, 23 December 1938.
49. Ibid., 5 May 1933.
50. *Bedfordshire Mercury*, n.d., quoted ibid., 9 January 1863.
51. *The Times*, 2 June 1840. Buxton and Shaftesbury (as Lord Ashley) spoke. Edward Baines MP also attended. The near-ubiquitous American philosemite Paul D. Cravath probably derived his outlook from his Quaker mother and his Congregationalist father, foundation President of Fisk University, who took a particular interest in negro education.
52. Ibid., 6 December 1890; *Jewish Chronicle*, 10 May 1895.
53. *The Times*, 2 February 1882.
54. *Jewish Chronicle*, 11 April 1919.
55. *The Times*, 4 July 1840.
56. Ibid., 19 October 1859; *Jewish Chronicle*, 28 October 1859.
57. *Outrages Upon the Jews in Russia*, p. 11. The obligation and desire of Englishmen to aid the oppressed was a recurrent theme at the rallies.
58. *Sydney Morning Herald*, 24 May 1881.
59. *The Times*, 11 December 1890.
60. Ibid. Argyll was active in the anti-slavery movement. See Christine Bolt, *The Anti-Slavery Movement and Reconstruction: A Study in Anglo-American Cooperation 1833–77* (London: 1969), pp. 11 et seq.
61. Adler, ibid., p. 136.
62. *Jewish Herald*, 1 December 1905.
63. Ibid., 12 January 1906.
64. *Jewish Chronicle*, 30 June 1933.
65. Walter Murdoch, preface to Chapman, op. cit., p. B (*sic*).
66. Ibid., *Jewish Chronicle*, 22 November 1918.
67. Ibid., 31 January 1896.
68. *The Times*, 2 February 1882, 11 December 1890; *Jewish Chronicle*, 8 October 1897.

69. Matthew Arnold, *The Great Prophecy of Israel's Restoration (Isaiah, Chapters 40–66)* (London: 1872); idem., *Letters* (London: 1895); *Jewish Chronicle*, 14 June 1872, 21 July 1876, 29 November 1895; Myer Domnitz, 'Matthew Arnold on Hebraism and Hellenism', *Jewish Chronicle Supplement*, 30 September 1938.
70. *Jewish Chronicle*, 19 June 1903, 5, 12 June 1895.
71. Rubinstein, '"A Noble Sight to See"', pp. 424–62.
72. See, for instance, *Evening Post* (Louisville, Ky.), quoted in Adler, op. cit., p. 320.
73. Information on black philosemitism from Professor Julius Lester (USA) at a conference in Paris, December 1996; Adler, op. cit., p. 113; *Argus*, 23 May 1903, 2 August 1881; *The Times*, 5 January 1906.
74. See Davitt, op. cit., p. ix; *Jewish Chronicle*, 5 November 1897, 26 June 1903 (White), 6 January 1922, 31 October 1930, 5 April 1935, 29 May 1936 (Wells), 5 March 1920 (Haggard), 15 September 1933 (Steed); Henry Wickham Steed, *Through Thirty Years 1892–1922: A Personal Narrative* (London: 1924), vol. 2, pp. 390–3; A.G. Austin, ed., *The Webbs' Australian Diary, 1898* (Melbourne: 1965), pp. 68–9. John Masefield, a Beilis protest signatory, altered a reference in his poem 'London Town' derogatory to Jews. *Jewish Chronicle*, 11 July 1930. See also Rubinstein, *A History of the Jews in the English-Speaking World: Great Britain*, especially chapter 5.
75. Ibid., 5 April 1907.
76. *New York Call*, n.d. quoted in *New York Times*, 4 January 1915.
77. Gladstone to Dr Samuel Montague, 13 May 1896, describing himself as 'strongly *anti*-anti-Semitism', *Jewish Chronicle*, 29 May 1896. (Emphasis his.) For his ambivalence see ibid., 20 October, 3, 17 November 1876, 18 May 1877, 29 March, 16 August 1878, 17 January, 26 December 1879, 13 November 1891, 31 December 1909; Gladstone to Olga Novikoff, 13 February 1895, in *Christ or Moses: Which?* (London: 1895), pp. iv–viii. For Camilla Wedgwood's privately confided preference for 'the non-Aryan Christian refugee to the Jewish', see D. Wetherell and C. Carr-Gregg, *Camilla: C.H. Wedgwood 1901–1955. A Life* (Kensington, NSW: 1990), p. 40. Conservative protesters could also harbour ambivalence towards Jews. See, for instance, *Jewish Chronicle*, 5 March 1920 (Rider Haggard), but contrast Morton Cohen, *Rider Haggard: His Life and Work* (London: 1968), quoted in Gould, op. cit., p. 165; 31 October 1924 (Curzon); *American Jewish Yearbook 5699* (Philadelphia: 1938), p. 163 (Londonderry).
78. See, for instance, Robert S. Wistrich, ed., *The Left Against Zion* (London: 1979), and idem., *Revolutionary Jews from Marx to Trotsky* (London: 1976).
79. Robert S. Wistrich, 'The Ghost of Leon Trotsky', 'Global Anti-Zionism in the 1980s', and 'The New War Against the Jews', in *Modern Antisemitism and Jewish Identity* (London: 1990); W.D. Rubinstein, *The Left, the Right and the Jews* (London: 1981), pp. 99–117; Michael Lerner, *The Socialism of Fools: Anti-Semitism on the Left* (Oakland, Cal.: 1992).
80. On American aspects of this association see Harvey Klehr, *The Heyday*

of American Communism: The Depression Decade (New York: 1984); Arthur Liebman, *Jews and the Left* (New York: 1979); Irving Howe and Lewis Coser, *The American Communist Party* (Boston: 1957); Beth S. Wenger, *New York Jews and the Great Depression: Uncertain Promise* (New Haven: 1996). On Britain see Henry Felix Srebrnik, *London Jews and British Communism, 1935–1945* (London: 1995); Rubinstein, *A History of the Jews in the English-Speaking World: Great Britain*, pp. 241–6.
81. Srebrnik, op. cit., pp. 38–64.
82. Ibid.; Joe Jacobs, *Out of the Ghetto* (London: 1978); Robert Skidelsky, *Oswald Mosley* (London: 1990).

7 'THE DEEPEST DEBT'

1. *The Times*, 2 February 1882.
2. Ibid., 11 December 1890.
3. W.H. Fitchett, *Argus*, 6 June 1903.
4. Bishop of Oxford to O.J. Simon, 2 January 1906, *Jewish Chronicle*, 6 January 1906.
5. *American Jewish Year Book 5675*, p. 80. See also Samuel Hinds Wilkinson's preface to *New Light on the Jewish Question in Russia by C.A.* [i.e. Count K.K. Palen] (London, [1908]); Samuel Hinds Wilkinson and Sir Andrew Wingate, *Antisemitism: its Causes and Cures* (London: [1907]). Wilkinson was a British Israelite with several relevant publications.
6. *Jewish Chronicle*, 9 December 1938.
7. *Times*, 17 June 1938; see also Snoek, op. cit., p. 91.
8. See, for example, the Reverend Baptist Noel, *Jewish Chronicle*, 19 September 1857; the Reverend Thomas Raffles, ibid., 11 July 1856; Canon Archdall, *Jewish Herald*, 19 June 1903.
9. Quoted in Tuchman, op. cit., p. 81.
10. J.C. Wedgwood, *The Seventh Dominion* (London: 1928), pp. 119–21.
11. 'A Foreigner' [i.e. Benisch], *Voice of Jacob*, 6 September 1841; John M. Shaftesley, 'Dr. Abraham Benisch as Newspaper Editor', *Transactions of the Jewish Historical Society of England*, vol. 21 (1968), p. 217.
12. David S. Katz, 'The Phenomenon of Philosemitism', *Studies in Church History*, vol. 29 (1992), pp. 327–61; quotation at p. 327. See also idem., *Philo-Semitism and the Readmission of the Jews to England, 1603–1655* (Oxford: 1982).
13. Roger Ingpen, ed., *The Autobiography of Leigh Hunt*, 2 vols. (London: 1903), vol. 1 pp. 111–12.
14. Interview, *Jewish Chronicle*, 31 January 1908; cf. ibid., 16 October 1896. Ignatius' real name was the Reverend Joseph Lyne. See *Church Times*, 3 September 1932.
15. *Voice of Jacob*, 8 July 1842; Harry Golden, *Forgotten Pioneer* (New York: 1963), pp. 66–7; Golden, 'Jew and Gentile in the New South,' pp. 403–4.
16. Father Ignatius, 'The World's Debt to the Jews', *Jewish Chronicle*,

16 October 1896; Emily Marion Harris, 'The Late Mrs. Fitzgerald', ibid., 4 August 1899; see also, for example, *Mormon Times*, n.d., quoted ibid., 19 December 1856; James Simpson, *Voice of Jacob*, 22 July 1842; Lew Grade, *Still Dancing: My Story* (London: 1987), pp. 116–17.
17. *Jewish Chronicle*, 28 July 1854.
18. Ibid., 18 January, 6 August 1897; Rev. M.G. Hart, *Ballarat Star*, 8, 9 June 1903.
19. *Christian Lady's Magazine*, January 1843, pp. 63-8; *Jewish Chronicle*, 31 January 1908; ibid., 3 August 1934 (Inspector Thomas Eveson).
20. Ibid., 21, 28 January, 4 February 1876; some English parishes even appointed practising Jews as churchwardens! Ibid., 26 August 1864, 5 May 1876. See also chapter 8, note 11.
21. F.C. Burkett, 'The Debt of Christianity to Judaism', in Edwyn R. Bevan and Charles Singer, eds., *The Legacy of Israel* (Oxford: 1927), pp. 69–96.
22. Rev. J.D. Sir to M.L. Mozley, *Voice of Jacob*, 8 December 1843.
23. *Christian Reformer*, ca. November 1851, quoted in *Jewish Chronicle*, 12 December 1851.
24. Mrs. S.C. Hall, 'The Grave of Grace Aguilar', ibid., 10 October 1851. Emphasis in original.
25. *New York Times*, 27 December 1880; *Jewish Chronicle*, 13 July 1877; see also the stirring speech of Rev. Labagh of New York, *Voice of Jacob*, 8 May 1846.
26. Rev. Dr. David Paton, *South Australian Register*, 20 August 1881.
27. *The Times*, 2 February 1882.
28. Anne Fraser Bon, *Argus*, 23 May 1903.
29. Rev. Dr. Frank Oliver Hall (Universalist) to Rev. W.C. Stiles, in Stiles, op. cit., p. 281.
30. *Jewish Chronicle*, 31 January 1908.
31. Ibid., 31 October 1913.
32. Ibid., 6 December 1935; cf. Snoek, op. cit., pp. 71–2 and *Church Times*, 12 May 1944.
33. See Gidney, op. cit., for the Society's activists; for the Society's Australian patrons, see Rubinstein, '"A Noble Sight to See"', pp. 440, 447, 459, 460; for Paget see *Church Times*, 24 March 1922; for Blackstone see especially Yaakov Ariel, 'A Neglected Chapter in the History of Christian Zionism in America: William E. Blackstone and the Petition of 1916', in Jonathan Frankel, ed., *Jews and Messianism in the Modern Era: Metaphor and Meaning* (Oxford: 1991), pp. 68–85 and idem., *On Behalf of Israel,* for Blackstone and other American millenarians. By the 1920s most overt conversionist activity in Britain had subsided owing to Jewish remonstrations, *Jewish Chronicle Supplement*, 26 August 1921. Architect Basil Champneys, who protested the pogroms, was the son of the conversionist Rector of Whitechapel, who signed the Mortara protest.
34. See Kenneth Hylson-Smith, *Evangelicals in the Church of England 1734–1984* (Edinburgh: 1988); D.W. Bebbington, *Evangelicism in Modern Britain: a History from the 1730s to the 1980s* (London: 1989); Sherwood Eliot Wirt, *The Social Conscience of the Evangelical* (London: 1968).

35. *Liverpool Mail*, 21 September 1841, quoted in *Christian Lady's Magazine*, May 1843, p. 435; cf. ibid., June 1843, p. 540.
36. Ibid., see also Henry Downes, *Voice of Jacob*, 27 October 1843 and Bishop of Stepney, *Jewish Chronicle*, 6 December 1912.
37. See, for instance, Hugh McNeile, *Popular Lectures on the Prophecies Relative to the Jewish Nation* (London: 1830); idem., *Sermons on the Second Advent of Christ* (London: 1865); see also chapter 8, *infra*.
38. Her anonymous work *The Perils of the Nation* (London: 1843), influenced factory legislation. *Voice of Jacob*, 24 November 1843, Tonna, *Personal Reflections*, pp. 408–9; G.M. Young, 'Portrait of an Age', in idem., ed., *Early Victorian England 1830–1865*, vol. 2 (London: 1934), p. 460. She has attracted attention from scholars of Victorian literature, but her importance as an Evangelical writer and catalyst for social reform remains virtually unexplored. The only study of her attitude to Jews is Rubinstein, 'A Pioneering Philosemite'. Monica Correa Fryckstedt, 'Charlotte Elizabeth Tonna & the *Christian Lady's Magazin*e,' *Victorian Periodicals Review*, vol. 14, no. 2 (Summer 1981), pp. 433–51, in presenting Tonna's antipathy to popery as atypically fanatical appears to underestimate the robust anti-Catholicism prevalent in Victorian Britain. A highly tendentious interpretation of Tonna, Elizabeth Kowaleski, '"The Heroine of Some Strange Romance": The Personal Recollections of Charlotte Elizabeth Tonna', *Tulsa Studies in Women's Literature*, vol. 1 (1982), pp. 141–53, especially pp. 143, 152, similarly misunderstands English religious history. Frank Felsenstein, *Anti-Semitic Stereotypes: A Paradigm of Otherness in English Popular Culture, 1660–1830* (Baltimore: 1995), pp. 312–13, seems to class her among the judeophobes, as a result of using the 1841 edition of her memoir, which lacks the essence of her opinions concerning Jews found in the 1843 edition.
39. *Christian Lady's Magazine*, January 1843, pp. 63–8; May 1843, pp. 438–45; June 1845, pp. 556–7; *Israel's Ordinances. A few thoughts on their perpetuity, in a letter to the Right Rev. the Bishop of Jerusalem, by Charlotte Elizabeth* (London: 1843); Tonna, *Personal Recollections*, pp. 399–400, 404.
40. W.J. Conybeare, 'Church Parties', in his *Essays Ecclesiastical and Social* (London: 1855), pp. 81–4; this work first appeared in the *Edinburgh Review* during 1853; cf. *Voice of Jacob*, letter, 10 May 1844, 6 September 1844; letter, *Jewish Chronicle*, 11 January 1856; J.C. Budgett Meakin, ibid., 6 August 1897.
41. Tuchman, op. cit., p. 174.
42. *Christian Lady's Magazine*, May 1843, p. 396; May 1844, pp. 434–42; cf. the Dean of Lincoln's remarks in a debate on the prayer book, *Jewish Chronicle*, 20 February 1920.
43. See Rubinstein, 'A Pioneering Philosemite', pp. 221 et seq.
44. 'A Gentile Reader', *Jewish Chronicle*, 15 June 1855; cf. James Finn to Earl of Malmesbury, 9 August 1852, Hyamson, op. cit., vol. 1, pp. 204–5.
45. Shaftesbury (when Lord Ashley), to Tonna, 9 May 1843, quoted in *Jewish Chronicle*, 8 May 1908.
46. *Voice of Jacob*, 10 May 1844, hoped for the best of the self-styled (in

Hebrew characters) 'Sarah Abigail'; the *Jewish Chronicle*, 19 February 1858, revealed the worst; see also 29 May, 5 June 1874. 'We have never seen the name of a Conversionist in the list of donors to any Jewish charity', ibid., 6 October 1876, was fundamentally, although not entirely, true.

47. *The Times*, 19 October 1859.
48. *Voice of Jacob*, 13 May 1842.
49. Spurgeon to Morris Lissack, 19 December 1874, in *Jewish Chronicle*, 8 January 1875; cf. ibid., 24 December 1871, 5 January 1872.
50. Exceptions to this rule were few. For a naked example see ibid., 19 January 1917.
51. Bishop of Liverpool to Alderman A.B. Forwood, n.d., in *Aberystwyth Observer*, 28 January 1882.
52. *Massacre of the Jews in Russia*, pp. 34–5.
53. *Church Times*, 12 May 1944.
54. *Jewish Chronicle*, 19 October 1877.
55. George F. Magour, 'The Chicago Jewish Christian Conference', *Our Day* (Lexington, Mass.), vol. 7 (1890), pp. 266–77; Ariel, *On Behalf of Israel*, pp. 69–70.
56. Quoted in Magour, p. 267n.
57. Ibid., p. 268; see also *Jew and Gentile. Being a Report of a Conference of Israelites and Christians regarding their mutual relations and welfare* ... (New York & Chicago: 1890).
58. Rev. Hugh Hulton, describing his friendship with Rev. Morris J. Raphall, *Jewish Chronicle*, 12 October 1849. For an example of Christian pro-Jewish emancipation see *Christian Examiner*, n.d., quoted in *Voice of Jacob*, 11 April 1845.
59. 'A Christian Minister', letter, *Manchester Free Lance* [n.d., 1874], quoted in *Jewish Chronicle*, 8 January 1875. Like many anti-conversionist Christians he observed that Jews won over by missionary activity seldom proved sincere and pious: the London Jews' Society offers 'a premium for the worst kind of hypocrisy'.
60. Ibid., 16 June 1854.
61. Ibid., 28 July 1854. Mills had reportedly gone to London from Wales in order to undertake missionary activity among Jews. See Mills and Jones, *Buchdraeth y Parch. John Mills*, chapter 6. Whatever the case, the quoted passage and the fact that he was courted by Benisch and other leading Jews implies that he had effectively jettisoned such designs.
62. Letter, *Jewish Chronicle*, 18 September 1874, emphasis his; cf. 31 October, 14 November, 26 December 1873, 6 March 1891; Voysey's son, Rev. Ellison A. Voysey, was a philosemite. Ibid., 3 February 1899.
63. Ibid., 26 July 1912; see also Rev. Morris Joseph's tribute, ibid., 13 September 1912; cf. ibid., 6 December 1872. Voysey's followers reportedly included John Ruskin, the two Darwins, Benjamin Jowett, Viscount Amberley, the Earl of Harrington, and a former Bishop of Norwich.
64. Quoted ibid., 26 July 1912.
65. Ibid., 31 January 1908; 28 May 1897.
66. Ibid., 18 October 1844.

Notes

67. Emma Willis, North Kensington, ibid., 14 May 1897.
68. Samuel Smith, Sedgley, ibid., 29 October 1858; cf. letter from 'an Unorthodox Christian,' Hanley, enquiring as to the principles of Judaism. Ibid., 21 July 1876.
69. John Oxlee, *Three letters, humbly addressed to the Lord Archbishop of Canterbury, on the inexpediency and futility of any attempt to convert the Jews to the Christian faith, in the way and manner hitherto practised ...* (London: 1843); see also *Voice of Jacob*, 31 March 1843, *Jewish Chronicle*, 15 January 1858.
70. Alexander Espline, Monimail, ibid., 27 December 1850, 10 January, 11, 25 April, 13 June 1851, 2 December 1853, 7 April, 17 November 1854, 19 November 1858, 25 November 1859. Emphasis his.
71. Ibid., 17 November 1854. Emphasis in original. See also excerpts from two Fifeshire newspapers praising Jews, ibid., 24 November 1854.
72. E.R. Norman, *Anti-Catholicism in Victorian England* (London: 1968); *Christian Lady's Magazine*, January 1840, p. 89.
73. Tonna, *Personal Recollections*, pp. 406–7, cf. p. 151.
74. Harriet Martineau, *The History of England during the Thirty Years Peace 1816-1846* (London: 1850), quoted in *Jewish Chronicle*, 1 March 1850. Many Protestants, including Mrs Tonna, came to support Jewish emancipation, perhaps because Catholics, who ranked with idolators, were allowed to take their seats. For Tonna see *Voice of Jacob*, 11 April 1845, cf. *Protestant Magazine*, 1 April 1841, 1 May 1842 which she edited anonymously. The question divided Evangelicals. See Scult, 'English Missions to the Jews', pp. 13–16.
75. *The Times*, 11 December 1890.
76. See, for example, 'Parliament and the Persecution of Jews in Germany' [speeches], *The New Judaea*, April 1933, p. 99; Sir James Barrett, *Argus*, 28 April 1933; Wyndham Heathcote, *The Jew in History: A Plea for Tolerance: Lecture Delivered ... at the Real Estate Institute, Sydney, August 21st, 1938* (Sydney: 1938), pp. 2–3. Heathcote was a Unitarian minister.
77. *The Times*, 2, 4 July 1840; Salbstein, op. cit., pp. 38–9; Bolt, op. cit., pp. 10, 16, 20, 55, 102; *Jewish Chronicle*, 31 May 1872, 1 January 1897 (regarding Joseph Fry). See also ibid., 18 March 1938 for a bequest of £10,000 for distribution among the Jews of Palestine from an anonymous Christian Englishman, reportedly a Quaker; and ibid., 1 January 1937. R.N. Fowler left the Quakers in 1858, and was baptized an Anglican in 1865. But his outlook retained some of that Quaker legacy. Malchow, op. cit., pp. 172–3.
78. Ibid., 26 April, 31 May 1872; Henry Richard, *Memoir of Joseph Sturge* (London: 1864).
79. *The Times*, 11 December 1890. Similarly, J.E. Budget Meakin compared the persecution of Jews in Russia with that of Evangelicals, *Jewish Chronicle*, 6 August 1897.
80. *Argus*, 6 June 1903; *New York Times*, 20 December 1880, 2 May 1882.
81. *Massacre of Jews in Russia*, p. 34. Although not specified, Green was obviously meant.
82. *Jewish Chronicle*, 31 October 1913.

83. See, for instance, *Presbyterian Review*, March 1936, cited in *Voice of Jacob*, 22 December 1843; Sir Alexander R. Simpson, *The Unconsumed People* (n.p., n.d.: reprinted from *The Expositor*, August 1912); Thomas Jones, *Rhymney Memories* (Llandysul: 1970, first published 1938), pp. 119–20, 122, 124, 147; Derec Llwyd Morgan, 'The Welsh Biblical Heritage', *Caernarvonshire Historical Society Transactions*, vol. 49 (1988), pp. 7–26; Dr Ellis Edwards, a Beilis protest signatory, *Jewish Chronicle Supplement*, 31 October 1913; the Reverend John A. MacCallum, Philadelphia Presbyterian, *Jewish Chronicle*, 6 April 1928.
84. *Jewish Chronicle Supplement*, 29 May 1925, cf. *Jewish Chronicle*, 3 September 1926, 7 July 1933, 16 March 1937.
85. Ibid., 7 September 1934.
86. Henry Hawkes, *Position of the Jews: A Sermon ...* (London: 1842); speech, *Voice of Jacob*, 1 December 1842, extract, ibid., 3 February 1843. Hawkes was a Portsmouth Unitarian minister close to the town's Jewry. Ibid., 21 December 1849, 13 December 1850, 9 February 1855. See also letters from 'S.S.', a Unitarian, *Jewish Chronicle*, 27 September 1861 and 'A Unitarian', ibid., 7 April 1876; the Reverend George Walters, Sydney, *Jewish Herald*, 19 June 1903.
87. *Jewish Chronicle*, 29 January 1913. For the United States generally, see Yaakov Ariel, *On Behalf of Israel: American Fundamentalist Attitudes Towards Jews, Judaism, and Zionism, 1865–1945* (Brooklyn, N.Y.: 1991).
88. *Jewish Chronicle*, 9 January 1915.
89. *Protestant Magazine*, 1 June 1840; cf. *Christian Lady's Magazine*, September 1841, pp. 367–8.
90. *Jewish Chronicle*, 5 April 1861.
91. Quoted ibid.
92. Ibid., 24 May 1872, 25 February, 17, 24, March 1876.
93. See, for example, *Christian Lady's Magazine*, September 1843, pp. 254–61, October 1843, pp. 335–46, March 1844, pp. 202–5, 259–65, June 1844, pp. 491–2; *Protestant Magazine*, 1 September, 1 December 1843; *Ipswich Express*, 22 August 1843.
94. See, especially, *The Times* editorials, 11, 19 September 1899, letters, 21 September 1899; Frederick C. Conybeare, *Roman Catholicism as a Factor in European Politics* (London: 1901) which reprints his pro-Dreyfus articles from the *National Review*. See also Cardinal Vaughan, *The Times*, 18 September 1899; Canon Armitage, *Jewish Chronicle*, 22 September 1899.
95. Rubinstein, '"A Noble Sight to See"', pp. 436, 438, 467; *Vigilant*, 5, 19 February 1920; criticism of Roman Catholics when they indulged in antisemitism can be found in the *Vigilant*, organ of the Victorian Protestant Federation and founded by Albiston (e.g. 14 February 1933, 14 May 1937) and in various pamphlets issued by the Loyalist League in Victoria. Henley, who contrasted the trouble-free Jews with the troublesome Catholics (ibid., 19 February 1920) attended Sydney's rally protesting Nazi persecution, *Sydney Morning Herald*, 19 May 1933. Albiston's uncle and Leeper's son signed the pro-Kimberley manifesto. *Argus*, 1 December 1939. For British Roman Catholics and the Dreyfus Affair see letters, *The Times*, 18, 19 September 1899.

96. Details in Rubinstein, "'A Noble Sight to See'", pp. 432, 434, 436, 457; Thornton-Smith, op. cit., pp. 57 et seq.
97. See Thurston, op. cit.; *American Jewish Year Book 4675*, pp. 79–82; *The Times*, 9 June 1903, 6 May 1912; *New York Times*, 28 October 1913; *Jewish Chronicle*, 1 December 1899, 19 June 1903, 29 April 1921, 4 January 1934.
98. *Sydney Morning Herald*, 24 May 1881; *The Times*, 2 February 1882, 10 December 1890; *Jewish Chronicle*, 4 February 1938, 2 January 1891.
99. Ibid.
100. *Hebrew Standard*, 19 November 1942.
101. *Jewish Chronicle*, 7 July 1939.
102. Ibid., 14 May 1852.
103. See, for example, [Henry Hart Milman], *The History of the Jews*, 3 vols. (London: 1829); Rev. John Anderson's introduction to *Lays and Laments for Israel. Poems on the Present State and Future Prospects of the Jews* ... (Edinburgh: 1845); *The Anglo-Hebrews; their past Wrongs and Present Grievances* ... *Written for all Classes of the British Public by a Clergyman of the Church of England* (London: 1856), and the works by Chapman, Dark, Hawkes, Heathcote, Richard Jones, Peters, Stiles, and Thurston, all cited *supra*. Rev. J.H. Adeney, author of *The Jews of Eastern Europe* (London: 1921) was active in missionary work among Roumanian Jewry.
104. Rev. William Yate, Dover, *Jewish Chronicle*, 26 February 1864.
105. Quoted in Adler, op. cit., p. 115; cf. the Roman Catholic J.H. Plunkett QC, Sydney, *Jewish Chronicle*, 27 February 1863.
106. See, for instance, *Jewish Chronicle*, 11 June 1847, 14 February, 21 March, 5 June 1851, 16 February 1866, 13 September 1872. Donations were often generous, including £20 given to the North Shields synagogue appeal in 1866 by the Duke of Northumberland.
107. Rev. Labagh, at New York Hebrew Benevolent Society dinner, 5 November 1845, in *Voice of Jacob*, 8 May 1846. Dialogue, of course, required cooperation from Jews, whose leaders in the United States (perhaps owing to the development of Reform Judaism there) pioneered the trend earlier than their British counterparts. See, for instance, Feldman, *Dual Destinies*, pp. 124–8. See also Chief Rabbi Hertz's participation at a Christian-organized rally to protest religious persecution in Soviet Russia, *Jewish Chronicle*, 27 December 1929.
108. Ibid., 6 April 1928.
109. Snoek, op. cit., p. 83; cf. *Jewish Chronicle*, 8 December 1933 (U.S. church leaders' support for the Boycott Movement); 17 June 1938.
110. Ibid., 16 June 1939. This statement launched the Committee of Catholics to Fight Anti-Semitism.
111. Ibid.

8 'THE AGE-LONG DREAM'

1. In addition to the works cited in chapter 1, note 33, see N.A. Rose, *The Gentile Zionists: A Study in Anglo-Zionist Diplomacy, 1929–1939*

(London: 1973) and Mayir Vereté, *From Palmerston to Balfour: Collected Essays of Mayir Vereté*, ed. Norman Rose (London: 1992); Ruth P. Goldschmidt-Lehmann, comp., *Britain and the Holy Land 1800–1914: A Select Bibliography* (London: 1995); Milton Plesur, 'The American Press and Jewish Restoration During the Nineteenth Century', in Meyer, op. cit., pp. 55–76; Rubinstein, *A History of the Jews in the English-Speaking World: Great Britain*, pp. 163–5. Paul C. Merkley, *The Politics of Christian Zionism 1891–1948* (London: 1998), deals mainly with the United States.
2. On George Eliot, see Alice Shalvi, ed., *Daniel Deronda: A Centenary Symposium* (Jerusalem, 1976); Gordon S. Haight, *George Eliot: A Biography* (Oxford: 1968), pp. 456–99; Ruth Levitt, *George Eliot, the Jewish Connection* (Jerusalem: 1975).
3. Vereté, 'The Restoration of the Jews in English Protestant Thought 1790-1940', pp. 3 et seq.; Hylson-Smith, op. cit., pp. 94–6; Bebbington, op. cit., pp. 62, 81–5, 92; Mel Scult, *Millenial Expectations and Jewish Liberties: A Study of the Efforts to Convert the Jews of Britain up to the Mid-Nineteenth Century* (Waltham, Mass.: 1978). See also Samuel H. Levene, 'Palestine in the Literature of the United States to 1867', in Meyer, op. cit., pp. 21–38.
4. Tonna, op. cit., pp. 247–8.
5. *Christian Lady's Magazine*, September 1841, pp. 367–8.
6. Ibid., January 1840, pp. 88–9.
7. Ibid., February 1841, pp. 189–90. It is not known whether these proposals were acted upon.
8. Charlotte Elizabeth Tonna, *Judah's Lion* (London: 1843); Kobler, op. cit., pp. 71–2. Kobler is seemingly unique among historians of gentile Zionism in mentioning Mrs. Tonna, whose importance has been overlooked perhaps because of her gender. See also Rubinstein, 'A Pioneering Philosemite', pp. 215 et seq.
9. *Christian Lady's Magazine*, January 1840, pp. 8–9.
10. Ibid., February 1844, p.107. Emphasis in original.
11. Warder Cresson, *Jerusalem the Centre and Joy of the Whole Earth and the Jew the Recipient of the Glory of God*, 2nd edn (London: 1844), reviewed in *Christian Lady's Magazine*, September 1844, pp. 270–2. For the remarkable career of Cresson, his conversion to Judaism, and the dismissal of the 'insanity' charge consequently brought against him by his wife and son, a landmark ruling which ensured that in America religious belief could never again be a test of a person's mental state, see Abraham J. Karp, 'The Zionism of Warder Cresson', in Meyer, op. cit., pp. 1–20; Frank Fox, 'Quaker, Shaker, "Rabbi": Warder Cresson, The Story of a Philadelphia Mystic', *The Pennsylvania Magazine of History and Biography*, vol. 95 (1971), pp. 147–94.
12. Bickersteth, op. cit., p. 197; cf. *A Collection of the Prophecies Concerning the Gathering of the Jews from all Parts of the Earth to their Own Land ...* (London: 1842), issued by L. and G. Seeley, Evangelical publishers. See also Samuel H. Levine, 'Palestine in the Literature of the United States to 1867', in Meyer, op. cit., pp. 21–38; Will of Rev. T. Hannay (Canada), *New York Times*, 22 April 1882; Louis Golding, 'The

Proto-Zionist Mystery', *Jewish Chronicle Supplement*, 26 August 1927.
13. Lecture, 'The Destiny of England in the Prophetic Record', *Jewish Chronicle*, 19 October 1860. See also John Cumming, *Apocalyptic Sketches* (London: 1848).
14. *Voice of Jacob*, 12 May 1843, cf. *Jewish Chronicle*, 2 November 1860. The *Mormon Times*, n.d., quoted ibid., 19 December 1856, expressed it thus: 'they will be gathered to their own lands in unbelief. Many societies of Christendom, overlooking this fact, or ... not believing that it would be so, are making strenuous efforts to convert the Jews, flattered, no doubt, with the hope that they will be successful.'
15. Adam Cairns, *The Jews: Their Fall and Restoration. Two Discourses Preached in the Chalmers' Church, on September the 3rd, in Behalf of the Suffering Jews of Palestine* (Melbourne: 1854), pp. 31, 17.
16. *Argus* (Melbourne), 31 December 1861.
17. Cairns, op. cit., p. 17; *Jewish Herald*, 21 October 1881.
18. George Gawler, *Tranquillization of Syria and the East. Observations and practical suggestions in furtherance of the establishment of Jewish Colonies in Palestine; the most sober and sensible remedy for the miseries of Asiatic Turkey* (London: 1845), excerpted in *Voice of Jacob*, 4 July 1845. Emphasis in original.
19. Letter, op. cit., 13 February 1846; Tuchman, op. cit., p. 217.
20. *Voice of Jacob*, 13 February 1846.
21. See Franz Kobler, 'Charles Henry Churchill', *Herzl Year Book*, vol. 4 (1962), pp. 1–66.
22. *Jewish Chronicle*, 11 January 1850. In 1849 Gawler accompanied Montefiore on an exploratory tour of Palestine. See also ibid., 16 November 1849 and 3 June 1853, 1 June 1855 (Jews' Orphan Asylum donations), 16 June 1854 (Palestine Jewry appeal), 2 February 1855 (Sussex Hall committee).
23. Letter, *Voice of Jacob*, 13 February 1846.
24. Ibid., 4 July 1845. In preferring Gawler's scheme the paper professes to cast no aspersions on the 'purity' of intent of other Christian Zionists, such as the Reverend Samuel Bradshaw, author of *A Tract for the Time, being a plea for the Jews* (London: 1844), and the Reverend T.T. Crybbace, who in 1845, styling himself 'the representative of the British and Foreign Society for Restoring the Jews to the Land of their Fathers,' gave a lecture in London entitled 'Restoration of the Jews to Palestine,' *Jewish Chronicle*, 13 June 1845.
25. *Voice of Jacob*, 13 February 1846, 18 July 1845. Dr Alexander Alexander of Exeter was optician to both William IV and Queen Adelaide; for his tribute to the latter see ibid., 29 August 1845. See also letter from the Canadian Henry Wentworth Monk, ibid., 6 November 1863.
26. *Jewish Chronicle*, 3 July, 7, 14 August 1874, 30 June 1876 (emphasis in original); see also 7, 14 January, 4 August 1876.
27. Ibid., 7 July 1876.
28. Ibid., 31 July 1925.
29. Ibid., 24 December 1852.
30. Ibid., 28 July 1854.

31. Ibid. Emphasis in original. See also Mills and Jones, *Buchdraeth y Parch. John Mills*, chapters 6, 7, 8.
32. E.L. Mitford, 'An Appeal on Behalf of the Jewish Nation in Connection with British Policy in the Levant' (London: 1845) reproduced under the title 'A Time for Mighty Changes', *Midstream*, Autumn 1961, pp. 17–31. The *Spectator* believed that a Jewish colony should be under the protection of Britain 'or a Committee of European Powers'; extract in *Voice of Jacob*, 1 August 1845. See also Edward Cazalet, *England's Policy in the East: our relations with Russia and the future of Syria* (London: 1879).
33. Anon., 'The Jew and his Land', *The Witness*, n.d., quoted ibid., 24 May 1861.
34. *Prophecies Concerning the Final Restoration of the Jews, and their Return to the Land of Judea. By a Christian* (London: 1861), quoted ibid., 14, 21 June 1861.
35. Thomas Clarke, *India and Palestine, or the Restoration of the Jews, viewed in relation to the nearest route to India* (London: 1861); letters, *Jewish Chronicle*, 28 June 1861, 27 June 1862. Clarke's pamphlet is so reminiscent of *Prophecies Concerning the Final Restoration* as to suggest a common authorship.
36. Letter, ibid., 28 June 1861; *Liverpool Standard*, 24 February 1846, commending Gawler's scheme; extract in *Voice of Jacob*, 13 March 1846.
37. Quoted in Tuchman, op. cit., p. 178.
38. [Shaftesbury], 'State and Prospects of the Jews', unattributed review (when Lord Ashley) of Lord Lindsay, *Letters on Egypt, Edom, and the Holy Land*, 2 vols. (London: 1838) in *Quarterly Review*, vol. 63 (January/March 1839), pp. 166–92, quotation at p. 178.
39. Diary entry, 24 August 1840, quoted in Frankel, op. cit., p. 303.
40. See ibid., pp. 291–6, 302–10; *The Times*, 17 August 1840.
41. 'State and Prospects of the Jews', pp. 187, 192; see also his statement in *Jewish Chronicle*, 23 May 1856.
42. Ibid., 27 February, 6 March 1891.
43. John Bidwell to W.T. Young, 31 January 1839, in Hyamson, op. cit., vol. 1, p. 2; James Finn, *Stirring Times: Records From Jerusalem Consular Chronicles of 1853 to 1856* (London: 1878), vol. 1, pp. 104–21, 126–7.
44. Ibid., vol. 2, pp. 76, 67.
45. James Finn to Earl of Malmesbury, 9 August 1852, Hyamson, op. cit., vol. 1, pp. 204–5; Finn, op. cit., vol. 2, p. 73; see also pp. 77, 81. There was considerable ill-feeling among Anglo-Jewish leaders towards the Finns, and Mills failed to allay assumptions that conversionism underlay their 'kindness' towards Jews. *Jewish Chronicle*, 12 July 1850, 2 May, 22 August 1862. Compare that newspaper's bitterness towards them with the Philadelphia *Occident*, run by the Reverend Isaac Leeser, towards Mrs. Clorinda S. Minor, Palestine-based American millenarian: 'She was a true friend of Israel, notwithstanding her notion that conversion was the best method of making us happy. By her practical labours in horticulture ... she has proved that Palestine may be made to bloom again ... and when the land of Israel again smiles with plenty

'... let the name of its benefactress ... be remembered with a blessing.' Quoted ibid., 11 April 1855.
46. Laurence Oliphant, *The Land of Gilead* (London: 1880); idem., 'Jewish Tales and Jewish Reform,' *Blackwood's Magazine*, vol.132 (1882), pp. 639–53; *The Times*, 15 February, 7 April 1882.
47. Margaret Oliphant, *Memoir of the Life of Laurence Oliphant and of Alice Oliphant, his Wife*, 3rd edn (Edinburgh: 1891), vol. 2, pp. 171, 183, 342. Oliphant's second wife, an American, was a dedicated millenarian. See Rosamond Dale Owen, *My Perilous Life in Palestine* (London: 1928), especially pp. 277, 295–300, and *Supplement* [n.p. 1935], p. 10. See also *Jewish Chronicle*, 26 July 1907, for her outstandingly philosemitic remarks concerning the future endurance of Jewry.
48. See Cyrus Hamlin, 'International Aid for the Jews', *Our Day* (Lexington, Mass.), vol. 8 (1891), pp. 1–8. Ariel, *On Behalf of Israel*, p. 73, rejects the suggestion that signatories were motivated by reluctance to see large-scale Russo-Jewish refugee immigration into America.
49. Ariel, 'A Neglected Chapter', pp. 80–1. See also Ariel, *On Behalf of Israel*, pp. 80–1, 87–8. The petition was based on the text of resolutions passed by the Chicago Methodist Preachers Meeting following Kishinev in 1903; US Protestant bodies endorsed the petition and prominent Protestant denominational leaders formed a committee to present it to President Wilson. In 1891 Blackstone had acted on his own initiative; this time, in concert with Zionist leaders.
50. *Jewish Chronicle*, 2 October 1903.
51. See *The American War Congress and Zionism* (New York: 1919), issued by the Zionist Organization of America.
52. Bebbington, op. cit., pp. 192–3; Christabel Pankhurst, *Pressing Problems of the Closing Age* (London: 1924), pp. 73–80.
53. *Jewish Chronicle*, 26 July 1907: the ministers were A.B. Aylesworth (Justice) and William Patterson (Customs). Their presence caused a 'sensation', as being the first time a Canadian government had shown support for Zionism.
54. *Sydney Morning Herald*, 24 May 1881.
55. *Jewish Herald*, 15 December 1905.
56. Finn, op. cit., vol. 2, p. 99; *Jewish Chronicle*, 21 February, 17 April, 29 May, 10 July 1896; 9 September 1910.
57. Sir Alfred E. Turner, *Sixty Years of a Soldier's Life* (London: 1912), pp. 323–4; Turner disclosed that he had a Jewish great-grandmother, *Jewish Chronicle*, 14 May 1915.
58. *Jewish Herald*, 15 December 1905.
59. *Jewish Chronicle*, 14 April 1899, 4 September 1903, 16 April 1909, 28 November 1913. Although not ostensibly a conversionist, Johnston believed that if Jews 'did regain Palestine, with Jerusalem as their capital, they will come under the influence of the greatest Jew who has ever lived, and conform to essential Christianity.' Another notable Zionist around this time was Sir Charles Wilson. Ibid., 7 June, 14, 22 July, 22 December 1899.
60. Ibid., 8 November 1912.

246   *Philosemitism*

61. Ibid., 2 February 1917.
62. Ibid., 9 January 1906.
63. Diary entry of Lord Bertie of Thame, British Ambassador to Paris, 24 December 1917, quoted ibid., 24 October 1924. See also John Marlowe, *Milner: Apostle of Empire* (London: 1976), pp. 330–3.
64. Ibid., 9 May 1912.
65. Ibid., 19 December 1913.
66. Ibid., 1 November 1918; *The Times*, 7 October 1920.
67. Speech, ibid., 5 December 1930.
68. Ibid., 18 October 1918; cf. 25 March 1921, 24 April, 1 May 1925, 5 December 1930.
69. Ibid., 16 July 1920, 4 April 1930.
70. Speech, 31 December 1876, ibid., 5 January 1877; see also ibid., 25 September 1903.
71. Ibid., 28 November 1924; cf. 10 February 1939.
72. See, for instance, ibid., 9 November, 14 December 1917, 16 July 1920, 3 April 1925, 18 November 1927, for numerous sympathetic public figures and many press extracts. See also R.H.S. Crossman, 'Gentile Zionism and the Balfour Declaration', *Commentary*, vol. 33 (1962), pp. 487–94.
73. *The Christian*, n.d., quoted *Jewish Chronicle*, 9 November 1917.
74. John Annan Bryce MP, ibid.
75. Ibid., 16 July 1920.
76. Ibid., 20 October, 24 November 1922.
77. Quoted in Smith, op. cit., p. 317. See also John Buchan, 'Ourselves and the Jews', *Graphic*, 5 April 1930.
78. Ibid., 16 July 1920, 1 November 1918. Other noteworthy examples of gentile Zionism can be found ibid., 1 March 1918 (T.P. O'Connor MP), 30 January, 19, 26 March 1920 (Lt. Col. J.H. Patterson), 38 October 1921 (Sir Andrew Wingate), 27 February 1920 (Ormsby-Gore), 27 June 1924, 21 January 1927, *Supplement*, December 1931, pp. iv–v (Kenworthy), 7 December 1917, 16 January 1925 (Cecil), 12 March 1926 (Allenby), 20 October, 3 November, 24 November 1922, 13 February 1925, 4 February 1927 and *Supplement*, 27 April 1923, April 1927 (all E.P. Hewitt KC). See also Wilkinson and Wingate, op. cit., 'Lord Balfour and Zionism', idem., *Portraits and Criticism* (London, 1925), pp. 95–110; Norman Bentwich, *Sir Wyndham Deedes: A Christian Zionist* (Jerusalem, 1954).
79. For Sidebotham's many pro-Zionist publications see chapter 5, note 149.
80. Ibid., 20 July 1923; cf. 1 June 1923, 26 December 1923.
81. Ibid., 1 November 1918, 4 November 1927.
82. Article, 'The Jewish National Effort: Its Political Significance,' ibid., 11 January 1929. Birkenhead's philosemitism was probably honed by his admiration for Lords Reading and Melchett.
83. C.V. Wedgwood, *The Last of the Radicals: The Life of Josiah Clement Wedgwood M.P.* (London: 1951), pp. 182, 189; *Jewish Chronicle*, 14 December 1917, 7 January 1927, 29 September 1922, 25 May 1917. Among the League's founders were Liberal MPs Sir Martin (later

Baron) Conway and Sir Robert Hamilton, Labour MP J.M. Kenworthy, and Conservative MP Sir Leslie Scott KC.
84. Ibid., 26 October 1917, 9 September 1927, 7 January 1927, 29 September 1922, 16 July 1920 (his emphasis).
85. *Jewish Chronicle Supplement*, 29 May 1925; *Jewish Chronicle*, 3 September 1926, 29 May 1925; cf. 28 November 1930. Among other Welshmen to make similar points were David Davies MP, ibid., 1 November 1918, and, after the establishment of the State of Israel, on numerous occasions by George Thomas MP (Lord Tonypandy), for example in 'A Welshman Looks at Israel', *CAJEX*, vol. 7, no. 3 (1957), pp. 75–6. See also Thomas Jones, op. cit., pp. 119–20, 122, 124, 147.
86. Article, 'Zionism and Palestine: A "Just Demand"', ibid., 20 July 1923, reprinted from *Daily Chronicle* and *Daily Telegraph*. Asquith was certainly wrong in his diary, 13 March 1915, that Lloyd George 'does not care a damn for the Jews or their past or their future'. Extracted ibid., 11 May 1928.
87. See *The American War Congress and Zionism*, especially pp. 136, 140–1, 154–5, 214.
88. For text and signatories, see ibid., 23 November 1928; see also speech of Acting Prime Minister F.S. Malan, ibid., 21 February 1919. Like Sykes and other gentile Zionist politicians Malan stressed that the establishment of a Jewish National Home would not interfere with the citizenship and status of Diaspora Jews, a principle enshrined in the Balfour Declaration.
89. Ibid., 4 November 1927, 10 March 1922, 1 November 1918.
90. Ibid., 31 October 1930; cf. 28 November 1930. Amery, Austen Chamberlain, Baldwin, and Churchill also protested. See, for example, speeches by Amery and Churchill, House of Commons, 22, 23 May 1939, speech, Zionist Organization of America luncheon, ibid., 24 January 1930.
91. Jan Christian Smuts, Telegraph to Ramsay Macdonald, ibid., 31 October 1930. Smuts was not Prime Minister at that time; his links with organized Zionism in South Africa were strong and his feelings ran deep. See also Leonard Stein, 'General Smuts and Palestine', ibid., 21 August 1936.
92. See, for example, ibid., 7 November 1930, 14, 28 October, 4 November 1938; John Haynes Holmes, *Palestine To-Day and To-Morrow* (London: 1930).
93. Ibid., 13 August 1937.

9 'THE GLORIOUS INHERITANCE'

1. *Liverpool Mail* ('a staunch conservative organ', n.d.), quoted in *Voice of Jacob*, 11 April 1845. See also, for example, 'Remarks on the Civil Disabilities of the Jews. By a Conservative', quoted in ibid., 8 November 1844. This was apparently co-authored by 'a Dignatory of the Church of England' and a Jew.
2. Charlotte Elizabeth Tonna, 'Mogador and the Jews', *Christian Lady's Magazine*, March 1845, quoted in *Voice of Jacob*, 14 March 1845. She

wrote of the 'high lineage' of the Jewish people. *Christian Lady's Magazine*, March 1843, p. 223.
3. For anti-Bolshevism see Rubinstein, *A History of the Jews in the English-Speaking World: Great Britain*, pp. 214-16.
4. Edmund Burke, 14 May 1781, regarding the mistreatment of Jews in the Dutch West Indies, quoted in Allan Gould, comp. and ed., *What Did They Think of the Jews?* (Northvale, N.J.: 1991), p. 70.
5. *The Times*, 4 July 1840.
6. Ibid., *Voice of Jacob*, 16 February 1844; *Sydney Morning Herald*, 19 September 1854; cf. Reginald G. Russell, 'In defence of Jews / Let us not forget Europe's debt to their culture,' *Vigilant*, 14 January 1939 (reprinted from *British Weekly*, n.d.).
7. *Jewish Chronicle*, 24 November 1865.
8. See Rubinstein, '"A Noble Sight to See"', p. 461.
9. Ibid., 31 May 1872; *The Times*, 11 December 1890.
10. *Outrage Upon the Jews in Russia*, p. 25
11. Maxse, 'M. Cavaignac's Vindication of Captain Dreyfus', p. 822.
12. (Sir) Herbert Phillips, *Jewish Herald* (Melbourne), 1 December 1905.
13. *Massacre of Jews in Russia*, pp. 28-9; *Jewish Chronicle*, 28 August 1903, 9 May 1912.
14. Letter, *Morning Post*, 19 October 1922. Hewitt was 'a prominent member of the "Die Hard" Party' of extreme Tories. *Jewish Chronicle*, 20 October 1922.
15. Ibid., 9 January 1931.
16. Ibid., 22 January 1932.
17. For Barrett, President of the Royal Empire Society in Victoria, a correspondent of Leopold Amery, and active within the National Party, see Hilary L. Rubinstein, 'Sir James Barrett (1862-1945): Australian Philo-Semite', *Australian Jewish Historical Society Journal*, vol. 12, part 1, 1993, pp. 91-100, and Barrett Papers, University of Melbourne Archives. But note (cf. Rubinstein, op. cit., pp. 96-7) that Barrett's name (unlike Merrett's) does not appear in the list of signatories to Melbourne's pro-Kimberley manifesto. See *Argus*, 1 December 1939. As President of the British Medical Association of Australia Barrett defied a substantial proportion of his membership in championing the admission of refugee physicians. Merrett was President of the British Empire Union in Melbourne. For the *Sydney Morning Herald*'s attitude see Blakeney. op. cit., pp. 71 et seq.
18. *Sydney Morning Herald*, 5, 23 March 1863. Melbourne's conservative newspaper was also sympathetic towards Jews, as in 1936 when it deplored an Australian's antisemitic speech. See *Argus*, 8 December 1936.
19. *Daily Mail*, 30 June 1934. According to the *Jewish Chronicle*, 6 July 1934, the *Evening News* carried a similar editorial.
20. *Daily Mail*, 30 June 1934.
21. *The Times*, 11 December 1890; *Jewish Chronicle*, 13 November 1903. Rowton, a cousin of Shaftesbury, became close to the English Rothschilds.
22. *The Times*, 11 December 1890.

23. *Massacre of the Jews in Russia*, p. 39.
24. *The Times*, 9 January 1931.
25. For Meath, Colomb and Curzon, see chapter 3; for Queen Victoria see chapter 3, and chapter 4, note 16; for King Edward see *Jewish Herald*, 1 December 1905; *Jewish Chronicle*, 14 October 1927; the King's initiative came following requests from his friends, the Rothschilds.
26. Sir George Houston Reid, *My Reminiscences* (London: 1917), pp. 154–5.
27. Rubinstein, '"A Noble Sight to See"', p. 432; *Argus*, 30 July 1878; A Patchett Martin, *Australia and the Empire* (Edinburgh: 1889), pp. 65–75.
28. *Jewish Observer* (Perth, W.A.), 1 May, 1 July 1920.
29. *Jewish Chronicle*, 26 May 1933; see also Walter Elliot, Minister of Agriculture, Primrose League demonstration, Albert Hall, ibid., 12 May 1933; *Daily Mirror*, n.d., quoted ibid., 7 April 1933, extracted in chapter 5; Heathcote, op. cit., p. 8.
30. Ibid., 22 October 1937. Banks had married a Mrs Eva Epstein.
31. Ibid.; Michael Cathcart, *Defending the National Tuckshop: Australia's Secret Army Intrigue of 1931* (Ringwood, Vic.: 1988), pp. 40–3, 113, 115–16, 139; Geoffrey Serle, *John Monash: A Biography* (Melbourne: 1982), pp. 526–7. Monash was a highly visible Jew. He served as Honorary President of Australia's Zionist Federation and his funeral was conducted in Melbourne's largest synagogue by the city's best-known rabbi.
32. Francis Galton, *Hereditary Genius: an Inquiry into its Laws and Consequences*, London, 1914 (first published 1869), pp. 3–4; 'Eugenics and the Jew' (interview), *Jewish Chronicle*, 29 July 1910.
33. *The Times*, 6 May 1912. Pearson was Galton Professor of Eugenics at the University of London. See also Elazar Barkan, *The Retreat of Scientific Racism: Changing Concepts of Race in Britain and the United States between the World Wars* (Cambridge: 1992), citing *Annals of Eugenics*, vol. 1 (1925), p. 127. The attitude towards Jews of Galton and Pearson should be set alongside Paul Rich, 'The Long Victorian Sunset: Anthropology, Eugenics and Race in Britain, *c*.1900–48', *Patterns of Prejudice*, vol. 18, no. 3 (1984), pp. 2–11.
34. John Stuart Mill, *Considerations on Representative Government* (New York: 1961), p. 51, quoted in Gould, op. cit., p. 145.
35. Dr David Wilkie, Honorary Physician to the Melbourne Jewish Philanthropic Society, *Australian Israelite*, 31 January 1873; see also *Jewish Herald*, 17 April 1885.
36. B.W. Richardson, *Health and Life* (London: 1878); idem., *The Son of a Star: A Romance of the Second Century*, 3 vols. (London: 1886); *Jewish Chronicle*, 13 March 1876, 26 April 1878, 26 April 1895, 27 November 1896. Richardson was founder and editor of the *Journal of Public Health and Sanitation Review*. A synopsis of his views can be found in a lecture he gave before the National Eisteddfod at Denbigh on 21 August 1882, published as *Race and Life*, London [*c*.1882] (reprinted from *Fraser's Magazine,* September 1882), especially pp. 19–20.
37. W.E.H. Lecky, 'Israel Among the Nations', *Forum* (New York), vol. 16 (1893), pp. 444, 445–6, 449. See also, for instance, G.F. Abbott, *Israel in Europe* (London, 1907), pp. 327–8, and Madison Peters' lecture, *New*

York Times, 8 May 1899 and his *Justice to the Jew*, pp. 319–20.
38. *New York Daily Times*, quoted in *Jewish Chronicle*, 11 July 1856; [Bernard Cracroft] 'The Jews of Western Europe', *Westminster Review*, n.s., vol. 23 (1863), pp. 428–70, quotation at p. 428. See also Anderson, op. cit., p. 369: 'The Jews are ... eminently an intellectual people.'
39. G.C. Stigant, quoted in *Voice of Jacob*, 16 February 1844.
40. Quoted in Israel Porush, 'The Story of State Aid to Jewish Establishments in New South Wales', *Australian Jewish Historical Society Journal*, vol. 1, part 10, (1943), p. 345.
41. *New York Evening Post*, January 1867, quoted in Peters, *Justice to the Jew*, p. 219.
42. Quoted ibid., p. 108; for Curtis on Jews see also *New York Times*, 5 April 1890. Poet James Russell Lowell, editor of the *Atlantic Monthly*, was conscious to the point of obsession of Jews as extraordinarily high achievers. While his inherent attachment to fair play made him staunchly supportive of Jews, he allegedly harboured a measure of ambivalence towards them. See Gould, op. cit., pp. 126–30.
43. Dowd, *Life of Zebulon B. Vance*, p. 370.
44. *The Public Ledger of Philadelphia*, 13 January 1863, quoted in *Jewish Chronicle*, 20 March 1863. For the orders in question see ibid., 11 December 1862.
45. [Anon.], 'The Jew and his Land', ibid., 24 May 1861. The writer was not Jewish. See n. 68 *infra*.
46. Benjamin R. Plumley, quoted ibid., 5 July 1872. In his inaugural presidential address at Williams College, Williamstown, Mass., Professor Franklin Carter warmed to the same theme, but showed disapproval of Jewish exclusiveness. See *Jewish Herald* (Melbourne), 21 October 1881 for text of Carter's speech.
47. Mr Justice (later Sir John) Mellor, quoted in *Jewish Chronicle*, 12 April 1872. Of Unitarian upbringing, Mellor was a former Liberal MP.
48. *Argus* (Melbourne), 2 August 1881; *Jewish Herald*, 12 August 1881.
49. *Sydney Morning Herald*, 24 May 1881; see also the Melbourne-based *Presbyterian Messenger*, 19 June 1903, which in part is so reminiscent of Mark Twain's (ambivalent) 'Concerning the Jews', *Harper's Magazine*, vol. 99 (September 1899), pp. 527–35, especially p. 535, as to to suggest plagiarism.
50. *Aberdare Times*, 11 February 1882 (Fleming sermon); *South Wales Daily News*, 16 January 1882 (Farrar article).
51. *The Times*, 11 December 1890.
52. Dr Edwin A. Alderman, quoted in Adler, op. cit., pp. 106–8.
53. W.C. Stiles, *Out of Kishineff: the Duty of the American People to the Russian Jew* (New York: 1903), p. 50. In the original Zangwill and Rubinstein are misspelled.
54. Rev. Edwin Watkin to B.H. Alston, 11 November 1905, quoted in *Jewish Herald*, 1 December 1905.
55. *Jewish Chronicle*, 15 January 1909. Liberal MP L.A. Atherley-Jones took a similar line to Burt in his lecture.
56. *South Wales Weekly Post*, 2 September 1911; cf. the leftist, Welsh-language *Llais Llafur*, 2 September 1911 (translated for the present

authors by Huw Roderick).
57. Thomas D. Schall, Minnesota, quoted in *The American War Congress and Zionism*, pp. 134–5.
58. Thorstein Veblen, 'The Intellectual Pre-Eminence of Jews in Modern Europe', in Leon Ardzrooni, ed., *Essays in Our Changing Order by Thorstein Veblen* (New York: 1934), pp. 219–31 (reprinted from *Political Science Quarterly*, vol. 34 (March 1919)).
59. J.H. Corah, quoted in *Jewish Chronicle*, 16 June 1933.
60. Walter Besant, *The Rebel Queen*, London, 1893, quoted in Peters, *Justice to the Jew*, p. 148. Besant was Secretary of the Palestine Restoration Fund (established 1864), 1868–86, and wrote or co-wrote several relevant works. He was also Secretary of the Palestine Pilgrims Text Society, founded in 1884 under the directorate of Sir Charles Wilson to translate old narratives of pilgrimages to the Holy Land.
61. The Honourable John Schroers, quoted in Adler, op. cit., p. 189; *Evening Post* (Louisville, Ky.), 21 July 1903, quoted ibid., p. 321.
62. Lloyd George, speech to the Jewish Religious Education Board, *Jewish Chronicle*, 7 July 1933.
63. Bertrand Russell, 'Why are the Jews Persecuted?', *Time and Tide*, 12 January 1935.
64. Introduction, *The Yellow Spot*, p. 6.
65. Haim Genizi, 'American Non-Sectarian Refugee Relief Organizations (1933–1945)', *Yad Vashem Studies*, vol. 11, Jerusalem (1976), pp. 164–220; Laura Ferni, *Illustrious Immigrants: The Intellectual Migration from Europe, 1930–1941* (Chicago: 1967).
66. C.P. Snow, Introduction to Arnold A. Rogow, *The Jew in a Gentile World*, 1961, pp. xv–xvii. Snow popularized the old notion (see, for instance, *Jewish Chronicle*, 29 June 1877, citing Galton's book, *Hereditary Genius*) that the disproportionate number of Jewish intellectuals derives from the many centuries when the rabbinate married and produced offspring but the Christian clergy were celibate.
67. *Spectator*, n.d. [1845], quoted in *Voice of Jacob*, 1 August 1845.
68. [Anon.], possibly Thomas Clarke MD, 'The Jew and his Land', *Jewish Chronicle*, 24 May 1861.
69. Henry W. Nevinson, lecture on 'Palestine,' quoted ibid., 7 March 1930.
70. St John Ervine, *A Journey to Jerusalem*, London, 1936, pp. 273, 300–8. Ervine, a playwright and drama critic, returned a passionate Zionist: '[Palestine] would be better with fewer Arabs and more Jews ... the Jews, after several thousand years of misrule everywhere, are able to make five acres of stony soil in Palestine do as much work as an Arab can extract from sixty acres!' Ibid., pp. 302, 305.

10 THE JEWISH EMERGENCE FROM POWERLESSNESS

1. Yehuda Bauer, *The Jewish Emergence from Powerlessness* (Toronto: 1979).
2. On this development in British detective fiction (which actually began in the 1930s following Hitler's ascendancy), see Rubinstein, *A History*

of the Jews in the English-Speaking World: Great Britain, pp. 292–3, 303–4.
3. See, for example, R.J.B. Bosworth, *Explaining Auschwitz and Hiroshima: History Writing and the Second World War, 1945–1990* (London: 1993).
4. On these processes, see Rubinstein, *The Left, the Right and the Jews* and idem., *Jews in the English-Speaking World: Great Britain*, pp. 374–80.
5. See Elliott Abrams, *Faith or Fear: How Jews Can Survive in Christian America* (New York: 1997), pp. 59–69.
6. Braybrooke, op. cit., p. 13.
7. Ibid., p. 14.
8. Ibid., pp. 20–4. Claims that the Council proposed practical measures to assist the Jews under Nazi domination, but that the British government failed to act upon them are, however, misleading. Virtually the only concrete proposal which the Council could make was to advise Britain to admit more refugees. Unfortunately, the Jews of Nazi-occupied Europe were not refugees but prisoners, and could not escape. In common with other persons of goodwill in the West, the Council in essence could think of nothing which might save significant numbers of European Jews. See Rubinstein, *The Myth of Rescue*.
9. Braybrooke, op. cit., p. 24.
10. Ibid., p. 25.
11. Ibid., pp. 135–7.
12. For instance, 'Resolution 1' of the Resolutions approved by the 1978 Lambeth Conference (the international gathering of churches in communion with the Anglican Church, held every ten years at Lambeth Palace), when this movement was probably at its apogee, consisted of a 1,000-word denunciation of the Western world and capitalism, with every left-wing cliché well to the fore, e.g. 'We need to recognise that at present all over the world there tends to be a growing urbanisation. Many cities are in crisis due to the growing number of people with little hope of freedom of choice. The gap between the rich and the poor, between the powerful and the powerless, continues to grow ... We need to help the developed industrial nations and the people who live in them to face the necessity of a redistribution of wealth and trading opportunities' (Roger Coleman, ed., *Resolutions of the Twelve Lambeth Conferences, 1867–1988* (Toronto: 1992), p. 175.
13. See Rubinstein, *The Left, the Right and the Jews*.
14. Braybrooke, op. cit., p. 136.
15. On the Australian situation, which is very similar, see W.D. Rubinstein, *The Jews in Australia: A Thematic History, Volume II: 1945 – Present* (Melbourne: 1991), pp. 464–7. On America see Edward S. Shapiro, *A Time for Healing: American Jewry since World War II* (Baltimore: 1992), p. 212.
16. 'Indicators', *The American Enterprise* (February–April 1995), p. 19, cited in Abrams, op. cit., p. 67.
17. Ibid.
18. Cited in Abrams, op. cit., p. 41.
19. Ibid., p. 45.

20. Truman was crucially influenced by his Jewish former Kansas City business partner, Eddie Jacobson, a keen Zionist.
21. W.D. Rubinstein, *The Jews in Australia: A Thematic History*, pp. 516–20.
22. Peter Gross, *Israel in the Mind of America* (New York: 1983), p. 262.
23. *Jewish Chronicle*, 2 June 1967.
24. Ibid.
25. Ibid., and 9 June 1967.
26. Ibid., 9 June 1967, citing *Daily Telegraph*, 6 and 7 June 1967.
27. Ibid., 16 June 1967.
28. Ibid., 9 June 1967.
29. *Jewish Chronicle*, 23 June 1967; *Sunday Truth* cited in W.D. Rubinstein, *The Jews in Australia: A Thematic History*, p. 534.
30. In Britain, the left had already turned perceptibly against Israel during and soon after the 1967 war, with the *Guardian* newspaper repeatedly accused by responsible sources of anti-Israeli bias. Just after the war 15 far left Labour MPs sponsored a motion in the House of Commons 'which declares invalid Israel's occupation of ... the Old City of Jerusalem'. Rubinstein, *A History of the Jews in the English-Speaking World: Great Britain*, p. 375.
31. Seymour Martin Lipset and Earl Raab, *Jews and the New American Scene* (Cambridge, Mass.: 1995), pp. 124–5.
32. On aspects of this question, see J.J. Goldberg, *Jewish Power: Inside the American Jewish Establishment* (New York: 1996), esp. pp. 3–21; Samuel Halperin, *The Political World of American Zionism* (originally 1961; Silver Springs, Maryland: 1985), pp. 293–316; and David Schoenbaum, *The United States and the State of Israel* (Oxford: 1993).
33. Lord John Russell was a lifelong liberal and advocate of religious toleration who was the principal author of the Great Reform Act of 1832. Yet as Prime Minister in 1850, he turned passionately and publicly against the attempts by the Vatican to re-establish a Catholic ecclesiastical hierarchy in Britain after a lapse of over 300 years. The movement for Irish Home Rule in the late nineteenth century led to a major split in the Liberal Party, with anti-Catholicism a factor among many (known as the Liberal Unionists) who left the party.

Index

Abercorn, James Hamilton, Duke of, 48
Abercrombie, Lascelles, 89
Aberdeen, John Campbell Hamilton Gordon, Earl of, 49, 159
Abergavenny, William Nevill, Marquis of, 48
Academic Assistance Council (renamed Society for the Protection of Science and Learning), 87, 89
Adam Smith, Sir George, *see* Smith, Sir George Adam
Adams, Vyvyan, 85, 86, 224
Addams, Jane, 72, 76, 82
Addington, Lord, *see* Hubbard, J.G.
Adelaide (South Australia), 19; public meetings at: (1882), 46, 131; (1903), 53; (1905), 56, 57, 121
Adelaide, Queen, 115, 154, 243
Adler, Herman (Chief Rabbi), 176, 179
Adler, Nathan (Chief Rabbi), 18, 44, 153
Age, The (Melbourne), 177
Ailesbury, George William Brudenell-Bruce, Marquis of, 165
AJA, *see* Anglo-Jewish Association (AJA)
Albemarle Association, 71
Albert, Prince, 154
Albiston, Walter, 146, 240
Aldenham, Lord, *see* Gibbs, Henry Hucks (Baron Aldenham)
Alexander I, Czar, 70
Alexander II, Czar, 39–40
Alexander III, Czar, 40, 49–50, 51, 52
Alexander, Alexander, 243
Alexander, Hooper, 221
Alexander, Major-General, 30, 210

Alexander, Prince, of Romania, 32
Alexandria, 8
Aliens Act (UK, 1905), 54, 215–16
Allen, Elizabeth A., 225
Allenby, Edmund Henry Hynman Allenby, Viscount, 164, 246
Alma-Tadema, Lawrence, 68
Amalgamated Society of Railway Servants, 62
American Board of Commissioners for Foreign Missions, 24
American Christian Fund for Jewish Relief, 107
American Committee for a Jewish Army, 103
American Episcopal House of Bishops, 58
American Federation of Labor, 169, 170
American Federation of Teachers, 82
American Jewish Committee, 74
American Medical Association, 77
American Palestine Committee, 107
American Writers Committee to Aid the Jews in Poland, 83
American Youth Congress, 82
Amery, Leopold, 93, 163–4, 166, 175, 177, 248; Jewish background of, 224
Ancona, 23; anti-Jewish decree at, 13–14, 146
Angell, Sir Norman, 94
Anglicans, 9, 11; conversionists among, 132–42, 159–61, 236, 237–8; *see also* clergymen, philosemitic; Evangelicals
Anglo-Israel Association (British Israelite movement), 154, 235
Anglo-Jewish Association (AJA), 31, 32–4, 137; Romanian Committee of, 33; Russo-Jewish Committee of, 45, 50

Index

Anschluss, 90, 94, 100; American clergy and, 100, 107
Anti-Nazi Council to Champion Human Rights (Great Britain), 90
Anti-Nazi League (USA), 100
Antisemitische Weltdienst, 108
Antisemitism since 1945, 190–3; in Great Britain, statement condemning, 95–6, 127–8; the United States, petition against, 81–2
Antonelli, Giacomo, Cardinal, 22
Archdall, Mervyn, 132
Argyll, George Douglas Campbell, Duke of, 48, 121
Armenians, persecution of, 120
Armitage, Robert, 80
Arnold, Matthew, 41, 44, 48, 122
Arthur, Richard, 56
Arthur, Sir George, 96
Artists' Refugee Committee, 95
Ashburnham, Dowager Countess of, 18
Ashley Lord (later 8th Earl of Shaftesbury), 29; *see also* Shaftesbury, Anthony Ashley Cooper, 7th Earl of
Ashton-under-Lyne, public meeting at (1882), 44
Asquith, Herbert Henry (later Earl of Oxford and Asquith), 112
Asquith, Margot, 83, 90, 94, 224
Association for Promoting Jewish Settlement in Palestine, 18, 154–5
Association of Writers for Religious Liberty, 91
Atholl, Katherine Marjory Stewart-Murray, Duchess of, 90
Atlanta, public meeting in (1919), 221
Atlanta Journal, 74, 75
Attlee, Clement, 90, 93, 195
Attwood, Matthias Wolverley, 10, 18
Auschwitz, 193, 194, 198
Australia, 19, 41, 112, 122, 175–6, 177, 182, 184, 192, 199; and

Beilis Affair, 68, 69; and Dreyfus Affair, 66; and Kishinev pogrom, 53–4, 127, 129; and Nazi antisemitism, 104–6; Jewish–Christian dialogue in, 108; Jews in, 112, 118; philosemitism in, xi, 19, 118; public meetings in: (1881), 45–6, 131; (1903), 53–4, 127; (1905), 56; (1933), 104; religious sectarianism in, 146, 202
Australia-Palestine Committee, 106
Australian Council for Jewish Rights, 106
Avebury, Lord, *see* Lubbock, Sir John
Aveling, Edward, 52
Aveling, Eleanor, 52
Aylesworth, A.B., 245

Baillie, Sir James, 90
Baines, Edward, 36, 233
Baker, Ray Stannard, 82
Baldwin, Stanley (Earl Baldwin of Bewdley), 95
Balfour Declaration (1917), 80, 93, 101, 161, 164, 165, 167, 168
Balfour, Arthur James Balfour, Earl, 55, 67, 119, 162
Balfour, J.H., 26
Ballarat, public meetings at: (1882), 46; (1903), 53
Baltimore, and Blackstone petition, 52
Bangor, Christopher Bethell, Bishop of, 18
Bank of England, 34; *see also* City of London
Banks, Sir Reginald Mitchell, 177
Baptists, philosemitic, 42, 47, 57–8, 77, 80, 132, 136, 144
Barker, Sir Ernest, 87
Bar Kochba, Simeon, 179
Barkley, Alben W., 103
Barlow, George, 61–2, 146
Barnett, David, 232; quoted, 117
Barrett, Sir James, 175, 248
Bauer, Yehuda, 189
Bazley, Sir Thomas, 37

Beaconsfield, Earl of, *see* Disraeli, Benjamin
Beauchamp, William Lygon, Earl, 63
Beaufort, Henry Charles Fitzroy Somerset, Duke of, 28
Bedford, Hastings Russell, Duke of, 35
Bedford, public meeting at (1877), 38
Beecher, Henry Ward, 131, 212
Beecher, John, 17
Beilis Affair (1911–13), 66–72, 83–4, 119, 127, 131, 132, 139, 144, 162, 178, 219
Beilis, Mendel, 59, 66–72
Belfast, public meeting at (1919), 80
Belleville (Kansas), 65
Belloc, Hilaire, 63
Bendigo, and Dreyfus Affair, 66; public meeting at (1882), 46
Benisch, Abraham, 18, 19, 128, 238
Benn, Sir Ernest, 83
Benson, Edward White, 49, 50
Berkeley, F.W.F., 29
Berlin, Congress of, 37, 176
Besant, Sir Walter, 48, 183, 251
Best, Sir Robert, 146
Bevan, Llewelyn D., 144
Bevan, Robert Cooper Lee, 132
Beveridge, Sir William (later Baron Beveridge), 88, 89, 98
Bible, impact of on Britons, 128–9, 131, 133
Bickersteth, Edward, 12, 151
Birkenhead, F.E. Smith, Earl of, 166, 246
Birkett, Norman, 92
Birmingham, 117; and Nazi antisemitism, 90; public meetings at: (1882), 44; (1890), 51; (1938), 90
Bismarck, Otto von, 131, 202–3
Black, Adam, 29
Black, James, 92
Blacks, 73, 74, 120, 233; contrasted with Jews, 5, 122, 183–4, 220; support for Jews among, 19, 71, 82, 101; *see also* slave trade
Blackstone, William E., 52, 132, 138, 160–1, 214, 245
Blaine, James G., 52
Blok, Alexander, 67
Blood libels, 53, 70; western condemnation of, 5–13, 32, 53, 67–72, 107, 119, 144, 176, 214
Blyden, Edward, 122
B'nai B'rith organisation, 72; and Kishinev pogrom, 54–5; awards to Theodore Roosevelt and Grover Cleveland, 58
Board of Deputies of British Jews, 16–17, 20, 24–5, 28, 90, 94, 137
Bohemia, blood libel in (1899), 53
Bologna, 22, 26; Archbishop of, 22
Bolshevism, Jews and, 79, 173
Bonar Law, Andrew, 69
Bond, Robert, 93
Bone, Sir Muirhead, 95, 221
Bonham Carter, Lady Violet, 93, 98, 112
Booth, William, 49
Boothby, Robert (later Baron Boothby), 85
Borah, W.E., 77, 101, 169
Boston (Mass.), and Blackstone petition, 52; pro-Frank petition in, 77–8
Bourne, Francis, Cardinal (Archbishop of Westminster), 56, 67
Bowater, Sir Frank, 95
Bowring, Sir John, 10, 120
Bowyer, Sir George, 44, 146, 209
Boycott of German goods, movement for, 89–90, 100
Bradford, 224; Bishop of, 96
Bradshaw, Samuel, 243
Bragg, Sir William, 89
Brailsford, H.N., 80, 118–19
Brest-Litovsk pogrom (1937), western condemnation of, 82
Bridges, Sir Brook, 29
Bright, Jacob, 34
Bright, John, 48
Brighton, public meeting at (1882), 44
Brisbane, public meeting at (1933), 104

Index

Bristol, public meeting at (1890), 51; Bishop of, 96
Britannia, 15
British and Foreign Bible Society, 19, 29
British Australian and New Zealander, 105
British Council of Churches, 196
British Federation of University Women, 84
British Israelite movement, *see* Anglo-Israel Association
British Social Democratic Federation, 123
British Union of Fascists, 124
Brooks, Van Wyck, 83
Brophy, John, 91
Brougham, Henry Peter Brougham, Baron, 28
Browning, Robert, 41, 44, 122, 231
Bruce, Lord Ernest, 29
Bruce, Stanley Melbourne (later Viscount Bruce), 105
Bruce, Theo, 121
Bryan, William Jennings, 65, 81
Bryant, William Cullen, 180
Bryce, James Bryce, Viscount, 43, 119, 165
Buccleuch, Walter Francis Scott, Duke of, 115
Buchan, John (Baron Tweedsmuir), 85, 165
Bucharest, 36, 37; Montefiore's visit to (1867), 32, 34
Buckland, Sir Thomas, 46
Buckley, E.P., 29
Buckmaster, Stanley Owen Buckmaster, Viscount, 83, 87, 88, 89, 121
Budgett Meakin, J.E., *see* Meakin, J.E. Budgett
Bulgaria, persecuted Christians of, 120
Burdett-Coutts, Angela Burdett-Coutts, Baroness, 41, 48, 49
Burke, Edmund, 173–4
Burkitt, F.C., 130
Burn, T.H., 80
Burrell, Sir Charles, 29

Burroughs, John, 76
Burrows, Herbert, 68, 214
Burt, Thomas, 182
Butler, Nicholas Murray, 82
Butler, Richard, 57
Buxton, Sir Fowell, 119, 120, 143, 233
Buxton, Sir Thomas Fowell, 36, 143

Cabot Lodge, Henry, *see* Lodge, Henry Cabot
Cadman, Samuel Parkes, 107
Caine, Sir Hall, 42
Cairns, Adam, 151
Calder, William M., 81
Calthorpe, Frederick, 29
Calvinists, and philosemitism, 143, 144–5
Cambridge University, and Beilis Affair, 67–8; and Dreyfus Affair, 62; and Kishinev pogrom, 55; and Nazi antisemitism, 88, 89, 92, 99
Cambridge, Adolphus Frederick, Duke of, 115, 154, 230
Campbell, Beatrice Stella (Mrs. Patrick Campbell), 63
Campbell, Thomas, 9
Campbell-Bannerman, Sir Henry, 55, 64
Canada, 41, 121, 192, 227; and Beilis Affair, 72; and Dreyfus Affair, 66; and Nazi antisemitism, 103–4; and Russian antisemitism, 57; Jews in, 118; Jewish–Christian dialogue in, 108; public meetings in (1938), 103–4
Canterbury, Archbishops of: Edward White Benson, 48, 50; Randall Davidson, 55, 58, 67; William Howley, 141; Cosmo Gordon Lang, 82, 83, 87, 91; John Bird Sumner, 28; Archibald Campbell Tait, 41, 44; William Temple, 97
Carden, Sir Robert, 43
Cardiff, 62; and Nazi antisemitism, 91; public meetings at: (1882), 44; (1919), 80; (1938), 93

258 Philosemitism

Cardiff University, and Polish antisemitism, 82
Carnegie, Andrew, 57
Carpenter, William Boyd (Bishop of Ripon), 49, 56, 127
Carroll, Lewis, see Dodgson, Charles Lutwidge
Carson, Sir Edward, 67
Carter, Franklin, 250
Carter, Lady Violet Bonham, see Bonham Carter, Lady Violet
Catholic Encyclopedia, 71
Catholic Herald, 86
Catholic World, 106
Catlin, George, 224
Cave, Sir George (later Viscount Cave), 70
Cavendish-Bentinck, Lord Henry, 79
Cazalet, Edward, 143
Cazalet, Victor, 98, 143
Cazenove family, 143
Cecil, Lord Robert (later Viscount Cecil), 79, 85, 89, 97
Central British Fund for the Relief of German Jewry, 87
Chaloner, Richard, 69
Chamberlain, Sir Austen, 67, 85, 87, 88, 162, 164
Chamberlain, Joseph, 55, 69, 145, 154, 164
Chamberlain, Neville, 92, 101, 164
Champneys, Basil, 236
Champneys, W.W. (Rector of Whitechapel), 236
Chapman, Benjamin Burgoyne, 108
Chapman, Emmanuel, 107
Charles (Carol), Prince of Romania, 32
Charleston, Bishop of, 11
Charleston, public meeting at (1840), 11
Chavasse, C.M. (Bishop of Rochester), 137
Chesterton, G.K., 123
Chicago, 245; and Blackstone petitions, 52, 161; and Dreyfus Affair; 65; Jewish–Christian conference at (1890), 138–9; pro-Frank petition in, 77; public meeting at (1903), 54; (1915), 76; (1943), 103; Zionist rally at (1907), 161
Chichester, Bishop of (George Bell), 96, 223
Chinese in Australia and the United States, support for Jews among, 122
Chisholm, Sir Samuel, 80
Choate, Joseph H., 46
Cholmondeley, George Horatio Cholmondeley, Marquis of, 28
Christadelphians, millenarianism of, 161
Christian Aid (organisation), 196
Christian Lady's Magazine, 14, 15, 51, 133, 135, 150, 208
Christian Observer, 6
Christian Palestine Committee (USA), 107
Christian philosemitism, 11, 126 et seq., 171; and conversionist activity, x, 132–42, 159–61, 236, 237–8
Christie, Agatha, 123
Christie Murray, David, see Murray, David Christie
Church Missions to Jews (Great Britain), 137
Church of England Newspaper, 96
Church of Scotland, and Nazi antisemitism, 92
Church Times, 85, 96, 108, 200; see also Dark, Sidney
Churches, American, and Nazi antisemitism, 107, 148; churches, postwar, and Israel, 194–8
Churches' Peace Aims Group, 226
Churchill, Charles Henry, 153
Churchill, Sir Winston, 199
Cincinnati, 145
Cincinnati Businessmen's Club, 77
Citrine, Sir Walter, 90
City College of New York, 72, 170
City of London, 153; Jews and, 8, 9, 34, 38, 41, 43, 69–70, 86, 113–16, 146, 173, 174, 175, 205; see also London, public meetings at
Clark, Champ (James Beauchamp),

71, 81
Clark, Chase, 103
Clark, Sir Kenneth (later Baron Clark), 95
Clarke, Sir Edward, 56
Clarke, Thomas, 157–8
Clergy, American, and Nazi antisemitism, 107, 148
Clergymen, philosemitic, 11, 20, 28, 38, 45, 46, 47, 48, 51, 54, 56, 57, 65, 67, 70–1, 72, 76, 80, 82, 84, 86, 93, 95, 98, 101–2, 103, 105, 106–8, 118, 127 et seq., 148, 161, 168, 226, 245; *see also* names of individual clergymen
Cleveland, Grover, 54, 58
Cleveland, Henry Vane, Duke of, 28
Cleveland (Ohio), and Beilis Affair, 72
Clifton, Bishop of, 51
Cluse, W.S., 96
Cocks, Seymour, 227
Codrington, Sir William, 20
Colby, Bainbridge, 82, 99
Coleridge, John Duke Coleridge, Baron, 44
Coleridge, Samuel Taylor, 231
Colomb, Sir John, 49, 176
Columbus Chamber of Commerce, 77
Colville, Lady Cynthia, 96
Commission of Inquiry into Nazi Persecution (USA), 100
Committee of Catholics to Fight Anti-Semitism (USA), 147
Committee of Religious Minorities (USA), 81
Communism, 124; *see also* Marxists, Socialists
Conan Doyle, Arthur, 68, 232
Congregational Union of England and Wales, 29
Congregationalists, philosemitic, 57, 71, 144, 217
Congress (USA) and Nazi antisemitism, 101, 102–3; and Russian antisemitism, 58
Constantinople, 8
Continuing Terror (book), 98

Conway, Sir Martin (later Baron Conway), 247
Conybeare, F.C., 62, 146
Cooley, Charles, 223
Cooper, Lady Diana, 91
Copeland, Royal S., 170
Corbett-Ashby, Margery, 87, 94
Cornell University, 72; and Frank Affair, 77
Costigan, Edward P., 100
Cotton, William, 43
Coughlin, Charles E., 79, 107
Council of Christians and Jews (Great Britain), 108, 195
Cousins, Robert G., 58
Cravath, Paul D., 54, 82, 233
Crawford, Emily, 62
Crawford, Robert Wigram, 36
Crémieux, Adolphe, 8
Cresson, Warder, 151, 242
Crewe, Robert Offley Ashburton Crew-Milnes, Earl and later Marquis of, 63, 98
Cripps, Sir Stafford, 92
Cromer, Evelyn Baring, Earl of, 67, 162–3
Crosby, Sir Thomas, 67
Crossman, Richard, 199
Crozier, W.P., 120
Crum-Ewing, Humphrey, 37
Crybbace, T.T., 243
Cumberland, Ernest Augustus, Duke of, 230
Cumberland, Richard, 231
Cumming, John, 151
Curtin, John, 106
Curtis, Charles, 101
Curtis, George William, 108
Curzon, George Nathaniel Curzon, Marquis, 48, 165, 176, 234

Daily Chronicle, 63
Daily Mail, 176
Daily Mirror, 87
Daily News, 62
Daily Telegraph, 23–4, 33
Dalley, William Bede, 46, 147
Damascus Affair (1840), 5 et seq., 113, 119, 132, 140–1, 145, 150

Daniels, Josephus, 81
Dark, Sidney, 108
Darrow, Clarence, 82
Dartmouth, William Walker Legge, Earl of, 49
Darwin, Charles, 41, 48
Darwin family, 68
Daughters of the Confederacy, Chicago Chapter, 77
Davey, Sir Horace, 44
Davidson, Randall (Archbishop of Canterbury), 55
Davies, David, 247
Davis, Noah, 46
Davitt, Michael, 53, 123
Dawson, Bertrand Edward Dawson, Viscount, 83
Dawson, Sir Philip, 85
Day Lewis, C., 91
de Quincy, Thomas, 231
de Rothschild, Alfred, 35
de Rothschild, Lionel, xii, 114
Deakin, Alfred, 56
Dearborn Independent, 81
Debs, Eugene V., 76
Deedes, Sir Wyndham, 83, 88, 97, 246
De Lisle, Edwin, 212
Delafield, E.M. (Edmé Elizabeth Monica Dashwood), 91
Delano, Frederick A., 77
Denison, Sir William, 19
Denman, Sir Richard, 85
Denman, Thomas Denman, Baron, 113
Denmark, and Beilis Affair, 67
Dent, Mr, 206
Derby, public meeting at (1942), 98
Des Moines, public meeting at (1903), 54
Despard, Charlotte, 68, 90
Deutsch, E.O., 122
Devonshire, Spencer Compton Cavendish, Duke of, 55
Dewey, Thomas E., 103, 226
Dicey, A.V., 68, 69–70, 80
Dinsdale, Sir Joseph, 56
Disraeli, Benjamin (Earl of Beaconsfield), 4, 50, 87, 176, 177

Dixon, George, 34
Doane, William C. (Bishop of Albany), 65
Dobree, Bonamy, 93
Dodgson, Charles Lutwidge, 44
Dohm, Christian Wilhelm von, 114
Donaldson, Canon, 223
Donors, gentile, to Jewish causes, xii, 17–21, 43–7, 56, 57, 87–8, 95, 115, 154, 208, 231
Dougherty, Denis J., Cardinal, 107
Douglass, Frederick B., 122
Dover, public meeting at (1882), 44
Downer, Sir John, 46
Downes, Henry, 17
Dresden, bombing of, 193
Dreyfus, Affair (1894–99), 59–66, 119, 145, 146
Dreyfus, Alfred, 59, 60–6, 74, 175, 176
Dreyfus, Lucie, 64, 65, 66
Drumont, Edouard, 60
Dublin, Richard Whateley, Archbishop of, 28; Lord Mayor of, 29
Dublin, public meeting at (1882), 44
Dubois, W.E.B., 82
Ducachet, Henry W., 11
Dugdale, Blanche, 84
Duggan, Stephen, 83
Duke, Sir James, 30
Duncombe, Thomas, 118
Dunsany, Edward John Drax Plunkett, Baron, 93
Dunstan, Sir Albert, 106
Durham Miners' Association, 91
Durham, Bishop of, *see* Henson, Hensley

Eardley, Sir Culling, 24–6, 28, 30, 137
East End of London, and Beilis Affair, 68
East India Company, 153
Eastern Europe, Nazi massacre of Jews in, 96–7, 105–6; status of Jews in, 3–4
Edelstein, Alan, ix
Eden, Sir Anthony (later Earl of

Avon), 96, 97, 99
Edgeworth, Maria, 116
Edinburgh, Provost of (John Cook), 25
Edinburgh, public meeting at (1882), 44
Edinburgh Review, 68
Edison, Thomas, 76, 220
Edward VII, King, 175–6
Edward VIII, King, 154
Edwards, William, 80
Einstein, Albert, 88, 184
Eliot, Charles W., 81
Eliot, George (Mary Ann Evans), 149, 231
Ellicott, C.J. (Bishop of Gloucester and Bristol), 36, 40, 51
Ellis, Sir John Whittaker, 40, 43, 44, 48
Elmley, William Lygon, Viscount, 85, 223
Emancipation, Jewish parliamentary, xii, 4, 8–9, 23, 41, 113–14, 118, 119, 130, 146, 172, 179
Emanuel, Emanuel, 232; quoted, 127–8
Emergency Committee for German Jewry (Great Britain), 86
Enfield, George Henry Charles Byng, Viscount, 34
English Zionist Organization, 69, 81
English-speaking countries, status of Jews in, 4–5, 111–13
Episcopal Convention (USA), 71
Epstein, Jacob, 80
Erle-Drax, J.S., 29
Ervine, St. John, 251; quoted, 185
Esperanto movement, 71
Espline, Alexander, 239; quoted, 141–2
Esterhazy, Walsin, 60, 61, 65
Eton College, Headmaster of, 55
Eugenics, and philosemitism, 172, 178–9
Evangelical Alliance, 24, 25, 29, 31, 136, 137–8
Evangelicals, 6, 10, 23, 197; and Jews, 12, 14, 24–5, 129; and millenarianism, 149–51; conversionists among, 12, 132–7
Evarts, William M., 46
Evatt, H.V., 199
Evian Conference on Refugees (1938), 93–4
Exeter, 24; Bishop of (Frederick Temple), 34, 42
Exodus (ship), refugees on, 195

Fairbanks, Charles Warren, 57
Falconer, Sir Robert, 103
Falmouth, public meeting at (1882), 44
Farley, John Murphy, Cardinal, 71
Farrar, F.W., 42, 43, 44–5, 48, 131, 181
Farrar, Geraldine, 76
Farthing, John C. (Bishop of Montreal), 227
Fascism, 124
Fawcett, Dame Millicent, 49
Federal Council of Churches of Christ (USA), 101
Fellowships of Faiths (USA), 148
Ferrara, 23
Figaro, Le, 66
Finn, Elizabeth Anne, 159
Finn, James, 159–60
Firth, Sir Charles Harding, 68
Fish, Hamilton (junior), 101, 102
Fish, Hamilton (senior), 37–8, 46
Fisher, H.A.L., 83, 88
Fitchett, W.H., 235; quoted, 53–4, 127
Flaherty, James, A., 107
Fleming, Canon, 181
Flipper, J.S., 71, 122
Foot, Dingle, 85, 90
Foot, Isaac, 84
Forbes, Sir Charles, 9
Ford, Henry, 76, 81, 106, 220
Forster, E.M., 91
Forsyth, John, 11
Fort Smith (Arkansas), public meeting at (1903), 54
Fortnightly Review, 68
Foss, Eugene N., 77
Foster, John W., 46–7
Fowler, Sir Henry, 42

Fowler, Sir Robert N., 30, 36, 43, 48, 49, 174–5, 239
Fowler, William, 43
Fox, Sir Henry Edward, 19
France, 6, 24, 25, 28; Jews in, 3, 63
Frank Affair (1913–15), 72–8
Frank, Leo, 72–8, 123
Frankfurt-am-Main, pro-Israel rally at (1967), 200
Franklin, Jacob, 13, 15–16, 135
Frazer, Sir James, 68
Frederic, Harold, 52
Free Church Council (Great Britain), 56
Freeland League for Jewish Colonization, 105
Freemasonry, philosemitic tradition in, 18, 2, 115
Frelinghuysen, Frederick T., 47
Freud, Sigmund, 184
Friends of Jewry (organization), 86–7
Frontier societies, and Jews, 118
Frost, Robert, 82
Fry, J. Storrs, 51
Fry, Lewis, 51
Fuller, Melville W., 52

Gallup Poll, Australia (1944), 105; Great Britain (1943), 98
Galsworthy, John, 68, 219, 232
Galt, Sir Alexander (Canadian High Commissioner), 41, 43
Galton, Sir Francis, 178
Garbett, Cyril (Archbishop of York), 97, 98, 223
Garvin, J.L., 162
Gaskell, W.H., 219
Gaster, Moses, 90
Gawler, George, 18, 152–4
Gawler, J.C., 154, 243
Geelong, and Dreyfus Affair, 66
George III, King, 114
Georgia Society (New York State), 76
Gerard, James W., 99
German Emergency Committee (Great Britain), 87
German Refugees Assistance Fund, 87, 88

Germany, 202–3; antisemitism in, 144; and Beilis Affair, 67; see also Nazi antisemitism
Germany Emergency Committee, see Society of Friends Germany Emergency Committee
Ghetto benches (Poland), protests against, 82–3
Gibbons, James, Cardinal, 52, 147, 214
Gibbons, Sir Sills, 34
Gibbs, Henry Hucks (Baron Aldenham), 43
Gibraltar, fund for Jewish refugees at (1859), 20–1
Gibson, Charles Dana, 82
Gideon, Sir Sampson, 24
Gillis, James M., 106
Gilpin, Charles, 143
Gingrich, Newt, 202
Gladstone, William Ewart, 43, 123, 234
Glasgow, public meetings at: (1882), 44; (1913), 70; (1919), 80; (1938), 93
Glenesk, Algernon Borthwick, Baron, 56, 176
Gloucester, Bishop of (C.J. Ellicott), 36, 40
Glynn-Jones, W.S., 70
Goldsmid, Abraham, 114
Goldsmid, Sir Francis, 33, 35
Gollancz, Victor, 98
Gooch, G.P., 83
Gordon, Elizabeth Anna, 154
Gorki, Maxim, 67
Goudge, H.L., 96
Grant, Ulysses S., 37, 46, 180, 212
Granville, Granville George Leveson-Gower, Earl, 37, 43, 116
Great Britain, Jewish–Christian dialogue in, 108; status of Jews in, xii, 4, 111–16, 172, 192–3
Great Synagogue, London, 114, 129
Greater New York Federation of Churches, 107
Green, A.A., 144
Green, J.F., 53, 68

Green, T.H., 44
Green, William, 169
Greenberg, L.J., 154
Greer, David, 71
Grégoire, Abbé Henri, 114
Grenfell, David, 98
Grier, Sir Wyly, 103
Grimsby, public meeting at (1942), 98
Grimshawe, T.S., 12
Groves, Captain, 17
Guernsey Star, 15
Gurney, J. Henry, 29
Gurney, Samuel, 9–10, 29, 30, 120, 143, 231

Haggard, H. Rider, 68, 234
Hailsham, Douglas Hogg, Viscount, 175, 176
Haldane, J.B.S., 89, 90, 224
Haldane, J.S., 89, 224
Halifax (Nova Scotia), public meeting at (1938), 104
Halifax, Edward Wood, Earl of, 92
Hall, Anna Maria (Mrs S.C. Hall), 131
Hall, James, 222
Hamilton, Sir Robert, 247
Hannah, Ian, 227
Hannon, Sir Patrick, 85, 98, 223
Hanson, Sir Reginald, 43
Hardie, James Keir, 53, 64
Harding, Warren G., 101
Hardy, Thomas, 68
Harper's Weekly, 180
Harrison, Benjamin, 52
Harrison, Sir Eric, 106
Harrison, Frederic, 68
Hartington, Edward William Spencer Cavendish, Marquis of (later 10th Duke of Devonshire), 85
Harvard University, quota system at, 81
Hawkes, Henry, 145, 240
Hazlitt, William, 231
Hearst, William Randolph, 53, 102
Henderson, Arthur, 91
Henley, Anthony Henley Eden, Baron, 37
Henley, Sir Thomas, 146, 240
Henry VIII, King, 128
Henry, F.A., 72
Henry, Hubert, 59, 60
Henson, Hensley (Bishop of Durham), 86, 90, 184
Herberg, Will, 191
Herbermann, Charles G., 71
Herrick, Myron T., 77
Herschell, Solomon (Chief Rabbi), 145
Herzl, Theodor, 61, 162
Hewitt, E.P., 165, 175, 246, 248
Hexham, Bishop of, 84
Hill, A.V., 98
Hills, J.W., 85
Hindenberg, Paul von, letter to, 85
Hinsley, Arthur, Cardinal (Archbishop of Westminster), 93
Hiroshima, 194
Hitler, Adolf, 85, 89, 92, 102, 108
Hobart (Tasmania), 19
Hodgson, Kirkman, 36, 231
Hogg, Quintin (later 2nd Viscount Hailsham), 98, 175
Holland, 25
Holmes, John Haynes, 82, 99 100, 102, 169, 222
Holocaust, House of Commons and, 96; impact of and attitude to Jews, 190; *see also* Nazi antisemitism
Holroyd, William W., 223
Hooper, Sarah, 136
Hope, Anthony (Anthony Hope Hawkins), 68, 182
Hope Simpson, Sir John, *see* Simpson, Sir John Hope
Hopkins, Daniel, 93
Horder, Thomas Jeeves Horder, Baron, 94
Horsfall, T.B., 29
Horthy, Miklos, 197
Horton, R.F., 56, 137, 144
Houghton, Richard Monckton Milnes, Baron, 34–5, 37
Housman, A.E., 89

Philosemitism

Howard, Sidney, 100
Howden, Sir John Hobart Caradoc, Baron, 10
Howell, Rees, 92
Hubbard, J.G. (Baron Addington), 43, 49, 175
Huddersfield, public meeting at (1942), 98
Hughes, Charles Evans, 81
Hughes, Hugh Price, 48, 212–13
Huguenots, and philosemitism, 143
Hull, public meetings at (1919), 80; (1938), 93
Hungary, 25
Hunt, Leigh, 129
Hunt, W. Holman, 63, 161–2
Hutt, Sir William, 29
Huxley, Thomas, 48, 49, 122, 128
Hyde Park, anti-Nazi rally at, 90; pro-Dreyfus rally at, 64
Hyndman, H.M., 53, 68

Ickes, Harold, 120
Iddesleigh, Walter Stafford Northcote, Earl of, 84
Ignatius, Father (Joseph Leycester Lyne), 129, 130, 131–2, 140, 235
Illinois Bankers' Association, 77
Immigration League of Australia, 56
Institute for International Education, 83
Institute of Journalists (Great Britain), 68
Intellectual ability of Jews, as factor in philosemitism, 171–2, 179–84
International Committee for Securing Employment for Refugee Professional Workers, 87
International League for Academic Freedom, 82
International Peace and Arbitration Association, 53
International Social Service, 87
Ipswich Express, 14
Iran, Jews in, 193
Ireland, 20, 29, 122
Irish nationalists, philosemites among, 122, 146; *see also* Davitt, Michael
Israel, State of, 189, 197; and Jewish status, 189, 190, 194; churches and, 196–8; Marxists and, 194, 201
Italians in the United States, prejudice against, 73
Ithaca (New York), 161

Jabotinsky, Vladimir, 167
Jackson, John (Bishop of London), 41, 42, 43
Jacobs, Joseph, 40
Jakobovits, Immanuel (Chief Rabbi), 191
Jamaica, 215; Jews in, 112
James, Montague Rhodes, *see* Rhodes James, Montague
Jeffrey, G.B., 87
Jennings, Sir Patrick, 177
Jerome, Jerome K., 68
Jerusalem, Marxists and, 194, 196; public opinion and, 196–9; Vatican and, 198; Anglican bishopric in, 158
Jewish army, support for creation of, 103, 227
Jewish Chronicle, xii, 13, 18, 20, 21, 23, 24, 31, 34, 40, 50, 53, 117, 137–8, 141–2, 145, 147, 154, 157, 162, 164
Jewish–Christian dialogue, 11, 106–8, 138–9, 148, 195–7
Jewish–Christian relations, since 1945, 191, 195–200
Jewish Defence Association (USA), 57
Jewish Territorial Organization (ITO), 162
Jewish university, American plan for, 81
Jews of Morocco Relief Fund, *see* Morocco, Jews in, donations for
Jews' and General Literary and Scientific Institution (Sussex Hall, London), 114
Jews' College (London), 179
Jews' Free School (London), 115, 116

Jews' Hospital and Orphan Asylum (London), 114, 116
Jews' Orphan Asylum, *see* Jews' Hospital and Orphan Asylum (London)
Jews, perceived as an elite, 128–31, 171 et seq.; world population in 1840, 3; world population since 1945, 192–3
Jews, status of in 1840, 3–4
Jews, status since 1945, 189 et seq.
Joad, C.E.M., 83
Johannesburg, 218; Bishop of, 128
John Paul II, Pope, 198
John, Augustus, 95
Johnson, Edwin C., 103
Johnson, Hugh, 100
Johnston, Eric A., 103
Johnston, Harry H., 162
Joicey, James Joicey, Baron, 84
Jones, Sir George, 85, 86, 90
Jowett, Benjamin, 41, 44, 48
Judaism, post-war status of, 190–1

Kansas City, 65
Katz, David, 128–9
Kennan, George, 214
Kent, Victoria Mary Louisa, Duchess of, 115
Kenworthy, J.M. (later Baron Strabolgi), 79, 80, 85, 86, 90, 246, 247
Kenyon, Sir Frederic, 89
Kharkov, 40
Kilbec, E., 204
Kiley, J.D., 79, 80–1
Kimberley scheme (Australia), 195, 228, 240
King, William, 101, 102
Kingston (Ontario), public meeting at (1938), 103
Kinnaird, Arthur Kinnaird, Baron, 29, 37, 42, 56, 132
Kinnoull, George Harley Hay, Earl of, 90
Kishinev pogrom (1903), western condemnation of, 52–5, 103, 133, 161, 181–2, 183, 245
Knight, Holford, 84, 85, 86, 223

Knight, Dame Laura, 95
Knights of Columbus, 107
Know-Nothing Party (USA), 202
Knox, Philander C., 77
Kohn, Hans, 112
Kristallnacht (1938), western condemnation of, 91, 94, 100–1, 103, 104–5

Ladino language, 3
Lancaster, 20
Lancet, and refugee doctors, 94
Lane, Sir Arbuthnot, 91
Lang, Cosmo Gordon (Archbishop of York and later of Canterbury), 67, 82, 83, 98, 222
Lang, John Dunmore, 19
Langley, J.D. (Archdeacon of Sydney), 161
Lansbury, George, 85, 96, 222
Lansing, Robert, 81
Larpent, George Gerard de Hochepied, 10, 143
Laurier, Sir Wilfrid, 57, 121, 161
Lavery, Emmet, 107
Law, Andrew Bonar, *see* Bonar Law, Andrew
Lawrence, Sir William, 35, 40
Lebanon War (1982), 201
Lecky, W.E.H., 179
Leeds, George Osborne, Duke of, 28
Leeds, 132; public meetings at: (1882), 144; (1913), 70; (1919), 80: (1938), 90
Leeds University, and Nazi anti-semitism, 93
Leeper, Alexander, 146, 240
Leeser, Isaac, 245
Leicester, High Sheriff of, 183
Leighton, Frederic Leighton, Baron, 48, 122
Lemprière, Charles, 27–8
Lewis, John W., 100
Lewis, Sinclair, 100, 226
Liberal Ministers' Club (Philadelphia), 71
Liberals, and Jews, 23, 111 et seq., 171; and other minorities, 122

Lidgett, J. Scott, 84, 88
Lincoln, Abraham, 37
Lindemann, Albert S., x
Listowel, William Francis Hare, Earl of, 86
Littell, Norman A., 103
Liverpool, and *Kristallnacht*; 91; Jewish philanthropic society in, 116; public meeting at (1882), 44
Liverpool, Bishop of (John Charles Ryle), 137
Lloyd George, David, 93, 145, 167–8, 169, 184
Locker-Lampson, Oliver, 85, 86, 88, 223, 227
Lodge, Henry Cabot, 101
Lodge-Fish Resolution, 226
London, Bishops of: Archibald Campbell Tait, 30; John Jackson, 41, 42, 43, 127; Arthur Winnington-Ingram, 97; and Kishinev pogrom, 55
London, Jews in, 8, 9, 274–5; public meetings at: (1840), 9–10, 119, 120, 143, 145, 173, 174; (1872), 34–7, 119, 143, 174; (1882), 40–3, 119, 120, 122, 127, 131, 147, 175, 181; (1890), 48–50, 119, 120, 121, 122, 127, 143, 144, 147, 174–5, 176, 181, 182, 183; (1906), 55–6, 123, 144, 161, 176; (1913), 69–70; (1933), 83–4, 86; (1935), 90; (1937), 82, 4; (1938), 92–3, 95; *see also* City of London
London County Council, 52
London Jewish Board of Guardians, 45
London Peace Society, 143
London Society for Promoting Christianity Amongst the Jews, 7, 132, 133, 135, 139, 141, 151, 159, 160
London University, 9, 89; and Beilis Affair, 67–8; and Nazi anti-semitism, 88
Londonderry, Charles Vane-Tempest-Stewart, 6th Marquis of, 63
Londonderry, Charles Vane-Tempest-Stewart, 7th Marquis of, 84, 234
Longford, Earl of, *see* Pakenham, Frank
Lord Baldwin's Fund for Refugees, 95
Lord, James, 30
Lord's Day Observance Society (Great Britain), 29
Los Angeles, 161
Low, Seth, 54, 121
Lowe, Robert (later Viscount Sherbrooke), 180
Lowell, James Russell, 250
Lowther, James, 67
Lubbock, Sir John (later Baron Avebury), 37, 41, 48
Luce, Henry, 106
Lushington, Sir Godfrey, 62
Lustrat, Joseph, 74
Lyall, Edna, 63
Lyne, Joseph Leycester, *see* Ignatius, Father
Lyttleton, Edith, 88
Lytton, Victor Bulwer-Lytton, Earl of, 88

MacArthur, Robert S., 57–8
Macaulay, Rose, 91
Macaulay, Thomas Babington Macaulay, Baron, 112
MacCarthy, Desmond, 91
MacDonald White Paper on Palestine (1939), 80, 102
MacDonald, Ramsay, 67
Macfie, Robert, 44
MacLeish, Archibald, 83
Mackenzie, Sir Compton, 91
Macmillan, Harold, 191
Maimonides, Moses, 179
Malan, F.S., 247
Malcolm, Neill, 97
Malmesbury, James Howard, Earl of, 26, 27
Manchester, public meetings at (1840), 11; (1882), 44; (1890), 51; (1913), 70; (1919), 80;

(1933), 85
Manchester, Bishop of (James Fraser), 41
Manchester Guardian, 85, 120
Manchester University, 167; and Nazi antisemitism, 98
Mander, H.F., 144
Mann, Tom, 80
Manning, Henry, Cardinal, 41, 42–3, 48, 49, 52
Manning, Kathleen (Viscountess Simon), 154, 225
Manning, William T., 99, 107, 147, 228
Mansion House Fund (1882), 43–4, 46
Margesson, Lady Isobel, 94
Marley, Dudley Leigh Aman, Baron, 90, 223
Marshall, Sir Chapman, 10
Marshall, Louis, 74
Martineau, Harriet, 142–3
Martineau, James, 41, 48, 143
Marx, Karl, 52
Marxists, ambivalence towards Jews of, 123–5; and Israel, 194, 196
Masaryk, Jan, 97
Masefield, John, 68, 234
Massena (New York), blood libel at, 107
Masterman, John, 10, 174
Mathew, David, 97
Matthews, W.R., 96
Maxse, Leopold, 62, 175, 217
Maynard, Theodore, 107
McAdoo, William G., 81
McCaul, Alexander, 7–8, 132, 159
McConaughy, James L., 106
McCormick, Anne O'Hare, 100
McCormick, Cyrus, 52
McDermott, Allan L., 58
McGill University, anti-Nazi rioters from, 103
McKell, Sir William, 106
McKinley, William, 52, 65
McLauren, Anselm J., 58
McMichael, E.H., 74
McNeile, Hugh, 132, 133
Meakin, J.E. Budgett, 129

Meath, Reginald Brabazon, Earl of, 48, 50, 176
Mehemet Ali, 5, 8
Melba, Dame Nellie, 63
Melbourne, 19, 151, 177–7; and Dreyfus Affair, 66; and refugees from Nazism, 105; public meetings at: (1861), 152; (1881), 45, 181; (1903), 53–4, 127, 144; (1933), 104
Mellor, Sir John, 250
Menzies, Sir Robert, 103, 106
Merchant Taylors' Company, 18
Meredith, George, 49, 119
Merrett, Sir Charles, 175
Merthyr Tydfil, public meeting at (1882), 44
Methodist Times, 86
Methodists, philosemitic, 46, 47, 53, 71, 245
Mill, John Stuart, 178
Millenarianism, 12-3, 132, 149 et seq., 158–9
Mills, John, 18–19, 139, 154–5, 159, 208, 238
Mills, Ogden L., 99
Milner, Alfred Milner, Viscount, 56, 68, 162, 163, 175
Minneapolis, public meeting in (1915), 76
Minor, Clorinda S., 244–5
Minorities, contrasted with Jews, 122, 183–4
Mitchison, Naomi, 224
Mitford, Edward L., 155–6, 163
Modena, 23
Mogador atrocity (1844), donations for Jewish victims of, 17–18, 20
Monash, Sir John, 177–8
Monk, Henry Wentworth, 243
Montefiore, Claude G., 175
Montefiore, Sir Francis, 69
Montefiore, Sir Moses, 8, 9, 17–18, 22, 25–6, 28, 30, 32, 34, 114, 115, 117, 143, 153, 243
Montefiore family, 122, 231
Montreal, public meetings at: (1913), 72; (1938), 103, 227
Mormonism 243

Moody, Dwight L., 52, 65, 214
Moore, Henry, 95
Moore, Roger, 200
Morgan, J. Pierpont, 52
Morley, Samuel, 43
Morning Herald, 14, 15
Morning Post, 6, 56
Morocco, Jews in, donations for, 17–18, 19–20, 29
Morris, William, 52
Morrison, Herbert (later Baron Morrison of Lambeth), 85, 93
Morrison, Robert, 98
Mortara, Edgardo (Edgar), 22, 23, 24, 25, 26, 28, 30
Mortara Affair (1858–9), 22–31, 119, 145
Mortara Committee (Great Britain), 25, 30; petition of (1859), 28–31, 36, 120, 136, 210, 236
Moscow, 40, 48
Mosley, Sir Oswald, 79, 124
Mount Temple, Wilfrid William Ashley, Baron, 86
Mount-Temple, William Francis Cowper-Temple, Baron, 41
Muggeridge, Malcolm, 200
Müller, Max, 44
Mullock, Sir William, 103
Mumford, Lewis, 83
Mundella, Anthony, 37
Muntz, Philip, 34
Murdoch, Walter, 121
Murphy, Frank, 103, 227
Murray, David Christie, 61
Murray, Sir Gilbert, 88, 99, 121, 219, 222
Murray, Sir James, 68
Murray, John, 87
Mussolini, Benito, 92, 102

Nagasaki, 194
Napier, Sir Charles, 29
Napoleon III, Emperor, 25
Nash, Paul, 95
Nathan, Sir Matthew, 164
Nation, 68
National Committee for Rescue from Nazi Terror (Great Britain), 98
National Committee Against Nazi Persecution and Extermination of the Jews (USA), 103
National Conference of Jews and Christians (USA), 106
National Council of Catholic Men (USA), 101
National Council of Christians and Jews (USA), 191, 228
National Protestant Society (Great Britain), 27
National Review, 62, 217
National Union of Students (Great Britain), 82
Navarino, Battle of (1827), 149
Nazi antisemitism, gentile condemnation of, 79, 83 et seq., 112, 137, 148, 183
Nazi–Soviet Pact (1939), 125
New Orleans, public meeting at (1903), 181
New South Wales Council of Christians and Jews, 108
New South Wales, Jews in, 118
New York, and Beilis Affair, 131; and Frank Affair, 77; and Blackstone petitions, 52, 161; and Dreyfus Affair, 65–6; and Kishinev pogrom, 54, 119; and Russian antisemitism 57; public meetings at: (1882), 46–7; (1903), 54, 121; (1933), 98; (1937), 100; (1938), 100; (1943), 103
New York Call, 123
New York State House of Assembly, 71
New York State Legislature, 103
New York Times, 52, 65, 71, 75, 76, 78, 100
New Zealand, and Beilis Affair, 68; and Dreyfus Affair, 66
Newcastle, Henry Pelham Alexander Clinton, Duke of, 48
Newcastle upon Tyne, 62; Bishop of, 84; public meeting at (1933), 84
Newdegate, Sir Francis, 177
Nicholas I, Czar, 16

Index

Nicholas II, Czar, 52, 58, 70–1, 176
Nicholson, Sir Charles, 19, 174
Nicholson, George, 87
Nicolson, Harold, 91, 98, 99
Niebuhr, Reinhold, 107
Nobel Prize winners, among philosemites, 83, 88; Jewish, 184
Noel, Baptist, 10, 132, 235
Nonconformists, and philosemitism, 9, 11, 28, 46, 47, 56, 64, 67, 84, 127, 143–5
Norfolk, Henry FitzAlan-Howard, Duke of, 53, 67
Northumberland, Archdeacon of, 84
Nottingham, and Beilis Affair, 70; public meeting at (1933), 84
Nuremberg Laws (1935), gentile condemnation of, 90

O'Brien, John P., 99
Obshtchestvo Remeslenovo Truda, *see* ORT
O'Connell, Daniel, 10, 14, 120, 145
O'Connell, William Henry, Cardinal, 82
O'Connell, William John, 207
O'Connor, John N., 77
O'Connor, T.J., 84
O'Connor, T.P., 246
O'Donovan, W.J., 90
O'Reily, John, 57, 216
O'Ryan, John, 99, 107
O'Shanassy, Sir John, 122
Observer, 162
Odessa, pogroms at (1871), 31; (1881), 39
Odets, Clifford, 83
Oldroyd, Mark, 212
Oliphant, Laurence, 43, 160, 245
Oliver, George, 24, 145–6
Ormsby-Gore, W.G.A., 79, 85, 246
ORT (Society for the Encouragement of Jewish Handicraft), Parliamentary Advisory Council of, 90
Oslo Accords, 194
Oswego (Wisconsin), 66
Ottawa, public meeting at: (1905), 57, 121

Ottoman Empire, status of Jews in, 4, 5–6, 12, 31–3, 41
Overend Gurney and Company, 143, 231
Owen, Sir Hugh, 18
Owen, Rosamond Dale, 245
Oxford University, 27; and Beilis Affair, 67–8; and Dreyfus Affair, 63; and *Kristallnacht*, 92; and Nazi antisemitism, 88, 89, 92, 98, 99; and Russian antisemitism, 44, 119
Oxford, Bishop of (John Fielder Mackarness), 41, 127
Oxford, public meeting at (1943), 98
Oxlee, John, 141

Pacifico, Don, 167, 205
Paget, H.L. (Bishop of Stepney), 132
Paget, Lord Alfred, 29
Pakenham, Frank (Earl of Longford), 98
Palestine, 18–19, 92, 93, 94, 97, 129, 139, 149 et seq., 159, 174, 184, 185, 199; United States and, 101–3
Palestine Exploration Fund, 183
Palestine Federation of America, 169
Palmer, Edwin, 44
Palmerston, Henry John Temple, Viscount, 7, 8, 10, 158, 159, 167
Pankhurst, Christabel, 161
Pankhurst, Sylvia, 90, 223
Paris, Congress of, 32, 33, 36
Parkes, James, 98, 197
Parmoor, Charles Alfred Cripps, Baron, 80, 88, 120
Patterson, J.H., 246
Patterson, William, 245
Paul VI, Pope, 191
Peabody, George Foster, 54
Pearson, Charles, 18, 113, 231
Pearson, Karl, 68, 178
Pease, Sir Joseph, 49, 50, 144
Peden, Sir John, 103
Peel, Sir Robert, 8, 10, 11
Peixotto, Benjamin, 37

Percival, John, 44
Permanent Commission on Better Understanding between Christians and Jews in America, 107
Pershing, John, 107
Perth (Western Australia), and Dreyfus Affair, 66; public meeting at (1905), 56
Peterborough, Bishop of (William Connor Magee), 34
Peters, Madison C., 57–8, 76, 146–8, 216
Petlura, Simon, 79
Phelan, Thomas, 65
Philadelphia, 148, 150, 180; and Blackstone petition, 52; public meetings at: (1840), 11; (1882), 47; (1903), 54
Phillips, Sir Herbert, 248; quoted, 175
Phillips, Thomas, 19
Philosemites, ambivalence towards Jews among, x, 122–5, 214, 234, 250; impact of Nazi antisemitism on, 123; types of, 111 et seq., 126 et seq., 149 et seq., 171 et seq.
Philosemitism, defined, ix; ignorance, of, ix-x, xii; Christian, 8, 111, 126 et seq., 171; conservative and elitist, xi, 43, 111, 114, 171 et seq., liberal and progressive, 111 et seq., 171; postwar, 189 et seq.; Zionist, 111, 149 et seq.
Picquart, Georges, 60, 61
Piedmont, 25
Pieritz, George, 9
Pierrepont, Edwards, 46
Pilcher, C.V., 106
Pinckney, Henry L., 11
Pius IX, Pope, 22
Pius XII, Pope, 197
Pogroms (1919–20), gentile condemnation of, 79–81, *see also* Russia.
Poland, antisemitism in, condemned, 80, 82–3

Polhill-Turner, F.C., 38
Polk, Frank L., 99
Pomroy, Dr., 24
Ponsonby, Arthur Ponsonby, Baron, 90
Pontypridd, public meeting at (1933), 85
Portsea Hebrew Philanthropic Society, 116, 153
Portsmouth, 116, 117–18, 180; and Dreyfus Affair, 63; first Jewish Mayor of (Emanuel Emanuel), 117–18; Mayor of (Daniel Howard), 117; public meeting at (1933), 84
Potter, Sir Thomas, 11
Potteries, public meetings in the (1882), 44
Poynter, Sir Edward, 55
Presbyterianism, and philosemitism, 46, 71, 126–7, 129, 141–2, 144, 161
Pretoria, Bishop of, 168
Price, Thomas, 57
Priestley, J.B., 91
Primrose, Sir John Ure, 70
Primrose League, 176
Pritt, D.N., 90, 94
Pro-Palestine Committee (USA), 101
Procter, Henry, 175
Protestant Alliance, 29
Protestant Association, 6, 16, 26, 29, 30
Protestant Magazine, 6, 14
Protestantism, and philosemitism, 20, 23, 25, 128 et seq., 148; and Zionism, 149 et seq.; postwar, 197
Protocols of the Elders of Zion, 81, 82
Public meetings, purpose of, 38, 42, 38, 42, 51, 57; *see also* under names of cities and towns
Puritans, and philosemitism, 128–9

Quakers, and philosemitism, 30, 87, 114, 126–7, 143–4, 150–1, 239
Quarterly Review, 68

Index

Quebec, public meeting at (1938), 104
Quiller-Couch, Sir Arthur, 68

Radford, Sir George H., 70
Raffles, Thomas, 235
Rappaport, Solomon, ix
Rathbone, Eleanor, 85, 88, 90, 98
Ratti-Menton, Benoît, Count de, 6
Ravensworth, Robert Arthur Liddell, Earl of, 84
Rayleigh, Robert John Strutt, Baron, 89
Reade, Charles, 41–2
Record, 96
Redgrave, Vanessa, 200
Reformation, implication of, for philosemitism, 128–9
Reformation Society, 29
Reformed Church of America, 148
Refugee Assistance Fund (Great Britain), 88
Refugees from Nazism, Australia and, 104–6, 121; British efforts for, 87, 89, 93–9; Canada and, 103–4; United States and, 94, 99–103
Reid, Sir George, 46, 177
Reinach, Joseph, 60
Relief Fund for Palestinian Jewry, 19
Rhodes James, Montague, 68
Rhodes, blood libel case on, 5, 6, 8, 12
Rhondda, Margaret Haig Thomas, Viscountess, 94
Richard, Henry, 33, 37, 41, 143
Richardson, Sir Benjamin, 178–9
Ripon, Bishop of, *see* Carpenter, William Boyd
Ripon, George Frederick Samuel Robinson, Marquis of, 48
Roan, Leonard, 74
Robbins, Lionel (later Baron Robbins), 89
Roberts, Mrs, 17
Roberts, Frederick Sleigh Roberts, Earl, 67
Robertson, Sir John, 46, 120–1
Robeson, Paul, 122

Robinson, Frederick B., 170
Rochester (Kent), Mayor of, 30
Rochester (New York), public meeting at (1915), 76
Rockefeller, John D., 52
Roden, Robert Jocelyn, Earl of, 24, 132
Rogers, Will, 103
Rollit, Sir Albert, 50
Roman Catholics, xi, 6, 9, 11, 19, 20, 22–4, 145–7, 202–3; British prejudice against, 5, 13–14, 31, 119, 126, 136, 142, 145, 158, 197, 202, 203, 205; and blood libels, 6–7, 53, 67, 69, 70, 71; and Damascus Affair, 6–7, 11, 119; and Dreyfus Affair, 119; and Mortara Affair, 22–31, 119; and Nazi antisemitism, 84, 91, 93, 97, 98, 101, 104, 107, 123; and Russian antisemitism, 41, 42–3, 48, 49, 52, 53, 56, 122; relations with Jews since 1945, 197–9
Romania, 201; antisemitism in, 32, 193; western condemnation of, 33–8, 143
Rome, 25; Jews in, 146
Roosevelt, Franklin D., 100–3, 169, 199
Roosevelt, Theodore, 54, 161, 216
Root, Elihu, 99
Rose, Norman, x
Rosebery, Archibald Philip Primrose, Earl of, 67
Rothschild, Nathan Mayer, 143
Rothschild, Nathan Mayer Rothschild, Baron, 18, 53, 55
Rothschild family, 122; *see also* de Rothschild
Roupell, William, 231
Rowton, Montagu Corry, Baron, 176
Royden, Maude, 223
Rumbold, Sir Horace, 53, 214
Russell, Bertrand, 184
Russell, Charles Edward, 170
Russell of Killowen, Frank Russell, Baron, 53

Russell, Lord John, 30–1, 115, 116, 202, 253
Russia, antisemitism in, 3–4, 14–17, 39 et seq., 122, 123, 163, 176–7, 182, 193; pogroms in, 39, 40, 55, 136, 137, 161; pro-Beilis sentiment in, 67; public meetings protesting, 40–54, 69–71, 221; *see also* Beilis Affair; Soviet Union
Russian Jewish Relief Fund, 152
Russian Refugee and Colonization Fund (New York City), 47
Rutherford, Ernest Rutherford, Baron, 87, 88, 89
Rylands, Peter, 37

Sacks, Jonathan (Chief Rabbi), 191
Sadler, Sir Michael, 80, 88, 89
St John's Wood Synagogue, 122
St Jude's Church, Southsea, 44
St Louis, public meeting at (1903), 58, 183
St Petersburg, 40, 47, 48, 50, 51, 58; Metropolitan of, messages to, 55, 58
Salford, Bishop of, 85; Mayor of, 70
Salomons, David, 9, 113, 114, 118
Salt, Sir Titus, 29
Salvation Army, 69, 70, 80; *see also* Booth, William
Samuel, Sir Marcus, 53
San Diego Theosophical Society, 77
San Francisco, 65; public meeting at (1903), 54
Sankey, John Sankey, Viscount, 92, 98, 99
Savannah, public meeting at (1840), 11
Savory, Sir Joseph, 48, 50, 51, 143
Sayers, Dorothy, 96, 123
Scarsdale, Rev. Alfred Nathaniel Curzon, Baron, 41
Schurz, Carl, 54
Scotland, 20, 29, 142
Scott, Benjamin, 29, 30
Scott, Leslie, 69, 247
Scottish Reformation Society, 26
Scribner, Charles, 54

Second Vatican Council, 197
Seager, Sir William, 80
Selborne, William Waldegrave Palmer, Earl of, 67, 162
Serbia, Jews in, 33, 34, 37
Seton Watson, Hugh, 83
Seventh Dominion League, 167
Shaftesbury, Anthony Ashley Cooper, 7th Earl of, 12, 16, 26–7, 28, 35–6, 40, 120, 132, 135, 158–9, 233
Sharswood, George, 47
Shaw, George Bernard, 55, 68, 99, 221, 223
Sheffield, public meeting at (1913), 70
Sheffield, Mayors of, 18, 218
Sherrington, Sir Charles, 89
Sidebotham, Herbert, 108, 165, 229
Simon, Sir John, 34, 38, 225
Simon, Sir John Simon, Viscount, 96, 154
Simon, Viscountess, *see* Manning, Kathleen
Simpson, Sir John Hope, 226
Simpson, W.W., 108
Sinclair, Sir Archibald, 93, 95, 119
Sioux City (Iowa), public meeting at (1903), 54
Six Day War (1967), and political left, 124, 125, 18; gentile support for, 199–201
Slater, Oscar, 232
Slaton, John M., 72, 73, 75–6
Slave trade, philosemitic opponents of, 120, 135
Smith, Alfred E., 81, 99, 100, 101
Smith, F.E., *see* Birkenhead, F.E. Smith, Earl of
Smith, John Abel, 9, 18, 231
Smith, Sir George Adam, 89
Smith, Payne and Co., 231
Smith, Samuel, 29–30, 239, quoted, 141
Smith, W.H., 37
Smith, William Saumarez, 132
Smollett, Tobias, 231
Smuts, Jan Christian, 145, 168–9, 247

Snell, Henry Snell, Baron, 225
Snow, C.P. Snow, Baron, 184
Snowden, Ethel (Mrs Philip) Snowden,Viscountess, 166
Socialists, ambivalence towards Jews, 123–5; philosemites among, 123
Society for the Extinction of the Slave Trade, 120
Society for the Protection of Science and Learning, *see* Academic Assistance Council
Society for the Relief of Persecuted Jews, *see* Syrian Colonization Fund
Society of Friends, *see* Quakers
Society of Friends of Russian Freedom, 68
Society of Jews and Christians (South Africa), 108
Sokolow, Nahum, 101, 163
Somerset, Edward Adolphus, Duke of, 49
Somerville College, Oxford, 84
Sons of Italy Grand Lodge, 107
Souchay family, 143
Soulsby, Sir William, 41, 43
Soustelle, Jacques, 97
South Africa, 196, 208–9; and Beilis Affair, 68, 89; and Dreyfus Affair, 66; Jewish–Christian dialogue in, 108; Jews in, 118; status of Yiddish in, 175; Zionism in, 168–9
South Australia, 152
South-west London Protestant Institute, 27
Southampton, 117, 118, 174
Soviet Union, 125; Jews in and Israel, 123, 192; Nazi massacres of Jews in, 96–7, 105–6, 195
Spargo, John, 82
Spectator, 62, 68, 184, 244
Spencer, John Poyntz Spencer, Earl, 48
Spinoza, Baruch (Benedict), 122
Spurgeon, Charles H., 42, 136
Squire, Sir John, 97
Stamp, Sir Josiah (later Baron Stamp), 88
Stanley, Edward Lyulph, 43
Staples, Sir John, 43
Stapleton, Mrs, 17
Stead, W.T., 63
Steadman, W.G., 64
Steed, Wickham, 83, 123, 224, 234
Steel, Robert, 161
Stepney, Bishop of, *see* Paget, H.L.
Stevens, Sir Bertram, 103
Stewart, W.J., 223
Stock Exchange Journal, 114
Storrs, Sir Ronald, 91
Strabolgi, Baron, *see* Kenworthy, J.M. (later Baron Strabolgi)
Stratford de Redcliffe, Stratford Canning, Viscount, 30
Stroud, public meeting at (1882), 44
Stuart, Lord Dudley, 116
Students' Christian Movement, 84
Sturge, Joseph, 143
Sueter, Sir Murray, 85, 223
Sugden, Sir Wilfred, 223
Sunday Times, 108
Sunday Truth (Brisbane), 200–1
Sussex Hall, *see* Jews' and General Literary and Scientific Institution
Sussex, Augustus Frederick, Duke of, 18, 114, 115–16, 154, 205, 231
Swaffer, Hannen, 90
Swansea, 132, 144, 182; public meeting at (1882), 44
Swinburne, Algernon, 41
Switzerland, 25
Sydney, Archbishop of, 147
Sydney, and Dreyfus Affair, 66; and refugees from Nazism, 105; public meetings at: (1854), 19, 174; (1878), 177; (1881), 45, 46, 120–1, 147, 181; (1903), 53; (1933), 104; (1942), 106
Sydney Morning Herald, 69, 175–6
Sykes, Sir Mark, 166
Syria, Jews in, 193; *see also* Damascus Affair (1840)
Syrian Colonization Fund, 159

Tablet, 6–7, 145
Taft, William H., 81, 145, 222
Taggard, Genevieve, 83
Tait, Archibald Campbell, 28, 41
Tangier, Jewish refugees from (1859), 19–21
Tasmania, 19, 152; Bishop of, 19; plan for Jewish refugee settlement in, 105
Tawney, R.H., 226
Tecoma (Washington), public meeting at (1903), 54
Temple, William (Archbishop of York and later Canterbury), 89, 97, 98
Tennyson, Alfred Tennyson, Baron, 42, 48, 121
Terry, Ellen, 64
Thatcher, Margaret, 93, 191
Theistic Church (London), 139–40
Thomas (Tommaso), Father, 5
Thomas, G.N.W., 91
Thompson, Dorothy, 99, 100
Thompson, Sir Joseph, 89
Thompson, William, 10
Thorndike, Dame Sybil, 88, 91, 96
Thurston, Herbert, 69
Times, The, 6, 12–13, 14–15, 28, 30, 40, 53, 62, 63, 80, 91, 93, 98–9, 158, 205
Tolstoi, Aleksei, 67
Tolstoi, Leo, 48
Tolstoi, Lev, 67
Tonna, Charlotte Elizabeth, 14, 16, 17, 18, 51, 129–30, 133–5, 140, 142, 145, 149–50, 151, 172–3, 205, 207, 208, 237, 239, 242
Tooke, Mr, 206
Toronto, and Beilis Affair, 72; public meeting at (1938), 103–4
Trafalgar Square, pro-Beilis rally in, 70
Trevelyan, G.M, 89
Trevelyan, Sir Charles (junior), 84
Trevelyan, Sir Charles (senior), 37
Truman, Harry S., 199
Tuchman, Barbara W., 134
Tunis, antisemitic episode in, 120
Tunney, Gene, 107, 147

Turkey, 25, 149–50, 156, 162; Sultan of, 8, 32, 52; *see also* Ottoman Empire
Turner, Sir Alfred, 162
Tuttle, Archbishop, 58
Twain, Mark (Samuel Langhorne Clemens), 57, 250
Tweedsmuir, Lord, *see* Buchan, John
Tyndall, John, 41

Unitarians, and philosemitism, 126–7, 143, 145, 239, 240, 250
United Nations Ad Hoc Committee on Palestine, 199
United States, 4–5, 25, 111, 112, 129, 197, 214; and Beilis Affair, 70–2, 127, 131; and Damascus Affair, 11–12; and Dreyfus Affair, 65–6; and Frank Affair, 72–8; and Israel, 197, 201–3; and Nazi antisemitism, 94, 99–103, 148; and Kishinev pogrom, 54–5; and Palestine, 18–19, 92, 93, 94, 129, 139, 149 et seq., 159, 161, 168, 169–70, 182, 199–200; and pogroms (1919–20), 81; and Polish antisemitism, 82–3; and Romanian antisemitism, 37–8; and Russian antisemitism, 46–8; Jewish–Christian dialogue in, 106–7, 138–9, 148; Jews in, 4–5, 81, 112, 118, 191, 192, 201–2; petition condemning antisemitism (1921), 81–2; receptivity of to elite philosemitism, 184

Van Buren, Martin, 11–12
van Paassen, Pierre, 103, 227
Vance, Zebulon B.,180
Vatican, 30–1, 119, 197
Vaughan, Herbert Alfred, Cardinal (Archbishop of Westminster), 43, 146
Veblen, Thorstein, 183
Verdon, Sir George, 45
Vereker, C.S., 27

Index

Victoria, Queen, 7, 8, 16, 50–1, 150, 154, 176, 208, 217
Vienna, 53
Vincent, Howard, 176
Voice of Jacob, 13, 15, 135, 141, 142, 151, 153
Voysey, Charles, 139–40, 219, 238
Voysey, Ellison A., 238

Waco (Texas), and Frank Affair, 77
Wade, Thomas, 231
Wagner, Robert F., 107, 169
Waldegrave, William Frederick Waldegrave, Earl, 49
Wales, anti-Jewish riots in (1911), 182, 222–3; philosemitic tradition in, 18–9, 20, 29, 143, 144, 155, 168, 247
Wallace, Henry, 103
Walsh, Frank, 77
Walter, Bruno, 88
War Refugee Board (United States), 103
Ward, Mary Augusta (Mrs. Humphry Ward), 162
Ward, S.A., 19
Warner, Sylvia Townsend, 91
Washington, DC, and Blackstone petition, 52; public meeting at (1943), 103
Waterlow, Sir Ernest, 68
Watt, W.A., 103
Way, Sir Samuel, 46
Webb, Beatrice, 99, 123
Weber, John B., 214
Wedgwood, Camilla, 106, 234
Wedgwood, Josiah C., 80, 85, 90, 95, 106, 128, 165, 166–7
Weizmann, Chaim, 163, 167
Wellington, Arthur Richard Wellesley, Duke of, 28
Wells, H.G., 68, 88, 123, 224, 234
Welsh Calvinistic Methodist Church, and Jews, 18, 143, 144
Welsh, John, 47
West, Dame Rebecca, 91
Western Jewish Girls' Free School (London), 115
Westminster Review, 10

Westminster, Archbishop of (Cardinal Basil Hulme), 191; *see also* Bourne, Francis, Cardinal; Hinsley, Arthur, Cardinal; Manning, Henry, Cardinal; Vaughan, Herbert Alfred, Cardinal; Wiseman, Nicholas Patrick Stephen, Cardinal
Westminster, Dean of, 92
Westminster, Hugh Lupus Grosvenor, Duke of, 42, 49, 63, 120, 181
Whale, J.S., 97
Wheelhouse, William, 34
White, Arnold, 123, 234
White, Graham, 98
White, James, 37
White Australia policy, philosemitic supporters of, 122, 184
Whitla, Sir William, 80
Whitman, Charles S., 99
Whitwell, John, 34
Wichita (Kansas), 65
Wickersham, George W., 99
Wiesel, Elie, ix
Wilder, Thornton, 83
Wilkie, David, 249; quoted, 178
Wilkinson, Samuel Hinds, 235
William IV, King, 154
Willis, Emma, 239; quoted, 141
Willkie, Wendell, 103
Willshire, William, 17
Wilson, Sir Charles, 245, 251
Wilson, Woodrow, 82, 160–1
Wingate, Sir Andrew, 246
Winnington-Ingram, Arthur (Bishop of London), 77
Winnipeg, and Beilis Affair, 72
Wire, David, 8, 10, 18, 25, 29, 30, 113, 117, 120, 136, 231, 232
Wisconsin, protest against anti-semitism (1921), 222
Wise, Isaac Mayer, 145
Wise, Stephen S., 222, 227
Wiseman, Nicholas Patrick Stephen, Cardinal (Archbishop of Westminster), 24
Wolf, Simon, 37

Wolmer, Roundell Cecil Palmer, Viscount, 96
Women's groups, and Frank Affair, 76, 77; and Nazi antisemitism, 84; *see also* Feminists
Women's Peace Society, 77
Working Men's Education Society, 29
Working Men's International Club, 51
World Alliance for Combating Anti-Semitism, 86
World Council of Churches, 195
World Non-Sectarian Anti-Nazi Council to Champion Human Rights, 224
Writers, British, philosemites among, 116, 231–2

Yiddish language, 3, 166, 169, 175

Yom Kippur War (1973), 201
York, Archbishops of: Thomas Musgrave, 28; Cosmo Gordon Lang, 67, 80; William Temple, 87, 89, 93, 96; Cyril Garbutt, 97, 223
Young Men's Christian Association, 84

Zangwill, Israel, 162
Zionism, 4, 61; elitist philosemitism and, 175, 184–5; gentile support for, 12–13, 18–19, 80, 86, 93, 95, 101–3, 107, 143, 175, 178, 182, 241 et seq.; Marxists and, 124; millenarians and, 12–13, 132, 149 et seq., 158–9; postwar opponents of, 196–7, 200
Zionist Congress, 169
Zola, Emile, 60, 61, 64